THE WORKING CLASS IN AMERICAN HISTORY

Editorial Advisors

David Brody

Alice Kessler-Harris

David Montgomery

Sean Wilentz

A list of books in the series appears at the end of this book.

LAWYERS AGAINST LABOR

LAWYERS AGAINST LABOR

From Individual Rights to Corporate Liberalism

Daniel R. Ernst

UNIVERSITY OF ILLINOIS PRESS · URBANA AND CHICAGO

Library of Congress Cataloging-in-Publication Data

Ernst, Daniel R.
  Lawyers against labor : from individual rights to corporate liberalism
/ Daniel R. Ernst.
    p.   cm.
  Includes bibliographical references and index.
    ISBN 0-252-02168-1 (acid-free paper). — ISBN 0-252-06512-3 (pbk. :
acid-free paper).
    1. Boycotts—Law and legislation—United States—History.
  2. Trade-unions—Law and legislation—United States—History.
KF3431.E76   1995
344.73'01893—dc20
[347.3041893]   94-45058
                                                                  CIP

FOR MY MOTHER AND FATHER

———————————

Contents

Acknowledgments

In writing this book I have been fortunate to receive the help and advice of some extraordinary scholars, including Gary Gerstle, James E. Goodman, Hendrik Hartog, James Willard Hurst, Stanley I. Kutler, James Livingston, Louis P. Masur, Gary Peller, Daniel T. Rodgers, Mark V. Tushnet, and Robert H. Zieger. Above all, I am grateful to Stanley N. Katz, who guided me through the dissertation and whose example has provided me with a touchstone for my own career as a humanist.

A two-year fellowship from the Institute for Legal Studies of the University of Wisconsin–Madison Law School provided me financial support and the company of Professors Hartog, Hurst, and Kutler. I also thank Dean Judith Areen for grants from the summer writers' fund of the Georgetown University Law Center.

I received exceptional assistance from Richard Strassberg and the staff of the Labor-Management Documentation Center of the Martin P. Catherwood Library of the New York State School of Industrial and Labor Relations. Director Lucye Bolland and the staff of the Danbury Scott-Fanton Museum and Historical Society provided much-appreciated help in locating illustrations. For their willingness to share with me their materials and memories of Walter Gordon Merritt, and for their warm hospitality, I am grateful to Henry and Barbara Ingraham and Mary Shawah Merritt.

For their research assistance, I wish to thank Ross P. Andrews, Kyle Badger, Shana DeSouza, Inez Friedman, Elise Packard, Andrew Ringel, and Liza Velazquez. I am also grateful to Ross Andrews for sharing his research on the trial of *Seubert v. Reiff*.

Quotations from material in the Oliver Wendell Holmes, Jr., Papers are reprinted with the permissions of David de Lorenzo, curator of Manuscripts and Archives at the Harvard Law School Library. Quotations from and references to the R. G. Dun and Company Collection of the Baker Library of the Graduate School of Business Administration of Harvard University are made with the permission of the Dun & Bradstreet Company.

Portions of chapter 1 have previously appeared as "The *Danbury Hatters'* Case" in *Labor Law in American: Historical and Critical Perspectives* (1992), edited by Christopher L. Tomlins and Andrew J. King. These passages appear here with the permission of the Johns Hopkins University Press.

Of the qualities I admire in historians, I value none more than empathy. If I evidence any in this book it is because of my family: my wife, Joy, who possesses that trait in greater abundance than anyone I know; my children, Anna and Daniel; my sisters, Ellen and Ruth; my grandmother, Elinor Robinson; and my parents, Daniel P. and Ann R. Ernst.

LAWYERS AGAINST LABOR

Introduction

Those fellows are always strong for the law. They make it.

—Clarence Darrow (1915)

During the first decade of the twentieth century a remarkable change occurred in the law of strikes and boycotts in the United States. In the 1880s and 1890s most lawyers, judges, and legislators were alarmed by the economic power labor had acquired in the form of nationally organized trade unions and city and state federations. In retrospect, at least, most antebellum labor groups looked like the simple and wholly voluntary associations of independent citizens that Tocqueville celebrated. The new labor organizations, in contrast, seemed capable of overawing and oppressing individual workers or employers, driving their opponents from the markets, and subverting government and the electoral process. Much like Standard Oil or some other business "trust," the new labor groups struck the lawmakers as a threat to individual morality, the personal independence of workers and employers, the natural laws of competition, and equal rights before the law. In fact, many thought the analogy between labor and business combinations was so close that they employed a metaphor that conflated the two. The new labor unions, they wrote, were labor trusts, industrial factions equal to the business trusts in their danger for the public good.

By the time the United States entered World War I, organized labor had acquired a much surer footing in the law. Judges and legislators had challenged or discarded fundamental tenets of Victorian labor jurisprudence—above all, the notion that the individual, endowed by nature with inherent rights, was the basic unit of legal and political analysis. Often without acknowledging their innovation, the lawmakers took the "equity of functional groups" as their starting point in deciding cases or debating statutes.[1]

In rejecting the atomistic individualism of much late-nineteenth-century thought, they did not decide to honor any and all claims of group solidarity and group interest. Most refused to swap the individualistic laissez-faire of the Victorians for a collectivist equivalent; to endow groups with the same formal autonomy individuals once enjoyed was "to let things run along as best they may" when the situation demanded a more active and interventionist intelligence.[2] Thus the lawmakers rejected calls from trade unionists and their allies to let workers and employers alone as they formed themselves into associations and bargained collectively. They insisted on their right to distinguish legitimate from illegitimate assertions of group solidarity and to proscribe any assertion of class solidarity whatsoever.

Perhaps the lawmakers would have embraced collective laissez-faire had they believed workers naturally formed themselves into homogeneous groups—although even then they would have been troubled by the prospect that unions and associated employers could combine to gouge the consuming public.[3] But because the lawmakers recognized that deferring to labor leaders could preserve or strengthen inequality within a group of workers—that it would allow leaders to use group identity "to aggrandize and to wrap a cloak of legitimacy and authenticity" about themselves—they sought to preserve some autonomy for individual workers and employers, even as they recognized workers' right to organize and bargain collectively in the public interest.[4]

Few labor and legal historians have noted the rise of liberal pluralism in the American labor law before the New Deal. Until the early 1960s most scholars of the law of strikes and boycotts in the Progressive Era viewed the subject from the perspective of the skilled trade unionists of the American Federation of Labor (AFL). The most prominent of these "industrial pluralists" were the students of the labor economist John R. Commons. Like Commons, they were advocates of collective laissez-faire, which they worked hard to make the touchstone of national labor policy. In their efforts they tended to exaggerate the persistence of Victorian jurisprudence, to write as if the only alternative to their position was a benighted legal regime based on a wholly formal "liberty of contract." They did this even when responding to critics who joined them in opposing the injunction judges but insisted on treating trade unions as agents of an active state.[5]

In time, industrial pluralists and their counterparts in the law schools came under attack from their left. The "new" labor historians and the members of the critical legal studies (CLS) movement produced a stunning revision of the history of the New Deal's labor policy and its aftermath that showed how it undercut the radical aspirations of American workers. Given the nature of their revisionism, few thought it worth asking whether liberal pluralism affected labor law before the onset of the New

Deal.[6] The two scholars who did discovered a surprising fact: In the 1920s common-law judges treated trade unions as corporate bodies capable of enforcing collective bargaining agreements in their courts. But because this discovery did not aid them in their principal mission, using class analysis to debunk the pretensions of industrial pluralism, neither scholar used it as a point of departure for a sweeping revision of the law of industrial disputes along liberal-pluralist lines.[7]

Only recently has this project seemed worth undertaking. As historians and legal academics have increasingly become preoccupied with the implications of the diversity of human experience, even scholars who had been inclined to place class above all other aspects of human identity have felt obliged to acknowledge and account for ethnicity, religion, gender, race, and sexual preference in the American past.[8] As a rule, they have not revived the models of American social science during the heyday of pluralism in the 1950s.[9] Whether inspired by work on personal identity in American studies, by post-CLS writing on race, gender and the law, or by rational-choice and other social scientific models, they have started to produce a post-pluralist account of the rise of American pluralism. They have studied how some leaders managed to construct social and political groups out of heterogeneous and often narrowly self-interested constituencies, while others lacked the resources to build a politically effective force.[10] And they have shown that the actions of government officials were not simply the aggregates of conflicting interest-group pressure. The desire of officials to preserve or strengthen their positions within government and political parties also shaped their conduct in decisive ways.[11]

For many of these scholars, the early twentieth century has become a particularly intriguing period in the American past. In this era the problem of governance in a diverse society, polity, and economy first claimed the sustained attention of thoughtful minds writing for a wide audience. In intellectual life, the universalist epistemology and ethics of Victorian culture shared space with William James's admonition, "Hands off: neither the whole of truth nor the whole of good is revealed to any single observer." Seeking a middle way between the individual and the class, many settled on the group as the forum in which people received the shared understandings that gave meaning to their ideas and actions. Even then, however, the problem of governing "a world where truth and justice are to be carved from culture rather than found already etched in reason" was a puzzle. It remains one today.[12]

In politics, too, the early twentieth century was an age of the group. For much of the nineteenth century the party was the focus of American political life. Identification with the Democratic or Republican party was an important part of personal identity, regularly renewed in sharply contested elections in which large percentages of voters participated. The principal business of state and national government was not regulation but the promotion of economic development through the distribution of resources and privileges. With the turn of the twentieth century, the "party period" came to an abrupt end. To be sure, the political scientist Arthur Bentley exaggerated his case in pretending he could see "no political phenomena except group phenomena" at work in 1908. Political parties remained important, particularly in organizing the national government.[13] But Bentley did see (as historian Daniel Rodgers put it) that the parties were no longer "the single most important channel through which Americans tried to affect the policies of governments," that party loyalties had weakened considerably, that long-lived, issue-oriented pressure groups had formed around a bewildering array of interests, and that the leaders of the new groups were as likely to be found lobbying legislators, the staff of a recently established administrative agency, or other executive officials as attempting to influence a broad electorate.[14]

Finally, new forms of organization came to the American economy. Most industries were competitively organized for decades after the Civil War, and most employers were "proprietary capitalists," men "who owned and managed their plants, engaged in contentious but mutualistic relations with workers, and regarded their family and partnership enterprises as personal projects and legacies as much or more than as investments."[15] A prolonged depression and a wave of horizontal mergers between 1895 and 1904 upset this order, as leading firms and finance capitalists cajoled or bludgeoned proprietors in many vital industries into corporately organized, multiplant firms staffed by salaried managers and endowed with sufficient market power to administer prices and output. Proprietary firms persisted in the many industries unsuited to mass-production techniques. At the end of the first decade of the new century these firms were still more numerous than the corporations; still, they accounted for a smaller share of capital, employment, and value added in the national economy.[16]

Measured against United States Steel, Standard Oil, and the other industrial giants of the early twentieth century, the proprietary capitalist was a much diminished figure. Walter Lippmann, for example, dismissed him as a "little business monarch who brooded watchfully over every operation in factory and office, called his working men by their pet names, and was impelled at almost every turn by Adam Smith's 'natural propensity to truck and barter.'"[17] Even among the proprietors, many hoped to attain the benefits of organization for themselves by seeking ways of barring new entrants into the industry. Where labor made up a substantial portion of the costs of production, some employers found a barrier to entry in a union's monopoly of skilled labor. This "regulatory unionism" (as the historian Colin

Gordon has dubbed the phenomenon) held out the promise of comfortable profits for employers and wages for employees—a peaceable kingdom
erected on the industrywide collective bargaining agreement.[18]

This book views the rise of liberal pluralism in American social thought,
politics, industry, and law from the perspective of the American Anti-
Boycott Association (AABA), a group organized by proprietary capitalists
in 1902 to litigate and lobby against organized labor. For well over a decade, in cases before state and federal judges and in the halls of Congress,
the AABA and its general counsel Daniel Davenport staunchly defended
small employers from organized labor and Victorian culture from the corporate reconstruction of American capitalism.[19] After 1915 a younger lawyer, Walter Gordon Merritt, the son of a founder of the group, played an
increasingly important role in establishing policy. In the aftermath of World
War I, Merritt would commit the group to a corporate variant of liberal
pluralism under a new name, the League for Industrial Rights.

The AABA originated in a campaign by the United Hatters of North
America to impose standard wage schedules and work rules throughout the
hatting industry. Most manufacturers of "stiff" hats joined with the United Hatters in a typical experiment in regulatory unionism, but several refused. Among them were two proprietors of hat companies in Danbury,
Connecticut: Charles Hart Merritt and Dietrich Eduard Loewe. When the
union demanded that Loewe unionize his firm or face a strike and boycott, he and Merritt organized the AABA. Their credo appealed to other
opponents of industrywide collective bargaining, who similarly refused to
exchange complete control of their business and a competitive advantage
for a place in a union-regulated industry.

Merritt and Loewe recognized they needed a lawyer who was willing to
make their cause his. They found him in the person of fifty-year-old Daniel
Davenport, who practiced in Bridgeport, Connecticut. The opportunity to
lead the AABA came to Davenport at a decisive moment in his life. The
lawyer was steeped in the values of genteel Victorian culture learned as a child
and at Yale College after the Civil War. From classical literature, moral philosophy, and the political economy of William Graham Sumner, Davenport
constructed a calling for himself: the preservation of the immutable and
universal truths of his moral and economic upbringing. As an enthusiastic
foot soldier in the Democratic party of Grover Cleveland and as a lawyer to
private individuals and local politicians, Davenport acted the part of a Victorian Cicero, who stood up for the common good with compelling displays
of personal rectitude. Just as the demise of the party period denied Davenport and his fellow Cleveland Democrats the political stage they needed for
their classical dramas of republican virtue, the AABA held out the prospect
of a new theater of operations, the law.

Davenport thus saw the AABA as a chance to conduct Victorian politics by other, nonelectoral means. He did not intend to pioneer interest-group politics, and he would have been outraged to learn that future historians would count him as an early master of "pressure-group techniques."[20] Yet in providing members with the "selective benefits" of free legal advice, the possibility of AABA funding for their lawsuits, and the opportunity to participate in a great crusade for individual liberty, Davenport developed tactics that have become part of the standard repertoire of interest-group entrepreneurs.

Davenport believed litigation would be an effective vehicle for preserving Victorian values because so many of the late-nineteenth-century decisions on the law of strikes and boycotts were written by judges who shared his social and cultural background. Yet well before the founding of the AABA, a revolution in legal thought was underway that would ultimately eclipse the labor jurisprudence of the Victorian bench. The first development was the subsuming of the law of conspiracy within a larger category of intentional torts. In itself the change did not work a breakthrough to a new legal regime; while a judge in Ohio, William Howard Taft found the new framework could bear the assumptions of Victorian culture as easily as the old. Yet many of the same law professors and law writers who made labor law a part of intentional torts also attacked the immutable, a priori, and individualistic premises of Victorian jurisprudence. The Massachusetts judge Oliver Wendell Holmes, Jr., was only the most prominent advocate of a jurisprudence that acknowledged the historical contingency of all legal institutions and took the social consequences of legal rules as the proper test of their value. Well before the United States' entry into World War I, many law professors urged judges to treat groups as basic units of legal and political obligation and to see themselves as agents of social control.

The tendency of the judges to lag behind the highbrow legal thinkers was evident in the AABA's first campaign, a series of lawsuits intended to establish the illegality of all strikes and boycotts for the closed shop. Based on nineteenth-century precedents and an early AABA-sponsored suit, Davenport believed the courts would accept his view that the adoption of the closed shop in any plant violated individual rights and unlawfully aided the establishment of a monopoly of skilled labor. By 1915 Davenport's goal was no longer tenable, a victim of decisions written by judges influenced by the new labor jurisprudence. Although the judges suggested they would condemn the closed shop if established throughout an industry, they agreed that an isolated demand for its creation was a lawful act of group solidarity.

The AABA's two most famous cases also were watersheds in the new labor jurisprudence. The filing of Loewe's lawsuit against 239 members of the United Hatters won instant notoriety for the AABA. Labor historians remember the "Danbury hatters' case" for Chief Justice Melville Weston Fuller's holding that the Sherman Antitrust Act applied to organized labor. That issue was far less important to the lawyers arguing the case than a jurisdictional question, whether the union's boycott of Loewe's distributors interfered with interstate commerce. Resolving that question in the AABA's favor, Fuller readily concluded that the boycott of Loewe's hats was an unlawful breach of individual dealing in the marketplace—an intolerable violation of "the liberty of the trader." Justice Oliver Wendell Holmes, Jr., was obliged to join the chief justice's decision, albeit for quite different (and unstated) reasons.

Fuller's decision in February 1908 came just after the issuance of a sweeping injunction against Samuel Gompers and two other AFL leaders in another AABA suit involving a distributor-targeted secondary boycott. Like the Danbury hatters' case, the Buck's Stove and Range Company case started as a revolt against regulatory unionism, but it quickly escalated into a cause célèbre, as the company's president, James Wallace Van Cleave, who also headed the National Association of Manufacturers (NAM), and Gompers used the proceedings to marshal their respective constituencies behind their leadership. In December 1908 the lawsuit produced a sensational judicial endorsement of the AABA's position, but appellate judges undercut this victory by disposing of the case on narrow grounds that denied both sides the judicial vindication they sought.

Meanwhile, the Danbury hatters' case was making its slow progress toward a second decision in the Supreme Court in 1915. With the federal courts' jurisdiction over the dispute settled, Davenport and his young associate, Walter Gordon Merritt, turned to the task of establishing that each of the defendant hatters had performed acts which, by operation of law, authorized or ratified the United Hatters' boycott. After two trials Loewe finally received a verdict and saw it upheld in an opinion by Justice Holmes. The result was consistent with the Victorian model of the trade union as a voluntary association of independent workers, but it produced new calls for the incorporation of trade unions to free rank-and-file members from personal liability for the actions of their leaders. Although both Gompers and Davenport opposed this measure, it had enormous appeal for many pluralist lawyers and economists, including those firmly convinced that strong unions were potential agents of the common welfare. They would grant trade unions a legal status unknown to Victorian America, but regulate them in the public interest.

The same pluralist accommodation to the national trade union was also apparent in the AFL's campaign for an exemption from the antitrust laws. In the wake of Fuller's decision in the Danbury hatters' case, Gompers joined an attempt to revise the antitrust laws by corporate liberals associ-

ated with the National Civic Federation. In 1908 the Republican standpat-
ters' control of Congress kept the proposal in committee, but the revolt of
insurgent Republicans, the election of a Democratic majority and a disciplined "labor bloc" in the House of Representatives, and Woodrow Wilson's election in 1912 soon put the open-shop leaders on the defensive.
Neither Davenport's lobbying nor an outpouring of protest from the
NAM's members could prevent the passage in 1913 of a rider that denied
the Department of Justice funds to prosecute organized labor under the
Sherman Act. The open-shop forces rallied the following year when the
House passed the Clayton bill, with ambiguous language that threatened
to create an outright exemption for organized labor. With the assistance
of the NAM, Davenport ensured that Congress would not accede to the
AFL's demands for collective laissez-faire, but he could not hold a congressional majority to the individualistic views of law and legislation that triumphed in 1908. That organized labor could lawfully possess great collective power was beyond question in 1914. The battleground had shifted to
distinguishing lawful from unlawful exercise of that power—a task the
members of Congress were happy to leave to the courts.

An AABA-sponsored campaign against yet another instance of regulatory unionism, the refusal of New York City carpenters to handle woodtrim produced beyond the metropolitan area, shows how the courts handled this task. With Davenport dividing his time between Washington and
Bridgeport, Walter Gordon Merritt took the leading role in overseeing the
litigation. In the end, his lawsuits failed. The AABA's injunctions did not
break the boycott; the U.S. Supreme Court rejected the federal suit on technical grounds; and the New York Court of Appeals squarely ruled that the
boycott was a lawful expression of group solidarity, a holding in keeping
with a general trend toward greater tolerance of secondary pressure in the
building trades.

As his stature as a lawyer and expert on labor relations grew, Walter
Gordon Merritt increasingly came to articulate policies that broke with the
founding faiths of the AABA. For Daniel Davenport, law was an a priori
system, a manufacturing firm was the private property of its proprietor,
unions were voluntary associations of independent workers, and labor relations were a private matter into which the state had no business intrud-
ing. By 1917, Merritt, the product of a quite different education, publicly
parted company with his senior colleague on each of these points. After
his father's death in 1918, the lawyer committed the AABA to a "progressive" approach to industrial relations under a new name, the League for
Industrial Rights. In championing the proprietary capitalists, Davenport
believed that he championed the public interest. Merritt knew his father's

class of employers was only a part of the whole, and he undertook the dubious task of converting them to his pluralist vision of law and labor.

The history of the American Anti-Boycott Association thus shows that the common law of industrial disputes was not the reliable ally of a united class of employers in the war with organized labor. The notion that, as the labor economist Robert Hoxie put it, unionism was "in its very essence a lawless thing" has long been an unexamined truth among American historians of the Progressive Era.[21] The many defeats and pyrrhic victories of the AABA show that employers could not keep the judges of the Progressive Era from revising Victorian precedents in order to accommodate the rise of national trade unions. To be sure, Clarence Darrow's wisecrack contained a grain of truth: The law of strikes and boycotts was a human construction, and the open-shop lawyers had a great part in making it. But the product was quite different from what the open-shop lawyers wished. It is better understood as an attempt by lawmakers to incorporate organized labor into a pluralistic body politic and to regulate it in keeping with their independent estimate of their own and the public's interest.

ONE

Origins

A just man armed is potent for peace.

—AABA (1903)

When Louis Brandeis catalogued the evils of the trusts during congressional testimony in late 1911, his discussion of their effects on workers was particularly impassioned. "The destruction of trade-unionism appears to be a cardinal principle with trust builders," Brandeis declared. Once, when firms were small, workers could find powerful defenders in trade unions; now the annihilation of organized labor in trust after trust had helped create repression "as bad as any conditions of peonage found in the United States." Brandeis made clear that he opposed some of the practices of organized labor, as well he might given his experience as a lawyer for family-run firms in Massachusetts and such recent examples of union-sponsored violence as the bombing of the Los Angeles *Times* building. In particular, Brandeis singled out the closed shop as illegal and "radically wrong." "I think there is no body of men whose intelligence or whose character will stand absolute power," he explained, "and I should no more think of giving absolute power to unions than I should of giving to capital monopoly power." But such an event was quite unlikely, Brandeis claimed, given the trade unions' failure to organize the great trusts, and no special prohibitions were needed to curb unions' power. "The time has passed . . . when we have any reason to regard the combination of men in trade unions as a real menace," Brandeis concluded.[1]

Several weeks later, during the same hearings, Daniel Davenport took issue with Brandeis's "quite foggy" generalities. Davenport agreed that the steel, petroleum, and shoe machinery trusts endangered individual liberty in America, but he denied that labor unions were any less dangerous as a consequence. The closed shop, the secondary boycott, and the other un-lawful practices of organized labor had nothing to do with the trusts. "These practices, which were in vogue and used with all their vigor and power long before the formation of the United States Steel Co., have never been di-rected against any of these corporations," save only the American Tobacco Company, the target of a quite ineffective boycott by the AFL. "Weak men, weak concerns" were the target of organized labor, and national trade unionism was very much a threat to industrial liberty for such employers and their employees. If Brandeis dwelt on industrial conditions in oligop-olistic, corporately organized industry, Davenport detailed practices in the competitive hatting and building trades, where firms typically were man-aged by the men who owned them. If Brandeis denounced the great trusts for having "stabbed industrial liberty in the back," Davenport condemned a labor movement that aimed at "conquering all concerns and bringing them one after another under the control of the unions."[2]

One might well think that the best starting place for an understanding of the law of industrial disputes in the early twentieth century was Bran-deis's: the large business corporation. After all, corporate managers played a leading role in shaping public policy toward business combinations, rail-roads, banking, and industrial accidents, and their interests and beliefs sig-nificantly influenced judges, economists, party politics, and popular cul-ture.[3] In this light, Davenport's protest that the law of industrial disputes owed little to the giant business corporation seems disingenuous and self-serving, an unconvincing denial of the fact of corporate hegemony in American society and culture. And, indeed, the lawyer exaggerated his case: Large firms dependent on skilled labor at crucial stages in their produc-tive process sometimes joined the AABA and looked to the courts for help in labor disputes.

Nevertheless, Davenport's objection provides the better point of depar-ture. Great industrial firms founded upon unskilled labor and mass pro-duction had little need for anything so baroque as the law of industrial disputes; elementary principles of contract, which permitted them to fire workers for any reason or no reason at all, and property, which recognized their right to exclude union organizers from the workplace, were sufficient. In the first years of the new century the employers who bulked largest in the thinking of the judges (and the ranks of the AABA) were not the new corporate managers but proprietary capitalists. In fact, the AABA was the creation of two such men, the Danbury hat manufacturers Dietrich Edu-ard Loewe and Charles Hart Merritt. Both shared Davenport's commit-ment to individual dealing in competitive markets and saw themselves as the opponents of industrial combination rather than its agents.

THE HAT TRADE

By the 1880s, the American hatting industry was divided into two branches: the production of stiff hats, such as the derby, and the production of soft hats, such as the fedora. Some large companies, like the John B. Stetson Company, E. A. Mallory and Sons, and Henry H. Roelof and Company, produced both stiff and soft hats and kept all stages of production within their own factories. Many more firms specialized in producing either stiff or soft hats. Stiff-hatting centered in two Connecticut towns, Danbury and South Norwalk; soft-hatting centered in Newark and the Orange Valley of New Jersey. Firms also specialized in various stages of the production process. Some firms "made" partially shaped hat bodies and sold them through merchant houses to "commission shops" for "finishing" into either stiff or soft hats.[4]

As a rule, firms in the hatting industry were not large multiunit enterprises that employed the techniques of mass production and sold goods through a wholly owned distribution system. To be sure, the industry did include an exceptional giant or two. Stetson, for example, was incorporated, owned its own distribution network, and employed well over five hundred workers in a large factory complex. Stetson's workers enjoyed the latest in welfare capitalism, such as a company-sponsored Sunday school and a home savings club. The company could afford these benefits thanks to its solid and stable profits—more than $380,000 in 1899.[5] But the typical hat firm looked nothing like Stetson. It was managed and financed by a single proprietor or a handful of partners. Quite often these men had been hatters themselves before scraping together the several hundred dollars needed to start business as a commission shop. Firms generally employed fewer than a hundred workers in a single factory and marketed their output through independent chains of wholesalers and retailers.[6]

The lack of profits to be had in the industry was a constant lament. The trade journals rarely missed a chance to urge manufacturers to resist price-cutting, sometimes employing such aphorisms as, "Whatever is worth having should be of sufficient account to charge in the bill," and "There's always room at the top."[7] The established manufacturers agreed. A gathering in late 1902 lamented "an almost entire absence of profits in their business" and blamed their plight on the "unintelligent competition" of the "lower, profitless grades" of hats.[8]

Now and then, the manufacturers contemplated the kind of horizontal combination that flourished during the merger movement of 1895–1904. For example, in the summer of 1901 the trade journals reported efforts by an unnamed New York City law firm to convince proprietors to sell out to a holding company. Nothing came of this scheme, perhaps because of dis-economies of scale and the variability of fashion in the trade. In any event, proponents of combination would have had to overcome suspicion bred of years of mistrust among the hat manufacturers. "There is probably no in-dustry in the country where there is so much petty jealousy and underhand influences at work," a trade journalist wrote in dismissing the idea of a "Hat Trust." "Each manufacturer is sitting up nights in the effort to design some plan to circumvent his competitors."[9]

One consequence of this scheming was that wages did not keep pace with the rising cost of living at century's end. Many manufacturers had only recently left the workers' ranks and sympathized with calls for higher wages. None, however, would pay more if it meant being undersold by a rival. Thus, a trade journal claimed that "no manufacturer cares whether he pays $1.50 or $2 a dozen for finishing hats provided that his neighbor is made to pay the same rate for a similar grade. Both can make a corresponding advance in the selling price, and since one cannot undersell the other both can get the advance."[10]

Such sentiments were by no means unique to the hatting industry. "In my opinion the trouble is caused by each local union being permitted to make a scale of prices," declared the proprietor of a New York cigar mak-ing firm in 1886.[11] "In consequence some localities can manufacture cheaper than others. My judgment is this, make a uniform price for the entire United States; give men good pay, but make everyone pay alike for manu-facturing the same article. I am a friend of labor and would like to see it well paid." To take such employers at their word, Adolph Strasser and Samuel Gompers made uniform trade agreements a cornerstone of the cigar makers' "business unionism" during the Gilded Age.[12]

In a competitively organized, labor-intensive, and geographically dis-persed industry like hatting, employers and workers alike came to appre-ciate the promise collective bargaining held for stabilizing wages and block-ing the entry of new, "cut-throat" firms. The hatters' experiment in regulatory unionism commenced in the fall of 1885, when labor leaders offered to meet with hat manufacturers to discuss "the present state of the trade, and the way to improve it, and the condition of those engaged in it." Edmund Tweedy, the proprietor of one of Danbury's largest firms, took the lead in recruiting manufacturers for a meeting with the union. Tweedy's address to his fellow employers alluded to the labor strife of the day and to conditions in the hatting industry. "It is safe to say that in many a factory . . . the wheels have been turned for the sole benefit of the work-ers, while the owner has been content if the end of the year found him in no worse financial condition than the beginning." Tweedy conceded that "the workmen in our trade have not been satisfied with their share of the profits of the business," but he also observed that, with few exceptions, "the same remark will apply to the employers."[13]

Tweedy claimed the hatters had taken an important first step by inviting their employers to organize themselves into an association. The workers sincerely believed that "by mutual interchange of views, and by concert of action, it is possible to improve the condition of trade, remove many of its difficulties, and make it more profitable to all parties." Tweedy was well aware that many of his fellow employers regarded unionization as "a foretaste of the torments that await the wicked." He promised they would instead enjoy "a paradise on earth," if only they would give up a measure of individual freedom and follow common work rules and wage rates as policed by the union.[14]

New Jersey hat manufacturers, among whom were many of Tweedy's "injurious" competitors, rejected his proposal, but the Danbury proprietors established their own association to "maintain harmonious relations with our employés and unite with them in the adoption of such measures as will tend to improve the condition of the business and promote the general welfare of all employed in it." Despite these good intentions, the Danbury hat manufacturers grew restive as the New Jersey firms made serious inroads into their share of the market. The business collapse of 1893 provided them with an opportunity to break with the union. "The soft hatting industry has nearly left us and stiff hatting is rapidly losing ground," they complained in an open letter to the hatters in July 1893. The nonunion New Jersey firms could pay lower wages and use better machinery than the union permitted them. "We have the factories and the men," the employers asserted, "but the conditions surrounding the employment of men, owing to the restrictions of trade unions here, are such that it is impossible to successfully compete." After a lockout of almost ten weeks, eleven of Danbury's hatting companies, including C. H. Merritt and Son and D. E. Loewe and Co., reopened as independent shops.[15]

As the nation recovered from the depression of 1893–96, the hat finishers and hat makers merged their two organizations into the United Hatters of North America and commenced a new campaign of strikes and boycotts to organize the industry.[16] A major turning point was the capitulation in August 1900 of the largest soft-hatting concern in New Jersey's Orange Valley, F. Berg and Company. After Berg "went fair," the union quickly organized the remaining soft-hatting firms in the Orange Valley and Newark.[17]

As early as November 1900 Loewe had discussed unionization with James P. Maher, president of the Danbury hat makers' association and treasurer of the United Hatters.[18] Although willing to meet with a local man, Loewe told Maher that he did not care to talk to the national officials, who "were not Danbury people and had no interest in Danbury affairs." The following March, Loewe again met with Maher and Martin Lawlor (a local hat maker as well as the national secretary of the United Hatters), but he broke off negotiations after learning that many of his employees would not be given union cards were he to go fair. On April 22, 1901, Loewe defended his decision in a letter to the national leadership "care of James Maher" and braced for a strike and boycott.[19]

This surely would have ensued but for a spontaneous walkout three days earlier at Henry H. Roelof's Philadelphia factory. The national leadership suspended its plans for Loewe in order to mount a national boycott of Roelof's goods at an expense to the union of some $23,000. Roelof, a confirmed opponent of trade unionism, responded with civil and criminal conspiracy suits but finally came to terms with the union on July 19, 1902. Less than a week later, the United Hatters called out Loewe's work force. Even though Loewe's workers had never complained to the union about their employer, even though Loewe, with tears in his eyes, begged them to stay, they left rather than be blacklisted by the union and barred from the industry. Among those leaving was the son of Loewe's partner, a union member who was not later named a defendant in Loewe's suit against the hatters.[20]

In the days after the walkout, Loewe met with Maher and John Moffitt, president of the United Hatters, who had convened a meeting of the General Executive Board in a Danbury hotel. While these negotiations were in progress, a thousand workers struck another giant soft-hat firm, the Waring Hat Company of Yonkers, New York. This time, however, Loewe was given no reprieve, for when Maher and Moffitt left Danbury for Yonkers, they left behind a committee to continue discussions. Loewe soon broke off the negotiations with the declaration, "If I am to die, I am going to die my way." On August 7, 1902, the board authorized the national officers to proceed with a boycott of Loewe's hats.[21]

LOEWE

In hyperbolic moments, the open-shop press depicted Loewe in larger-than-life terms, as "the man of the hour" heroically defending individual liberty "in the face of tremendous odds and impending disaster." To one of his lawyers, he was "an obstinate German, who would much rather be ruined and free than . . . prosperous and subject to a commercial slavery." In 1902, Loewe himself explained his actions as the discharge of a duty to "the business, to the people still in the factory, to the town of Danbury." At a victory banquet in March 1908, he modestly protested, "You are making too much of me altogether. I have been doing my duty, trying to do so, at least, and if in doing my duty I have been able to help the cause along a little, I am glad of it, but I don't think I have done any more than that."[22]

Loewe's sense of duty flowed from the experiences of his own life. To more than one observer this "proletarian who, by the opportunities of this country, rose to the rewards of his native abilities" epitomized the workings of the free labor creed.[23] His origins in Germany were by no means impoverished, as his father, a farmer, held important local posts and gave his son brief periods of study at an agricultural college and technical institute, where he enjoyed courses in civil engineering and higher mathematics. Yet when the eighteen-year-old Loewe emigrated to the United States in June 1870 he brought with him few resources beyond this human capital. Over the next seventeen months he worked as a farmhand, a day laborer for a railroad, and a shipping clerk for a wholesale grocer before locating in Danbury and becoming a journeyman hat maker in Tweedy's factory. Over the next several years he learned the more specialized skills of hat finishing, and in 1876 became a foreman in the finishing department of a different firm. In 1879 he established a commission shop with the investments of two partners. Loewe's own contribution was $180.[24]

From the outset Loewe impressed business observers with his industry, honesty, and punctuality in meeting obligations. The firm was "gaining a little all the time," an informant wrote a credit-reporting service in 1883. Seven years later another reporter approvingly noted that Loewe's whole family, including his wife and daughters, still worked in the shop and that the firm was worth $10,000. "He enjoys the respect and esteem of all who know him and has achieved considerable prominence," the informant reported, not solely for his business success, but also for his service (as a Democrat) in the state legislature in 1887, as councilman for the Fourth Ward in 1890, and as an officer and board member of several local charities.[25]

Between 1885 and 1896 Loewe produced both stiff and soft hats, but in the latter year he decided to devote his entire plant to meeting the increasing demand for his soft hats, which he sold under his own name through several wholesalers and a retail store in New York City.[26] By the turn of the century, the firm, although no giant, had nonetheless become a significant producer in the soft-hat industry and a real threat to the newly unionized New Jersey concerns. Loewe's principal wholesaler recalled that his dealings with the manufacturer "gradually grew to quite a nice business in 1900. Then it grew quite rapidly up to 1902, when it was a very satisfactory business to us, and, I hope, to Mr. Loewe." Loewe's balance sheets told the same story: his profits in 1900 came to $25,000 (6 percent of his net sales). In 1901, the last full year before the strike, they totaled $28,000, an increase of 12 percent. At the time of the strike, Loewe's payroll of 246 workers placed him ahead of most Connecticut hat firms, although well behind Berg, Roelof, Stetson, and Waring.[27]

In large part Loewe's business had grown because he used more apprentices on his best-selling line than union regulations permitted. Notwithstanding this, the Danbury locals never complained to the national hierarchy about conditions in Loewe's factory. In fact, local hatters winked at this infraction, because it gave work to children who could not otherwise find employment in Danbury.[28] Nonetheless, this local arrangement jeopardized the efforts by the national leadership and union employers to realize Tweedy's paradise of stable wages and profits.

Loewe was convinced that a return to union work rules would destroy his business. "Our experience of 1885 to 1894 is still in our minds," he explained to Maher in April 1901, "and the knowledge then obtained convinces us that the increased cost would drive the production of our most popular grades of hats from Danbury, just as the increased cost of production occasioned by the unionizing of all the factories in 1885 drove the soft hatting from this town to other districts." Union conditions would force him to fire many valued employees who would not be "white-washed" into the United Hatters. As Loewe recalled, "I knew that all the employees were satisfied—and we as a firm were satisfied—with the way the business was running, and I felt that Danbury as a town was satisfied, and I couldn't see why it should be necessary to change the conditions. I wanted to be left alone."[29]

But Loewe could not be left alone, not if prices, profits, and wages in the hatting industry were to stay at comfortable levels. The divergence between the interests of a single, marginal firm and the larger industry became apparent when Loewe met with Maher shortly after the strike commenced. "If I should acquiesce in your demands to unionize the factory," Loewe explained, "I would soon have to make a higher class of goods here, and I would not find a market for them, or, in other words, I would soon die of dry rot." But Maher was adamant. "The manufacturers had tried for many years to control this industry," he insisted. It was now the union's turn.

"It would seem that you are called upon to right the wrongs of the hatting industry," Loewe retorted. "Well," Maher replied, "in a way. You may call this a trust, and perhaps it is a trust, but it is the only thing for us to do to get a good living out of the industry."[30]

That Loewe was not misstating his position became clear once the boycott commenced. The experience of Loewe's wholesale merchant in Richmond, Virginia, illustrated the manufacturer's plight. In December 1902, Thomas D. Stokes wrote Loewe about his recent meeting with a delega-

tion of local labor leaders. In response to their demand that he stop marketing Loewe's hats, Stokes pointed out the dilemma that Loewe would
face if he unionized his firm. Based on his general knowledge of the trade,
the merchant estimated that unionization would raise Loewe's costs by
more than 10 percent. Should Loewe maintain the quality of his hats, he
would have to raise his prices to those of the Berg firm. "I explained to them
that in this event we would not need both factories," Stokes reported to
Loewe. Because Stokes already bought a special line of hats from Berg, "We
no doubt would have to place our business with him to your detriment."
Should Loewe attempt to maintain his prices, the quality would slide to
an unacceptable level, and, once again, Stokes would take his business to
Loewe's competitors.[31]

Despite his initial resolve to stand by Loewe, Stokes quickly capitulat-
ed to the unionists' demands. Richmond retailers had been warned that if
they continued to sell Stokes's merchandise they would be placed on an
unfair list. "Since this was done our trade has virtually amounted to nothing in Richmond," wrote Stokes. Because he had "no chance whatever of
winning out single handed," Stokes reluctantly canceled his outstanding
orders with Loewe.[32]

Similar efforts targeting Loewe's other distributors were equally effective. In 1901, Loewe's profits totaled $28,000; his balance sheet for 1902
revealed a loss of $17,600, and losses continued in the following years. Small
wonder, then, that at the May 1903 convention of the United Hatters President Moffitt predicted the Loewe boycott would end just "as successfully
as . . . the other fights of like nature in recent years."[33]

MERRITT

What confounded Moffitt's prediction was the start of formal operations by the AABA in August 1903 after two years of planning by Loewe
and his close friend Charles Hart Merritt. The pair's friendship commenced
in the mid-1880s and was cemented by long walks in the wooded hills south
of Loewe's home, during which they often discussed the state of the industry. As president of the local association of hat manufacturers, Merritt
actively participated in the collective bargaining of the early 1890s, yet he
had none of Tweedy's enthusiasm for the union's work rules. Raised in a
wealthy Quaker family, known for his "strong, straightforward and earnest"
character, and related through his mother to one of the oldest and most
prominent of Danbury's families, Merritt deeply resented sharing control
over his family's business with union officials.[34] More than a decade after
the lockout of 1893, he could still tick off his grievances: the union's require-

ment that Merritt pay a sizable fee to cover the back dues of union members in his employ, its fining of a foreman who had disciplined a dishonest worker, and regulations prohibiting Merritt from docking workers' pay for inferior work and limiting the apprentices he could hire.[35]

Like Loewe, Merritt opened his plant on a nonunion basis in 1894. For the next several years he sold stiff hats through commission merchants, who marketed them under their own trademarks in several major cities. Merritt also produced for the low end of the market, a fact signaled by the firm's slogan, "Just a little better than the next best," and by the charge in the labor press that he and his son George ran "the cheapest non-union hat plant in Danbury." Loewe had prospered by adopting a similar strategy for soft hats, but Merritt's firm had less success, at least in part because of a quietly pursued boycott of his hats. In early 1900 Merritt added a line of soft hats but failed to reverse the firm's declining fortunes.[36]

In March 1904 Merritt tried to evade the boycott by marketing his hats with a counterfeit union label, which he brazenly registered as a firm trademark and denied was intended to deceive the public. A preliminary injunction granted in the summer of 1904 kept the manufacturer from using the counterfeit, but Merritt ultimately prevailed in an extraordinary decision of the Connecticut Supreme Court.[37]

In the interim, however, Merritt gave up the fight, so that by the summer of 1905 operations had ceased at his plant. By February 1906 the factory had been sold to another concern, the North American Hat Company, which moved the "Merritt" line to its main plant in Fall River, Massachusetts, "owing to the difficulties attending the manufacture of hats" in fully unionized Danbury.[38]

Merritt thus shared Loewe's sense that the United Hatters were the initiators of industrial strife, aggressors who threatened a family's property and heritage. During one of their walks in 1901, with Loewe facing the prospect of a boycott and Merritt suffering the consequences of another, the two hit upon the idea of forming an employers' association to combat such union campaigns though the law. By the end of the year they obtained tentative support from employers in the industrial Northeast, and in February 1902 they issued a general call for employers to join them in destroying "the unlawful and most un-American boycott" through "the machinery of existing law." Preliminary meetings followed in the fall of 1902, with the adoption of a constitution in December of that year. The framers provided that formal operations should not commence until a hundred charter members joined the organization. When this finally occurred in April 1903, Merritt became chair of the general executive board, a position he retained until his death fifteen years later.[39]

Founding Faiths

The new group adopted the motto, "A just man armed is potent for peace."[40] It was a revealing choice. It proclaimed, first, that the individual—the "just man"—was the fundamental unit of industrial life. In joining the AABA, the slogan promised, employers would retain their individuality and would simply be exercising their right as free and independent citizens to form voluntary associations. Trade unionists might denounce the group as a secretive, self-interested faction opposed to the public good, but the AABA's leaders maintained it had no corporate or collective interest apart from the will of its individual members. Rather, they charged, it was the trade union that violated the tenets of republicanism. Since the labor conspiracy cases of antebellum America, judges had denounced unions as "secret and unknown tribunals" seeking to subvert "this free and happy commonwealth."[41] The AABA's leaders needed only to update this critique by stressing the anticompetitive consequences of standardized work rules. If antebellum political economy directed critics of trade unions to political metaphors—to see in labor combination an *imperium in imperio*—the AABA reached for a metaphor from the world of industry and likened the national trade union with Standard Oil, American Tobacco, and the other great "trusts." Unions were "labor trusts," its officials held, which coerced and degraded workers who could not escape their grasp.[42]

The fundamentally individualistic outlook of the AABA is also significant when viewed in light of the rise of the large business corporation at the turn of the twentieth century. Historians of "corporate liberalism" and the "organizational synthesis" have shown how the new corporations served as models of collective action for many groups in progressive America. At its founding, the AABA was at odds with this trend. Certainly, its members appreciated the value of collective effort in an age of organization, yet they had little enthusiasm for the bureaucratic structures and administrative expertise through which corporate liberals hoped to attain industrial order and stability.[43] Most members joined the AABA to defend an older industrial order in which independent employers were subject only to the natural and impersonal workings of the market and such bargains as they negotiated with their workers. So deeply ingrained were these habits of independence that Charles Merritt often assumed an *aversion* to collective action on the part of his audience. Thus, writing from personal experience, Merritt praised employers' associations for giving manufacturers the chance to discover that their competitors were "men of integrity and ability, while before they have been estimated and described as the opposite."[44]

A second revealing aspect of the motto was its insistence that justice would be served through the AABA's litigation. The AABA's members looked to the law as a righter of wrongs, a protector of just men. The goal of making new law, so readily acknowledged by today's legal defense funds, was no part of the employers' plans for the AABA. To adopt such a goal would go against their deep conviction that existing law already recognized the justice of their cause. The "broad and patriotic work" of the association was simply the enforcement of rights *already* enshrined in the law. No less than Blackstone, the AABA's members believed the business of the courts was limited to "the protection of every individual's private rights." Were courts free to innovate in light of the times, they might well upset the just and vested rights of private parties and, in so doing, redistribute wealth. The AABA's rank and file would thus have joined the Victorian jurist who denounced the "pretence of public policy" as a "deadly weapon of socialism and communism."[45]

Third, the motto's promise of potency revealingly spoke to the proprietary capitalists' growing sense of powerlessness at the turn of the century. Although trade unionists might depict the proprietors as powerful tyrants, Davenport's description of them as "weak men, weak concerns" came closer to their self-conception. Their spokesmen insisted that "the immense body of employers" should not be lumped with the giant business corporations; indeed, the proprietors were "actually attacked by the very existence of huge combinations of capital."[46] The motto, then, spoke to the widely shared fears of the small employers. Although challenged by labor combinations on one side and business combinations on the other, the proprietary capitalists learned from the AABA that they could yet be the masters of their own destiny and a potent force within the emerging industrial order.

Finally, the slogan declared the ultimate aim of the AABA to be the attainment of industrial peace. This choice of an ultimate end had a calculated, rhetorical side to it, in that it implicitly cast labor leaders in the role of industrial aggressor. It also addressed the psychic needs of the employers on a more immediate and instinctive level, as an expression of a heartfelt desire to be left alone—left in peace—free from the impediments of business conspiracies, labor trusts, or ill-conceived legislation and subject only to the discipline of the market and a Christian conscience. When an AABA member nodded assent to some invocation of the principle of "laissez-faire," he did so not so much to endorse the whole structure of classical economic thought premised upon it, but because it spoke to many of the grudges and grievances he harbored as he went about his daily life.

The AABA's understanding of industrial peace was, of course, a profoundly partial vision, grounded upon assumptions that were under attack even as the group commenced its activities. Implicit in the employer's notion of being "left alone" were the beliefs that firms were the private prop-

erty of those who owned them, that a crucial element of the private ownership of a firm was untrammeled control over all facets of the business,
that an employee's interest in a firm was limited to the terms of the labor
contract, and that the public had no legitimate concern in an employer's
affairs unless they somehow endangered the health, safety, and welfare of
the citizenry as a whole. Each premise had been called into question by
mid-1903, not only in radical tracts and trade union periodicals, but also
in a great outpouring of middle-class, reformist literature and even in the
apologetics of the corporate liberals. Such arguments made little headway
in the thinking of the AABA's members. Their most common fate was to
be labeled a species of socialism and banished to a terra incognita of foolish or knavish schemes.

The collective bargaining agreements of the business unionist might
have fared better, because, as Edmund Tweedy's example suggests, some
employers found their way to ceding significant control over their work
force to the union. After all, employers often entered into long-term contracts with suppliers and wholesalers in which they surrendered much de-
cision-making authority in exchange for stability and predictability. Where
unions made good on their promise to organize the industry, employers had
little trouble reconciling themselves to the surrender of a measure of control over their employees. But the AABA's rank and file were more like
Loewe and Merritt than Tweedy. Some had tried collective bargaining and
seen it collapse after a period of erosion and decline; others knew without
a trial that they would suffer something like Loewe's fate; still others, secure in their position in the industry, wanted to introduce new production
techniques that would be prohibited in a collective bargaining agreement.
Nothing the unions offered such employers could induce them to bargain
away their freedom of action.

If Charles Merritt was convinced that large numbers of employers would
rally to an organization based on such principles, he also knew that he
needed a like-minded lawyer to oversee the day-to-day affairs and principal litigation of the AABA. As he recalled years later at an AABA banquet, "It was indeed almost ludicrous to observe the general shrinking from
such a just cause." At last, in early 1902, Merritt found his man: an able,
tenacious lawyer of "fine presence and personality," a man "free from political aspirations," a man who understood the mission of the AABA as its
founders did and who could present the cause in terms businessmen would
instinctively affirm. "You do not need to be told," Merritt remarked to his
audience, "that no mistake was made when we selected for this work our
General Executive Agent—Mr. Daniel Davenport."[47]

TWO

Davenport

Let one person believe and feel strongly on moral themes,
and he becomes at once a power with his fellow-men.

—Noah Porter (1885)

Sometime in 1901, on the verge of his fiftieth birthday, Daniel Davenport looked back on what had promised to be the most satisfying period of his professional and political career and regretted what he saw. "My history since 1893 has been that of a busy country lawyer of an obscure type," he confessed to his Yale classmates. "Like the annals of the poor, it is brief and simple. I have published nothing, written nothing except briefs, and done nothing worthy of mention."[1] In fact, Davenport wrote with undue modesty: by 1901 the lawyer had acquired a reputation as an able appellate advocate and an important figure in the Democratic party of Bridgeport, Connecticut. Yet Davenport was surely right in recognizing that President Noah Porter, Professor William Graham Sumner, and the other great men who taught the class of 1873 expected more momentous careers for their pupils. By virtue of their schooling in classical literature, moral philosophy, classical economics, and liberal political philosophy, these sons of the American gentry considered themselves the moral navigators of their generation. Davenport had tried to act this part since graduating from Yale. By 1901, however, he had good reason to doubt that his law practice and political experience would ever win him the respect and authority he thought he deserved.

A year after he wrote to his classmates, Davenport became the chief executive officer of the AABA and commenced a cross-country campaign to enlist members for the organization. To unravel why a moderately successful lawyer would swap his practice for an unprecedented venture like the AABA, we have to look back to Davenport's upbringing, education, and early legal and political career. What emerges from such a study is a more complicated and attractive portrait than one would expect from the conventional depictions of the antilabor bar as selfish and cynical manipulators of patently outdated rhetoric.

Davenport was tolerably representative of the most influential segment of the Victorian bar, who had similar origins in a social class that prized independence, manliness, and refinement and who were just as enthusiastic adherents to the civic humanist, Christian, and liberal traditions that comprised Victorian culture.[2] Lawyers of Davenport's class and generation still believed their authority as public actors came first and foremost from their devotion to these values rather than the mastery of an arcane body of knowledge. They had not yet undergone what historian Stow Persons has called "the uncomfortable transformation of gentlemen into professionals."[3]

Davenport's career also illuminates a parallel and general transformation in the way genteel lawyers participated in American politics. While his early success in seeking political office seemed to confirm his place among an elite of "virtue and talent," in the 1890s an electoral realignment threatened to exile gentry politicians to the margins of American political life.[4] When that happened, Davenport discovered in the AABA an ingenious device for promoting Victorian values in an increasingly pluralist age.

A Genteel Education

Daniel Davenport was born in Wilton, Connecticut, on January 13, 1852, to George A. and Mary Sturgis Davenport, the fourth of their six children. He was a child of the peculiarly American gentry class that grew up in the antebellum United States, whose members sought to maintain the authority of learning, manners, and moral character claimed by their English counterparts while rejecting the aristocratic exclusiveness and effeminate estheticism of the Old World. The American elite was, in the eyes of its members and apologists, a natural one, open to all who lived by (in Persons's phrase) "the great Emersonian principles of individualism and self-reliance." Although the antebellum social elite was in fact more permeable than its predecessors in the Anglo-American past, the character, training, and ability that distinguished the American gentleman were most often discovered in persons of the proper ancestry and parentage. These Davenport was fortunate to possess.[5]

Davenport could trace his ancestry back to the earliest years of colonial settlement, and he was not reluctant to do so if given the chance. On his father's side he counted as ancestors John Davenport, the Puritan cleric who founded the New Haven Colony; another seventeenth-century minister who founded Newark, New Jersey; and a petitioner for Connecticut's charter of 1662. Davenport's maternal grandfather had been a member of Connecticut's constitutional convention of 1818, a selectman and justice of the peace, and a leader of the Democratic party in the state legislature.[6]

Davenport's father was no less estimable a model of the cultured and independent gentleman. The son of a woolen manufacturer, George Davenport became a lawyer after attending lectures at Yale's law school. He attained some prominence in Fairfield County, serving as state's attorney in 1842, practicing in Norwalk with the future state chief justice Thomas B. Butler, and sitting for more than thirty years as judge of probate for Norwalk and vicinity. Davenport proudly recalled his father's independent nature, never better evidenced than when he stood with Connecticut's "War Democrats" in supporting the Lincoln administration during the Civil War. This decision must have brought bitter rebukes from the regular organization, controlled by the "Peace Democrats," yet such was the elder Davenport's reputation for integrity that he was regularly returned to the probate judgeship with large majorities. Davenport also found remarkable his father's love of learning, which led him to take up the study of Hebrew when he was more than eighty.[7]

George Davenport saw to it that his children would appreciate and participate in the genteel cultural tradition he cherished. Daniel and his two brothers followed their father into the legal profession, in Daniel's case after graduating from Yale, a stronghold of genteel education. Noah Porter, inaugurated president during Davenport's junior year, committed the college to producing men of "comprehensive thought" and refined, liberal culture, rather than teams of "specialists."[8] Four elements of the curriculum were especially important sources of genteel values: the civic humanism of the great works of Greek and Roman antiquity; Scottish "commonsense" moral philosophy; classical economics; and liberal political philosophy, as found in such textbooks as Francis Lieber's *Manual of Political Ethics* (1838–39) and *On Civil Liberty* (1856) and Whiggish accounts of English constitutional history.

Classical training left its mark on Davenport's legal and political career in two respects. First, it helped him master the "middling style" that audiences expected from the lawyers and politicians of his generation. A reference to some figure in classical literature and patterns of speech modeled on the orations of Demosthenes or Cicero flattered speaker and listener alike; when coupled with more colloquial speech it impressed listeners without alienating them from the speaker.[9] Davenport effectively employed the middling style in most talks of any formality, whether a jury summation, an after-dinner address, or a political stump speech. In one address during his brief stint as spokesman against the regulation of railroad shipping rates, for example, Davenport drew upon both the pastoral imagery of Virgil's *Georgics* and the interrogatives of Ciceronian oratory to charm the residents of Clarinda, Iowa. After contrasting the "fresh, untouched, unbounded, magnificent wilderness" of the American Midwest before European settlement with the comfortable prosperity of twentieth-century Iowa, he asked: "What has wrought this wonderful transformation in the brief space of my short lifetime, unparalleled as it is in all the past ages of the world? What factor is it that has brought here this great and prosperous population, exceeding that of all France when Napoleon ruled it and sold this land to us?" To buttress his answer (railroads unencumbered by the superintendence of "political bodies"), Davenport first borrowed from Sallust and then folksily admonished would-be regulators to "let sleeping dogs lie."[10]

Classical training also introduced Davenport to the political culture of civic humanism, in which he found a powerful vocabulary for comprehending political life. The classic authors in this tradition had profoundly influenced the revolutionary generation. As the historian Gordon Wood writes, "Classicism was not only a scholarly ornament of educated Americans; it helped to shape their values and their ideals of behavior."[11] Noah Porter shared the earlier generation's enthusiasm for classical literature. One simply could not translate Homer or Virgil, he claimed, without being attracted to the dignity and truth found in their works. Porter kept the study of Greek and Latin at the center of Yale's curriculum when other colleges were easing it aside.[12] Although in time the claims of newly professionalized social scientists to powerful expert knowledge triumphed over Porter's genteel universalism, for most of the nineteenth century Cicero, Sallust, Tacitus, and Plutarch were widely assigned texts, and the lives and sentiments of the classical authors remained valuable sources for legal and political rhetoricians.[13]

Two classical ideals were particularly important. First, many Victorians were attracted to ancient exemplars of public-minded citizenship. The notion that private wealth carried with it both the capacity to perceive the common welfare and the obligation to defend it from self-interested factions repeatedly appears in the genteel literature and polemics of the Gilded Age. College-educated lawyer-politicians were particularly likely to find their model republican in Cicero, the great advocate whose orations showed how "reason and speech" could awaken listeners to peril around them. Many took to heart his counsel in *De officiis* that public eloquence could persuade individuals to look beyond their private interests to that of "the whole body politic."[14]

A second teaching of civic humanism was the timeless nature of the public good and the corrupting nature of change. The virtuous republican resisted innovation, for this could only represent declension from ancient ideals. In Victorian America, the ancients' general equation of fundamental change with declension was given specific historical and geographic content to produce a rhetorical figure that the historian Dorothy Ross has dubbed the "republican jeremiad."[15] In Tocqueville's telling, for example, America was "an empty land waiting for inhabitants," its first settlers "the seed of a great people which God with His own hands [planted] on a predestined shore."[16] The mission of this exceptional nation (defined by the Jeremiah as his or her purposes required) was confirmed in the American Revolution, which stood "at once as the climax of history and the pattern of things to come." To be true to the American mission, any change had to be a mere elaboration of the Founders' institutions. Qualitative change was dangerous: It jeopardized America's exceptional nature and threatened to introduce the serpent of European class warfare into the American Eden. Accounts of ancient revolts against the innovations of tyrants inspired Victorian republicans like Davenport to exhibit their own manliness (*virtus*) by denouncing social practices and legislation that they believed threatened the political institutions of the Founders.[17]

A second fertile source of inspiration for Davenport's later career was the mental and moral philosophy curriculum taught during his senior year by President Noah Porter. Porter's greatest intellectual debt was to the commonsense faculty psychology of Thomas Reid, Dugald Stewart, and other Scottish philosophers, who developed moral philosophy as a kind of "a priori psychologism" in which scholars "abstracted 'truths' about human nature from moral and religious assumptions that they regarded as axiomatic, made great display of 'discovering' these truths as empirical 'facts' in their own consciousness, and from these facts drew inferences about society, nature, and the moral universe."[18] Far from seeing science and culture as incompatible with theology, Porter insisted that the more advanced that knowledge of the world became, the more "the transcendent attractions of the supernatural Christ" could be discerned.[19]

As one might expect from a psychologist who defined his field as "the science of the human soul," the most important axiom in Porter's psychology was theological, the existence of "an uncreated Thinker" whose will humans could discover by using the intellect He created in them. The "faculties" or endowments that constituted the human intellect were immutable, "natural to man and universal with the race." These "observing," "creating," "thinking," and "intuiting" faculties were the means for comprehending all human experience; consequently, psychology was the foundational science for all other disciplines, including ethics, politics, social science, law, esthetics, and theology.[20]

Porter taught his seniors the fundamentals of "intellectual science" in their first term; in their second he pressed on to ethics, the domain of the intuitive faculty. Here Porter's assumption of the divine origins of the intellect gave his ethics their universalist and certain character. Because God endowed everyone with the same intuition, each could draw the same distinctions between right and wrong. The Creator had thus wrought moral law into the nature of things, so that ethical rules were as certain and uniform as the laws of physics.[21]

One inference Porter drew for his students was that the dutiful person who publicly insisted on righteous conduct would in time win the assent and support of others. This was most evident when he presented the moral reformer as a Christian Cicero, whose simple but forceful proclamations could restore long-suppressed truths to their proper social authority. "Let one man believe and feel strongly on moral themes," Porter declared, "and he becomes at once a power with his fellow-men. The assertion of convictions by one earnest man evokes responsive convictions from all who hear his words." The auditors' common "assenting and consenting conscience" would transform them into "a resistless power, now a rushing stream, and then a sweeping torrent," until the hostility or indifference of the general populace was overwhelmed. "The effects," Porter assured his students, "are often surprising in power, rapidity, and permanence."[22]

Porter's last words to Davenport's class played on all these themes. The text for his baccalaureate sermon was a verse from the Gospel of John, "Who is he that overcometh the World, but he that believeth that Jesus is the Son of God?" Porter took the evangelist's question as a call to faith in "the personal and supernatural Christ of history," whose death and resurrection redeemed sinful humanity. He urged the students not to surrender this faith "at the suggestions of the last discovered fossil" for a more idealized notion of Christian virtue. Without Christ, there could be no grounds for positing a common faculty for divining duty and obligation; without this faculty, right and wrong had no certain and universal content; without such a universalist ethics, public officials could indulge "a hireling's greed for gain or reputation or power." Political, legal, or social science without faith would not suffice; it would make "an educated legislature a den of thieves, and a bench of justice a place where justice is more skillfully and learnedly betrayed." Only manly believers in a personal, historical Christ could save the world from such a fate, for only they possessed "a courage that will never flinch, a disinterestedness that cannot be bought, a patience that is never wearied, and a love that never fails to subdue and win."[23]

A generation later, social scientists would unseat moral philosophers as the leading experts on human affairs and recast the "labor problem" of the Gilded Age—a puzzle capable of decisive resolution if only manly citizens enforced the right principles—as "labor relations," an ongoing process specialists could guide but never conclude.[24] Davenport, in contrast, continued to act on what Porter taught him: that the same immutable principles of right conduct were knowable by all, and all could be appraised by the same universal standards; that in judging public actors one should consider above all the morality of their intentions; that social ills were invariably the product of moral shortcomings that were themselves products of human sinfulness; and that by zealously and courageously proclaiming his convictions, "one earnest man" could restore scorned truths to their proper place.

In 1904, for example, Davenport paused in a letter to Charles Eliot to remark that the social gospeller Lyman Abbott's rejection of a divine "great first cause" and his celebration of "a God who is in and through and of everything" had "a queer sound to one reared in the atmosphere that existed hereabouts forty years ago." It should; it was the very idealized Christianity Porter had attacked in his last address to Davenport's class. A few years later Davenport urged an audience to look charitably upon the Calvinism of the settlers of a Connecticut town. "The origin of evil, the ineradicable tendency of the human heart to sin and do evil, the mournful spectacle of ruin and desolation in the moral world, and the future life are the same inscrutable mysteries to us as to them," he cautioned. "If we have constructed or adopted a more comfortable theology, it is . . . perhaps because we have forgotten or refused to look at some things at which they did not blink." Still later, in a speech to his Yale classmates, he argued that the outbreak of World War I proved that peace could not come from human expertise, but would arrive only when the sublime doctrines of Christianity were "enthroned in the hearts of man."[25]

If civic humanism equipped Davenport with classical rhetoric and role models and Porter provided theological grounds for insisting that social problems be analyzed in moral terms, the liberal tradition provided Davenport with the substance of his social analysis. Again, his principal inculcation came during his senior year from an imposing figure: William Graham Sumner, just installed as professor of political and social science. The son of an immigrant artisan, educated at Yale and in the new German historicism at the University of Gottingen, Sumner came to New Haven after service as an instructor at Yale and as rector of a prominent Episcopalian church.[26] Although he scoffed at the "mandarinism" of Porter's curriculum, Sumner shared his president's conviction that the fate of the commonwealth rested upon "the fidelity, the self-control, and the conscientiousness of the individual man" and that the highest obligation of an educator was to awaken students to their individual responsibility for the public welfare.[27]

By all accounts Sumner was an imposing and inspiring teacher. Unlike the majority of Yale's faculty, Sumner was well connected with men of affairs and gentry politicians, and his worldliness carried over to the classroom, where he employed the novel technique of referring to the *New York Times* during his lectures.[28] "He broke upon us like a cold spring in the desert," a member of the class of 1874 recalled. A later graduate remembered his education at Yale as a search for a teacher who could free himself from "the old ways of thought" and be relied upon to speak "boldly, honestly, and clearly from the new point of view." He found his "intellectual leader" in Sumner.[29]

In the fall of 1872 Sumner's course in political economy remained in the tradition of the "clerical economics" taught in antebellum colleges. Sumner himself learned his economics from writers in the classical tradition: the English author Harriet Martineau and Francis Wayland, Protestant clergyman and president of Brown University, whose *Elements of Political Science* (1837) was scarcely less popular than his influential textbook on moral philosophy, *Elements of Moral Science* (1835).[30] That a moral philosopher would produce both an economics and an ethics text was not surprising, for both fields were thought to deal with sentiments wrought in humans by the Creator. In fact, as Wayland wrote, the principles of political economy were so closely analogous to those of moral philosophy "that almost every question in the one may be argued on grounds belonging to the other."[31] Just as God instilled the same moral intuitions into all, so did He endow humans with the instinct to seek pleasure and avoid pain, which was in turn the basis for the laws of supply and demand. Sumner's economics was therefore just as certain and universal as Porter's ethics, and for the same, divine, reason.[32]

The text Davenport and his classmates read for Sumner's class, Arthur Latham Perry's *Elements of Political Economy* (1871), updated Wayland without departing from the clerical tradition. "From beginning to end of Perry's popular text," Dorothy Ross writes, "God made frequent appearance." Perry believed God's goodness was nowhere more discernible than in the natural laws of supply and demand. So long as each person was free to engage in voluntary exchanges, society as a whole would benefit; "so long as capital and labor rest solely upon their natural rights, neither can have the advantage of the other," and each would make the other prosperous. But let government usurp the natural functioning of the market by granting monopolies and special privileges, protective tariffs, maximum-hours legislation, or usury laws, and the results for the nation's material well-being and moral fabric could be disastrous.[33]

On these fundamental points, Sumner's lectures reinforced the assigned text. The laws of supply and demand, he wrote in his lecture notes for 1874, "are fixed in the order of the universe. We may go still further and say [they are] God's laws." He was Perry's equal in attacking the protective tariff: "Everyone left his course in political economy a free trader," a student recalled.[34] If Perry believed the only just rule for exchanges between capital and labor was that "each party is bound to look out for his own interest, to know the market value of his own service, and to make the best terms for himself which he can make," Sumner likewise declared that between members of a highly organized society "justice can mean nothing but the unrestricted play of supply and demand."[35]

Finally, Perry and Sumner believed the United States had its competitive markets to thank for the absence of permanent social classes among its people. In the early 1870s neither saw any evidence of social stratification like that of the Old World. "In the United States the greatest freedom prevails," Perry wrote. "There is nothing to hinder any laborer from becoming a capitalist; nearly all our capitalists were formally laborers." Sumner agreed. "Let every man be sober, industrious, prudent, and wise, and bring up his children to be so likewise," he counseled, "and poverty will be abolished in a few generations."[36]

None of this would favorably dispose Davenport or his fellow students to trade unionism, and in fact the general tenor of Perry's and Sumner's specific discussion of strikes and boycotts was unfavorable. Yet here a difference between the two is worth noting. Perry subscribed to a rather strict version of the "wages-fund" theory of classical economics. Developed to explain a primarily agricultural economy, the theory was inspired by the obligation of masters to sustain their workers out of the savings from the previous year's harvest. From this observation classical economists from Adam Smith to John Stuart Mill reasoned that employers designated a portion of their working capital for the payment of wages. As capital accumulated, the size of this wages fund could grow, benefiting workers and capitalists alike. At any particular moment, however, the fund available for the payment of wages was fixed so that the average wage in an industry was simply and invariably the wages fund divided by the number of laborers.[37]

The consequences of the wages-fund theory for those who would try to increase wages by collective or governmental action were stark indeed. Such efforts, Perry wrote, were "a delusion," because they could at best improve the lot of some workers at the expense of others. "There is no use arguing against any one of the four fundamental rules of arithmetic," Perry admonished. "The question of wages is a question of Division." Not surprisingly, Perry emphatically and unequivocally denounced trade unions: "The spirit of Political Economy, which is the spirit of freedom, is against such associations." Strikes were "false in theory and pernicious in fact"; they sprung from "utter misapprehension of the true principles of wages"; they upset the divinely ordained, mutually dependent relations of employers and employees; and they almost never permanently benefited the workers themselves.[38]

If Perry's text thus left Davenport without the slightest grounds for approving labor unions, Sumner's lectures were more generous. While Sumner agreed with the classical economists that wages generally varied with the amount of capital and number of laborers in an economy, he denied that they were paid out of an employer's working capital. Wages and profits were not inversely related; they could be and often were high and low together. Wages were set by the "supply and demand of personal talents and capacities" at the time production commenced. Employers had to pay enough to make it worthwhile for their workers, and where, as in the United States, workers could choose to devote their time to their own freeholds and business schemes this sum could be considerable. The only limit on wages was what employers could successfully recover from consumers, which had no necessary relation to working capital. Thus, Sumner concluded, "it is a great error to treat [wages] as a simple ratio of arithmetical quantities."[39]

From this revised theory of the wages fund, Sumner derived a more tolerant position on trade unions and strikes. As currently practiced in the United States, trade unionism left much to be desired. "It teaches the men not to take pains, not to try to excel, not to do good work," Sumner complained. Its philosophy was that workers should "try not to produce, on the theory that if things are made scarce and dear and hard to get, that makes 'work,' and so makes wages high."[40] Yet collective action by workers was not necessarily evil; in fact, employer-employee conflict was "legitimate and necessary," for the law of supply and demand assumed that each party would "struggle to the utmost for its interests." Strikes in particular were not great evils; they were costly, but they tested the market. Labor unions that limited themselves to orchestrating voluntary withdrawals from an employment relationship simply aided workers as they exercised "the first prerogative of a free man": the right to make or unmake contracts. Only when labor unions struck for impermissible ends, such as to force an employer to hire only union labor, or when they pursued "monstrous" secondary boycotts did they become "industrial factions." Sumner's students thus learned to accept trade unionism, but only so long as the trade unionists accepted the basic tenets of free-market capitalism.[41]

Davenport retained Perry's and Sumner's belief in the natural working of supply and demand and also something like Sumner's position on trade unionism. Perhaps the most notable occasion for his defense of competitive markets came in 1908 during congressional hearings on the so-called Hepburn bill, a measure to revise the strict antitrust policy established by

the Supreme Court's *Trans-Missouri* case. Davenport led the opposition to
the bill, primarily because of its possible consequences for the AABA's suits
against organized labor and also because he rejected attempts by capitalists to limit output and fix prices for their goods at other than their "real
value." Thus he likened Elbert Gary of United States Steel to the czar in
that both usurped the natural law of supply and demand.[42] To bolster his
claim that competition was "part of the providential order of things," Davenport submitted an article by the French economist Charles Coquelin,
who found the competitive instinct to be part of "the very nature of man"
and declared it "the true motive power of progress in human society."[43]

Sumner was also the most important teacher of the final element in
Davenport's genteel education at Yale—liberal political philosophy and
history. Sumner's principal lesson came through clearly enough. Following Henry Maine's *Ancient Law* (1861), Sumner declared contract—"real-
istic, cold, matter-of-fact" contract—the only sound basis for civil society
in modern states because it alone provided "the utmost room and chance
for individual development, and for all the self-reliance and dignity of a
free man." When he turned to the state he found not the morally resonant
Rechtstaat of his German teachers but a thinner, contractual arrangement,
"a little group of men chosen in a very haphazard way by the majority of
us to perform certain services for all of us." The redistribution of wealth
through regulatory or other means was not among these agents' mandate,
for Sumner assumed it could not win universal assent. The only proper role
of the state was to maintain "neutral conditions of security"—"peace, order, and the guarantees of rights." Going further and favoring some group
with more than it could obtain through contract amounted to a reaction-
ary return to status. Labor legislation, for example, was objectionable because it reduced the independent American worker to the status of social
dependents, like "Indians, or freedmen, or women, or children."[44]

Davenport's understanding of Sumner's political philosophy seems never
to have proceeded beyond this point, which was hardly an advance on the
social contract of Locke's *Second Treatise*. In a manner similar to more famous laissez-faire jurists, such as Supreme Court justices Stephen J. Field
and David Brewer, Davenport combined a Jeffersonian assertion of inalienable rights with the free-labor rhetoric of his War-Democrat father to produce a powerful defense of unregulated capitalism. At the same congressional hearings in which he praised competition, for example, Davenport
referred to the Declaration of Independence as "the title deed of American institutions" and agreed with a congressman that Jefferson's words had
"saturated" the Constitution "with the fundamental inherent principles of
natural justice."[45]

In opting for a natural-rights theory of the political order, Davenport overlooked or rejected alternative positions, including that of Sumner himself. Noah Porter's moral philosophy, for example, held that humanity's divinely endowed social nature made the state a natural phenomenon and not a human artifice. Consequently, the state was not limited to defending "the so-called natural rights of life, liberty and property," but could act in a broader and less clearly defined domain fixed by "the traditions of the past, the habits of the present, and, above all, . . . the intelligence, the self-reliance, and the moral worth of the people."[46] Francis Lieber, whose popular text *On Civil Liberty* Davenport read for Sumner, also assumed humans were essentially social beings and that rights originated in human institutions. Like Henry Hallam's *Constitutional History of England,* assigned to Davenport during his last term at Yale, Lieber's influential work traced the gradual expansion of liberty until it reached a kind of apotheosis in recent Anglo-American constitutional law.[47]

Sumner's lectures may have reinforced Lieber's historicist approach. In the 1880s, Sumner followed Lieber in defining civil liberty as an inherited condition "created for the individual by laws and institutions" and treated the idea of natural rights as patently ridiculous. "Before the tribunal of nature, a man has no more right to life than a rattlesnake," he snorted. "He has no more right to liberty than any wild beast." An appreciation of the dangerously open-ended quality of natural-rights arguments led him to this stance. If on one occasion the Supreme Court's resort to "great, *a priori* principles . . . makes for us," Sumner wrote to a friend in 1881, "next time it will make for theirs." In contrast, history was a more secure place in which to discover rights, at least as long as it was the domain of genteel writers.[48]

Judging from the notes for his early lectures (reviewed by Donald Bellomy in an important study), in the 1870s Sumner similarly taught his students that rights were social in origin, but he did so without sharply distinguishing this historicist argument from earlier, natural-rights positions.[49] Davenport might well have failed to appreciate the imperfectly articulated historicism of his teacher's lectures. His wide reading in the sources of colonial and revolutionary history would certainly have made the language of natural rights familiar to him. (Given his ancestry Davenport might well have considered it a birthright.)[50] Upon graduating and plunging into politics, Davenport may well have discovered that talk of rights was a better vehicle for stirring campaign oratory. Whatever its origins, the choice of natural rights over historical jurisprudence had significant consequences for Davenport's later career as an antiunion lawyer.

These consequences do not include his opposition to certain kinds of strikes and boycotts. First, the natural-rights tradition could be used to defend such activities, as when trade unionists likened their boycotts to the patriots' nonimportation campaigns against the Townsend and Stamp Acts of the Revolutionary Era and invoked "the innate right of man" to bestow his trade in accordance with his moral and social convictions.[51] Second, these same activities could be attacked on historicist grounds so long as the opponent had a teleological understanding of historical development. Even someone who rejected the idea of natural *rights* might still believe (with Herbert Spencer) in the existence of natural *laws,* divinely ordained moral principles that became manifest as time unfolded. Any change inconsistent with the moral order of the universe, as understood by the observer, could be condemned as an illegitimate, artificial innovation.[52]

This was the lesson Sumner drew from Spencer's work. The United States might advance to a higher level of social development, Sumner allowed, but only by proceeding "in the direction of more complete realization of a society of free men united by contract." Secondary boycotts and strikes for the closed shop did not qualify as steps toward a higher cooperative plane in Sumner's reckoning; they were instead coercive acts running counter to the mainstream of historical development.[53] Similarly, some of the most notable treatise writers of the laissez-faire era, such as Thomas Cooley and Christopher Tiedeman, were simultaneously historicists and sharp critics of trade unionism.[54]

Where Davenport's preference for natural-rights jurisprudence did appear to have significant consequences was in his attitude toward the state. Certainly, historicists were not invariably more accepting of novel uses of state power. Sumner and Tiedeman, for example, employed the moral logic of historical development just as effectively against the regulatory state as they did against the excesses of trade unionism. For other jurists, however, historicism provided an answer to critics of modest regulatory innovations. Cooley, for example, became the first chair of the Interstate Commerce Commission, which the natural-rights jurist David Brewer considered an abomination.[55] Deeper and wider tolerance of trade unionism and governmental regulation awaited the dissemination of a secular, nonteleological historicism throughout the legal profession. Although Oliver Wendell Holmes, Jr., could comfortably fashion a jurisprudence premised upon neither the natural rights of the Declaration of Independence nor the natural laws of "Mr. Herbert Spencer's Social Statics," few if any other members of the Victorian bench could join in so atheistic an enterprise.[56]

Davenport's predilection for natural-rights jurisprudence helps explain his opposition to minimum wages and hours laws and the compulsory arbitration of labor disputes. For another illustration of Davenport's antistatism—turning on the right to procreate—consider his protest against the law Connecticut adopted in 1909 providing for the compulsory sterilization of the criminally insane. Drawing upon research in the manuscripts of the state library, he showed that the ancestors of the great Puritan theologian Jonathan Edwards had committed a variety of criminal and sexual-ly promiscuous acts in moments of mental instability. "It would seem that, if from such unpromising stock so many lines of noble descendants could spring," Davenport observed dryly, "it would be well to go a little slow in attempting to protect society from the descendants of anybody." In contrast, Holmes's historicist understanding of the state's demands upon its citizens led him to write *Buck v. Bell* (1927), his infamous decision upholding Virginia's eugenics program.[57]

In sum, by the time Davenport left Yale he had received formal instruction in the most important components of gentry culture in Victorian America. He learned from the classical exponents of civic virtue and a clerical instructor in moral philosophy that the revolutionary generation had founded the American republic on universal, a priori principles grounded ultimately in Protestant Christianity and that he should strive wherever possible to prevent or reverse departures from these timeless precepts. He learned from classical economics and liberal political philosophy that attempts to regulate prices and output upset the providential laws of supply and demand and trampled upon the rights of employers, workers, and consumers. Sumner in particular charged him to resist such threats to the permanent welfare and "political virtue" of the country.[58]

For almost three decades after leaving Yale, Davenport behaved as his teachers said he should, believing with Sumner that when the citizenry grew tired of their small-minded governors they would turn to the college-educated gentry "for men who know what ought to be done and how to do it."[59] By the turn of the century, however, Davenport had ample reason to conclude that that day would never come, notwithstanding the best efforts of a would-be Cicero such as himself. With electoral politics foreclosed, how then could he defend the cultural ideals of the Victorian gentry?

LAW AND POLITICS

Critics of the antiunion lawyers and injunction judges of the early twentieth century often attacked them for harboring biases built up over years of service to industrial concerns and confusing the interests of their clients with that of the whole society.[60] Davenport's legal and political career before 1902 was nothing like what one would expect from this critique. Although he was not quite the obscure "country lawyer" of his letter to his classmates, most of Davenport's cases appear to have involved the personal affairs of private individuals, and his commercial clients were rarely the proprietary capitalists or manufacturing concerns who would later join the ranks of the antiunion movement. Indeed, some of his most important legal work pitted him against large corporations; other cases allowed him to pose as a defender of working-class culture; still others grew out of partisan politics. Combining legal work for the Democratic party with his own campaigning for municipal office, Davenport did not sharply distinguish his professional from his political activities. No less than the Wall Street lawyers Robert Gordon has studied, Davenport believed he could exemplify in his private practice "the public roles demanded by conceptions of republican virtue."[61]

Davenport's dual career in law and politics commenced soon after his graduation in 1873, when he started reading law in the offices of Asa B. Woodward, who would succeed George Davenport as probate judge for the Norwalk district in 1878, and John H. Perry, who would serve with Davenport in the state constitutional convention of 1902. In early 1875 Davenport represented Wilton in the state legislature as a Democrat; in September he was admitted to the bar. He married a month later and by April 1876 had moved to the growing industrial city of Bridgeport to start a year's term as assistant city attorney and prosecutor. Over the next three decades Davenport became an active member of Bridgeport's legal community and Democratic party.[62]

Davenport's law partner for some seventeen years was William H. O'Hara, a second-generation Irishman who was also prominent among Bridgeport's Democrats. When Lord Bryce visited the United States in the early 1880s he found many two-person firms like Davenport and O'Hara, which Bryce believed quite sensibly paired courtroom spellbinders with office men better suited to managing "the thousand little things for which a man goes to his attorney."[63] In the case of Davenport and O'Hara, Davenport played the former role. While not adept at "the business side of a modern law practice," he was an imposing advocate before a jury or an appellate bench, thanks to his marvelous memory, his literary and historical allusions, and his ability to trace a principle of law "clear to its beginnings."[64] He was a large man, weighing some 250 pounds, but he exercised regularly so that his bulk increased the impression of command and forcefulness in the courtroom. "Nature gave him a stalwart physique, an engaging personality, an abundance of physical stamina," O'Hara recalled. He combined a commanding presence, "praetorian dignity," and "a rare sweetness of nature," which led him to greet his old friends in the Bridgeport bar cordially, even after he attained national prominence through his work for the AABA. Although he sometimes sparred in court with his fellow Connecticut Democrat and lawyer Simeon Baldwin, Davenport joined Baldwin's American Bar Association and supported the founders' goal of promoting the ethics and learning of the bar under the leadership of its "best men."[65]

In the 1880s and 1890s, such gentry lawyers expressed almost as much

alarm over the rise of large business concerns as they did about the newly formed, nationally organized trade unions. Democrats in particular
were quick to spot corporations' corrupting influence in politics and the
market, if only because they were less likely to enjoy the benefits of corporate lobbying. Algernon Sydney Sullivan, a southern Democrat who
co-founded the Wall Street firm of Sullivan and Cromwell, for example,
took the dedication of New York City's Consolidated Petroleum and
Stock Exchange in September 1887 as an occasion to denounce the business corporation as a "dangerous contrivance" that could indefinitely ac-
cumulate money and power, smother competition, and swindle the public. Individual proprietorship, whether that of a small manufacturer, a
professional, or even a worker, was a different matter altogether, because
each was subject to the disciplinary machinery of the market, and none
was likely to maintain great wealth over many generations. In contrast,
Sullivan's young partner William Cromwell Nelson, a pioneer corporation lawyer, largely gave up the courtroom for the more lucrative office
work of corporate mergers and reorganizations.[66]

So far as we can tell, Davenport's law practice gave him no occasion to
build up allegiances to new business corporations; in fact, his work for industrial clients of any variety was infrequent. Of the fifty-one disputes
in which Davenport appeared before the Connecticut Supreme Court between 1876 and 1907, forty involved public entities or the personal or political troubles of private individuals, including sixteen cases growing out
of the probate of estates. Nine appeals involved the business affairs of individuals or proprietorships, and Davenport represented business corporations in only two appeals. [67]

Davenport's appellate clients included none of the metalworking and
manufacturing concerns that were turning Bridgeport into one of New
England's most important industrial cities. Most prominent businessmen,
as Davenport noted, were Republicans and favored Republicans when looking for a lawyer. As a result, most of Davenport's commercial and industrial clients were individuals or small concerns: a high school principal, a
law tutor, a construction contractor, a hotel-keeper, a retailer, a real-estate
broker, and a manufacturer of phosphate manures and fish byproducts.[68]
Once he represented the Chemical Bank of New York when its interest in
a farm was threatened by a suit to foreclose a mechanics lien. On another
occasion he defended the Pennsylvania Railroad in a suit brought by an
attorney, Alberto Roraback, for professional services rendered.[69] Republican lawyers might well have declined to represent the railroad, because the
plaintiff and his brother were powerful figures in the state party. Davenport, in contrast, would have welcomed the opportunity to oppose a leader of the Republican machine.[70]

A third corporate case, also with political overtones, was fought out before the Interstate Commerce Commission in 1890–91. In the late 1880s, after years of close cooperation between the two boards of directors, the New York, New Haven and Hartford Railroad and the Boston-based New York and New England Railroad started to compete actively for shipments between Boston and New York. Looking about for a railroad to complete its route to New York City, the New York and New England considered two options. One was a connection along the Connecticut coast via the Housatonic Railroad, a line built and owned by Bridgeport businessmen, including the Democratic politician William H. Barnum. Another was via the New York and Northern, a line running along the New York–Connecticut border quite near Danbury, Connecticut. The Boston railroad chose the Housatonic and insisted that it stop allowing Danbury's manufacturers and merchants to use through bills of lading over its line between Danbury and Brewster, New York, the connecting point with the New York and Northern. This effectively deprived the New York and Northern of the Danbury trade. "It was like two ladies with one gentleman paying attention to both," Davenport later explained. "When he selected one the other was left . . . in the condition of an old maid."[71]

The New York and Northern responded by filing suit before the ICC and hiring the prominent Wall Street lawyers Sherman Evarts and William A. Day. The New York and New England seemed to have left the selection of defense counsel to the Housatonic, which chose Davenport and O'Hara. The New York and Northern produced a small army of Danbury businessmen to state their preference for its route. In their number was Charles H. Merritt, whose bristling exchanges with Davenport left the lawyer muttering about Danbury's unparalleled "assemblage of cranks and kickers and strikers."[72]

Evarts and Day charged the Housatonic with monopoly, fighting words to a lawyer schooled in classical economics. Davenport defended his representation of a large business concern by casting his client as an opponent of a larger, anticompetitive railroad. He did not stress the virtues and efficiency of combination, as corporate liberals later would. Rather, he insisted that his clients faced "the fiercest competition at almost every important point along the line." The most daunting competitor was the "Consolidated Road," the New York, New Haven and Hartford, notorious for its influence with Republicans in the Connecticut legislature. Davenport defended the injury to the "New York & Nowhere" as the price of relieving western Connecticut from the tyranny of the New York and New Haven. "Let me tell you gentlemen," he lectured the ICC commissioners, "George III was never such a tyrant in Connecticut as is that 'Consolidated Road.'"[73]

If such reasoning helped Davenport square his occasional representation of large business concerns with his gentry values, his occasional defense of more humble clients also helped him preserve his self-image as a republican lawyer in classless America. In defending William Clark, for example, who refused to answer a grand jury's questions about his purchases of liquor on Sunday, or in resisting the revocation of the liquor license of the hotel-keeper Clark patronized, Davenport stood with the urban, working-class, ethnic constituents of the Democratic party and against temperance-minded, rural, Yankee Republicans. If Davenport's clients included the occasional railroad, they also included Bertha Maisenbacker, a paper-box maker who sued Danbury's Concordia Society when she was forcibly ejected for "dancing in an indecent manner." Davenport won punitive damages for his client, who had been told she "was not a fit person" to mingle with the town's polite society.[74]

Partisan calculations lurked behind such disputes, and they were explicit in many other cases. "I have been a Democrat all my life," Davenport once declared, "and have eaten and drunk, and tasted and smelt and swum in and advocated Democracy from a thousand stumps."[75] He might have added that he had litigated Democracy in scores of courtrooms. In 1878 he successfully prosecuted Owen Harty's claim to the position of Bridgeport street commissioner after the common council had selected a rival during the absence of Mayor Robert E. DeForest, a Yankee Democrat lawyer much like Davenport. In 1884 Davenport and DeForest defended a predominantly Democratic common council against charges of procedural irregularity in the widening of the city's streets. Democratic candidates for the city's chief of police, registrar of voters, controller, and director of public works turned to Davenport or his firm in electoral matters, and on one occasion he defended the aldermen's decision to place official notices in the Democratic Bridgeport *Farmer* and the independent *Post* instead of the Republican *News*.[76]

Interspersed with such litigation were Davenport's duties as the holder of a string of elective or appointive offices for the city of Bridgeport. He was assistant city attorney in 1876–77; justice of the peace from 1879 to 1881 and 1887 to 1889 (the source of the honorific "Judge" sometimes used by Davenport's antiunion comrades); a member of the common council from 1879 to 1880; president of the board of charities from 1889 to 1893; and city attorney from 1893 to 1895.[77] Law and politics were inseparable for Davenport; courtrooms and hustings were simply different venues for a single-minded advocacy of gentry ideals. His early career as a lawyer cannot be understood apart from the political history of Connecticut and, in particular, the rise and fall of the Cleveland Democracy in the state.

When Davenport won election to the state legislature in 1875, Connecticut's Democrats were in the midst of their first sustained period of electoral success since before the Civil War. For most of the 1880s and 1890s, Bridgeport's administration remained safely in the hands of Democrats, whose constituency of first- and second-generation immigrants grew steadily over the period.[78] Other Connecticut cities registered similar gains, yet a scheme of apportionment that gave small, rural, and usually Republican towns the same representation in the lower house as the largest municipalities deadlocked politics on the state level. In 1884, 1886, and 1888, for example, Democratic gubernatorial candidates won pluralities in the popular vote, yet failed to take office when the legislature (whose concurrence was required if no candidate received a majority) selected the Republican nominee.[79]

In this period the state Democratic party was dominated by the wealthy iron manufacturer William H. Barnum and Alexander Troup, a newspaper editor with a large following among the state's workers and immigrant groups. Arrayed against this machine of "iron and Irishmen" was a reform or Yankee wing, the political home of George and Daniel Davenport, which was predominantly comprised of native-born advocates of civil service, low tariffs, and limited government. The Yankee Democrats were largely ineffectual in statewide matters until they formed an alliance with Connecticut's "Mugwumps," genteel Republicans appalled by bossism in their own party. These disaffected Republicans included Davenport's teacher Sumner, his fellow lawyer Simeon Baldwin, and Mark Twain, whose sardonic commentary on political affairs was an invaluable asset. ("Suppose you were an idiot," Twain once wrote. "And suppose you were a member of Congress. But I repeat myself.")[80] The tentative cooperation between the Yankee Democrats and Mugwumps during Grover Cleveland's first presidential campaign in 1884 was solidified during his second run in 1888, so that by 1890 the two groups could merge into an expressly Democratic organization, the Connecticut Democratic Club.[81]

The genteel politicians triumphed over the machine Democrats at the state convention of 1890 and selected a slate of reform nominees, including the Bridgeport lawyer and former mayor Robert E. DeForest, who would go on to win his election to the U.S. House of Representatives.[82] This alliance enjoyed considerable success until it collapsed in the critical election of 1894, which commenced sixteen years of unbroken Republican rule in the state, and the capture of the national Democratic party in 1896 by its "free silver" wing led by William Jennings Bryan. Thereafter, the state party was controlled by ethnic political leaders, primarily Irish Catholics, but also Italians and Russian Jews. Baldwin, DeForest, and a few other prominent Yankees stayed in the party, but most either bolted to the Republicans or consigned themselves to the political limbo of independency.[83]

One can understand how a genteel politician like Davenport experienced this quarter century of political history by considering three different episodes: his vigorous support of the presidential candidacies of Grover Cleveland, his call as city attorney for strict oversight of the construction of Bridgeport's street railway, and his service in the Connecticut Constitutional Convention of 1902. Cleveland's significance as a political icon can easily be overlooked today, when he is recalled, if at all, as a rather large, mustached, unreflective, and determined man who presided over one of the nation's worst economic depressions. Yet his meteoric rise from mayor of Buffalo in 1881 to the governorship of New York in 1883 to the presidency in 1885, vetoing at each step the boodle of grafting politicians, thrilled the normally cautious gentry politicians. "From the first I have been one of your supporters because you seemed to me to represent the principles in which I believe more fully than any man now in public life," gushed Brooks Adams in a fan letter in 1884. Woodrow Wilson saw Cleveland's first election as the spontaneous choice of "the body of the people." Progressive editor William Allen White agreed: Cleveland reached the presidency borne "by the tidal power that was moving in the protesting hearts of the people"; he was the champion of a people "sick with politics" and "nauseated at all politicians." Cleveland, in short, was the gentry's ideal public figure. A holder of political office, he was nonetheless no "politician." Duty, not ambition, propelled him upward to the presidency.[84]

Davenport demonstrated admiration for Cleveland by stumping for him in each of his three presidential campaigns. Davenport certainly could identify with Cleveland, for their resemblance went beyond their stout physiques and walrus mustaches. Both were genteel lawyers with political ambitions that depended upon the support of working-class voters. Both prided themselves on their ability to mingle with the working classes. If Cleveland comfortably drank beer alongside German workers in Buffalo's saloons, Davenport could call Bridgeport's workingmen his friends. "Whatever I had in this world in the way of political preferment," he once declared, "I owe to them." And if Cleveland's progress seemed to show that the public would acclaim and reward courageous opponents of political corruption, Davenport may well have hoped higher office would follow his own stand against graft in city government.[85]

Davenport's Ciceronian moment came in 1894 during his tenure as city attorney. That summer, the construction methods of the Bridgeport Traction Company, formed to build and operate a street railway for the city, provoked wide public complaint. The company enjoyed the support of a large majority of the common council, but Davenport and the editor of the city's independent newspaper were outraged by the company's grade work, unnecessary blockage of city thoroughfares, and shoddy construction materials. Davenport urged the common council to act quickly to remedy these problems, yet the aldermen did nothing.[86] The dispute came to a head after the acting mayor (Davenport's partner William O'Hara) vetoed a resolution of the common council that in all likelihood would have absolved the company from making the necessary repairs and improvements. As the aldermen considered overriding the veto, Davenport warned in an open letter that doing so would amount to a total surrender of the city's interests.[87] When the aldermen contended that the special act the company had obtained from the state legislature barred them from proceeding, Davenport fired off another salvo:

> The fault, gentlemen, is not in the law, but in yourselves that the city's interests are not better looked after. The most absolute and sweeping power over the whole matter is placed in your hands, and it is only by the neglect on your part to exercise it with intelligence, firmness and vigor, that those interests are jeopardized. . . . If there is just cause of complaint on the part of the citizens on account of the quality of work done, or the method of doing it, the responsibility rests with you.[88]

"Thank God we have a fearless law advisor," wrote one grateful taxpayer to the Bridgeport *Post*, which weighed in strongly against the traction company and aldermen. Whatever satisfaction Davenport might have taken from such support was short-lived, however, because the common council overrode the veto the day after receiving his letter. "Traction Company in Clover," the *Post*'s headline declared. "Can Now Do Anything They Like with City." Construction on the roadbed proceeded as before, and when Davenport reviewed the project in the summer of 1895 he found it substandard from start to finish.[89]

In 1882 Cleveland had escaped the maw of urban politics, thanks to the intervention of a strong state party in search of a gubernatorial standard-bearer. In 1895 Connecticut's Democratic party could provide Davenport with no similar means of ascent because its gentry wing had already started to disintegrate.[90] Davenport was left alone with the machine politicians he had opposed during the traction fight, and they had little inclination to reward him with another public office. Local observers judged that O'Hara's veto meant that his political fortunes were "ready to be reviewed by the coroner"—also an apt observation for Davenport.[91]

Davenport, in turn, grew increasingly dissatisfied as the advocates of protectionism and the free coinage of silver captured the machinery of Bridgeport's Democratic party.[92] In 1896 he voted against Bryan, whom he considered a "populist" rather than a true Democrat, and in 1898 he voted for the Republican industrialist Ebenezer J. Hill over the Democratic nominee for Congress.[93] Davenport's political prospects were no brighter in

1901, when he wrote his self-pitying note to his classmates. That fall he and the other "gold men" successfully supported an antimachine candidate for mayor, Denis Mulvihill, a coal-shoveler who ran on the agreeable slogan "rugged honesty" and was swept into office with great majorities in the working-class wards. Whether a Yankee Democrat could ever provoke such enthusiasm was doubtful, and Mulvihill's election did nothing to improve Davenport's chances of obtaining a major political office. What Davenport won instead, possibly as the price of the Gold Democrats' support of Mulvihill, was the Democratic nomination to represent Bridgeport in the state constitutional convention scheduled to convene in Hartford on New Year's Day, 1902, the first since the 1818 convention attended by Davenport's grandfather. Davenport easily beat his Republican rival, although with a considerably smaller majority than Mulvihill enjoyed.[94]

To most observers, the convention promised to be a quixotic affair. For years Connecticut's urban politicians had called for a revision of the constitution to end the disproportionate representation of small towns. Urban Democrats were particularly eager for reapportionment, as they had regularly seen their legislative proposals blocked by small-town representatives, who were widely thought to be the pawns of lobbyists for the Consolidated Road and the state's insurance industry. Davenport, for example, had accused the Republicans of willful partisanship on the question as early as 1894. With the Republicans enjoying an overwhelming majority among the convention's delegates (122 members to the Democrats' forty-nine), to expect a different outcome one needed an enormous faith in the justice of the urbanites' cause and the power of public opinion.[95]

These Davenport possessed. His performance at the convention impressed genteel commentators who still believed that manly, articulate calls to duty would win public acclaim and support, that strong moral convictions could make a person "a power with his fellow men." No delegate introduced more resolutions, including proposals to secure the right of trial by jury for plaintiffs suing for injuries in the workplace, to outlaw lobbying by corporations and the issuance of free railroad passes to legislators, and to prevent trusts from pricing goods at other than their "real value."[96] He even introduced a resolution in favor of woman suffrage, explaining that he would vote for it to give female taxpayers the equal representation he sought for all the state's citizens. Davenport won a laugh from his fellow delegates—and acknowledged the anxiety they felt in contemplating the prospect of women as political actors—by disavowing "personal reasons" for supporting the resolve. His wife and daughter were "bitterly opposed" to woman suffrage, he assured his male counterparts.[97]

Davenport's grandest moments came in leading the urban delegates' fight for greater representation in the legislature. His first major speech of the convention was an attack on the principal constitutional objection of the small towns. Their "great argument," as Davenport rendered it, was that Connecticut's towns were "earlier in the order of their existence than the state, and that in Connecticut history the idea of the township carries with it the right to representation in the General Assembly." Once attained, a town's representation in the legislature could never be reduced. To demolish this theory, Davenport provided the delegates with a tour-de-force review of the formation of individual towns and their widely varying representation in the assembly. "For three hours [he] held that body in intense interest," a friend recalled thirty years later. "Without a note, dates, places, facts and incidents fell from his lips in their right order, giving to them their most dramatic effect in words so chosen that they fitted in his story with all the symmetry the chiseled stone of a majestic cathedral fits into its designated place."[98]

Davenport urged the Republicans to follow the wisdom of Connecticut's founders, who took "the great principles of human equality and human liberty and human rights" from the Declaration of Independence and made them a part of the fundamental law of the state. Proportionate representation was a simple deduction from those principles, to which each delegate had solemnly sworn obedience. Just as Davenport had warned Bridgeport's common council that the public would demand an accounting of their dealings with the street railway company, so did he now remind the Republican delegates that "the people, knowing you have the power, will hold you responsible for the use you make of it."[99]

Davenport's threat was no more effective in 1902 than in 1894. With the small-town forces firmly marshaled by Donald T. Warner of Salisbury, the convention remained deadlocked for a month. Then, after a proposal backed by Warner carried in the Committee of the Whole, Davenport caused what the Hartford delegate Charles H. Clark later termed "probably the most intense incident of the convention." Davenport commenced the proceedings on February 13 by offering a resolution denouncing the composition of the convention, declaring its immediate adjournment, and calling upon the governor to convene another in which large towns would be properly represented. As the nature of the resolution became clear, the convention's president (a member of Warner's "Litchfield County Caucus") pounded his gavel until he stopped the clerk from reading further. "Then Mr. Davenport produced a duplicate and read the rest himself," Clark recalled, "shouting with his stentorian voice so as to overcome the racket of presidential protest." Although the convention came very close to dissolving in chaos, the crisis passed. The proceedings ground on until May 15, when the delegates adjourned after adopting, with little enthusiasm, a compromise plan of representation. The product of their heated debates was rejected by a two-to-one margin in a referendum in which only 15 percent of the electorate bothered to vote.[100]

Before the referendum took place, Davenport had decided to lead the AABA. The reportage of his exploits at the constitutional convention brought him to the notice of a statewide audience for the first time in his career, and the publicity and the admiration of Connecticut's genteel politicians must have confirmed his own conviction that he could play a larger role in the defense of the moral, economic, and political values of genteel Victorian culture. Yet the indifference of the populace to his philippics and the capture of Connecticut's Democratic party by ethnic, working-class politicians must have soured him on partisan politics. If in 1902 Davenport struck Charles Merritt as being "free from political ambitions," this was because the lawyer had given up the doubtful struggle to reconcile his Victorian values and the requirements of electoral politics in a pluralist age.[101]

The attractions of the AABA are also clear in light of Davenport's recent political history. If the realm of electoral politics had fallen to the barbarians, a final bastion of genteel culture, the judiciary, still stood. In 1884, one of Davenport's fellow members of the American Bar Association, dismayed by the legislative tendencies of his day, concluded an address by challenging his brethren to lift their clients "above the passions of the hour" and bring their causes to the "inner Republic" of the courts, where judges and lawyers of "wisdom, moderation, and patriotism" could resolve disputes as morality and intellect required.[102] A decade or so later, Holmes noted the same sentiment, albeit from a very different intellectual perspective. The fear of socialism, or something like it, he declared in 1897, "has led people who no longer hope to control the legislatures to look to the courts as expounders of the Constitutions," with the result that in some decisions "new principles have been discovered outside the bodies of those instruments, which may be generalized into acceptance of the economic doctrines which prevailed about fifty years ago."[103]

Holmes wrote to confront gentry lawyers with the partial nature of their values, to show that they were in fact "taking sides upon debatable and often burning questions" and not simply working out the implications of the uncontroversial, permanent, certain and universal principles they had imbibed at the fonts of genteel culture.[104] From this insight and from related developments in the humanities and social sciences, later lawyers, judges, and legal academics would develop a full-blown pluralist and relativist jurisprudence and use it to recast the Victorian law of industrial disputes. Davenport, however, would never acknowledge these developments. For him, lawyering would remain one of several ways to enforce and defend genteel values, and he would always think of his work for the AABA as gentry politics pursued by nonelectoral means.

To judge from the eulogies delivered at his death in 1931, Davenport's strategy worked. By litigating and lobbying on behalf of the AABA he at last realized his ambitions to play a genteel Cicero on the national stage. Thus, to Connecticut Supreme Court justice George W. Wheeler, Davenport typified "the brave man who will do his duty whatever comes." To William O'Hara he was "courageous in combat" and an "idealist in things to promote the general welfare." Both men were convinced that Davenport's work for the AABA would stand (in Wheeler's words) as "an everlasting monument to his strength and capacity as a lawyer." But Wheeler and O'Hara had been Davenport's colleagues in the Victorian bar and Cleveland Democracy; they were genteel lawyer-politicians remembering the last of their fellows as they would have themselves be remembered.[105] A less sympathetic observer might have noted how few people shared Davenport's premises, how imperfectly his beliefs comprehended the pluralist state and society of the day, and how great a debt Davenport owed to the long-discarded notion that moral sentiments had "a self-executing and self-propelling capacity," that they possessed innate, "efficacious powers."[106]

THREE

A Liberty League

It is more than a league to protect manufacturers engaged in interstate commerce against conspiracies to ruin by boycott. It is a league to do battle for individual liberty.

—John C. Spooner, in AABA, *Liberty League* (1908)

Soon after the constitutional convention adjourned, Daniel Davenport set out on a cross-country tour in search of members for the AABA. The zeal he brought to the task became part of the folklore of the organization. "He has not been merely the hired advocate of a cause," marveled former U.S. Senator John C. Spooner at an AABA gathering in 1908. "He has been a devotee of the cause for principle's sake." No Revolutionary or Civil War soldier, Spooner claimed, had been "more steadfast, more heedless of his own comfort, keener of eye, more loyal and determined in the discharge of the duties which this Association has imposed upon him."[1] Davenport himself described his labors in apostolic terms. "I traveled more miles than ever Saint Paul traveled in his fourteen journeys to found the infant church," he boasted to a congressional committee in 1908. "While he was said to have fought with beasts at Ephesus, I fought with bedbugs at Aurora, Illinois."[2]

Davenport may have set out on his travels with little more than Noah Porter's faith in the self-propagating nature of moral sentiment and a belief in the justice of Dietrich Loewe's cause, but he and his fellows quickly discovered that more calculated efforts were needed to establish the AABA on a lasting basis. Looking back on their efforts with the help of recent theorists of interest-group formation, we can see that the AABA's founders confronted three basic obstacles in establishing their organization and used what are now the standard tactics of pressure-group politics to surmount them.[3]

Davenport's first task was to convince potential members that they faced a common danger in the trade-union movement. Here he enjoyed considerable advantages over, say, a leader of one of today's environmental groups, struggling to bring home the dangers of global thermal warming. By the summer of 1903 most proprietary capitalists thoroughly appreciated the consequences of closed-shop unionism and secondary boycotts for their businesses. Many had themselves been the target of organizational campaigns; the rest knew of the AFL unions' demands from newspapers, trade journals, or the activities of their trade associations. Davenport valued the access to politically mobilized employers the trade associations provided, and he worked hard to maintain good relations with their leaders.

Davenport's second task was to convince his employers that their common peril required a collective response: an association to fund precedent-setting litigation against the closed shop and secondary boycotts. Against such practices, Davenport argued, the individual employer could not be counted on to produce the needed court decisions. The problem was not a lack of fortitude but the economics of planned litigation. "You may talk as much as you please about men not having backbone," Davenport told an employers' group. "Men are so situated often that if they have backbones they cannot rely on them." What was needed was an organization to spread the costs of suing trade unions and developing legal expertise on the labor problem, and this was what the AABA would provide.[4]

As a final task, Davenport needed to provide incentives to employers who not only understood the value of collective legal action but also realized they would benefit from the AABA's litigation whether they joined the group or not. Davenport hit upon what has become a familiar tactic for addressing the temptation to take a "free ride" on the contributions of others: the provision of "selective" benefits, enjoyed only by the members of the AABA. Some of these were intangible, such as the satisfaction of contributing to a momentous cause. Some were tangible—most notably the right to consult Davenport and his staff on labor questions. By appealing to their constituents' self-interest as well as their public-spiritedness, the AABA's leaders produced a stable and effective organization, just as the theory of interest-group formation would predict.

The social-science literature explains much of the structure and early activities of the organization, but understanding the AABA's unique place in the development of American political institutions requires a more time-bound account of Davenport's efforts. Davenport stood at the close of "the party period" of American politics, with its strong partisan attachments and universalist rhetoric. Before him lay the issue-oriented, weak-party, extra-electoral, and pluralist politics of the twentieth century.[5] Davenport, of course, lacked this bird's-eye view. Further, as a devotee of the genteel political tradition he did not set out to invent the role of interest-group politician, a figure he could only have understood in pejorative terms. Labor leaders, he would have protested, led interest groups. *He* led "a liberty league."

To capture this ironic aspect of the founding of the AABA—to see how a genteel Victorian contributed to the destruction of the political regime he hoped to preserve—the behaviorialist perspective of interest-group theory must be set aside and Davenport's own explanation of the AABA attended to. His basic speech performed two now-familiar tasks in the formation of interest groups, but Davenport did not understand himself to be pioneering the tactics of a new political regime. In fact, his speech followed the well-established conventions of a particular style of nineteenth-century political oratory, the republican jeremiad. Because the rhetoric Davenport used to win votes for Grover Cleveland proved just as effective in gaining converts for the AABA, he apparently never felt compelled to take stock of the changing terrain of American politics. He could retain the genteel notion that universal moral truths were self-propagating and irrepressible because that faith was well suited to the task of birthing an interest group.

Common Cause

The first task Davenport faced was convincing potential members of the AABA that trade unionists' demands for the closed shop jeopardized the well-being of employers throughout the nation's industries. The cost of mobilizing so large and dispersed a constituency would have quickly exhausted Charles Merritt's resources had the job been the AABA's alone. Fortunately for the AABA's leaders, most employers were well prepared for the message Davenport brought.

Many employers had firsthand experience with the new demands of organized labor. The turn of the twentieth century saw an explosion in trade-union membership and a dramatic shift in the goals sought by striking workers. The total membership of American trade unions more than doubled in the three years after 1899. By 1902, union membership totaled almost 1.4 million; in 1903 it stood at just under two million. During the same period more strikes were called to force employers to sign standardized, industrywide, closed-shop contracts than ever before. As a rule, earlier demands for the ouster of nonunion workers and for the observance of "shop rules" had been local affairs and not part of a nationally organized campaign to standardize wages and working conditions throughout an industry. Between 1898 and 1901, strikes for the recognition of the union and union rules increased 500 percent, accounting for 36 percent of all strikes in the latter year. Encounters like Dietrich Loewe's confrontation with the United Hatters had become a familiar part of industrial life.[6]

The trade and general press reported on many demands for the closed shop, but two incidents became particularly well known nationally as Davenport stumped for the AABA. The first, a great strike in the anthracite coal fields of northeastern Pennsylvania, commenced in May 1902 and ended with the miners' return to work in late October. Throughout the strike and its investigation by a federal commission appointed by President Theodore Roosevelt, city newspapers extensively covered the demands of the United Mine Workers, the imperiousness of the coal operators and railroad managers who controlled the industry, and industrial conditions in the coal fields. In March 1903 the commission rejected the UMW's call for the closed shop and denounced the miners' boycotts of businessmen who dealt with strikebreakers.[7] (Davenport would later attribute the attack on the boycott to his intercession with David Willcox, the general counsel of the Delaware and Hudson Railroad and the valedictorian of Yale College's class of 1872.)[8]

A second episode unfolded over the spring and summer of 1903, when the chief of the Government Printing Office dismissed William A. Miller, an assistant foreman, to avoid a strike by union bookbinders. The local had expelled Miller in mid-May for a variety of reasons, including his introduction of labor-saving machinery into the GPO's bindery. After a favorable decision by the Civil Service Commission, Roosevelt ordered Miller reinstated in July, with a strong endorsement of the open shop, which was widely praised in the nation's newspapers. "So much has been said and written in magazines, trade journals and daily press on the question of the open and closed shop," a labor journalist complained in 1904, "that to the average disinterested reader the question is becoming, figuratively speaking, nauseating."[9]

Many employers came to a more immediate understanding of the peril of closed-shop unionism through the meetings and activities of employers' associations. These included scores of state and local groups as well as nationally organized bodies like the National Association of Manufacturers (NAM), the National Metal Trades Association (NMTA), the National Founders' Association (NFA), and the National Erectors' Association (NEA). Often formed to promote a variety of functions, including collective bargaining, many employers' groups turned "belligerent" between 1901 and 1906. At the forefront of the "Open Shop Drive" was the NAM, whose president David M. Parry diverted the group from its original mission of promoting international trade to combating "the Great Muscle Trust."[10]

Davenport could dramatically lower the costs of communicating the perils of trade unionism and the mission of the AABA if he could appear before these groups and "piggyback" on the organizational efforts of their leaders.[11] The metal-work industry, for example, was thick with potential members, thanks to the aggressive organizational drives of the machinists', iron molders', and metal polishers' unions. So scattered and numerous were its firms that Davenport could not hope to reach a sizable percentage without help. Fortunately, the leaders of the NMTA allowed the lawyer to address the group's annual convention in April 1903. "There is not one man here who is running a factory whose treasury today is not liable to be raided regardless of what business conditions warrant," Davenport warned. "There is not a man who works for you but is liable to be forbidden the privilege to work." So impressed were the NMTA's leaders that they urged its members to support the AABA and promoted the group in their house periodical.[12]

Even more important to the AABA were good relations with Parry and his successors at the NAM, which Davenport established during his first organizational efforts and maintained for more than a decade. In part, cordial relations were valuable to ensure the access to the NAM's three thousand members. AABA officials addressed NAM conventions in 1904, 1905, and 1909, and the NAM's journal, *American Industries,* regularly reported on Davenport's work. A cooperative spirit became even more important as Davenport joined NAM lobbyists in opposing federal legislation on labor matters. Between 1904 and 1912 Davenport appeared with NAM lobbyists at four committee hearings on eight-hour legislation, six on anti-injunction legislation, and several on antitrust law and other matters. Davenport could maintain no more than polite relations with the NAM's first congressional lobbyist, the querulous Marshall Cushing, but he developed a warm friendship with James A. Emery, who replaced Cushing in 1906.[13]

As the business historian Thomas Cochran noted, the two men "did much to perfect pressure-group techniques." Davenport provided a fund of legal argument and the confident manner of a seasoned trial lawyer, while Emery and the NAM mobilized the proprietary capitalists. In one forty-eight-hour period in May 1908, for example, the NAM's call to arms sent ten thousand letters and telegrams raining down upon an anti-injunction bill, a feat the AABA could not hope to duplicate on its own.[14] Davenport was careful to credit the NAM at the group's annual convention in 1904. "The work that was done there was not half so much that of those of us who appeared before the committee," Davenport told the NAM members, "as it was the great work of organization which was from first to last brought to bear upon the committees of Congress."[15]

Such outward displays of unity masked occasional, behind-the-scenes quarreling between the AABA and other employers' groups. As allies in a mass offensive against organized labor, the open-shop leaders had enormous respect for Davenport's talents, but as rivals for the beneficence of employers they deeply resented the pretensions of lesser AABA officials. After a legislative triumph in 1908, Parry's successor, the St. Louis stove manufacturer James W. Van Cleave, wrote Davenport, "With you in Washington there is no such word as defeat."[16] Yet less than a year later Van Cleave was "sick at the stomach" over the complaint of Walter Gordon Merritt, son of the founder Charles Hart Merritt and Davenport's second-in-command, that the AABA had not received enough credit for recent lobbying efforts. He dismissed the young Merritt as "a grown up boy" and groaned at the suggestion that AABA secretary Frederick Boocock address the upcoming NAM convention. "Boocock is not fit to speak, he is far too prolix," Van Cleave protested. "If Davenport would in a short address simply state the facts, well & good; but Boocock—I hardly think I could stand for that."[17]

When he learned of the squabble, James Emery counseled conciliation. While deploring Merritt and Boocock for taking exclusive credit for the lobbying triumphs of the open-shop movement, Emery warned that "no feeling of any kind should be permitted to arise that would interfere with our joint work." Davenport should be praised not only "as an earnest of our good feeling," he wrote, "but as a deserved tribute to the great work the Judge has done and the spirit in which it has been accomplished."[18] Emery apparently succeeded in smoothing over this controversy: Boocock appeared at the NAM's annual convention and delivered the verbose speech Van Cleave predicted.[19]

Another spat broke out in 1911 between Frederic Herman Lee (Boocock's successor) and Walter Drew, the NEA's commissioner and general counsel. While attending an AABA banquet, Drew and Emery noted that some of the group's literature slighted the contributions of other open-shop organizations. Drew brought this to the attention of John Kirby, Van Cleave's successor as NAM president, and then protested to Lee. Drew wrote Lee that he had always encouraged members to join the AABA. (In fact, he had just recently praised the organization to an NEA member for its "big splendid work in taking up and carrying to final conclusion cases involving different phases of the labor problem.") In "the best possible spirit," Drew asked Lee to stop implying that his association was "the only one that is doing anything." Given the value of the AABA's work to the other open-shop groups, Drew wrote, "You would naturally receive their support, unless you yourselves conjured up and emphasized a conflict of interest and a competitive condition which have no real existence."[20]

Lee replied testily that while he and his associates sometimes stated the AABA's accomplishments in "broad and emphatic terms," they never pretended to do work best left to trade associations, and they always advised employers to support those groups before contributing to the "broader" and more fundamental mission of the AABA's legal experts. Drew retorted that he had handled "quite a little litigation myself," but he concluded as Emery had, on a conciliatory note. He declared he would continue to credit Davenport for his great work and ignore the zealous overstatements of his underlings.[21]

The exchange between Drew and Lee highlights the second challenge facing the AABA: how to convince employers that the special efficacy and importance of the AABA's work deserved their patronage when local or trade groups offered more tangible services, such as strikebreakers, or the opportunity to consult attorneys like Drew, who had considerable expertise on labor matters. Davenport's answer, echoed in Lee's response to Drew, was to argue that the law of industrial disputes was too important to be left to the trade associations. Walter Drew might perform valuable services for the structural steel firms in the NEA—as he did in prosecuting the union officials who dynamited the Los Angeles *Times* building in 1910—but the "broader," more fundamental work of defending "the liberty of the individual" required a less parochial and partial organization.[22]

THE AABA AND "REPEAT PLAY"

When the AABA was founded, the law of strikes and boycotts had only recently become a familiar feature on the landscape of industrial disputes. Although prosecutions of trade unions for violating conspiracy laws date from the start of the nineteenth century, these cases were exceptional before 1890 and rarely influenced the calculations of proprietary capitalists when confronted with a strike or boycott. For example, when a strike broke out at the principal factory of the Yale and Towne Manufacturing Company in 1890, even so worldly and knowledgeable an employer as Henry R. Towne did not consider turning to the courts. "The significant fact is that during this time of stress and trial," this titan of the hardware industry recalled at an AABA banquet in 1907, "no thought ever entered the minds of those responsible for the management of the company that they had any right to protection from the civil authorities or any recourse to the courts." Although Towne called upon the police for help, "the idea of appealing to the law for protection in our civil rights was not dreamed of. . . . The truth is simply that we were ignorant of our lawful rights."[23]

The popularization of the labor injunction in the great railroad boycotts of the 1890s and the ensuing debate on "government by injunction" ensured that by 1903 few employers would be so ill-informed. Injunctions provided an effective remedy when, "because of supineness or worse" (as a railroad executive put it), local police failed to control picketing or strike-related violence to an employer's satisfaction. In such cases, amounting to perhaps two-thirds of all injunctions sought between 1880 and 1932, employers had little need for collective action.[24] Because temporary restraining orders and preliminary injunctions could be granted on the basis of hastily prepared affidavits, relief was quick and inexpensive. The case law permitting injunctive relief in such cases was settled by the start of the twentieth century, and the drafting of court papers required no great legal expertise. Enforcement was also rather simple, particularly when the actual audience for the injunction was a police force whose discretion was to be cut down.[25]

Given this state of affairs, the AABA made no special effort to develop the law of picketing and limited its efforts in the area to counseling members on how to obtain relief on their own. In an exceptional case, Davenport took a more active role, traveling to Cleveland to advise a manufacturer of dynamos, air compressors, and motors who was caught up in a machinists' strike in 1907. "If it had not been for Mr. Davenport's presence here," the grateful employer wrote the association, "I fear the negotiations leading up to the application for our injunction would have been indefinitely postponed." With Davenport's assistance, the firm obtained the court order it sought, which the pickets "were extremely careful to observe."[26]

The cases the AABA decided to finance, in contrast, dealt with less-settled issues and circumstances in which an individual employer could not be counted upon to procure solid precedents. One large part of its docket before 1915 involved an effort to prohibit strikes to force the signing of closed-shop contracts. The remainder of its cases sought to outlaw the whole range of secondary pressure going under the name of "boycotting." Between 1903 and 1921 the AABA sued unions for targeting the distributors of hats, stoves, cigars, and other consumer goods; for refusing to handle woodtrim, electrical equipment, and other building products; and for strikes against employees who used the wooden boxes, brewery equipment, photoengraved material, or freight-hauling services of proscribed firms.[27]

In such cases the AABA possessed considerable advantages over the lone employer. First, the AABA was able to file or influence litigation throughout industrial America. Although proprietary capitalists might sometimes make out a claim under federal legislation and produce a decision that was national in scope, more often their disputes were local affairs that did not sufficiently affect interstate commerce to bring them within the jurisdiction of the federal courts.[28] As a result, they looked to the common law of their state for the relevant rule of decision. When the AABA commenced operations, most state supreme courts had not yet spoken on the legality of closed-shop contracts, and none had passed judgment on the whole range of secondary tactics employed by AFL unions. Resolute and prosperous employers might persevere and create a strong precedent in their states, but this would still leave the issue open in other jurisdictions. A nationwide policy against closed-shop strikes and most kinds of secondary pressure required multistate litigation, which a lone proprietary capitalist was rarely in a position to undertake.[29]

A second advantage of the AABA was its ability to spread the costs of litigation across several hundred employers through modest fees and dues that were no more burdensome than an annual donation to a local hospital.[30] As a rule, attorney fees were much higher in closed-shop and secondary-boycott cases than in antipicketing suits. An adequate evidentiary record often required substantial investigation of a trade union's aims and methods. The record Davenport and Walter Gordon Merritt built in Loewe's case, for example, contained many pages transcribed from often-inaccessible union journals and convention proceedings, as well as the affidavits of trade unionists and merchants from across the United States. Similar documents collected in the *Buck's Stove* case filled a brief three hundred pages long. Enforcement could also be more difficult when the enjoined conduct took place in construction worksites or scattered retail establishments rather than on the streets near a factory gate. The expense could overwhelm a proprietary capitalist. The *Buck's Stove* case cost the AABA between $8,000 and $10,000; Loewe's case, between $20,000 and $30,000.[31]

A final advantage was the AABA's ability to develop expertise on labor law. When it came to the law of closed-shop strikes and secondary boycotts, the proprietary capitalist was a typical example of what legal sociologist Marc Galanter has termed the "one-shotter."[32] Demands to sign closed-shop contracts and the travails of secondary boycotts were at most occasional experiences for employers, whose main concern was to resolve such disputes as cheaply and quickly as possible. They could expect no great return from investing the time in mastering a field of law, testing and revising legal documents or arguments, or setting precedents. If employers could have turned to a well-developed labor bar, backed by detailed treatises and specialized reporting services or newsletters, they might have been able to overcome this disadvantage. When the AABA was founded in 1902, however, labor specialists were rare at the bar, and the legal literature on industrial disputes was quite weak. Only a handful of lawyers connected to local employers' associations in major metropolitan areas devoted the bulk of their work to labor matters. The first proper treatise devoted solely to the law of industrial disputes did not appear until 1910, and no substantial periodical on labor law appeared until 1919, when the AABA commenced publication of the journal *Law and Labor*.[33]

The AABA's legal staff brought the advantages of "repeat play" to labor litigation. At its office in New York City, Walter Gordon Merritt maintained an unrivaled collection of briefs, pleadings, court orders, contracts, legislation, and judicial decisions, "a great national storehouse and clearinghouse on all that relates to the law of the Labor Problem."[34] Daniel Davenport directed the day-to-day activities of the AABA for much of the first decade of the group's existence, although the younger Merritt gradually assumed this role as Davenport's lobbying required longer and longer stays in Washington, D.C.

Other lawyers augmented the AABA's legal team for varying periods of time. Commencing in the autumn of 1903 and continuing until 1909 or 1910, Davenport shared power with a more eminent lawyer, James Montgomery Beck (1861–1936). Like Davenport, Beck started his political and legal career as a Gold Democrat in an eastern city. Unlike Davenport, Beck unambiguously left Philadelphia's Democrats for the Republican party in 1900 and served as an assistant attorney general in the McKinley and Roosevelt administrations. In that capacity he gained national prominence by directing the early stages of Roosevelt's antitrust suit against Northern Securities Company. After winning the case in the trial court, Beck left the administration for a lucrative position with the Wall Street law firm of Shearman and Sterling, in a move that prompted sarcastic commentary from eastern newspapers. As the AABA's general counsel, he brought the group considerable prestige and brilliant appellate advocacy, and he was regularly consulted by the executive board. In practice, however, Beck's work at Shearman and Sterling kept him from playing as important a role as his title implied.[35]

Commencing in 1905, the AABA also developed or tapped legal expertise through a loose network of district counsel located in major industrial cities. Some of these lawyers had considerable experience in labor affairs before affiliating with the AABA. Dudley Taylor, for example, was already counsel for the Employers' Association of Chicago, and the law firm of Wilkerson, Cassels, Potter and Gilbert, which provided the AABA with two district counsel, had a considerable labor practice of its own. Other district counsel were (as an AABA bulletin put it) "younger attorneys with a limited law practice who wish an opportunity to make themselves known." Such men included Thomas Hewes of Hartford, Connecticut, and Alexander C. Allen, who assisted in AABA cases in Chicago until he suffered a life-threatening beating from a "union slugger."[36]

The AABA employed its resources selectively. It chose only to fund those cases which squarely presented the legality of open-shop contracts or boycotting. The legal staff rejected cases for which a strong evidentiary record could not be built, and it insisted that the employer-client cede to Davenport and his staff the authority to terminate or continue a suit.

Thanks to the advantages of repeat play, the AABA enjoyed great success in its litigation. Five years after its founding, Boocock could still boast that the group had never lost in court, a feat he attributed to "the marked ability of our legal staff."[37]

In sum, Davenport, the Merritts, and the other leaders of the AABA quickly mastered many of the challenges of pressure-group politics. They communicated to a large segment of the AABA's constituency that it offered a unique and powerful solution to the organizational campaigns of the AFL affiliates. They shrewdly exploited media coverage of widely noted controversies involving the closed shop; they established a modus vivendi with existing associations of politically mobilized employers; and they developed a clearinghouse and other resources that would become the standard tactics of public-interest lawyers later in the century.

For all that, the AABA's leaders would have failed to construct a durable association had they not overcome a final obstacle: the possibility that too many employers would decide not to contribute to litigation that would benefit them whether they joined the AABA or not. Long before political theorists catalogued solutions to the "free-rider problem," the AABA's leaders discovered that even shrewd and tightfisted businessmen could be persuaded to contribute to an interest group if it provided members with the right mix of self-interested and altruistic reasons for doing so. In Davenport's case, discovering the proper mix required no fundamental rethinking of the nature of law and politics. He had only to restate the pieties of his genteel Victorian upbringing.

THE LOGIC OF COLLECTIVE LITIGATION

Viewed from the perspective of a political economist, a legal rule is a kind of "collective good"; that is, the "consumption" of a legal rule cannot feasibly be limited to those who contributed to its creation. After 1908, for example, any employer facing an interstate, distributor-targeted boycott could bring suit under the Supreme Court's first decision in *Loewe v. Lawlor*.[38] Knowing that he could not be excluded from the benefits of planned litigation, how should a perfectly informed, wealth-maximizing employer respond to an appeal to join the AABA? If too few employers contributed, valuable legal precedents might never get established, a point that should dispose him to join. On the other hand, the employer would also recognize that his dues paid for only a small fraction of AABA's operations. If he did not join the organization but enough of the thousands of other proprietary capitalists did, the AABA's litigation would go on anyway. If he decided to join but too many others did not, the AABA would lack sufficient funds to proceed, notwithstanding his efforts. Such reasoning would lead an employer to take a free ride on the contributions of others. Calculations that were rational from the standpoint of individual employers could thus produce an irrational outcome for employers as a whole.[39]

Political scientists have identified several tactics used by interest groups to circumvent the free-rider problem. The most important is to give members benefits which, unlike the collective good, only they can enjoy. Some of these "selective benefits" are tangible: an informative newsletter, for example, or cheap insurance. Even persons who were indifferent to the larger goals of an interest group might join to obtain these rewards. In the long run, however, such individuals were a poor constituency for an interest group, because they would stop contributing as soon as their demand for the selective benefits was met more cheaply by entrepreneurs who did not have to bear the cost of producing collective goods.[40] The most successful interest groups have provided their members with pleasures they could not receive from conventional transactions in the marketplace.[41]

Scholars of interest groups have identified two classes of these "intangible" benefits: the fun and friendship accompanying the act of associating ("solidary" benefits) and the satisfaction of having helped advance a worthy cause ("expressive" benefits). Solidary and expressive benefits are cheaper to provide than tangible rewards and can be quite powerful when they address a preexisting sense of collective identity, such as that shared by businessmen in a particular trade or industry. On the other hand, near substitutes are often close at hand in the solidary and expressive activities of other business groups. Further, as a variety of luxury goods, the intangible benefits of group membership are among the first things people sacrifice in hard times. Once again, a mix of tangible and intangible benefits has proven to be the best strategy for the creators of interest groups.[42]

The organizational efforts of the AABA's staff is fully consistent with this model of interest-group formation. AABA officials regularly mixed appeals to self-interest and public-spiritedness, emphasizing one or the other as the occasion demanded. To end his stirring address to the NMTA convention on an exalted note, for example, Daniel Davenport chose to downplay self-interest. Employers formed groups like the AABA, he explained, "not so much for their own individual benefit, not so much to protect themselves in their individual trade, but for the purpose of protecting and securing the rights of all as American citizens." If an AABA flyer carefully detailed the tangible benefits of membership, it also urged the employer to regard membership "not from the narrow standpoint of direct benefit but as a public-spirited obligation." In opening the 1904 convention, Charles Merritt congratulated the rank and file for looking "beyond immediate return for the investment made." Later in the day, however, Henry Towne noted the "egotistic" reasons for joining the AABA.[43]

The AABA offered its members two tangible benefits, one assured, the other contingent upon the approval of the general executive board. The first was the advice of "able, experienced and resourceful counsel upon labor problems" when labor lawyers were rare and none were as well apprised of national developments in the law. In one four-month period in 1916, for example, the AABA answered requests for legal advice from thirty-five cities across the industrial North. Commencing in 1915, the group made its special "open-shop" contracts available to members, and after World War I, it prepared plans for "company unions" tailored to the local circumstances of its members.[44] On occasion, Davenport personally answered calls for help in lobbying against organized labor's bills in state legislatures, but after 1907 the AABA usually limited its role to briefing local employers, who would then testify on their own.[45]

On at least a few occasions the AABA's lawyers lent their expertise and court papers to lawyers in closely related cases. Walter Gordon Merritt shared affidavits with a lawyer who also attacked a boycott of nonunion woodtrim by the carpenters of New York City, and he worked closely with Henry S. Drinker, the Philadelphia lawyer whose suit against the United Mine Workers for the Coronado Coal Company raised many of the same issues as a lawsuit sponsored by the AABA.[46] As a rule, however, AABA officials advised only its own members. When Justin Seubert, a cigar manufacturer in Syracuse, New York, wrote for help in 1915, he received in reply an application form, a pamphlet describing the objects of the AABA, and the assurance that joining would put at his disposal "the most expert counsel in the country on labor questions."[47]

As it happened, the AABA determined that Seubert's case would be an apt vehicle for attacking the union label in the cigar industry. The general executive board voted to assume the costs of the litigation and sent Walter Gordon Merritt to Syracuse for the trial. The possibility that the AABA would finance a member's lawsuit was a second tangible benefit held out to employers, albeit always with the qualification that the decision lay within the discretion of the board. Between 1903 and 1918, the AABA agreed to support at least twenty-seven cases originating in Arkansas, California, Connecticut, Illinois, Indiana, Maryland, Massachusetts, Minnesota, New York, and Washington, D.C.[48]

Along with these tangible benefits (expanded in 1919 to include a subscription to *Law and Labor*), the AABA offered its members a collective setting in which to assert and have confirmed their sense of patriotism, principle, and masculinity. At the early annual conventions, AABA officials depicted the rank and file as a beleaguered band of heroes who manfully struggled to defeat the tyrannous practices of trade unionism. They also brought forward like-minded employers to articulate the ideals and personify the fortitude they knew their members admired.

One such employer was Joseph Emmett Patterson (1839–1925). At the 1907 convention, Patterson, a proprietor of several lumberyards in and near Wilkes-Barre, related his experiences when a delegation of carpenters had asked him to recognize their union. "But how is it about the rest?" Patterson demanded. "There are some other people under the same conditions, in the same business, have they got to do the same as we have?" When the carpenters replied that they were proceeding one lumber manufacturer at a time, Patterson answered, "Then you have taken just the right man. If you don't whip the others until you have got me whipped, they will have peace for a long, long time." He brought suit against the union, paying the legal fees out of his own pocket. "As a free American citizen," he told the AABA convention, "I do not see how I dare do anything else, if I desire to leave a free inheritance to my children. It is not a question of dollars and cents; it is not a question of policy; but it is a question of principle." Patterson's concluded his remarks with patriotic, martial, and familial imagery that was sure to win the applause of his fellow proprietors. "As a grandson of a revolutionary soldier, I dare do nothing else but continue this fight if I am to be true to the inheritance that he left me and protect it for my children."[49]

Consider as well Benjamin S. Atwood, an employer of 120 workers in a box-and-rack factory in East Whitman, Massachusetts. In December 1903 Atwood found his work force halved and important customers scared off by a strike and boycott over the closed shop. "I have not made any money in the last nine months," he wrote a labor researcher in September 1904, "but I have had the satisfaction all the time of believing I was doing my duty as a patriotic American citizen"—just as the abolitionists William Lloyd Garrison and Wendell Phillips had done in addressing "the old Antislavery question." At an AABA convention two months later Atwood related the sense of solidarity he felt after receiving the well wishes of his fellow businessmen. When greeted with a hearty, "Hulloa, Atwood, how is the strike going on?" the employer explained, "I feel as if I were doing good work for the community I live in, whether I landed on Plymouth Rock or fought in '61 or not; I am fighting the battle that comes along."[50]

With the March 1908 general meeting, called to celebrate the Supreme Court's decision in Loewe's case, the annual gatherings became elaborate affairs, normally held at the Waldorf-Astoria Hotel. Members gathered to enjoy many courses of fine food and to hear stirring addresses by national figures. (Princeton's president, Woodrow Wilson, passed up an invitation to address the 1910 banquet, as did former president William Howard Taft in late 1913.) During the 1920s, at least, employers and their companions danced to the music of a full orchestra.[51] With these trappings the gatherings were no longer the proper place for inspiring tales of hardship and republican virtue, but they remained occasions for fostering camaraderie and linking the AABA to the most potent symbols of American patriotism. At the outset of the 1929 banquet, a rustic observer reported to the *New York Times*, "The lights were dimmed and a large and waving American flag was illuminated and we all sung some piece about it waving over the land of the free. As we sat down a neighbor says to me, 'But for this outfit it wouldn't wave so strong, by darn.'"[52]

A VICTORIAN JEREMIAH

Thus, the AABA was a carefully constructed force, like the patriotic outpouring at the 1929 banquet. Many other groups, however, gave employers the chance to wave the flag. What was it about the AABA that made Henry Towne consider its aims "deeper, more far-reaching, and more permanently effective" than those of any other employers' association?[53] The answer can be seen in the address Davenport gave during his early stumping on behalf of the AABA. Far more than the staged display of 1929, this speech, delivered (in Davenport's words) "man to man . . . from the bottom of my heart to my fellow citizens about their duty and my duty as citizens," explains the AABA's unique appeal—for its members and for Davenport.[54]

In structure the speech followed the basic conventions of the nineteenth-century republican jeremiad. Davenport commenced by recalling a heroic age in the American past, when the nation was simultaneously created and dedicated to a single, consensual, and permanent mission. At Wilkes-Barre in 1904, for example, Davenport commenced by invoking what Sacvan Bercovitch has called "the two quintessential moments in the story of America—the twin legends of the country's Founding Fathers—the Great Migration and the War of Independence."[55] As he traveled to Wilkes-Barre from New York City, past Pennsylvania's "green fields and steepled cities," its great rivers, blue hills, and frowning mountains, Davenport recalled the revolutionary and colonial eras: the fortitude of Washington's troops at Valley Forge during the desperate winter of 1778, the Declaration of Independence, and the first English settlers of America, who fled not only to acquire religious liberty but also to escape the monopolies of the Stuart monarchy. In the New World—"an uncivilized and unexplored territory"— they created their own political institutions, grounding them on a fundamental freedom unrecognized in feudal Europe: "the right to be men, to use the faculties that God had given them, their own brains, their own hands, their own strength and their own dexterity, to support themselves and their families."[56]

In his address before the Springfield Young Men's Lyceum, Abraham Lincoln similarly praised the Founders for taking possession of "the finest portion of the earth" and constructing political institutions based on civil and religious liberty:

We toiled not in the acquirement or establishment of them—they are a legacy bequeathed to us, by a *once* hardy, brave, and patriotic, but *now* lamented and departed race of ancestors. Their's was the task (and nobly they performed it) to possess themselves, and through themselves, us, of this goodly land; and to uprear upon its hills and its valleys, a political edifice of liberty and equal rights; 'tis ours only, to transmit these, the former, unprofaned by the foot of an invader; the latter, undecayed by the lapse of time, untorn by usurpation to the last generation that fate shall permit the world to know.[57]

Davenport faithfully followed Lincoln in contrasting the generative past with a conservative present. At the NAM's convention in May 1905 he declared, "It is not given to us to act the part of Solon and Lycurgus, and other founders of states (our fathers acted that part), yet there rests upon us of this generation a great duty of defense and preservation." Six months later, Davenport urged another assemblage to stand as a "bulwark of the principles of government which we received from our fathers and which we are duty bound to transmit to posterity."[58]

After establishing the nation's historic mission, a republican Jeremiah then detailed the actual state of the country and lamented the chasm between it and the American ideal. True to form, Davenport detected "a spirit rising up in the hearts of the people of America which is hostile to the very foundation of the principle of American institutions." Nowhere was this more evident than in the spread of the closed shop. Mobilizing every facet of his cultural heritage, Davenport then denounced the closed shop for violating the Declaration of Independence, divine will, the fundamental laws of economics, and the principles of Victorian masculinity.

His first instinct was to pillory the closed shop for violating "the free rights of every American citizen." The Declaration had recognized that every man had an equal right to life, liberty, and the pursuit of happiness, Davenport argued, yet the labor movement sought to "exclude others from the opportunity to work, although those others are of the same condition in life as themselves and have nothing but their hands and their dexterity by which to live and support their families." He then shifted from the laws of nature to nature's God. How could trade unionists dare to keep the nonunion worker from employment, Davenport asked, when God had given him "faculties to work and imposed upon him the solemn obligation to work to support himself and his family"? How could they hope to keep nonunion workers cowed when "every man, I don't care who he is, has implanted in his heart the deep seated love of liberty"? Davenport resolved to fight the closed shop, not out of animosity to labor unions ("It is my proud boast and claim that I have been throughout my life the truest friend of the workingman that I can be"), but "to do the poor man good; for whatsoever reward I expect in this world or the world to come is dependent upon my fulfilling my duty to my fellow citizens."[59]

The closed shop was no more defensible when one considered "the fundamental, permanent, enduring facts" of economics. First, the closed shop kept employers from hiring whomever they wanted and therefore denied them the absolute control they required if they were to risk their capital in an enterprise. Without this control, the material welfare of the community would certainly suffer, but more important would be the loss of manliness among the nation's employers. At Wilkes-Barre, Davenport offered the example of a Philadelphia employer, who, although his business was in sight of "Independence Hall and the Old Liberty Bell," had no more control over his hiring decisions than if he had lived in Turkey! "Though that man had all the feelings of a gentleman and American citizen," Davenport sadly concluded, "he was so intimidated he had become a slave."[60]

The closed shop also violated economic laws by ending competition among laborers, which was "as fundamental a necessity as the air we breathe." It would bring to America the very monopolies the first settlers had fled, and it would reduce workers to the servile status of their Old World counterparts. Under the closed shop, the worker lost the chance to "make a man out of himself" and "to develop his faculties as best he can." Society would regress to Old World despotism, a point Davenport underscored at Wilkes-Barre with an anecdote about the restrictive practices of "the Chinese Water Carriers' Union."[61]

Normally, Davenport drew upon Victorian notions of masculinity by parading before his audience such "unmanned" men as the Philadelphia employer, a tactic that addressed the businessmen's anxieties over the loss of authority in their own workplaces and homes. At the NAM convention in 1905, Davenport related an anecdote keyed to another facet of Victorian masculinity, the male's obligation, as head of his household, to protect his dependents. During the Chicago packinghouse strike of 1904, Davenport recalled, he witnessed an atrocity that still made his "blood boil":

> I saw a young lady there, a good looking, well-dressed young lady—any man would have been proud to call her sister or daughter—come up to the gate with the intent to go into work. A howling mob surrounded her, and as she insisted on going in, she said: "I must go to work; I struck with the rest of you, but my mother is home, sick, and I must earn money to take care of her." They seized that girl, they rolled her in the mud, they disfigured her, and they subjected her person to indignities not fit to be described in your presence.

With this anecdote Davenport again challenged employers to assert their masculinity by opposing the closed shop, although now as the protector of dependents—of female workers in their work force, likened to their own sisters or daughters—rather than as the champion of independence among male employers and workingmen.[62]

After showing how the present age had betrayed the mission of the founders, the republican Jeremiah moved to his final task: urging the benighted nation to return to its historic course. This is where Davenport made an original contribution to the jeremiad—and at last made clear the unique mission of the AABA. He restated his premise that the Revolutionary Era was America's last generative moment: "The institutions of this country are founded upon the principle of the liberty of the individual. It is expressed in the Declaration of Independence in the phrase, 'We hold these truths to be self-evident: that all men are created equal; that they are endowed by their Creator with certain inalienable rights; that among these are life, liberty and the pursuit of happiness.'" He then argued that the divine truth Jefferson knew still lived, sheltered by the law:

> The Supreme Court of the United States has repeatedly declared that the Constitutions of the United States and the several states are to be construed and interpreted in the light of that principle, and that every contract, combination, conspiracy, or law which assails it in its true meaning is to be condemned. This right of the individual is covered . . . by a panoply of law entirely adequate to its full protection. And that law is beyond the power of any body of men in this country to repeal or alter until the Constitution is overthrown or until those appointed to interpret it shall betray their trust.

With this, Davenport arrived at his conclusion. All that was needed to keep faith with the Founders was the proper enforcement of the law of the land.[63] "Stand for the enforcement of the laws," he declared; "bring all the influences of society back of that position, and the evil will be gone!"[64]

Davenport's jeremiad thus made clear the profound and uniquely powerful nature of the AABA's work. Other organizations might address the immediate concerns of the employers, say, by providing strikebreakers or maintaining a labor exchange. The AABA's lawsuits transcended such mundane tactics. Its cases promised to restore "the grandest heritage that ever was transmitted to a human being" to its proper social authority. They would safeguard and advance the great enterprise set for the nation by the Founding Fathers and "the author of our being."[65]

With the benefit of interest-group theory, we can appreciate how, in equating the interest of the employers with the commonweal, Davenport heightened the selective, expressive benefits of membership in the AABA. We can also see how his exalted notion of planned litigation differentiated the AABA from other contenders for the contributions of politically engaged employers. Davenport, we can assume, was shrewd enough to know that his references to the courage and wisdom of the Founding Fathers, to divine prescriptions to work and do justice, to the natural laws of competition, and to the responsibilities of true men would resonate with such employers as Dietrich Loewe, Joseph Patterson, and Benjamin Atwood. Of course, their enthusiastic support for the AABA was not an unintended consequence of Davenport's actions.

But if in these respects Davenport behaved like later leaders of interest groups, he measured himself against the very different ideals of genteel Victorian politics. To succeed in those terms he had to be more than a mere "hired advocate of a cause" (to return to Spooner's encomium); he needed to believe in the AABA's cause "for principle's sake." When Davenport likened the open-shop crusade to nineteenth-century campaigns against slavery and free silver, he surely was attempting to persuade his audience to join the AABA, but he was also attempting to persuade himself that his work for the group kept faith with the War Democracy of his father and the Gold Democracy of his earlier political career.[66] Flattered though he must have been when Spooner compared him to a revolutionary soldier and placed him at the head of "a liberty league," nothing less would have justified the course Davenport had chosen.

In his study of American jeremiads, Bercovitch observed that their authors "were berating the present generation for deviating from the past in order to prod it forward toward their vision of the future. In ritual terms, they were asserting consensus through anxiety, using promise and threat alike to inspire (or enforce) generational rededication."[67] Davenport's jeremiad was well calculated to raise anxieties among his audiences of employers. It spoke to their own sense that trade unionism posed an imminent threat to individual proprietors' right to manage their business as they saw fit. The address also offered employers a hospitable version of social consensus to be preserved into the future, one limned by the values they acted upon in their factories and communities.

With the filing of the AABA's first lawsuits in the summer of 1903 and his appearances before congressional committees the following winter, Davenport commenced the work of advancing his consensual, universalist approach to the labor problem in far less congenial settings than the annual conventions of employers' associations. Particularly at the outset of the AABA's activities, many judges, legislators, and other public officials shared Davenport's Victorian outlook, worried with him over the demise of America's exceptional, historic mission, and joined him in asserting a consensus governed by the values of the genteel Victorian. Other public figures, of course, sharply contested their claims. In 1912, for example, Theodore Roosevelt condemned the AABA in the language of civic humanism as a self-interested faction, "an association of manufacturers whom I have always found to be influenced by as noxious a class spirit as any labor organization."[68] A more subtle but ultimately more devastating critique would in time be made in terms of interest-group pluralism. Like Roosevelt, the pluralists would debunk the putatively universal values advanced by Davenport and argue that they were merely the beliefs of an increasingly unimportant portion of the business community. But where Roosevelt condemned the "class spirit" of the AABA as a political aberration, the pluralists would take Davenport's work as the ordinary practice of political actors. In pluralist accounts, Davenport's apocalyptic crusade would be recast as the workaday business of interest-group politics.

FOUR

From Conspiracy to Tort

We have said here more than once that these points will never be
cleared up until we leave off talking about conspiracy and malice.

—Sir Frederick Pollock (1904)

"Ever since the foundation of Anglo-Saxon civilization," Daniel Davenport once claimed, "the principle of conspiracy" condemned combinations
to overwhelm individuals in the exercise of their rights.[1] No new principles were needed to abolish the closed shop, the secondary boycott, or the
other tactics with which the trade unions menaced the proprietary capitalists of the AABA. All that was required was for judges to enforce the
ancient proscription of combinations that pursued an unlawful purpose or
a lawful purpose by unlawful means. Although to modern eyes the terms
of the conspiracy doctrine seem hopelessly vague, Davenport thought them
substantial because he invested them with the lessons of his genteel education. Although later jurists would insist that the legality of an act could
not be determined apart from its consequences, Davenport quite comfortably reasoned to his conclusions from abstract and a priori definitions of
rightful conduct. And although later jurists would find ways to acknowledge the social nature of individual rights—their origins in the collective
action of the group or society—Davenport never relinquished a jurisprudence founded upon natural right.

As Davenport planned his first cases for the AABA, a rival approach
to the law of industrial disputes was already sweeping leading law faculties. Notwithstanding Davenport's best efforts, it would also triumph in
the courts. The new approach owed nothing to the trade unionists' attacks
on the injunction judges. Like Davenport, the labor leaders argued from
the jurisprudential high ground of natural rights. Rather, the new labor ju-

risprudence originated in the efforts of law professors to organize the un-
wieldy and unsystematic causes of action of the common law into an intellectually satisfying framework, a general and "scientific" law of torts.[2] By
the turn of the century the legal academics had successfully recast the old
conspiracy doctrine as a species of intentional torts. By 1904 judges who
persisted in the older analysis risked being chided by the Oxford law don
Sir Frederick Pollock in the pages of the *Law Quarterly Review*.

The American law professors read into the general theory of international torts the empiricism, utilitarianism, and pluralism that were revi-
talizing social and political thought in the Progressive Era. Most of the
younger legal academics encountered the historicist insight in collegiate
or legal texts, while students or colleagues of historicist social scientists,
or in works of German jurisprudence. Like Roscoe Pound, they joined
"the march of the sciences away from . . . predetermined conceptions" and
toward "the adjustment of principles and doctrine to the human conditions they are to govern." Many were content with erasing the gap between lagging law and evolving society. Others went further. Keeping step
with the social scientists, they set out for the more ambitious goal of
controlling society itself. In 1915, Daniel Davenport still believed the law
was the embodiment of timeless principles of truth and right. In contrast,
Pound's protégé Felix Frankfurter thought law "a vital agency for human
betterment" and hoped the legal profession would act as "the director of
social forces."[3]

In this, the law professors stayed several steps ahead of the judges, who
were reluctant to surrender the pretense that their decisions were compelled
by logic and who were doubtful of their competence and authority to make
explicit calculations of social welfare. Nevertheless, as the nation prepared
to enter the Great War, a pragmatic and regulatory approach to the law of
industrial disputes could claim important adherents on the American
bench. What was once a law of "first things, principles, 'categories,' supposed necessities" was remade by judges who could not help but think of
labor law in terms of "last things, fruits, consequences, facts."[4]

Conspiracy Doctrine in the Great Upheaval

Although Davenport turned to King Alfred's time for the origins of
American labor law, a sufficient and more proximate point of departure
would be the "Great Upheaval" of the mid-1880s, when the American labor movement enjoyed a period of astounding growth in size and organization. National trade unions, organized along craft lines, emerged from
the depression of the 1870s with unprecedented strength as labor leaders
regularized procedures and imposed restraints on the autonomy of local

unions. The model for the new bureaucratic approach was the cigar makers' union, organized on "a business basis" by its leaders Adolph Strasser and Samuel Gompers in a successful attempt to force employers to establish better working conditions throughout the industry.[5]

Organization across craft lines grew dramatically as well. The most spectacular example was the Knights of Labor, an association open to workers in almost all industries and formally organized as a hierarchy of national, district, and local assemblies. After more than a decade of slow growth, the Knights' membership exploded, from just under twenty thousand in 1881 to a hundred thousand in 1885 and seven hundred thousand in 1886. Although the organization's successes in 1885 and 1886 seemed to herald the arrival of a powerful and united working class, the control of the national executive over local assemblies was more apparent than real. After cresting in 1886, membership declined dramatically as a series of unauthorized strikes ended in costly defeats. As the Knights fell, the American Federation of Labor gradually assumed the leadership of the labor movement,

Organization across industrial lines also improved markedly on the local level. The district assemblies of the Knights and the longer-lived city centrals affiliated with the American Federation of Labor became regular features of urban life in the mid-1880s. The bodies brought together the trades of the city to deliberate on a range of matters, including the mobilization of local workers into campaigns against proscribed employers.[6]

In the mid-1880s this organizational activity tended to produce lawsuits in two kinds of disputes. One was the strike to force the ouster of nonunion labor. The other was the secondary boycott, the concerted withdrawal of patronage or labor to prevent others from buying or using the wares of a proscribed firm. The latter in particular was not new—trade unionists conducted "non-intercourse" campaigns in the early years of the republic— but the founding of permanent central unions routinized what had been a sporadic practice. The names of the offenders were "usually posted conspicuously in the places of meeting of affiliated societies," the business journal *Bradstreet's* reported in 1885, "and in some instances lists have been prepared on cards for the use of members."[7] Special committees passed on requests for boycotts, policed the conduct of the campaigns, and called them off when the underlying disputes were settled.

Restaurants, taverns, grocers, bakers, and breweries with a local, working-class clientele often were brought to terms by primary boycotting by trade unionists and their sympathizers. Other employers could be reached indirectly through secondary boycotts. The printers quickly mastered the technique of overwhelming a nonunion newspaper by driving away advertisers who were themselves dependent upon working-class patrons. Another strategy was to attack employers through the union workers of firms that used their wares in producing their own goods. Such "materials" boycotts included the refusal of carpenters to handle woodtrim or nails made in nonunion factories and of brewery workers to use barrels proscribed by the coopers' union. Finally, boycotters sometimes targeted the wholesalers and retailers of an offending firm's goods. In 1885 union hatters were already using the techniques they would later employ against Berg, Roelof, and Loewe.[8] The printers organized boycotts of news agents who sold proscribed publications, and the retailers of consumer goods like carpets, stoves, and cigars were regularly called upon to cease distributing the wares of offending manufacturers.[9]

The majority of the first wave of cases including closed-shop strikes and secondary boycotts were criminal proceedings. Employers rarely found civil suits attractive. Damage suits were time-consuming, expensive, and ended in judgments that could not be collected from penurious workers or their unincorporated unions, and only a few lawyers thought to seek injunctive relief for their clients. Criminal prosecution was much more appealing, because the public bore the expense. Although the refusal of local officials to act would become a common lament among employers, public prosecutors could not ignore the vocal and effective constituency for criminal proceedings that the Haymarket bombing and other spectacular events in 1886 produced.[10]

The law the judges applied in these cases was an English inheritance and had a long American career before the dramatic events of the 1880s. Simply stated, the doctrine of criminal conspiracy held individuals liable if they joined a combination formed to accomplish an unlawful purpose or some lawful purpose by unlawful means. An unlawful purpose was one that tended to "prejudice the public or to oppress individuals"; unlawful means included force, threats, and other forms of coercion.[11]

Appellate judges regularly upheld convictions in cases involving the forced discharge of a nonunion worker under the "unlawful purpose" branch of the conspiracy doctrine. Prosecutions of secondary boycotts were upheld under either branch, and sometimes under both. Even when peacefully conducted, some judges claimed, the secondary boycott coerced employers and was therefore an unlawful means of labor combinations. Others argued that the purpose of the trade unionists made their combination unlawful. Whatever the ultimate goals of the boycotters, they insisted, their immediate purpose was to interfere with the right of employers to choose their own employees, suppliers, and manufacturing techniques.

Conspiracy doctrine gave the judges a point of departure, but its open-ended terms did not compel them to reach the results they did. Rather, the shared assumptions of genteel Victorian culture carried them to their conclusions. Two decisions written in 1887 by members of state supreme courts in Vermont and Connecticut illustrate this point. The first was *State v. Stewart*. The case grew out of a labor dispute between a Vermont branch of the nationally organized stonecutters' union and the Ryegate Granite Works over the employment of two nonunion men, James O'Rourke and William Goodfellow. Charles Stewart and five others were indicted for conspiring to force the discharge of O'Rourke and Goodfellow, to destroy "free competition in the price and value of labor," and to force Ryegate to conform to the rules and regulations of the national union. They were also charged with employing the unlawful means of forbidding its members to work on granite quarried in Ryegate or with the "scabs" O'Rourke and Goodfellow.[12]

The decision was written by H. Henry Powers (1835–1913). Like Davenport, Powers traced his lineage to seventeenth-century America and had been the recipient of an orthodox collegiate education, in Powers's case at the University of Vermont. The judge mixed a profitable law practice in northern Vermont with an active political life. A Republican, he held a variety of offices in state government, including the chair of the committee of the whole in the constitutional convention of 1870, and he represented Vermont in the U.S. House of Representatives from 1891 to 1901.[13]

The Connecticut case was *State v. Glidden*, a decision condemning a boycott of advertisers and subscribers by printers who sought to oust nonunion workers at a local newspaper. Its author was Elisha Carpenter (1824–97). Carpenter counted among his ancestors the founders of the New Haven Colony and soldiers in the Revolutionary War, prepared for college in Connecticut's common schools and a local academy, and (according to a eulogist) was "strong in his political and party predilections."[14] As a Republican legislator he oversaw the supplying of Connecticut's regiments in the Civil War.[15] A judge who served with Carpenter on the Supreme Court thought "the polar star which guided his course in every discussion seemed to be his love of right. He always wanted to put some right in the place of some wrong." The judge also noted Carpenter's "profoundly religious nature" and belief in "the realities of the spiritual world and the higher life."[16]

Both men concluded that the aim of ousting nonunion workers was an unlawful purpose under the conspiracy doctrine. "It is a criminal offense for two or more persons corruptly and maliciously to confederate and agree together to deprive another of his liberty or property," Carpenter explained in *Glidden*. The union printers had denied that they acted out of malice. They inflicted the economic loss on the publisher not as an end in itself, but to better their own condition. Carpenter's response would be followed by generations of jurists: Whatever the ultimate purpose of the unionists, the "direct and primary object must be regarded as the destruction of the business" of the newspaper.[17]

Both judges condemned closed-shop unionism in terms borrowed from the civic humanist tradition, in particular its hostility toward factions that selfishly put private interest before the public good. Powers, for example, distinguished between legitimate associations of workers—in which unionists set "their own wages, fraternize with their own associates, choose their own employers, and serve man and Mammon according to the dictates of their own conscience"—and the "secret association of conspirators" in the case before him, issuing anathemas against independent employers and workers. Carpenter similarly invoked the lessons of "all history" on the danger of investing any group with irresistible power. "Like the taste of human blood by tigers," Carpenter warned, it creates "an unappeasable appetite for more."[18]

Both judges were unabashedly moralist in their approach to law. Powers thought the demand for the closed shop was utterly inconsistent "with every principle of justice that permeates the law under which we live." Carpenter also conflated moral and legal considerations. The printers' motive was "a selfish one—to gain an advantage unjustly, and at the expense of others," he wrote, "and therefore the act was legally corrupt." He saw his verdict not as sound social engineering, but as protecting "the weaker party" from evil worked by a powerful combination.[19]

So far as their political theory is discernible in their opinions, both judges seemed to subscribe to something like the teleological historicism of Francis Lieber, William Graham Sumner, and Thomas Cooley. Powers in particular described the development of the legal status of workers in Whiggish terms reminiscent of Hallam's *Constitutional History of England.* "All the legislation in England and America has been progressively in the direction of according to laborers the enjoyment of equal rights with others." Medieval statutes prohibiting combinations to raise wages were indeed "harsh, illiberal, and tyrannical," but they were simply "the reflex of the prevalent notions of class distinctions that shaped and guided the social and political polity of those days." Since then English law had been "liberalized and Christianized" until "to-day, in England as here, workmen stand upon the same broad level of equality before the law."[20]

Neither Powers nor Carpenter took the view of the strict version of the wages fund that all strikes were illegitimate. In fact, both assumed that combinations to raise wages were lawful. But both also believed that competition was the great engine of economic prosperity, that it was as vital in markets for labor as in markets for products, and that it required that the decision making of individual workers and employers not be constrained by the demands of their combined rivals or the state. Powers, for example, did not distinguish between the right to work and the right to manage in condemning the closed shop. "Every man has the right to employ his talents, industry and capital as he pleases, free from the dictation of others," he declared. "The labor and skill of the workman, be it of high or low degree, the plant of the manufacturer, the equipment of the farmer, the investments of commerce"—all were forms of property the law must protect to promote the common welfare.[21]

The great evil of the closed shop, judged in terms of classical economics, was that it upset the system of rewards and penalties through which the market disciplined economic actors. Any dictation to employers by labor organizations threatened an obscene inversion of the work ethic, permitting the vicious and slothful to prosper and the virtuous and industrious to fail. Carpenter was amazed by the printers' demands, which he rendered as: "You shall discharge the men you have in your employ, and you shall hereafter employ only such men as we shall name. It is true we have no interest in your business, we have no capital invested therein, we are in no wise responsible for its losses and failures, we are not directly benefited by its success, and we do not participate in its profits; yet we have a right to control its management and compel you to submit to our dictation." "The bare assertion of such a right is startling," Carpenter remarked. If it were upheld, no employer could safely engage in business, for he would never know if "intelligence or ignorance" was to control his affairs.[22]

Labor's advocates denied that the secondary boycott was coercive or that it and closed-shop strikes were incompatible with the free labor creed. On the contrary, they argued, strikers and boycotters were simply exercising the rights to work and make contracts as they saw fit—rights that American patriots had exercised in nonimportation campaigns against the Townsend and Stamp Acts of the Revolutionary Era. "A man has not only the right to buy where he pleases," a trade unionist wrote, "but he has the right to advise another man to buy or not to buy of friend or enemy." Bestowing one's trade in accordance with one's moral and social convictions was nothing less than an "innate right of man."[23]

The judges solved this puzzle of rights in conflict by a sleight of hand. While conceding that workers generally had a perfect right to do what they would with their own, they insisted that in the exercise of their rights the workers must not violate the rights of others. For this proposition they cited an ancient common-law maxim, *sic utere tuo ut alienum non laedas* (so use your own as not to injure another). That workers violated this maxim when they boycotted or sought to oust nonunion workers was obvious to most judges; that employers did not in employing nonunion workers was equally apparent.

Powers took this approach in *Stewart*. "By the law of the land," he wrote, the defendant granite cutters "have the most unqualified right to work for whom they please, and at such prices as they please. By the law of the land,

O'Rourke and Goodfellow have the same right." Faced with such a conflict, later judges would attempt to "balance" these rights or to test them against the dictates of public policy. But Powers thought a mere invocation of the *sic utere* maxim justified his conclusion. "While the law accords this liberty to one," he wrote, "it accords a like liberty to every other one, and all are bound to so use their own liberties and privileges as not to interfere with those of their neighbors."[24]

A General Theory of Intentional Torts

The conspiracy doctrine and the *sic utere* maxim were all judges like Powers and Carpenter needed to bluster past the objections of the trade unionists and their allies. As the century drew to a close, however, two independent developments combined to prompt law professors and intellectually ambitious judges and treatise writers to rethink the theoretical basis for Great Upheaval cases. By 1900 legal essayists and law writers increasingly considered the law of strikes and boycotts as a special case of a general theory of intentional torts. Their systematizing prepared the way for the full-blown reception of consequentialism and pluralism into the law of industrial disputes.

The first development was a procedural innovation, the rise of the labor injunction. *Stewart, Glidden,* and the other leading cases of the Great Upheaval were public prosecutions for the offense of criminal conspiracy. Although a New York master tailor had successfully enjoined strikers in 1875, American employers did not generally recognize the advantages of injunctive relief until the 1890s.[25] The main checks on their use were the seemingly well-established principles that courts could only enjoin violations of property rights and could not enjoin criminal acts. As judges expanded their notion of property to include a broad range of intangible rights, they increasingly saw strikes and boycotts as injuries to employers' property in their employment contracts with their workers and their unrestricted access to labor and product markets. At the same time, judges decided that the fact that a strike or boycott could be prosecuted criminally did not foreclose an independent suit in equity.[26]

Several decisions by federal courts during the tumultuous railroad strikes of 1893–95 firmly established the employer's right to injunctive relief in labor disputes. William Howard Taft played a leading role in popularizing the device, in granting injunctions against the chief executive of the Brotherhood of Locomotive Engineers in 1893 and officers of Eugene V. Debs's American Railway Union during its 1894 boycott of Pullman railroad cars.[27] Any lingering doubts about the doctrinal basis for the labor injunction were settled for most legal commentators by Supreme Court Justice David Brewer's opinion in *In re Debs* (1895). By the end of the decade, "government by injunction" had become a household phrase. Employers sought them in greater numbers in each succeeding decade. During the 1920s, fifty injunctions a year were issued in New York state alone.[28]

As employers' requests for injunctive relief brought more and more strikes and boycotts into civil courts, the basis for liability in labor disputes shifted from the terms of criminal conspiracy statutes to the common-law causes of action. At first, the move from criminal to civil liability did not change the structure of the judges' reasoning. Anglo-American courts had long recognized conspiracy as a private cause of action, quite apart from the criminal law. If legal professionals had been content with a jurisprudence of discrete, heterogeneous categories of civil liability, no new theory of labor law would have emerged. As it happened, however, the rise of the labor injunction coincided with the emergence of a new kind of legal expert, the full-time, professional law teacher, whose raison d'être was to study law "scientifically," as a systematic body of knowledge. The professors' systematizing made possible a new way of thinking about the law of labor disputes.

Christopher Columbus Langdell best exemplified the new breed of jurist. Appointed dean of the Harvard Law School in 1870, Langdell tried to make the pursuit of systematic thought central to legal education, just as Harvard president Charles W. Eliot tried in remaking the antebellum college of "discipline and piety" into a modern center of research and writing.[29] Langdell's task was, if anything, greater than Eliot's. In 1870 legal educators had no secure and exclusive claim to the body of learning that would-be lawyers were expected to master before entering the profession. Decades after Langdell's appointment, most lawyers were still admitted to the bar after law-office apprenticeships and self-study.[30]

One consequence was that law professors, unlike scholars in other academic disciplines, who successfully marginalized the claims of amateurs, had to share the process of defining the scope and contents of their subject with judges and lawyers who did not always share their enthusiasm for systematic exposition. The scientific study of the law was vital for Langdell and his followers. It explained to their satisfaction why they belonged within the walls of academe and why they, and not the practitioners, were the better expositors of legal doctrine. In contrast, lawyers valued precedents for the immediate authority they added to some claim in a particular case. Whether a precedent could be reconciled with a broad and abstract principle of law was at best a secondary concern. Langdell bent his efforts to reducing the law of contracts to a handful of essential doctrines and concepts such as offer, acceptance, and consideration. While a practicing lawyer might feel obligated to account for a contrary precedent, Langdell, with his mind set on discovering abstract principles, felt free to dismiss inconvenient holdings as "useless or worse than useless for any purpose of systematic study."[31]

When Langdell published his casebook on contracts, he could build on what was already a long tradition of treatise-writing on the law of contracts. Legal thinkers were much slower to think of torts in the same terms. The causes of action based on the old writs of trespass, case, trover, nuisance, and conspiracy still seemed too intractable to be reduced to a coherent legal category. The first substantial Anglo-American treatise on the law of torts, prepared by the Boston law writer Francis Hilliard, did not appear until 1859.[32] It was a jumble of poorly related causes of action and included substantial discussions of property and criminal law. Surveying the field in 1871, Holmes declared that, as currently conceived, the field of torts was "not a proper subject for a law book"—although he also challenged his friend Nicholas St. John Green, a lecturer at the Harvard Law School, to tackle the job.[33] As late as 1886, Melville M. Bigelow, a law professor at Boston University, could find only a few "common elements" among the various causes of action, and nothing like Langdell's fundamental principles. "One tort is as perfect as another," Bigelow insisted. "There has been no common centre from which all have been worked out."[34]

A "scientific" approach to torts triumphed in the 1880s, thanks largely to Holmes and his friend Frederick Pollock. In 1873 Holmes answered his own call for a "theory of torts" with an article-length treatment, which he later expanded in *The Common Law* (1881). Pollock built on Holmes's work in his own treatise, published in 1887. "This is a book of principles if it is anything," Pollock wrote in a prefatory letter addressed to Holmes. "Details are used, not in the manner of a digest, but so far as they may seem called for to develop and illustrate the principles." In 1899 Holmes surveyed work on torts since Hilliard and assured himself that "the generalizing principle" would ultimately triumph. In 1907 even Bigelow joined the systematizers with the eighth edition of his treatise.[35]

As the law writers worked hard to shape the causes of action into a coherent theory, they became increasingly troubled by the conspiracy doctrine. All conceded that conspiracy was a criminal offense, but most struggled to account for it as an independent ground for civil liability. The issue troubled few of their predecessors, who took conspiracy to be one of the many discrete causes of actions that constituted the Anglo-American common law. Powers, for example, was so sure that the infliction of economic loss in *Stewart* gave the Ryegate Works a private right of action for damages that he never bothered to offer supporting authority for the claim. Similarly, legal commentators on the Great Upheaval cases saw nothing remarkable in conspiracy as a category of civil liability.[36]

Nevertheless, the treatise writers had difficulty finding room for conspiracy in their increasingly bold efforts to systematize the law of torts. The "unlawful means" branch of the doctrine struck most commentators as redundant. If threats, intimidation, and duress were already actionable when performed by single individuals, why was a special rule needed when more than one person engaged in the conduct? The "unlawful purpose" branch was no less problematic. If every step taken by strikers or boycotters was lawful, how could the sum of their actions be unlawful? Thomas Cooley in particular was troubled by this branch, and he urged that it be collapsed into the first. "The general rule," he explained, "is that a conspiracy cannot be made the subject of a civil action unless something is done which, without the conspiracy, would give the right of action."[37]

By and large, the law writers followed Cooley in disregarding the collective element in labor combinations. They made liability turn on the lawfulness of the acts of the individual defendants, just as it did in cases of other intentional torts. But as they returned their focus to the lawfulness of the acts of the workers, they confronted a new problem: Should the legality of the individual act turn on the "motive" or "purpose" of the actor? Labor's advocates insisted it did not. "While a bad motive may make an illegal act worse," a lawyer protested in 1900, "it cannot make unlawful that which in its essence is lawful. The law does not undertake to regulate the consciences of individuals, but only their acts."[38] A handful of cases, all of them suits by businessmen against their rivals, supported this position.[39]

With little dissent, however, the treatise writers argued to the contrary that mental state of an actor could make an otherwise lawful act unlawful. This was true when a striker or boycotter acted from actual malice, that is, the desire to inflict harm "for its own sake and as an end in itself."[40] Most commentators realized that trade unionists rarely acted out of unalloyed ill-will toward an employer. As a rule, strikes and boycotts aimed at some concrete goal, such as the adoption of uniform work rules or the ouster of an unpopular foreman. Should liability turn on motive in these cases as well? The treatise writers quickly decided it should, and they called on judges to develop a typology of lawful and unlawful motives on a case-by-case basis.[41]

Pollock provided the clearest and most influential early discussion. Although in general liability did not turn on the mental state of the tort-feasor, Pollock allowed, several exceptions were firmly established, such as malicious prosecution and malicious procurement of breach of contract. The general rule made sense, given the difficulty of proving underlying motive. "The evil of letting a certain kind of churlish and unneighborly conduct, and even deliberate mischief, go without redress . . . may well be thought less on the whole than that of encouraging vexatious claims." In some cases, however, "the balance of expediency" weighed in favor of taking motive into account. The most common examples involved harm inflicted as a byproduct of defendants' "exercise of common rights." In such cases, defendants could argue that considerations of private right or public expediency justified their conduct, and that they should therefore not be held liable to the plaintiff. The harm, the defendants maintained, was simply *damnum absque injuria* (loss without legally compensable injury).[42]

In passing on defendants' claim of justification by reason of common right, Pollock explained, judges often did not look further into the mental state of a defendant. For example, judges upheld the common right of landowners to develop property by building a "spite fence," a barrier with no other function than to vex a neighbor. They adopted a different course in cases involving the right to contract. They refused to compensate plaintiffs for loss suffered through the normal business competition of a rival, because (as Pollock explained), "To say that a man shall not seek profit in business at the expense of others is to say that he shall not do business at all, or that the whole constitution of society shall be altered."[43]

Other kinds of business rivalry fell into "a kind of obscure middle region" and were not "exempt from search into their motives." Pollock gave the example of a defendant who induced a party to breach a contract. When the defendant counseled the party to suffer the risks of breach "with all honesty and without ill-will to the other contracting party," Pollock felt the loss should go unredressed. When the defendant acted to obtain "some advantage to himself at the plaintiff's expense," the defendant should be held liable.[44]

American treatise writers and legal scholars generally agreed with Pollock that the lawfulness of labor combinations turned on the lawfulness of the individual participants' acts and that the lawfulness of those acts turned in some degree upon the motives of the actors.[45] At the same time, they questioned the need to retain conspiracy as a distinct cause of action. Early law writers, cautious about excluding civil conspiracy cases from their treatises, voiced their doubts but retained chapters on the subject.[46] By the first decade of the twentieth century, however, most law writers devoted little space to the doctrine. Pollock, for example, confessed "to great difficulty in understanding why . . . it was necessary to say so much about conspiracy" because defendants' actions were unlawful for the same reasons as those of single wrongdoers. Conspiracy should count only as a "matter of aggravation," he held.[47] Similarly, Bigelow gave conspiracy only a paragraph in the introduction to the 1907 edition of his treatise. He analyzed labor combinations in two new chapters, headed "Procuring Refusal to Contract" and "Procuring Breach of Contract."[48]

As conspiracy lost ground in the treatises, a rival formula gained favor

among the treatise writers and became the principle around which they
organized the whole field of intentional torts. Although the doctrine had
surfaced before the Great Upheaval, notably in the Massachusetts decision
Walker v. Cronin (1871), the most influential statement of the principle
appeared in Sir Charles Bowen's opinion in *Mogul Steamship Co. v. McGregor, Gow & Co.* (1889).[49] In *Mogul,* several English merchants involved in
the Chinese tea trade sued their rivals for maintaining a boycott of their
shipments. Bowen refused to analyze the boycott as a "malicious" wrong.
"The terms 'maliciously,' 'wrongfully,' and 'injure' are words all of which
have accurate meanings, well known to the law," Bowen declared, "but
which also have a popular and less precise signification, into which it is
necessary to see that the argument does not imperceptibly slide."[50]

Bowen proposed a different starting point for the case: "intentionally
to do that which is calculated in the ordinary course of events to do damage, and which does, in fact, damage another in that other person's property or trade, is actionable if done without just cause or excuse." This formula substituted for the morally resonant word *malice* a new standard, the
absence of "just cause and excuse."[51] The new language, in itself, was consistent with an a priori approach to intentional torts. In fact, American
judges sometimes invested the notion of "just cause" with moral significance. Nevertheless, Bowen's formula gave legal thinkers dissatisfied with
the middlebrow moralism of the American bench an opportunity to sidestep precedents and to fashion a new labor jurisprudence grounded on the
social consequences of human action.

Pollock, for example, championed Bowen's formula in the later editions
of his treatise. Exasperated by the opinions in *Quinn v. Leathem* (1901), he
urged the House of Lords to stick to the simple principle that "all damage
wilfully done to one's neighbour is actionable unless it can be justified or
excused." A plaintiff could make out a cause of action by showing that the
defendant intended to perform acts injuring the plaintiff and that the defendant's conduct did in fact cause the injury. After the plaintiff had thus
established a prima facie case, it was up to the defendant to justify the
injury. Only at this point, Pollock argued, should the judge consider the
motive of the plaintiff. Pollock acknowledged that some judges believed
making justification turn on motive introduced uncertainty into the law,
but he downplayed this concern. "The Common Law has already succeeded
in defining many grounds of justification and excuse, and is surely competent to define others as new facts bring them into prominence."[52]

As a rule, American law writers similarly used Bowen's formula as the
organizing principle for the law of intentional torts. Holmes made it the
centerpiece of his influential essay "Privilege, Malice, and Intent" (1894).[53]
Between 1898 and 1907 the eminent law professors James Barr Ames, Ernst

Freund, Ernest W. Huffcut, William Draper Lewis, Jeremiah Smith, and Bruce Wyman all pitched their studies of labor law as a search for the limits of justification. Law students soon followed suit, critiquing the latest strike or boycott case in light of Bowen's formula as stated in *Mogul* or Holmes's essays and opinions.[54]

TAFT AND HOLMES

In general, the courts were much slower to switch to Bowen's formula. Two nineteenth-century judges were exceptional in approaching the task of writing judicial decisions with the law writers' concern for systematic exposition when most of their brethren willingly sacrificed clarity to build a majority or dispose of a case quickly. In the hands of a young Ohio judge named William Howard Taft, Bowen's formula was a tool for a modest refurbishing of the labor jurisprudence of the Great Upheaval. It helped Taft tame an unruly set of precedents without resorting to the circularity of the *sic utere* maxim or jettisoning the orthodox learning he acquired at Yale College, which he entered a year after Davenport graduated. In contrast, Holmes made Bowen's formula the centerpiece of an all-out assault on the genteel tradition in American jurisprudence.

Taft first employed the new approach to labor law in *Moores & Co. v. Bricklayers' Union No. 1* (1890), a damage suit brought by a supplier whose building materials were boycotted by bricklayers to punish the supplier for dealing with nonunion building contractors. At the outset, Taft confronted the argument that in refusing to work with Moores's products, individual bricklayers had simply exercised their absolute right to dispose of their labor as they pleased.[55] Earlier judges would have replied that the bricklayers' right was not absolute, that the bricklayers had committed a moral and legal wrong in "so using their own as to injure another." But Taft departed from the quite different premise Pollock advanced in his treatise. "We are dealing in this case with common rights," the judge wrote. "Every man, be he capitalist, merchant, employer, laborer or professional man, is entitled to invest his capital, to carry on his business, to bestow his labor, or to exercise his calling, if within the law, according to his pleasure." In exercising these common rights, Taft explained, it sometimes happened that one person inflicted loss on a rival, as when two merchants settled in a town big enough to support only one. "In this legitimate clash of common rights, the loss is *damnum absque injuria*," and neither merchant had a cause of action. Strikes for higher wages or against the use of dangerous materials fell into this category of justifiable harm, but other losses—those "willfully caused to one another in the exercise of what otherwise would be a lawful right, from simple motives of malice"—were not justifiable and could be remedied by a court of law.[56]

For Taft, as for Bowen, malice meant nothing more than "intent to injure another without cause or excuse"—a proposition he advanced with citations to *Mogul* and *Walker*. Was the conflict of interest between the bricklayers and Moores, like the competition of two business rivals, sufficient justification to make the loss *damnum absque injuria?* Later commentators would answer the question with a freewheeling inquiry into the social consequences of privileging the defendants' conduct. Taft's response was to fall back on an a priori understanding of the legitimate scope of economic conflict he learned at Yale from William Graham Sumner. Just as business rivals competed to gain the best terms from customers, so did workers in the normal case compete to obtain the best terms from employers. Contract thus fixed the limits of legitimate economic struggle. "If the workmen of an employer refuse to work for him except on better terms at a time when their withdrawal will cause great loss to him, and they intentionally inflict such loss to coerce him to come to their terms," Taft wrote, "they are *bona fide* exercising their lawful right to dispose of their labor for the purpose of lawful gain." Between the striking bricklayers and Moores, however, there "was no competition or possible contractual relation . . . where their interests were naturally opposed." The economic loss Moores suffered was the consequence of economic coercion, not competition. It was intended to demonstrate "to the building world what punishment and disaster necessarily followed a defiance of their demands." It could not be justified.[57]

Taft's approach was typical of the jurists who were dissatisfied with the reasoning of the Great Upheaval cases but who thought of labor strife in terms borrowed from genteel Victorian culture.[58] More fertile for the legal reformers of the Progressive Era was Holmes's reworking of Bowen's formula in the decade from 1894 to 1904. An early and thoroughgoing critic of the genteel tradition, Holmes drove a priori moralism from the law of intentional torts, leaving the field open for jurists who would make calculations of social utility the touchstone of labor jurisprudence.

Like Bowen, Holmes believed that the prevailing legal terminology of his day encouraged judges to conflate general and specialized meanings of words and to mistake their particular moral predilections for general principles of law. "For my own part," he observed, "I often doubt whether it would not be a gain if every word of moral significance could be banished from the law altogether, and other words adopted which should convey legal ideas uncolored by anything outside the law." In a sense, the law did consult moral standards, Holmes allowed, but not by slavishly adhering to some "system of morals" such as those advanced by Kant, Hegel, or the American moral philosophers. Legal liability "falls far within the lines of any such system, and in some cases may extend beyond them, for reasons drawn from the habits of a particular people at a particular time."[59] The morality the law heeded was morality as "generally accepted," as found in "the actual feelings and demands of the community, whether right or wrong."[60]

Holmes first worked out the consequences of this general approach for intentional torts in the early 1890s and published his position in 1894. Earlier judges had made malice—in the sense of actual ill-will—part of the plaintiff's prima facie case, something needed to establish the moral culpability of the defendant. Holmes, in contrast, insisted that the plaintiff need only show the defendant performed acts that were certain—or at least very likely—to produce an injury that actually occurred. In assessing the plaintiff's prima facie case, then, "The standard applied is external, and the words malice, intent, and negligence, as used in this connection, refer to an external standard." Only when judges reached the defense of justification would Holmes permit them to consider the actual malice or the other motive of the defendant. As Holmes wrote in *Aikens v. Wisconsin* (1904), on the question of justification defendants could not argue that their motives were immaterial and "the standards of the law are external. . . . That is true in determining what a man is bound to foresee, but not necessarily in determining the extent to which he can justify harm which he has foreseen."[61]

Holmes rejected the trade unionists' argument that the infliction of loss through nonviolent strikes and boycotts was a natural right. Whether workers should be held liable was "a question of policy," in which the "advantages to the community on the one side and the other, are the only matters entitled to be weighed." Justification certainly did not turn on "empty general propositions" like the *sic utere* maxim or the claim that motive could never make unlawful an otherwise lawful act.[62] True, judges sometimes privileged defendants' conduct regardless of motive. Defendants could hate business rivals or neighbors, but so long as they engaged in simple acts of business competition or built a spite fence on their own property, the resulting loss to plaintiffs was only *damnum absque injuria*. But sometimes motive mattered. Thus, advice not to employ a doctor was privileged if offered in a sincere attempt to benefit others. It was actionable if motivated by actual ill-will toward the physician.[63]

Holmes employed his framework in two great dissents while serving on the Massachusetts supreme judicial court. Holmes analyzed *Vegelahn v. Guntner* (1896) in terms of Bowen's formula (for which he cited *Walker*) and voted to privilege the defendants' strike over hours and pay. The strikers' motive, he explained, was not to inflict damage for its own sake, but to win "a victory in the battle of trade." He noted that many people did not consider this battle the normal operation of business competition. But for Holmes, unlike Taft, the limits of justification were not fixed by the truths of classical economics or even the notion that "free competition is worth more to society than it costs." The "most superficial reading of industrial history," Holmes felt, showed that the age of individualistic competition was rapidly passing. The wiser course for the policy-minded judge was to give way to the inevitable organization of the world and to privilege loss inflicted in simple labor disputes as part of the "free struggle for life."[64]

In *Plant v. Woods* (1900), Holmes applauded as a majority of his brethern discarded the conspiracy doctrine for the formula of *Walker* and *Mogul,* but he dissented when they refused to privilege loss inflicted during a jurisdictional strike between rival unions. Holmes agreed justification could turn on the motive with which the defendants acted, and he volunteered that strikes for the purpose of overriding the jurisdiction of the courts would be actionable. The freedom to refuse work, then, was not absolute, natural, and unvarying, but was historically contingent, like every other right in Holmes's jurisprudence. But if the purpose of raising wages was sufficient justification, Holmes argued, so was the motive of strengthening a union in order to "make a better fight" for higher wages. "I think that unity of organization is necessary to make a contest of labor effectual," Holmes declared, "and that societies of laborers may employ in their preparation the means which they might use in the final contest."[65]

A Regulatory Law of Industrial Disputes

In retrospect, Holmes's belief that judges should consult "considerations of policy and of social advantage" may make him look like an advocate of aggressive social engineering—and all the more so once one remembers his praise for "the man of statistics and the master of economics."[66] Yet Holmes's notion of consulting public policy was more modest than that of later legal scholars. Judges should not "undertake to renovate the law," Holmes insisted. "That is not their province." Their mission was to determine whether a given legal rule advanced "a social end which the governing power of the community has made up its mind that it wants." Social science helped judges see more clearly by overcoming their "often blind and unconscious" estimates of the relative strengths of conflicting social ends. It was not a mandate for independently imposing a particular notion of the public good upon society.[67]

The legal progressives who wrote on labor law in the twenty years after the *Debs* injunction followed Holmes in seeing the field as a special case in the general theory of intentional torts and in stressing the collective, particular, and historically contingent origins of individual rights. Like other progressive reformers, the lawyers used the language of "social bonds" to describe human relations.[68] "Few, if any, rights are now recognized as absolute," a law professor forthrightly declared in 1910. "We are coming more and more to measure our approval or disapproval of acts by the effects they have upon society as a whole, and public opinion is fast approaching a stage where it will no longer approve an act which though beneficial to the individual is detrimental to society." "Even competition is only a permission," another wrote, "granted when its operation is best for established society, forbidden when it is prejudicial to the industrial order."[69]

Beyond this point, however, the law professors broke ranks, taking up contradictory and potentially conflicting positions on two important issues. First, they differed over whether legal reformers could control the direction of social change. The dominant theme in the "sociological jurisprudence" of Roscoe Pound (1870–1964) took social change to be organic, inevitable, and, on the whole, benign. Legal reformers could safely limit their efforts to noting where legal doctrine had lagged behind society, leaving a gap between "the law in the books" and the "law in action." Pound urged lawyers to contemplate the "actual social effects" of legal rules. If they did, he felt sure they would discard outdated doctrines and settle on ones better suited to the novel conditions of their day.[70] In contrast, younger legal scholars, educated after the notion of social control had gained currency among American social scientists, took a more aggressive stance.[71] For them, law reform was less a matter of erasing a gap between law and society than the use of law to remake society itself. In their writings, Bowen's notion of "just cause and excuse" became a charter for social engineering in the law of industrial disputes.

The law professors also divided over whether organized labor should enjoy greater freedom under the new jurisprudential regime. Melville Bigelow (1846–1921) was certain that the tides of history were running against trade unions. When he encountered historicist jurisprudence in the 1870s, Bigelow was a doctoral candidate in Harvard's history department and a member of Holmes's circle of legal scholars. Throughout the nineteenth century his writings kept to the safe path of teleological historicism, but after 1900, inspired by his friend Brooks Adams, he took up a relativistic position.[72] Law was but "the resultant of conflicting social forces," offset by "the conservatism of courts and legislatures." With an analogous view of law, Holmes thought the balance of social forces called for judges to provide greater freedom for labor organizations. Bigelow held the contrary to be the case. Holmes's opinion in *Vegelahn* went "against the direction of economic energy," he declared in 1907. Decisions favoring capital and turning aside labor's demands for the closed shop took the wiser course.[73]

A member of the first wave of historicist legal scholars, Bigelow never lost his generation's conviction that the development of the law was an organic and largely autonomous process. Yet even younger men, trained as American social science swapped historicism for institutionalism and social control, could agree that labor unions required strict policing. William

Draper Lewis (1867–1949) most strikingly illustrates how the new labor jurisprudence could be turned against the trade unions. A lawyer and a student of the heterodox economist Simon N. Patten, Lewis was less than thirty when he was appointed dean of the University of Pennsylvania's law school in 1896, and thereafter supported a variety of progressive causes.[74] In the 1890s he sharply criticized labor injunctions for denying workers the right to a jury trial.[75] When the *Debs* decision settled the law against his position, Lewis turned from procedural considerations to the substantive law of industrial disputes. In this new context he became a strong critic of labor activism and of organized labor's claim of an absolute right to strike and boycott.

Like his mentor Patten, Lewis believed that all rights were social in origin and were legally cognizable only insofar as they advanced the collective good. Trade unionists might argue that strikes were among those acts which "man has an inherent right to do, irrespective of the circumstances under which he does them," but in fact no such acts existed. Ultimately, the lawfulness of any act turned on the circumstances in which it was performed and whether some "corresponding benefit to the community" offset the harm inflicted. "A state cannot recognize the existence in the individual of an inherent right to injure his fellow-man," Lewis flatly proclaimed, for it would then find itself unable to keep pace with industrial combination and other social change. Claims of inherent rights only clouded legal analysis. Judges would do better to consider "the fundamental position of our common law—that he who injures his fellow-man is liable for that injury, unless he can show that the community regards his act as conducive to the public welfare." If they did, they would be sure to hold against the closed shop and many other aims of organized labor.[76]

Other rebels against the a priori jurisprudence of the Victorian bench looked more favorably on trade unionism. Ernst Freund (1864–1932), for example, was an early exponent of a "sociological" case for granting labor unions more freedom to organize. Born in New York City but raised in Germany, Freund was educated at the universities of Berlin and Heidelberg, where he learned to think of human institutions in historical terms.[77] Like Bowen, Pollock, and Holmes, Freund believed the ultimate question in labor cases was the presence of lawful cause or excuse. This "ought not to be called malice," Freund maintained, because the presence or absence of actual ill will was only one of the factors "social sentiment" regarded in setting the limits of legal justification. In 1898 Freund thought judges were sufficiently attuned to changing popular attitudes toward the working class to make a "liberal exception" for nonviolent strikes and boycotts. Eight years later, disillusioned by *Lochner v. New York* (1905) and similar cases, he wrote that "legislative regulation" was required.[78]

In the next decade, more legal academics argued that labor law should be grounded in social needs. With the passing of Powers's and Carpenter's faith in a priori legal reasoning, some law writers even ventured that courts were incapable of fashioning proper rules for the settlement of industrial disputes. One was James Wallace Bryan (1884–1973), a Baltimore lawyer who received a doctorate in political science from Johns Hopkins University in 1908.[79] The scope of trade unionists' privilege to inflict economic loss, Bryan argued in 1910, was "a complex problem of economics and sociology" requiring "a competent and exhaustive investigation of the facts of modern industrial life and organization." Courts simply were not up to this task. The "elaborate but palpably unconvincing reasoning" of the judges notwithstanding, the true basis of decision in labor cases was the bench's "pre-determined economic views" informed by only the most rudimentary understanding of the social context of industrial disputes. Bryan urged that the whole field be governed by statutes drafted by legislative commissions of qualified experts.[80]

In the years before the United States entered World War I, other young lawyers joined Bryan in arguing that labor law could not be left to the "atomistic theory of justice" imbedded in the common law. "The working-out of the destiny of so important an institution as a labor union should never have been committed to the decision of the court, working, necessarily, with a conservative tradition which ignores the needs and progress of society," declared Albert Kocourek (1875–1952) in 1912.[81] Social scientists and activist lawyers continued the assault on the common-law of labor relations, most notably in the final report of the United States Commission on Industrial Relations, published in 1915. Headed by the liberal labor lawyer Frank P. Walsh and the labor economist John R. Commons, the commission urged the adoption of an American equivalent to the British Trade Disputes Act of 1906, which would deny the courts jurisdictions in labor disputes. In its place, Commons and his researchers called for an industrial commission staffed by trained experts, such as themselves.[82]

In sum, just as the AABA commenced operations, a substantial body of literature produced by full-time law professors and a handful of other highbrow legal thinkers had rejected the conspiracy doctrine as the framework for the common law of industrial disputes. A taste for systematic thought started the law writers on the search for a general theory of liability for intentional torts, which they found in Bowen's *Mogul* decision, Pollock's treatise, and Holmes's essays and opinions. Holmes's generation of American legal scholars historicized Bowen's formula, arguing that the privilege for intentionally inflicted injury varied with the social circumstances prevailing in a particular time and place.

The next generation of legal scholars combined the historicist notion that labor law should be tailored to fit existing social conditions with the idea of social control to produce a more activist jurisprudence. No longer would highbrow legal thinkers dismiss labor's claims of privilege by invoking the syllogism, the *sic utere* maxim, and the tenets of genteel culture. Rather, they would require that trade unionists show how their conduct promoted social welfare, notwithstanding the loss suffered by individual employers. The new approach would by no means privilege all of the organizational tactics of the labor movement at the turn of the century. It never satisfied Samuel Gompers or the other leaders of the AFL, who preferred an a priori jurisprudence of their own based on the absolute, natural, and individual right to strike and boycott. Nevertheless, the new approach promised unprecedented acceptance of the collective power of workers and their unions so long as it could be shown to be necessary for the promotion of the broader public good.

When the AABA commenced operations most judges still clung to the conspiracy doctrine and refused to confess that the true grounds of their decisions were "considerations of policy and social advantage"—much to the consternation of the law professors.[83] The judges' continued resort to conspiracy doctrine was enormously encouraging to Davenport as he launched his campaign against the closed shop. A more scholarly and reflective lawyer might have been troubled by the rise of the general theory of intentional torts, the substitution of "just cause and excuse" for the morally resonant term *malice,* and the increasing eagerness of legal scholars and judges to make justification turn on the social consequences of a particular act. Bolstered by the case law, however, Davenport convinced himself that the law of industrial disputes still followed principles laid down in the 1880s. Whether he could convince the judges of the new century was another matter.

FIVE

The Labor Trust

How can the right of combined action be curtailed without depriving individual liberty of half its value; how can it be left unrestricted without destroying either the liberty of individual citizens or the power of the government?

—Albert Venn Dicey (1905)

In the summer of 1904 Daniel Davenport debated the merits of the closed shop with Samuel Gompers in a small town in upstate New York. Well into his speech, Davenport used a metaphor that was already a favorite among the leaders of the open-shop movement. "Now, the purpose of and the plan of the labor unions," Davenport declared, "is the establishment of a labor trust."[1] In the first years of the new century, as historian Daniel Rodgers suggests, the urban middle class "discovered" the octopus—the problem of industrial combination—decades after it first alarmed the rural populations of the American South and West. When Davenport spoke, Ida Tarbell's serial exposé of the Standard Oil Company was already scandalizing the readers of *McClure's Magazine,* and the Supreme Court had recently upheld Theodore Roosevelt's antitrust prosecution of the Northern Securities Company, a giant railroad combination midwived by the nation's leading financial houses. Even then, of course, a cadre of economists, lawyers, corporate managers, and publicists were at work fashioning a defense of the new holding companies, making the case for the superiority of administered prices and output over the booms and busts of entrepreneurial capitalism.[2] But Davenport was surely right in assuming that the perils of industrial combination were more apparent than its promise in the summer of 1904, and he was probably correct in calculating that many in his audience would accept the analogy between the business trust and the labor union. Both taxed consumers to fatten the privileged and powerful few. Both upset the delicate system of rewards and punishments that made competitive markets "a kind of disciplinary machinery for the development of character."[3] And both subverted the democratic process by corrupting legislators and executive officials with graft and the votes of its self-interested constituents.

When Davenport spoke, the AABA had already launched a "trust-busting" campaign of its own, a series of cases to outlaw even peaceably conducted strikes and boycotts when intended to force employers to adopt closed-shop contracts. Davenport and his associates pitched their arguments in the still-potent terms of the labor jurisprudence of the Great Upheaval. Ignoring the tort-based approach of the law professors, the lawyers argued that the closed shop was an unlawful purpose under the conspiracy doctrine, rendering any labor combination to advance that aim illegal, regardless of the actual social and economic effects of unionization in the particular case. They did not seek the regulation of labor disputes in the name of social utility; they asked the courts to vindicate individual liberty. The individual remained the fundamental social and political unit in their analysis; the group, endowed with legitimate, collective interests beyond that of its individual members, had no place in their thinking.

This chapter chronicles the AABA's campaign against the closed shop between 1903 and 1915. Cases decided between the Great Upheaval and the founding of the AABA held great promise for Davenport, but at best they provided a point of departure, and one precedent, at least, was an undeniable obstacle to the complete judicial outlawry of the closed shop. AABA-sponsored litigation provided the occasion for some harsh judicial words on trade unionism, but Davenport never produced a precedent unambiguously declaring the closed shop an unlawful aim under the conspiracy doctrine. Although the arguments of labor leaders and their lawyers won some support, ultimately the terms of accommodation tracked the new labor jurisprudence of the law professors. A priori, categorical analysis under the conspiracy doctrine gave way to discussion of whether the actual harm inflicted on employers and union workers was justified by the benefit of the closed shop to the union and the larger public.

Of course, the courts never acceded to organized labor's demands for complete immunity for the nonviolent, economic loss they inflicted on nonunion workers and employers. The jurisprudential absolutism of the trade unionists was just as incompatible with the new sociological jurisprudence as was that of the AABA. Not all claims of autonomy deserved protection, according to the legal reformers, only those that permitted the individual to "work for a common end."[4] Even so, the courts ended up privileging varieties of industrial coercion that would have outraged the bench of the 1880s. Well before the United States entered World War I, the judges glimpsed a solution to Dicey's conundrum and suggested the terms on which organized labor could be welcomed into the nation's emerging pluralist polity.

STATUS QUO ANTE BELLUM

Stewart, Glidden, and similar cases dating back to the Great Upheaval provided Davenport with the foundation for his campaign against the closed shop. These precedents had established that strikes and boycotts aiming to force the discharge of nonunion workers were unlawful combinations under the conspiracy doctrine. Valuable as they were, the cases did not in themselves amount to the weapon open-shop leaders needed to turn back the organizational campaigns of the business unions of the AFL. Such disputes usually commenced, as Loewe's did, with a demand that an employer sign a standard-form, closed-shop trade agreement. What the employer most sought in such circumstances was a legal basis for enjoining the union from any efforts to force the adoption of the agreement. Signing such a contract did not necessarily oblige employers to discharge any workers, because the union could accept all of the employees into its membership. This possibility distinguished the facts of the turn-of-the-century disputes from those of the 1880s, in which a targeted employee had already been discharged.

Davenport's task was to convince the courts to ignore the distinction and treat strikes to force the adoption of a closed-shop agreement as the equivalent of strikes to oust nonunion workers. Labor's advocates responded by insisting on the difference, arguing as Gompers did in his debate with Davenport that "the whole world is invited to come in and join the ranks of labor."[5] They also argued from the jurisprudential high ground of natural right that workers could quit work and purchase goods for no reason or any reason whatsoever. In a mirror image of the open-shop lawyers' defense of the employers' liberty of contract, Gompers proclaimed the workers' rights fundamental, inalienable, and "under the protection of the Constitution of our country." They were absolute, immune from abridgement or qualification in the name of social utility. No less than Davenport, Gompers reasoned from the individualistic, a priori terms of Victorian jurisprudence and mistrusted the implicit utilitarianism of the new tort-based approach. He would not concede that trade unionists' freedom from liability in nonviolent labor disputes ultimately depended upon the judges' calculations of social welfare, rightly sensing that the labor movement and the judiciary had conflicting understandings of the public interest.[6]

In fact, when the AABA commenced operations, few judges welcomed an expressly utilitarian approach to the law of industrial disputes. Long after Taft, Holmes, and the treatise writers had envisioned the law of strikes and boycotts as a subfield of intentional torts, most cases were decided under the conspiracy doctrine.[7] Holmes stood virtually alone in forthrightly basing his prolabor decision on explicit calculations of social advantage; the handful of other judges who joined him in supporting trade-union defendants usually adopted the a priori, formal arguments of the unionists themselves.[8]

As Davenport surveyed the legal terrain in preparation for his campaign against the closed shop, two decisions of the influential New York Court of Appeals were foremost in his mind. *Curran v. Galen* (1897), a unanimous, per curiam decision, was a cause for optimism, a promising bridge between the Great Upheaval cases and the outlawry of the closed shop. *Curran* was the damage suit of an engineer discharged for refusing to join a brewery union and unable to obtain employment at his trade in any other local brewery. Thus far the case was no novelty: *Stewart* and *Glidden* imposed liability on trade unionists on similar facts. The new and, for Davenport, encouraging aspect of the case involved the trade union's defense. Curran, the defendants pointed out, had been discharged in accordance with a closed-shop contract made with a local employers' association. This agreement, they argued, justified the loss Curran suffered.[9]

The New York court agreed with the union's framing of the issue. "If such an agreement is lawful," it wrote, "then it must be conceded that the defendants are entitled to set it up as a defense to the action." The judges then argued that closed-shop contracts were illegal. They remarked that in themselves trade unions were "proper and praiseworthy," and they noted the defendants' claim that the closed shop would promote public policy by avoiding "disputes and conflicts." In 1897 this tentative statement of the social benefits of the closed shop made less of an impression on the judges than the perils it held for the rights of individual workers and the public. Unions that advanced the common welfare of their members were well and good, but the defendants in *Curran* had gone further. They had used their collective might to injure others. They had attempted to oust "the individual who prefers by single effort to gain his livelihood." They had interfered with Curran's "constitutional right freely to pursue a lawful avocation, under conditions equal as to all." Like the judges of the Great Upheaval cases, the New York court saw labor disputes as a matter of individual right and wrong—of determining whether the defendants had "so used their own as not to injure others"—and it relied upon the most fundamental tenets of genteel Victorian culture to arrive at its conclusion.[10]

In his early speeches on behalf of the AABA, Davenport proclaimed that *Curran* had established "for all time" that closed-shop agreements were illegal in New York and that any person who entered into one was liable for damages.[11] Still, he must have recognized that the case was at most a first step toward the holding that any attempt to establish the closed shop was an unlawful purpose under the conspiracy doctrine. True, the *Curran* court had unanimously declared that coercing other workers into joining the union through contracts with employers violated "the spirit of our government and the nature of our institutions."[12] That bold proposition, however, was limited by the facts of the case, in which an identifiable worker had proved that an agreement kept him from finding suitable employment anywhere within the city of his residence. *Curran* was not good authority for the claim that any attempt to force the closed shop on an unwilling employer was illegal or that simply by signing such an agreement an employer broke the law. Thus, writing in 1900, a lawyer advised a New York City employer that simply entering into a closed-shop contract with a union was not unlawful under *Curran*, but that the employer could be held liable if he hired a nonunion worker and then fired him in compliance with the agreement.[13]

If *Curran* posed an opportunity for the open-shop movement, *National Protective Association of Steam Fitters v. Cumming* (1902) presented an obstacle. The case involved a jurisdictional dispute between two unions in the construction industry in New York City. By a 4-3 vote, the New York Court of Appeals rejected the suit of the members of the rival union who were denied employment under a closed-shop agreement. Judge Irving G. Vann (1842–1921), a Yale-educated Republican, forcefully made the case against the closed shop under the conspiracy doctrine in terms that closely tracked *Curran*. This time, however, the position claimed the support of only three judges.[14] Squarely opposed to them were three other judges led by Alton B. Parker (1852–1926), a stalwart Democrat who remained in the party after Bryan's ascendancy and who was rewarded for his regularity with the presidential nomination in 1904.[15] Much to the dismay of the law professors, Parker's reason was just as individualist and a priori as Vann's. William Draper Lewis, for example, contrasted Parker's reasoning from the absolute right to work or not to work with Holmes's "radically different" approach in *Plant v. Woods*.[16]

The seventh and decisive vote, cast in favor of the union, was that of John Clinton Gray (1843–1915), a Democrat educated at the University of Berlin, New York University, and the Harvard Law School.[17] Much of Gray's opinion looked back to the Great Upheaval cases. For example, Gray spoke of "the absolute freedom of the individual to work for whom he chooses and to make any contract upon the subject that he chooses." He stooped to the tautology of the *sic utere* maxim, writing at one point that trade unionists could advance their interest as they saw fit, so long as they did nothing illegal.[18]

Yet Gray's opinion also anticipated later and better developed attempts to find a place for organized labor in a pluralist model of social relations. He agreed with Vann that if the defendants' only aim was to limit employment for no other reason than the power and wealth it would bring them they would have been liable. The trial court's findings, however, did not establish that fact. Rather, they showed that the plaintiff had failed to pass the defendant union's examination, established to ensure that only competent and efficient workers were employed in the field. Gray believed this was a proper motive for the union to pursue, notwithstanding the fact that it would produce "unhappy results in individual cases."[19]

Gray did not explain why limiting employment to efficient workers justified the harm inflicted on others. Perhaps he viewed the matter from the standpoint of an employer and posited a willing trade of his unqualified right to hire for the union's guarantee of a competent work force. The union would then act in a corporate capacity as a de facto hiring agent for the employer. Perhaps Gray viewed the matter from the standpoint of the public, who might benefit if incompetent workers were driven from the field. Then the union in its corporate capacity served as a de facto licensing agent for the public. In either case the union would exercise a collective authority that did not originate in a voluntary delegation from the individual workers who made up the union's rank and file.

It would take more than Parker's and Gray's opinion (and a few, less prominent judicial endorsements of labor's case) to convince Daniel Davenport that the judiciary had renounced the timeless truths of the Great Upheaval cases—particularly because Gray refused to overrule *Curran* in *Cumming*.[20] When the AABA officially commenced operations in the summer of 1903, Davenport was already searching for a test case to make unlawful even peacefully conducted strikes for the closed shop. "We looked around for a case where we could bring up this question about the illegality of a combination to compel a person to unionize his shop," Davenport recalled. "Fortunately for the people of this country, the opportunity arose in Chicago."[21]

The *Christensen* Precedent

Davenport's test case was an injunction suit commenced by the Kellogg Switchboard and Supply Company in the spring of 1903. The firm employed between five hundred and six hundred workers, 90 percent of whom belonged to one of fourteen different unions. In May the overwhelming majority of the work force struck to obtain contracts granting the closed shop, limiting the use of apprentices, and permitting sympathetic strikes. For three weeks the strike continued without incident, but when the plant began operating with nonunion workers, isolated assaults took place. On May 25, Judge Jesse Holdom of the Cook County Superior Court granted a sweeping injunction drafted by Kellogg's attorney, Alexander C. Allen. The injunction banned "any act whatever" (including peaceful persuasion) that furthered the unions' conspiracy to obstruct Kellogg's "free, uninterrupted and unhindered control and direction of its business and affairs."[22]

The strike escalated dramatically in June and early July when Chicago's powerful teamsters struck in sympathy with Kellogg's workers and blocked the movement of freight to and from the premises. Violence against nonunion workers stepped up, and wild riots erupted when nonunion teamsters, accompanied by a guard of four hundred policemen, moved several shipments in and out of Kellogg's plant. In retaliation, the teamsters' union threatened to halt coal deliveries to the city's power plants. On July 20, Allen (now financed by the AABA) convinced Judge Holdom to extend the injunction to include the teamsters. As an observer wrote, the order helped convince "that large neutral element which is not permanently enlisted on either side of the labor-capital struggle" that the unions were in the wrong.[23] This certainly was the lesson that the employers drew for the public. "If it has come to this, that either the law or the labor unions must go," Davenport declared, "the latter might as well get ready to leave."[24] The public outcry led conservative leaders in Chicago's labor movement to withdraw their support, and on the evening of July 23 the teamsters formally ended their sympathetic activities. The strike dragged on for months, but in the end Kellogg succeeded in maintaining open-shop conditions.[25]

Holdom's injunction was a model of aggressive judicial intervention in labor disputes that faithfully followed the logic of the conspiracy doctrine. Its sweeping terms prohibited not only threats, intimidation, force, and violence, but also peaceful picketing and other forms of persuasion that advanced the unlawful purpose of obtaining the closed shop. As Holdom later explained, "There must be no attempt by coercion to destroy competition affecting the Union, or concerted action to force an employer to yield his right to select his own workmen, or to force him to submit himself against his will to the dictation of the Union."[26]

Clarence Darrow, attorney for the defendants, contested the injunction in an interlocutory appeal in July 1903. Arguing while strike-related rioting was at its height, Darrow conceded that some injunction should issue but insisted that it should only prohibit violent conduct.[27] The strikers' purpose in seeking the execution of the closed-shop contract, he declared, was the wholly lawful one of raising wages and bettering working conditions. It was "absurd," it was "farcical," to charge them with an unlawful purpose, Darrow claimed. One might as well have charged the defendants with a conspiracy to build a church, organize a lodge, or help the poor.

Organized labor was simply exercising the same freedom to compete that businessmen exercised in selling their wares, a right guaranteed by "all the organic law of the land." Workers were absolutely privileged in the exercise of this right through peaceful picketing, patrolling, and persuading. In ordering otherwise, Darrow declared, Holdom had helped Kellogg divert attention from its "assassination of liberty to the fisticuffs of outraged labor."[28]

Allen and James H. Wilkerson replied on Kellogg's behalf with a brief shrewdly calculated to produce the decisive precedent the open-shop movement sought.[29] The case presented "a much broader question than that of the lawfulness or unlawfulness of the specific acts prohibited," they announced. It turned on the legality of the purpose of the workers' combination, which was to force Kellogg to adopt a closed-shop contract. Such conduct was illegal because it interfered with Kellogg's "right to manage its own business in its own way and as its judgment might dictate." Further, "the agreement in itself was unlawful," quite apart from its being forced upon Kellogg, because it limited employment to union workers and obligated Kellogg to respect sympathetic strikes, in direct contravention of public policy, "the spirit of our government, and the nature of our institutions."[30]

The two lawyers scoffed at Darrow's invocation of constitutional principle. "In high sounding generalities we may talk about the right of free speech," they declared, "but every man must take the legal consequences of words spoken in furtherance of a conspiracy and as part of a plan to injure another." The injunction did not forbid workers from quitting, either individually or en masse. Nor was the right of the workers to speak or walk the streets assailed. This conduct was enjoined only when in aid of a conspiracy to force employers to adopt "a disastrous business policy" and execute unlawful agreements. No matter how innocent an act might appear in the abstract, it became unlawful when performed for such unlawful purposes.[31]

The appellate court quickly issued a per curiam opinion that condemned the closed shop in harsh terms (borrowed from *Curran*) but stopped well short of producing the precedent Davenport sought. "We are not to be understood as holding that a request to appellee [Kellogg] to enter into an agreement to employ none but union men was in itself unlawful," the court cautioned. But it also refused to overturn or modify Holdom's injunction, as Darrow sought. While it suggested that peaceful picketing should not be enjoined, it was satisfied that Holdom had forbidden only "so-called persuasion, backed up by acts of violence." Such conduct Holdom had ample authority to proscribe.[32]

The AABA's lawyers stuck to their original theory in the wake of the decision. Every contract that excluded nonunion men from "the free opportunity to earn his living" was criminal, Davenport insisted. "Every proposition to that effect by union men to their employers is criminal. Every act done to carry out such a contract to the exclusion of the non-union men is criminal." Darrow also saw no reason to modify his understanding of the case. Although Holdom's injunction remained in effect, he advised the strikers that they could continue to walk the streets near Kellogg's plant and speak to replacement workers as long as they limited themselves to purely peaceful means of persuasion.[33]

Holdom was outraged by what he saw as Darrow's impertinence. "An astute counsel issued his written manifesto to the union men," he later complained, "in effect telling them the court was in error."[34] Holdom responded by citing several strikers for contempt of court. The strikers appealed, and in May 1904 Judge Frances Adams affirmed the contempt citations. Issued during the flood tide of the open-shop movement, *Christensen v. People* at once became the subject of considerable debate and conflicting interpretations.[35]

Adams offered two independent bases for his decision. First, after reviewing the strikers' menacing comments, threats, assaults, and mass picketing, he condemned the strike under the "unlawful means" branch of the conspiracy doctrine. This was, given the case law of the time, a quite unremarkable ruling. If the case stood only for the proposition that violent picketing was unlawful, it posed no new threat to the labor movement.[36]

Adams went on, however, to declare the strikers' purpose unlawful for two reasons. First, the closed-shop agreements they sought would, if executed, "tend to create a monopoly in favor of the members of the different unions, to the exclusion of workmen not members of such unions." It was enough for Adams that the tendency of the agreement, determined in accordance with his a priori understanding of free competition, was toward monopoly; he saw no need to inquire into what actual effects Kellogg's adoption of the closed shop would have on local labor markets. Second, the closed-shop agreements violated criminal statutes prohibiting combinations to deprive owners of the lawful use and management of their property and to prevent persons from obtaining employment.[37] Adams's reasoning along this branch of conspiracy doctrine paralleled the statements in *Curran* and seemed to realize the earlier case's promise for the open-shop movement.

In the wake of *Christensen*, Davenport insisted on reading the case as condemning the closed shop under the "unlawful purpose" branch of the conspiracy doctrine. "Any combination of men to compel another man to do something against his will is an unlawful combination," he explained to a convention of the open-shop Citizens' Industrial Alliance of America (CIAA) in November 1905. "Every act, otherwise innocent, which is done to carry out that conspiracy, is unlawful by reason of the fact it is done in aid of such conspiracy." "Do I stand upon the street; do I visit a man; do I attempt to persuade a man; do I do any other act which I would have a perfect right to do if I were not doing it in carrying out that conspiracy?" If so, Davenport maintained, "I am liable . . . to the restraining act of the court."[38]

Other lawyers for the open-shop movement shared Davenport's interpretation of *Christensen*. "It is impossible to exaggerate the importance of this decision," declared Horace K. Tenney, one of Wilkerson's associates. "It will even be a crime to submit a closed-shop agreement in the future to an employer for his signature," another lawyer predicted. An attorney for the Illinois Manufacturers' Association believed that even employers would feel the deterrent effect of the decision. "When the employer of labor in this state awakes to the situation that he is a party to a criminal conspiracy the floodgates will open and non-union labor will . . . receive the protection that all the injunctions and processes of the courts have hitherto been unable to give them." No wonder the editor of the journal of the National Metal Trades Association heard the "death knell of the closed shop" in Adams's opinion.[39]

Always ready to expect the worst from the courts, Samuel Gompers read the case as the employers did. The open-shop movement had long sought a decision against the closed shop, Gompers charged. "At last they have succeeded."[40] But a different, more lawyerly interpretation of *Christensen* was possible, one that minimized the significance of the case as an anti-union precedent. Under this reading, the true basis for Adams's decision was his holding that the strikers used unlawful means in pursuit of their goals. His remark that the closed shop was an unlawful purpose was superfluous and did not bind other judges.

The strongest advocate of this position, and one of the most thoroughgoing critics of *Christensen*, was Louis D. Brandeis. In his contribution to a symposium sponsored by the National Civic Federation, Brandeis argued that the case merely applied "the well established and sound rule that picketing attended by intimidation and coercion is unlawful and will be enjoined." Adams's apparent holding about the closed shop was therefore but "an elaborate dictum."[41]

JUDICIAL ACCOMMODATION

In the years after *Christensen*, the AABA worked to establish its reading of the case. "Our idea has been to get, in as many States of the Union as we can, test cases where some application may be made of the immortal principles recognized in that decision," Davenport told the CIAA in

November 1905.[42] Already he could point to three cases that followed Adams in condemning closed-shop contracts for violating the "utmost freedom of the citizen to pursue his lawful trade or calling."[43] Two months after Adams's decision, a Milwaukee judge cited *Christensen* in dissolving a temporary injunction obtained by a tailors' union to enforce a closed-shop agreement against an employer. In *Jacobs v. Cohen,* decided in December 1904, an intermediate appellate court in New York rejected a suit by the United Garment Workers to collect on a bond given by a tailoring firm to secure its observance of a closed-shop contract. And in June 1905 the Massachusetts Supreme Judicial Court decided *Berry v. Donovan,* which upheld a verdict awarding $1,500 to a worker discharged pursuant to a closed-shop agreement. If the closed shop were treated as a legitimate object of trade unionism, Chief Judge Marcus Knowlton warned, "Every employer would be forced into membership in a union, and the unions, by a combination of these different trades and occupations, would have complete and absolute control of all the industries in the country."[44]

As much as Davenport must have enjoyed hearing these judges spout the dogmas of the open-shop movement, the three cases brought the AABA no closer to its goal of an unambiguous precedent declaring that even purely peaceful strikes for the closed shop were unlawful under the conspiracy doctrine. As Brandeis wrote of *Berry,* "The Court expressly limits its decision to the case of causing the discharge of a non-union man employed at the time of making the contract, and leaves open for further consideration the case of a contract which is to operate only as to the future."[45] Further, courts in Connecticut and North Carolina held that closed-shop strikes and boycotts did not violate the criminal laws of those states.[46]

Worse yet, the AABA's campaign suffered a damaging setback just days after Davenport appeared before the CIAA. In a 4-2 decision, the New York Court of Appeals reversed the intermediate court's decision in *Jacobs* and concluded that the particular closed-shop contract under review was fully "consonant with public policy, and enforceable in the courts of justice in this state."[47] As in *Cumming,* Vann dissented with an opinion that might have been written by an open-shop lawyer. The closed shop was "a form of slavery, even if voluntarily submitted to," he declared. "A labor trust in restraint of free labor is opposed to sound public policy the same as a trust of capital in restraint of free production, and any agreement by which either object is sought to be accomplished is illegal and void." For Vann, as for Adams, it was enough that the "object" or tendency of the contract was to prevent competition, regardless of the consequences of the contract under the conditions prevailing in the relevant market for labor.[48]

Gray now spoke for a majority of the court, in an opinion that sought a middle way between Vann's absolute condemnation of the closed shop and the trade unionists' absolute defense of the practice. Gray stressed that the defendant employers had voluntarily entered into the contract to obtain the benefit stated in its recital, access to union workers in good standing. Vann was wrong to see holding the employer to its agreement as a species of slavery. In fact, enforcing the agreement promoted freedom of contract by ensuring that parties would be held to their commitments.[49] Gray would find for the employers if the agreement actually operated "generally in the community to prevent craftsmen from obtaining employment and from earning their livelihood," as had the closed-shop arrangement in *Curran*. But *Jacobs* was a very different case. If the contract "might operate to prevent some persons from being employed by the firm, or, possibly, from remaining in the firm's employment," Gray explained, "that is but an incidental feature." The record did not show that the contract had deprived nonunion workers of "all opportunity of pursuing their lawful avocation." Short of that, the members of the United Garment Workers were simply exercising their right to "freedom of action" in the collective pursuit of mutual and lawful interests. "If surrender of individual liberty is involved in combination," Gray concluded, "that is, nevertheless, but an extension of the right of freedom of action."[50]

Gray thus broke with the labor jurisprudence of the Great Upheaval in two important respects. First, Gray required that judges look beyond a priori definitions of competition to the social consequences of the particular closed-shop agreement at issue in a tort or contract case. "I do not think that competition is invariably a public benefaction," Gray had earlier written, "for it may be carried on to such a degree as to become a general evil."[51] Judges should determine whether a decision for the union would in fact realize the monopolistic potential of the agreement. Read with *Curran*, *Jacobs* made legality turn on the extent of closed-shop conditions within an industry and community. Thus, in 1910 a treatise writer reconciled the two New York cases by distinguishing between "an association of all the employers of labor engaged in the same line of business in a single community" and a closed-shop contract between "an individual employer and a labor union." The former was against public policy and void; the latter, enforceable.[52]

Although a significant departure from the a priori jurisprudence of the Great Upheaval, Gray's opinion provided an uncertain rationale for the closed shop. Gray would protect a union's attempt to establish the closed shop only insofar as the effort fell short of its goal, the establishment of union conditions throughout an industry. A stable basis for closed-shop unionism required something more—a judicial acknowledgment of the public benefits of exclusive union contracts. Readers of Gray's opinions in *Cumming* and in *Jacobs* could catch glimpses of this in his suggestion that closed-shop unionism provided employers with a skilled, stable, and disciplined work force, but Gray himself did not make much of the point, probably because by advancing it he would assume the role of policymaker. For Gray, at least, the notion that he should balance the competing social utilities of industrial stability against the anticompetitive consequences of closed-shop unionism was too great a break with the Victorian understanding of the judge as a doer of corrective justice.[53]

Gray's tolerance for some "surrender of individual liberty" was a second notable break with the labor jurisprudence of the Great Upheaval. Under the "voluntarist" model of trade unionism affirmed by Powers, Carpenter, Davenport, and Vann, labor unions could claim no authority or legitimacy beyond that delegated to them by their free and independent members. This position followed from the premise that the individual, endowed by nature with certain inalienable rights, was the fundamental unit of social and political organization.[54] Gray's claim in *Jacobs* that "organization, or combination, is a law of human society" echoed the historicism of Holmes's dissent in *Vegelahn*—and, perhaps, Gray's own exposure to historicist thought at the University of Berlin.[55] Earlier judges would have balked at sanctioning any "surrender of individual liberty." In the wake of the great merger movement, Gray sensed that corporate economic power was an irreversible fact of industrial life that necessarily entailed some sacrifice of individual freedom, at least as it was understood in an economy dominated by proprietary capitalists. Gray did not solve Dicey's conundrum in *Cummings* and *Jacobs*, but he did perceive it, and in so doing he heralded a more explicit reception of pluralism into American law.

Jacobs galvanized the leadership of the AABA. Secretary Frederick Boocock quickly issued a bulletin assuring the rank and file that "our Association had no connection with this case whatsoever, and it is a marked example of the unfortunate results that may follow the absence of such management and supervision as our Association furnishes." AABA lawyers huddled with the employer's counsel and convinced them to apply for a rehearing on the "Constitutional question as to the freedom of workingmen"—namely, whether the due process clause of the Fourteenth Amendment required that the contract not be enforced.[56] With this "federal question" raised before the New York courts, the case could then be carried to the U.S. Supreme Court. Unfortunately, the request was denied, leaving Boocock to grumble that the AABA was now "obliged to watch for another case of a similar nature."[57]

In the interim, *Jacobs* left the legal status of strikes and boycotts in a state of considerable uncertainty.[58] In 1908 Walter Gordon Merritt still insisted that a majority of American jurisdictions considered the attainment of the closed shop an unlawful purpose for labor combinations, although even he conceded that judges divided on the issue. For several years legal commentators frankly confessed that the law was unclear and offered no firm rule on the subject.[59] At last two decisions by leading state supreme courts brought an end to the AABA's search for an antiunion precedent. Neither case absolutely privileged loss inflicted by labor unions in pursuit of the closed shop. Neither announced the policy of total judicial noninterference that organized labor sought. Both contained strong expressions of concern for the fate of individual workers and the general public once industries became fully unionized. Taken together, however, they helped make the common law of labor disputes markedly more tolerant of trade unions' nonviolent but coercive exercises of collective power.

The first case, *Kemp v. Division No. 241*, was decided by the Illinois Supreme Court in 1912. In *Kemp*, eight employees of the Chicago Railways Company sued their former union after being fired pursuant to a closed-shop agreement. The employees had quit the union over a $1,200 contribution to a mayoral candidate who advocated the municipal ownership of Chicago's street railways. Few cases could have better embodied a genteel Victorian's fears about labor combinations. That rank-and-file workers were coerced by their leaders into supporting a political cause they opposed was bad enough; that the cause was somewhat doubtful under classical economic theory made matters worse; that the full economic power of union had been brought to bear upon the few workers manly enough to stand up for their rights was horrifying.[60]

The seven-judge court split three ways, much like the New York Court of Appeals in *Cumming*. The three most senior judges voted in favor of the plaintiffs and the sacred right of every worker to "dispose of his labor as he may choose for himself and those dependent upon him." A disgruntled employee might be "but one asserting his right against the dictation of the many"; still, that employee deserved the protection of the law—unless the union could justify the loss as the exercise of some equal or superior right, such as business rivalry.[61] Three other judges upheld the closed shop in an opinion reminiscent of Parker's in *Cumming*. Although they cited Holmes's dissent in *Plant*, the prounion judges ultimately rested on the most unHolmesian ground of "an absolute right" of workers to combine voluntarily in pursuit of their mutual interest.[62] The seventh and decisive vote was cast by a judge who, like Gray, sought a middle way between these two positions, but who was more willing than Gray to advance an expressly policy-oriented and regulatory approach to the law of industrial disputes.

Born in 1854, Orrin Nelson Carter received his undergraduate degree from Wheaton College in 1866, taught school for more than a decade, and then studied law with Murray F. Tuley, an influential appellate judge with a long interest in labor relations.[63] As general attorney for the Chicago

Sanitary District, Carter oversaw the start of work on the city's great drainage canal. After serving several terms as a trial judge, Carter was elected to the Illinois Supreme Court as a Republican in 1906. Unusually receptive to the work of the law professors, Carter organized the judicial section of the American Bar Association to help judges become "not only learned in the law, but well grounded in many other departments of knowledge" and to encourage them to consult "the learned and searching articles in the leading law magazines of today." Above all, Carter counseled lawyers to reform the law in light of social change. "Law is and must be a progressive science; growing with our growth, and expanding with our needs," Carter told his fellow judges in 1915. "It rests largely with our profession to see to it that the law keeps step with the changes of society and civilization."[64]

Carter's own opinion in *Kemp* drew heavily from articles by the Harvard law professors Jeremiah Smith and James Barr Ames. He followed the law professors in assuming that loss inflicted in labor disputes was actionable as an intentional tort unless the defendants could show justification or excuse.[65] His approach was in sharp contrast with earlier decisions, including Taft's a priori and individualist reasoning in *Moores*. For Taft, the individual came first, so that justification was a matter of sorting out individual rights in conflict. Further, justification was a categorical issue, a question of distinguishing the competition of "naturally opposed" rivals from that of persons having "not the remotest natural connection" to each other.[66] Carter, in contrast, started with a constitutive and historically contingent social order. "The legal right of every person is conditioned on the welfare of society," he declared, "and the latter is more important than the welfare of any individual or class." Moreover, Carter took a consequentialist approach to the law. The decision of labor cases depended "not upon arbitrary rules, but upon the peculiar and special facts in each case," he announced. They turned not on differences of kind, but differences "of degree, as 'most differences are, when nicely analyzed.'"[67]

The specific test Carter proposed for resolving the issue of justification in labor disputes closely tracked one advanced by Jeremiah Smith five years earlier. The Illinois judge would privilege a trade union's intentionally inflicted economic harm when (1) the labor dispute involved "real and substantial" demands relating to the employment of the persons involved; (2) the union's demands affected the "direct and immediate interests" of these persons; and (3) the loss suffered by the employer and the general public was reasonable when compared to the benefits sought by the defendants.[68]

Under this standard Carter would prohibit sympathetic strikes and secondary boycotts. Neither was within "the immediate field of competition"; they could only be justified "when revolution is."[69] Yet the closed-shop contract in *Kemp* passed Carter's test. Without discussing the political context of the case, Carter decided that the discharges were lawful because the contract was a real and substantial matter directly relating to the employment of the defendants. If innocent third parties or the general public were inconvenienced by strikes to force the adoption of such contract, this was true of all strikes, and "certainly no one in this day would argue that all strikes, no matter what their purpose, should be enjoined."[70]

Coming after such a setback, the decision of the Connecticut Supreme Court in *Connors v. Connolly* (1913) heartened the lawyers of the AABA. Like *Kemp*, the case involved a worker denied employment after falling out with his union. Dominick Connors struck with the rest of Danbury's hatters when the town's manufacturers of stiff hats unsuccessfully attempted to establish open-shop conditions in 1909. After resuming work, Connors demanded the union pay him the benefits he believed were owed him for his participation in the strike. With his demand outstanding, Connors refused to pay a special assessment levied by the national union. The local union responded by expelling Connors and had him fired from his job, in keeping with the closed-shop contract adopted by all of Danbury's stiff-hat manufacturers in the aftermath of the strike. Unable to find work in any local shop, Connors secretly called on Walter Gordon Merritt, well known in Danbury for his role in *Loewe v. Lawlor*, which was then in the midst of its long progress through the courts.

Merritt brought suit against the local hatters' union during a slump in the industry and tried the case in a Danbury courtroom packed with angry and unemployed union hatters. Notwithstanding Merritt's emphatic arguments from *Curran*, the trial judge, Ralph Wheeler, instructed the jury to find for Connors only if the consequences of the closed-shop contract were "unreasonable, under all the circumstances of the case," including the history, level of unemployment, and wages in the hatting industry. The jurors found for the defendants, and Merritt appealed.[71]

Writing for a unanimous court, Chief Justice Samuel O. Prentice (1850–1924) reversed the judgment and remanded the case for a new trial. Much of Prentice's opinion was thoroughly compatible with the AABA's case against the closed shop—as one would expect from one of Davenport's classmates at Yale.[72] Prentice was amazed by the defense counsel's claim that the United Hatters should organize the entire industry because the resulting benefits of a stable, skilled, and safe work force would outweigh any inconvenience suffered by "a few people desiring to obtain work." Under this "unique and astonishing proposition," Prentice declared, "monopolies might become transformed into blessings to be cherished, oppression into an agency of the public weal, and the tyranny of a majority into a benevolent factor of social progress."[73]

Prentice's declaration that the "whole theory of a free government" was opposed to the closed shop led Merritt to hale the case as "the most forceful and far-reaching decision upon this subject which has ever been rendered in the English-speaking countries."[74] Yet *Connors* revealed just how much the jurisprudential terrain had shifted since Prentice's predecessors decided *State v. Glidden* twenty-six years earlier. First, Prentice used Holmes's definition of an intentional tort rather than the conspiracy doctrine to frame his case. His standard for justification (whether the harm was "reasonably referable to the alleged object of lawful gain or advantage") owed more to Jeremiah Smith and Orrin Carter than to the judges of the Great Upheaval.

Second, the *Glidden* court could not conceive of a legal regime in which the right of nonunion workers to employment and the right of union workers to force their discharge were recognized simultaneously. "The two alleged rights could not possibly exist," Carpenter had declared.[75] In contrast, Prentice stopped short of condemning any and all contracts for the closed shop. Agreements taking in "an entire industry of any considerable proportions in a community," he agreed, were unreasonable, unlawful, and contrary to public policy, yet he saw no need to find every closed-shop contract unlawful regardless of the conditions in which it operated. Rather than confirm the open-shop lawyers' reading of *Curran*, he adopted the narrower, more tolerant rule of *Jacobs*.[76]

In the wake of *Kemp* and *Connors* a leading treatise writer at last resolved the conflict in the cases by stating as "the better view" the position that strikes to obtain closed-shop agreements were lawful.[77] By May 1915, even Daniel Davenport had given up the fight for a precedent declaring all closed-shop contracts unlawful. Testifying before the United States Commission on Industrial Relations, Davenport surprised Chairman Frank P. Walsh by insisting that, "apart from all questions of monopoly," the closed shop was not only legal but also constitutionally guaranteed. As a general proposition, Davenport explained, employers could insist on hiring only union workers, just as they could insist on hiring only nonunion workers. The closed shop was unlawful only when it created a monopoly of an industry within a community or otherwise interfered with the rights of third parties or the general public. Absent these circumstances, he declared, "The right of the closed shop entered into freely between the employer and the employee was as secure as the Government itself."[78]

Beyond the Labor Trust

"As the law in spirit is individualistic," the labor economist Robert Hoxie instructed his students at the University of Chicago, "the law cannot help being in spirit inimical to unionism. Unionism is in its very essence a lawless thing."[79] Hoxie's lecture tolerably summarized the labor jurisprudence of the Great Upheaval, founded on a priori systems of morality, economics, and politics. It overlooked the process of judicial accommodation that was well underway when he spoke. As a heightened sense of human interdependence and appreciation for "sociological" jurisprudence spread, more and more jurists became dissatisfied with the "atomistic theory of justice"—"the now unworkable individualistic doctrine"—of their predecessors.[80] Even a confirmed antitruster like Louis Brandeis rejected the jurisprudence of a priori tendency. If all contracts tending to the creation of a monopoly were unlawful, Brandeis reasoned in the wake of *Christensen,* "no large manufacturer could contract to increase his plant, or contract for an exclusive right to a patent which would cheapen production, for such a course tends inevitably towards securing a larger share of the market, thereby driving out competition and to that extent tending towards a monopoly."[81]

Brandeis's teacher, the Harvard law professor Jeremiah Smith, agreed that an a priori tendency toward monopoly was not enough of a reason to outlaw industrial combinations—whether of businessmen or workers. "That capitalistic combinations will in the near future be suppressed for the sole reason that they aim at monopoly, we, for our own part, do not believe," he wrote in 1907. And, "So long as the state does not suppress the capitalistic monopolies, it cannot suppress the labor monopolies without giving rise to revolution." Both must be regulated to curb their abuses and promote the public interest.[82]

The legal domestication of the labor trust had two phases. First, judges rejected many of the dogmas of Great Upheaval jurisprudence to give greater room for the exercise of Dicey's "right of combined action." In 1887 Elisha Carpenter asserted and defended an unqualified right to manage. In 1912 Orrin Carter declared that the "rights of employer and employees . . . are relative and not absolute."[83] In 1887 Henry Powers was certain he could draw a neutral line between unionists' right to strike and nonunionists' right to seek employment. By 1912 legions of judges and law professors joined Holmes in scoffing at the *sic utere* maxim.[84]

Although judges touched by historicist legal thought were the most outspoken practitioners of the new approach, even as orthodox a bench as the Massachusetts Supreme Judicial Court could not escape its influence. In *Pickett v. Walsh* (1906), for example, the court unanimously upheld a strike by bricklayers to force employers to give them the work of "pointing" and cleaning brick walls, even though other workers could do those jobs better and less expensively. "Imagine a judge fifty years ago . . . delivering with the assent of his colleagues such an opinion," exclaimed a commentator. "The fact that the contractors are forced to do what they do not want to do is not decisive of the legality of the labor unions' acts."[85]

Mindful of trade unionists' collective rights, the judges were also (to quote Dicey) jealous of "the liberty of individual citizens" and "the power of government." They refused to swap the individual laissez-faire of their predecessors for the collective laissez-faire of the AFL's leadership. Gradually and without much regard for the larger implications of their reasoning, the judges moved toward a consequentialist and pluralist understanding of their job. No longer comfortable with their traditional role as defenders of the rights of "self-independent" individuals, they entertained the notion that they should strike a balance between the competing and often collective interests to promote the needs of society and the interest of the public. John Henry Wigmore, dean of Northwestern's law school, caught the new temperament in a comment on *Kemp*. "The only solid way to settle these issues," he declared, "is to look the ugly facts in the face, and then decide if we can sanction them in law."[86]

As Holmes's writings on intentional torts grew in influence, labor's lawyers were increasingly called upon to show how trade unionists' conduct advanced the public interest.[87] Two strong arguments were articulated at the outset of the Progressive Era. First, closed-shop unionism promoted order and stability on the shopfloor. "It is for his own interests that the employer should run a union shop," the AFL leader Lee M. Hart declared in the wake of *Christensen*. "If it is unionized the union is responsible" for the firm's workforce, he explained. If unorganized, nonunion workers would disrupt production and lower workers' care and skill to their lowest common denominator. Repeated in the recitals of closed-shop contracts, echoed in opinions of sympathetic judges like John Gray, the idea that a strong union could promote industrial peace and stability would become a touchstone of American labor policy in the decades ahead.[88]

A second public-regarding justification turned on how a union's control of skilled labor could drive marginal firms from the industry, end "cutthroat" competition, and eliminate unsafe or unhealthy working conditions. Chief Justice Prentice might have recoiled at the suggestion that "monopoly" had its advantages, but unrestricted competition seemed the greater peril for at least some who read of the horrors of the sweatshop. As early as 1894, the Texas judge B. D. Tarleton was rocked by an account of conditions in the needle trades of New York City. "In the presence of such a picture," he imagined, "it would be difficult to preserve an air of decorous composure." In 1912 many more would agree with the New York lawyer who argued that organized labor had "done much benefit to us all," including working for the abolition of child labor ("that blot on civilization"), making the workplace more healthy, and requiring the use of safety devices to "protect the lives and limbs of all workers from loss and mutilation."[89]

These two arguments made judges more tolerant of industrial combination, but neither convinced them to privilege any and all economic loss inflicted by trade unionists. The law of the closed shop suggested one limit: When a union's control of a labor market approached a monopoly, competing concerns about individual freedom and consumer welfare tipped the balance in favor of the nonunion worker or employer. The AABA's two most famous cases, *Loewe v. Lawlor* and *Buck's Stove and Range Company v. Gompers,* would help fix another limit. In mounting distributor-targeted boycotts of consumer goods, unions did not advance a "direct and immediate" interest of their members. They went beyond the legitimate interest of the group to advance the interest of a class. The cases not only circumscribed the unions' activities, but they also provided occasions for thoroughgoing reassessments of the old law of labor disputes. At their conclusion, many observers concluded that trade unions must be treated as corporate bodies within a pluralist polity and that the policing of strikes and boycotts could not safely be left to judges, once that task was conceived in regulatory terms.

SIX

The Liberty of the Trader

The AABA's efforts to outlaw the closed shop represent one type of planned litigation, an attempt to establish a favorable legal rule in multiple jurisdictions. Often such campaigns are little noticed beyond the affected parties and their lawyers. In contrast, the AABA's best-known lawsuits, *Loewe v. Lawlor* (1903–17) and *Buck's Stove and Range Company v. Gompers* (1907–14), were significant less for their contribution to legal doctrine than for their impact on leading political figures and public debate. The lawsuits put the law of industrial disputes high on the national agenda for the first time since the *Debs* litigation of 1894–95. With each step in their long progress through the courts they unleashed waves of public comment, with significant consequences for congressional and presidential elections between 1906 and 1912 and on federal legislation between 1908 and 1914.

The place of these two cases in American law and politics is the subject of the next three chapters. I will start with Daniel Davenport's attempt to frame the Danbury hatters' case as a Victorian melodrama in which the public-spirited Loewe was set upon by an immense faction directed by the tyrannous Samuel Gompers. This portrayal, presented to the U.S. Supreme Court by Davenport and James Montgomery Beck, helped persuade Chief Justice Melville Fuller to rule that Loewe had a valid cause of action against the hatters under the Sherman Act. Holmes joined Fuller's opinion, albeit for quite different reasons. Although this might seem inconsistent with Holmes's dissents in *Vegelahn* and *Plant,* the justice believed the result followed from the historicist jurisprudence that informed those opinions.

Fuller announced his decision in February 1908 in a political climate charged by developments in the *Buck's Stove* case. Chapter 7 commences with the origins of that dispute in a distributor-targeted boycott mounted to discipline a manufacturer who rejected the terms of an industrywide collective bargaining agreement. Despite this similarity to *Loewe,* the *Buck's Stove* case differed in several crucial respects. Dietrich Loewe headed a marginal firm that would surely go bankrupt if forced to adopt union work rules. The Buck's Stove and Range Company, in contrast, was a leader in the stove industry. Its president, James Wallace Van Cleave, eagerly sought a fight with his unions. The desire to free his company from union rules was by no means Van Cleave's most important reason in bringing the suit. Assuming the presidency of the National Association of Manufacturers in early 1906, he pursued the litigation as part of a broad strategy to unite proprietary capitalists into a politically effective force, and he persisted even though settlement would clearly have improved the financial condition of his company.

On the AFL's side, as well, the *Buck's Stove* case served as a crucible of interest-group formation. Gompers's personal conviction in the justice of his cause cannot be doubted, but he also realized the instrumental value of the dispute, the way in which it produced "expressive benefits" of considerable use for building support for the AFL's executive officials within a contentious and often divided labor movement. The case also solidified ties between the AFL's leaders and the national Democratic party, thanks largely to the close relations between Samuel Gompers and Alton B. Parker, who wrote *National Protective Association v. Cumming,* ran for president in 1904 on the Democratic ticket, chaired the platform committee of the Democratic Convention in 1908, and led the defense in the *Buck's Stove* case.

Clashes between the NAM and AFL in national elections, congressional lobbying, and in the policymaking of the federal executive impressed contemporaries with the growing significance of interest-group politics. The thought that legislators and executive officials might become the minions of a pressure group was troubling enough, but the *Buck's Stove* case raised the still more alarming specter of a politicized judiciary. The trial court's initial order in the case prompted Roosevelt to deliver a special message to Congress on injunctions just three days before *Loewe* was announced. The case would figure prominently in national politics throughout 1908 and provoke widespread legal and popular comment down to its ambiguous conclusion in early 1914.

The later stages of the *Loewe* case (chapter 8) were just as significant. After winning in the Supreme Court, the AABA's lawyers turned to the task of convincing a jury that the named defendants were personally liable for the decisions of their leaders. Davenport's spellbinding performances produced favorable verdicts, which, after an initial setback, were upheld on appeal. Although the result followed the law of agency, the possibility that the individual hatters might lose their homes over a decision they had no real part in making troubled many observers. They concluded that the gap between the de jure and de facto status of the labor organizations should be abolished by the mandatory incorporation of trade unions. They advanced a pluralist vision of the labor movement in which groups were not the voluntary associations of Victorian jurisprudence but political and juridical units in their own right.

"Million against One"

Loewe concluded his April 1901 letter to the United Hatters with the warning that he would, if attacked, use "all lawful means to protect our business interests." In August 1902, with the assistance of Charles Merritt, Loewe published a notice in the Danbury newspapers to warn "all the members of all Labor Unions" that he intended to hold them individually and collectively responsible for the unlawful acts of their leaders and agents, regardless of whether the individual members personally approved of the boycott. At the same time, he sent copies of the notice to every hatter listed in the Danbury directory, along with the text of an injunction against a similar secondary boycott.[1]

Laying aside the work of organizing the AABA, Daniel Davenport turned to the task of drafting a complaint for Loewe's suit against the hatters. To say that Davenport was proud of the result would be an understatement. "It took me a month to draw it," he boasted to the Supreme Court justices in 1907. "I claim there is more thought, there are more pains in that single complaint than in any similar document in the English language—unless it be Grey's Elegy in a Country Church Yard, which they say took him seven years to write."[2] In seven legal pages of fine print Davenport laid the jurisdictional foundations for a damage suit under the Sherman Anti-Trust Act. Just as important were passages calculated to persuade readers beyond the courts that the case was a war of a "million against one, a conspiracy to crush the 'open shop.'"[3]

Davenport based the suit on the Sherman Act's prohibition of contracts, combinations, and conspiracies in restraint of interstate trade. The federal statute held considerable advantages over the common law of Connecticut from the AABA's standpoint.[4] First, a section of the statute gave successful plaintiffs treble damages as a kind of bounty for bringing conspirators to justice. Connecticut law had no such provision. Second, a victory in federal courts would establish a precedent binding on federal courts throughout the United States. A decision of Connecticut's Supreme Court would only be controlling within the state. Finally, an appeal to the U.S. Supreme Court would bring the AABA's campaign against "the Labor Trust" before a national audience. Not only would the case go to "the highest court of this land," the AABA promised, but it would "also go to the still more potent and almost omnipotent tribunal—public opinion. It is the judgment of this tribunal which we invoke."[5]

The Sherman Act was not without its disadvantages, however. One question, whether the act applied to trade unions as well as business combinations, did not seem to trouble Davenport. True, the Supreme Court had never squarely ruled that the statute reached labor organizations, but Davenport knew that the legislative history was not unfavorable to his position. Congress had considered an explicit exemption of labor and farm organizations before settling on a general prohibition of "every" restraint of interstate trade and commerce.[6] Prior to the passage of the Sherman Act, state courts interpreting anticonspiracy legislation did not distinguish between business and trade-union combinations; presumably, courts should do likewise in interpreting the federal antitrust statute. In the 1890s, several trial judges upheld prosecutions of workers under the act—all in cases involving interstate or international transportation. The most famous case was the contempt prosecution of Eugene Debs for violating a court injunction in the Pullman boycott of 1894, where the circuit court of appeals expressly relied upon the Sherman Act. When the case reached the Supreme Court, Justice David J. Brewer sidestepped the issue and based his decision on the general power of the federal government to regulate commerce under the commerce clause of the U.S. Constitution. Yet Brewer also explained that he should not be read as disagreeing with the reasoning of the lower court. The Supreme Court justices simply preferred "the broader ground" of the commerce power in Debs's case.[7]

Davenport was far more troubled by a jurisdictional issue. Congress enacted the Sherman Act under its authority to regulate interstate and international trade under the commerce clause. The commerce power clearly reached the regulation of railroads and other forms of interstate transportation, but just how far Congress could supplant the states in policing industries whose production processes took place within a single state was debated throughout the 1890s. In *United States v. E. C. Knight Company* (1895), the Supreme Court held that a combination to monopolize sugar refining was not punishable under the Sherman Act. According to Chief Justice Melville Fuller, the record contained no indication that the manufacturer intended "to put a restraint upon trade or commerce." Rather, Fuller concluded, whatever effect the combination had on interstate commerce was indirect and incidental to its main purpose, the refining of sugar, a manufacturing process conducted within a state.[8] The Supreme Court followed *Knight* in 1898 in two cases involving Kansas City's stockyards. Once again, the Court, now speaking through Justice Rufus Peckham, found that "the purpose of the agreement was not to regulate, obstruct or restrain [interstate] commerce, but that it was entered into with the object of properly and fairly regulating" a livestock exchange. The effect on interstate commerce was "indirect and incidental." But in *Addyston Pipe & Steel Company v. United States* (1899) the Court at last upheld a conviction under the Sherman Act, satisfied that the defendants' agreement to divide the market for steel pipe was intended to and did directly and immediately restrain interstate commerce.[9]

The distinction between manufacturing and commerce set out in *Knight* and glossed in the Kansas City stockyard and *Addyston* cases was Davenport's legal concern as he drafted Loewe's complaint. Some of Davenport's allegations involved what, under the case law, were purely intrastate matters, such as the claim that the United Hatters called Loewe's workers out on strike. This gave the AFL's lawyers some basis for arguing that Davenport wanted to "federalize" the entire law of industrial disputes. Yet those allegations could also be read as supporting detail for Loewe's gravamen: the nationally conducted, distributor-targeted boycott of his hats. And here Davenport was careful to allege that the bulk of Loewe's sales went to merchants outside of Connecticut, that the unionists' boycott was intended to prevent Loewe and his out-of-state customers from carrying on interstate trade, and that Loewe's interstate trade declined dramatically as a direct result of the boycott.[10]

Interspersed with these jurisdictional allegations were statements intended for those—on the bench and off—who might be inclined to see the case as something more than a quarrel over the reach of the federal courts. Davenport used the complaint to argue the AABA's case for Loewe as a hero of industrial liberty pitted against a great, single-minded, tyrannous labor conspiracy. Loewe, the complaint announced, had conducted his business "upon the broad and patriotic principle of not discriminating against any person seeking employment because of his being or not being connected with any labor or other organization." Massed against him were the nine thousand members of the United Hatters, who sought to unionize the entire industry "in a manner extremely onerous and distasteful" to the employers. The United Hatters, however, were but a cog in a much larger and more powerful machine, the American Federation of Labor, with its 1.4 million members, 110 international unions, twelve thousand locals, twenty-eight state federations, and five hundred central labor unions. The "chief agent" of the combination was Samuel Gompers, who marshalled a thousand organizers and pronounced his anathemas on employers though a "ready, convenient, powerful and effective" organ, the *American Federationist*.[11]

This vision of organized labor bore little relation to the real structure of power and administrative capacities of the AFL. In fact, the labor movement was riven with actual and potential conflict. The AFL's executives were officially committed to the bedrock principle of the autonomy of the international unions. Further, the leaders of even the best organized internationals struggled to control local and district bodies. Many of the business unionists faced sharp challenges from socialist dissenters, who challenged Gompers himself in AFL conventions. Finally, state and local federations sometimes strayed from the voluntarism and business unionism of the AFL.[12] Thus unity of purpose and action within the labor movement was not a fact but a project, and it was never as successful as the open-shop leaders pretended. Not the least of the ironies of the AABA's litigation is that it helped call its own enemy into being. Just as Davenport used the threat of the closed shop to make the AABA a rallying point for proprietary capitalists, so Gompers discovered that the *Loewe* and *Buck's Stove* cases could recruit new workers to the AFL and persuade dissenters to close ranks behind his leadership.

Although Davenport cast Gompers as the evil genius behind the boycott, the defendants he actually named in his complaint were far more obscure. He could not win damages against the United Hatters itself. As an unincorporated association, it could not be sued as a collective entity at common law, and its funds, held in trust for all the members, could not be reached unless every member could be shown to have authorized or ratified the boycott. Loewe's only remedy was against the individual hatters who authorized or ratified the unlawful action of the union's leadership. The law thus treated the rank-and-file hatters as principals who authorized their agents, the national officials of the United Hatters, to conduct the boycott. This was true even though the leaders had in fact ordered the boycott without first consulting the membership.[13]

Most employers would find little comfort in the right to recover from individual workers and union officials. Because the assets of any one defendant were bound to be modest, a large judgment could be satisfied only by suing a large number of trade unionists. The lone employer could not afford to identify rank-and-file unionists, prove their knowledge and support of the boycott, and locate and attach their assets. Further, in most states a defendant's assets could only be attached after the plaintiff had won a judgment, with the result that workers sometimes hid or otherwise placed them beyond the plaintiff's reach.

Loewe, however, was not alone, and his situation as an employer in Connecticut's hatting industry was not typical. Thanks to the AABA he could afford legal bills that would have overwhelmed another proprietor. As a rule, his defendants, the hatters of Danbury and its environs, were relatively prosperous and sedentary. Moreover, Loewe could identify them easily, thanks to published union records and city directories. Finally, under a Connecticut statute the hatters' assets could be attached with the filing of Loewe's complaint.

Thus it was that Davenport, with the assistance of the freshly minted lawyer Walter Gordon Merritt, identified 239 members of the United Hatters who owned homes and had savings accounts in Danbury, Bethel, and Norwalk. Most had never worked for Loewe or held significant positions in the union. Davenport selected them solely because they owned property susceptible to pretrial attachment. The service of the writs of attachment on September 12, 1903—just after Labor Day—brought the case instant celebrity, which the AABA readily exploited. The dispute was "of the greatest moment to this nation," Walter Gordon Merritt wrote to the editor of the New York *Sun* later that month. "Fortunately for the industrial interests of this country the plaintiff is backed by the American Anti-Boycott Association, which will undoubtedly carry the suits to the United States Supreme Court, if necessary, in order to make them test cases." Merritt denied that the AABA intended to crush unionism. Rather, he claimed, it sought to encourage the "intelligent, conservative and law-abiding element" in the United Hatters to check the lawless ways of their leaders. It was a wake-up call to the respectable workers to exercise their suffrage within the union and monitor the conduct of their agents, to be the vigilant members of a voluntary association Victorian law presumed they would be.[14]

The United Hatters were not eager to see the case go to trial, and their lawyers took full advantage of the wide range of pretrial motions available in Connecticut. "The defendants have used every species of dilatory tactics known to the law," complained the AABA's secretary in late 1904. Two more years passed before federal district judge James P. Platt finally ruled on the hatters' demurrer to the complaint. Platt was unsure whether the hatters' boycott amounted to an interference with interstate commerce, and he was reluctant to order a long and expensive trial only to learn from an appellate court that he never should have heard the case in the first place. To settle this jurisdictional issue in advance of trial Platt sustained the hatters' demurrer.[15] The circuit court certified the case to the U.S. Supreme Court, which set oral argument for early December 1907.

"The Meaning of Certain Words"

The personnel and recent decisions of the Court gave Davenport good cause for optimism. Presiding over the Court was Melville Fuller, who, although almost twenty years Davenport's senior, shared the lawyer's New England origins, familiarity with the genteel tradition (acquired, in Fuller's case, at Bowdoin), enthusiasm for Grover Cleveland (to whom Fuller owed his nomination), and disgust over the Bryanites' capture of the Democratic party.[16] True, Fuller had written the *Knight* decision, but he had since joined in *Addyston, Montague & Co. v. Lowry* (1904) and *Swift & Co. v. United States* (1905), each of which expanded the reach of the Sherman Act.[17]

Swift was an especially favorable precedent for Loewe. A cornerstone of Theodore Roosevelt's antitrust campaign, this federal prosecution of the "beef trust" was upheld in an unanimous opinion written by Justice Holmes. Attorneys for Swift argued that because all the actions through which the company obtained its monopoly occurred in a single state, the effect of the combination on interstate trade was merely indirect and incidental, and *Knight* should control. In response Holmes distinguished *Knight*. The evidence admitted in that case, Holmes wrote, established that the direct object of the combination was monopoly of manufacture "within a State." In *Swift*, in contrast, the government's lawyers had shown that "the very point of the combination is to restrain and monopolize commerce among the States." The effect of the beef trust on interstate commerce was not "accidental, secondary, remote or merely probable"; interstate commerce "no less, perhaps even more, than commerce within a single State" was an object of attack.[18]

Eight of the nine justices who voted to uphold the *Swift* verdict still sat in December 1907 when the AABA's test case finally reached the Supreme Court.[19] Appearing for Loewe, Daniel Davenport and James Montgomery Beck were confident of success. The hatters' counsel, the Connecticut lawyers John H. Light and John Kimberly Beach, had a more daunting task. Perhaps they hoped that Holmes harbored prolabor sympathies that would counteract his stand in *Swift*. (Some commentators on the justice's appointment thought they detected them in his dissents in *Vegelahn* and *Plant*— much to Holmes's disgust.)[20] But the hatters' lawyers could not reasonably expect a sympathetic hearing for organized labor from the rest of the Court, which included Justice David J. Brewer and four of the justices who helped him send Debs to jail in 1895.

The oral argument commenced with Beck's presentation of the case for Loewe. It was a formidable performance. Beck was self-confident, precise, and forceful, and he displayed an exceptional command of federal antitrust law, the product of prosecuting the Northern Securities Company and advising the corporate clients of Shearman and Sterling.[21] Sharp questioning from William Moody, who had argued *Swift* as Roosevelt's attorney general, and the Court's other antitrust experts could not shake his argument that, after *Swift*, a suit against the hatters' boycott was clearly within the commerce power and the jurisdiction of the federal courts. Beck conceded that some allegations of the complaint dealt with matters "wholly concerning the police power of the states," but the same was true of the complaint in *Swift*. In both cases, the alleged acts were "parts of a plan" whose object was the restraint of interstate commerce. As for the merits of the case, Beck had little difficulty in establishing that the boycott amounted to a conspiracy in restraint of trade, both at common law and under the broader reach of the Sherman Act.[22]

In the closed-shop cases, Davenport had attacked the labor trust on economic as well as political grounds—as an interference with natural laws of market competition as well as a violation of individual liberty. Before the justices, the corporate lawyer Beck refused to count himself among the celebrants of unbridled competition. As far as business combinations were concerned, he told the justices, "Many economists are now honestly questioning whether unrestricted competition on the one hand or restriction of competition on the other has a direct result upon the enhancement of prices to the consumer." At a later AABA banquet the difference between the two men would become explicit when Beck termed the Sherman Act "the most mischievous piece of legislation that has ever been put upon the Statute books of the United States," whereas Davenport dubbed it "the very Magna Charta of industrial freedom in this country."[23] But at oral argument Beck finessed the issue. The effect of unionization on prices was but "the apex of the pyramid," he explained. The much broader concern Loewe's plight posed was "the fundamental right of a man to engage in business as he thinks best, . . . the fundamental liberty of a trader to engage in business." Beck now called on the Court to give its support to the "obstinate German" Loewe, who manfully risked becoming "ruined and free" rather than "prosperous and subject to a form of commercial slavery" under the "real" defendant in the case, Samuel Gompers.[24]

If the Court upheld the boycott, Beck warned, "It is quite conceivable, if it is not probable, that the entire control, at least over the conditions of labor, will pass into the hands of an executive council in this city, whose edict . . . will be greater than the sovereign States themselves." Beck argued from the legislative history of the Sherman Act that drafters had refused, "out of any passing spirit of demagoguery," to exempt organized labor from its reach. Beck declared that Loewe and the AABA did not seek the outlawry of organized labor. "If the suggestion is made that on our theory of the case the mere existence of a labor organization is a restraint of trade, we disclaim such an idea." The lawsuit simply sought to demonstrate that no "self-constituted labor oligarchy" was above the law so long as America remained a republic.[25]

The arguments of Light and Beach were as weak as Beck's was strong. Neither lawyer argued that the drafters of the Sherman Act never intended it to reach organized labor. They opted instead for the jurisdictional argument grounded in *Knight*'s distinction between commerce and manufacturing. Light argued that the hatters had "no ultimate design upon interstate commerce as such"; their real purpose was to unionize Loewe's factory. Accept Beck's and Davenport's theory of the reach of the commerce power, Light declared, and every strike would be within the jurisdiction of the federal courts—an unthinkable result. Rather than see that happen, Beach told the justices, "We stand here for the State jurisdiction."[26]

The Court made short work of this argument by pointing out how it confused the hatters' motive with the narrower legal issue of intent. Several justices noted that the hatters' *motive* in conducting the boycott was irrelevant under the Sherman Act. Once they determined that the hatters *intended* to interfere with interstate commerce—that is, that they had performed acts whose "manifest tendency" was to interfere with interstate commerce—liability followed as a matter of course. Or, as Holmes, put it, Beach's argument, "would practically amount to this, would it not, that if the ulterior purpose of the people in the Northern Securities case had been to establish a Sunday School with the proceeds, the combination would have been all right?"[27]

After dismantling Light's and Beach's main argument, the justices turned helpful. They drew Light's attention to cases he had overlooked and held out various lifelines that might conceivably have saved the hatters' case, but the lawyers rejected every offer of assistance. At one point Justice Edward Douglass White had to assure a flustered Beach that his questions were intended to "help me, not to embarrass you." When Moody set the lawyer a hypothetical pointing toward a reformulation of the distinction between commerce and manufacturing, Beach steadfastly held to the wrong response, and he did so even after Holmes observed, "I think the question . . . rather invited you to deny, to give a negative answer."[28]

Light and Beach also hurt their cause by failing to rebut the AABA's claim that the AFL was the real party of interest in the case. This was relatively easy to do. As Gompers himself protested, the AFL's leaders had no notice of the hatters' boycott, and Loewe's name never appeared on the "We Don't Patronize" list published monthly in the *American Federationist.*[29] Light did commence with a sharp attack on Beck: "The gentleman's idea of liberty is the right of massed capital to do as it pleases with labor." But when Justice John Marshall Harlan wanted to know "what is the order of the Federation of Labor" in cases like *Loewe,* Light did not protest that the AFL had not ordered the boycott in the case. To make matters worse, he stated that the employer would be placed on "the unfair list"— a term the justices probably equated with the AFL's "We Don't Patronize" list, then much in the news as a result of the *Buck's Stove* case. The colloquy left the justices with the impression that Loewe's boycott was a major engagement in a class war directed by Samuel Gompers rather than a skirmish in an ongoing attempt of one craft union to bring order to a unprofitable, low-wage industry.[30]

With the hatters' case in shreds, Beach limped to his conclusion, a halting appeal to the man who once called upon judges to weigh the "considerations of social advantage" presented by their cases.[31] "The questions that we have to deal with in an argument of this kind are unrelated in the abstract to organized labor," Beach ventured,

> and yet it does seem as though in these times, when the trend of public opinion is toward letting these things more alone, letting them settle themselves—and I point, for example, to the English Trades Dispute Act as an evidence of it; and perhaps I might refer to the growing disposition on the part of people who have a right to have opinions about those things as to the use of injunctions in labor disputes—I say the general trend of affairs is towards letting the thing alone, and I think it would be perhaps, with submission, a mistake if this Court should pledge the power of the Federal Government to interfere.

Holmes's reply was simple and devastating. "Unfortunately all this Court has to do is to find out the meaning of certain words. That is all we can do."[32]

This remark, coupled with other evidence, helps explain why Holmes decided to join Fuller's unanimous decision upholding Loewe's suit. Had Holmes been free to decide whether the distributor-targeted boycott violated the common law of torts, he almost certainly would have found that the hatters were justified in inflicting loss upon Loewe. He would not have done so out partisanship for the cause of organized labor, for he prided himself on his impartiality. While *Loewe* was before the Supreme Court, Holmes dissented from two decisions striking down labor legislation under the Fourteenth Amendment, but he also wrote privately, "I suppose the capitalists think me dangerous and the labor people think me an eccentric slave of capital—so I hope I am all right. No one wants a dispassionate man."[33]

Rather, Holmes's dissents in *Vegelahn* and *Plant* suggest he would find justification for the United Hatters' boycott in the logic of history. Holmes did not consider the organization of workers a moral good—he insisted that trade unionists' gains came at the expense of their unorganized counterparts. Further, under some circumstances, such as a combination that denied the public vital resources or services, Holmes would hold their efforts illegal under the common law. "I have no doubt," he wrote in an unpublished opinion in 1917, "that when the power of either capital or labor is exerted in such a way as to attack the life of the community, those who seek their private interest at such cost are public enemies and should be dealt with as such."[34]

Short of such extreme cases, however, Holmes thought the economic loss inflicted by labor combinations was an unavoidable consequence of "the

organization of the world," a historical development that could not be reversed "unless the fundamental axioms of society, and even the fundamental
conditions of life, are to be changed." Although *Vegelahn* and *Plant* involved
strikes rather than boycotts, Holmes's writings provide no reason to suppose he would distinguish between the two. In *Plant*, Holmes wrote that
trade unionists could use either "the boycott or the strike" in order "to get
more than they now are getting." And just after he completed the Supreme
Court's second decision in Loewe's case, Holmes wrote to E. R. Thayer,
the dean of the Harvard Law School, that it went "wholly on the Sherman Act." As to the common law, Holmes explained, "I adhere to my views
expressed in Mass."—surely a reference to his dissents in *Vegelahn* and
Plant.[35]

Holmes's letter to Thayer suggests that he believed the presence of a
statute as the basis for decision in *Loewe* meant that his opinions and writings on the common law of torts were simply beside the point. "While at
times judges need for their work the training of economists and statesmen,
and must act in view of their foresight of consequences," he wrote in 1904,
"when their task is to interpret and apply the words of a statute, their function is merely academic to begin with—to read English intelligently—and
a consideration of consequences comes into play, if at all, only when the
meaning of the words used is open to reasonable doubt." To Holmes, a valid
statute was an authentic expression of the desires and needs of the social
masses—"the crowd" in his usage. The measure might be ill-conceived,
even "noxious"; still, Holmes considered it his job to execute the command
of the community, just as it had been his "blindly accepted duty" as a Civil
War soldier to execute commands he personally considered disastrous.[36]

In his dissent in *Northern Securities Co. v. United States* (1904), Holmes
offered an "intelligent reading" of the Sherman Act's prohibition of combinations in restraint of trade. The "exact words" Congress used prohibited every attempt by a combination to prevent outsiders from enjoying some
portion of a particular trade. Congress chose those words out of concern
for the outsiders and the "supposed consequent effect" on the public at
large.[37] In the Danbury hatters' case, the combination consisted of the
boycotting unionists and unionized employers, through whose efforts the
outsider Loewe was denied business to the conspirators' benefit. Holmes
would probably have upheld the United Hatters in a common-law case,
because he would have been free to act on his own understanding of the
social consequences of labor combinations. But once "the crowd" had condemned "every" contract and conspiracy in restraint of trade, Holmes's duty
was to implement its command.

No trace of Holmes's reasoning was discernible in the unanimous decision Chief Justice Fuller announced on February 3, 1908. According to

Davenport, Fuller spoke in a courtroom "packed to suffocation" and was well aware of the gravity of the occasion. "When all the other decisions had been announced," he told an AABA banquet, "the Chief Justice . . . , began to read his opinion in the Loewe case in a very low tone of voice, and you could have heard a pin drop all through that assemblage."[38]

Davenport declared himself fully satisfied with the opinion. He should have been: It closely tracked Beck's and Davenport's argument and borrowed whole passages from the AABA's brief. Under *Swift*, Fuller wrote, the hatters' boycott was clearly within the jurisdiction of the federal courts. Congress intended the Sherman Act to reach labor as well as business boycotts. "The act made no distinction between classes." And the United Hatters' boycott was a combination in restraint of trade as those words were used in the Sherman Act and understood at common law—a point Fuller made by quoting a passage from an English treatise Beck had read during oral argument. The chief justice was too reticent or circumspect to dwell upon the genteel Victorian premises underlying his reasoning, but he did repeat Beck's reference to "the liberty of a trader to engage in business" and Davenport's allegation that the AFL was leagued with the United Hatters against Loewe. Certainly, Davenport claimed, Fuller and his rather aged brethren saw the case as he did. "I have occasion to know the views of the Judges," he told the AABA. "Their idea was that this decision would be a bulwark against that rising tide which would, if not stopped, overwhelm the liberties of the individual citizen."[39]

Fuller's decision did not end *Loewe v. Lawlor*. The Supreme Court remanded the case to Judge Platt for trial, and it would remain in the federal courts for another nine years. Even so, in the days after the decision editorialists across the nation rushed to sum up the significance of the litigation. As a rule, they employed dramatic terms that scarcely seemed justified given the facts of the case. The issue of greatest concern to the lawyers, the scope of federal jurisdiction under the commerce clause, hardly surfaced in the editorials. Only an exceptional newspaper, like the New York *Journal of Commerce*, bothered to relate the case to the actual conditions of the hatting industry. And for all of the AABA's attempts to promote Loewe as a beleaguered hero of free labor, few commentators dwelt on the particulars of the employer's plight.[40]

Rather, most wrote about an abstract principle, equality before the law, and they wrote about it as if the Supreme Court had guided the nation through a great crisis. Any lawyer could have told the reporters that *Loewe* deprived organized labor of a particular type of organizational strategy, the distributor-targeted secondary boycott, effective only in industries in which manufacturers sold their goods through independent distributors to a largely working-class clientele. Why, then, did the newspapermen write as if decision had rescued the rule of law from great peril? "That the Supreme Court of the United States believes that the Constitution is menaced by present-day political tendencies in both parties is apparent," declared a Brooklyn newspaper. "That its members will stand together to uphold the Constitution is just as evident. It is also safe to prophesy that the 68,000,000 Americans who do not belong to labor organizations will see to it that the 2,000,000 who do, shall not be permitted to make the laws of the country." Other newspapers insisted that the Supreme Court had not "outlawed" trade unions, but had brought them "under the law" and made them "law-abiding bodies." Grant the United Hatters' plea for "exceptional rights, privileges or immunities," and "the United States would not be a fit place for human beings to inhabit."[41]

In fact, the public reaction to *Loewe* owed less to the facts of the case, the arguments of counsel, or Fuller's reasoning than to contemporaneous developments in the AABA's other great lawsuit, the *Buck's Stove* case, which placed labor law at the forefront of national politics for the first time since the *Debs* case. The circumstances that brought *Buck's Stove* such prominence raised troubling doubts over whether a government of laws could survive the rise of industrial combinations and an activist state. In such a supercharged environment, Fuller's understated opinion took on enormous importance, for it signified, to the satisfaction and evident relief of middle-class observers, that even the most novel and powerful economic forces were still subject to the rule of law and the commonweal.

SEVEN

The Politics of Law

The labor people have just cause of complaint with the Republican party taken as a whole, because Congress under the leadership of Cannon treated them badly; and the courts, representing both the old school Republicans and the old school Democrats, have been curiously disregardful of their interests.

—Theodore Roosevelt (1908)

"My dear Mr. Attorney General," Theodore Roosevelt wrote Charles J. Bonaparte on December 23, 1907, "is there no way by which the Government could interfere in regard to an injunction or contempt proceeding by a court which it regarded as improper? . . . It seems that if we thus acted on behalf of one or two labor organizations where we regarded the action as wrong, it would strengthen us when we regarded the injunction as right." Twice earlier Roosevelt had urged Congress to reform the procedure through which injunctions were issued. "It is a power that should be exercised with extreme care and should be subject to the jealous scrutiny of all men," he had declared in late 1906, "and condemnation should be meted out as much to the judge who fails to use it boldly when necessary as to the judge who uses it wantonly or oppressively." Now Roosevelt believed he had found an example of the latter in Ashley Mulgrave Gould, a judge on the Supreme Court of the District of Columbia, who had recently issued a sweeping injunction in what the *New York Times* called "the great test of strength between the National Manufacturers' Association and the American Federation of Labor."[1]

Roosevelt's public response to Gould's injunction came in a special message to Congress on January 31, 1908. "It is all wrong to use the injunction to prevent the entirely proper and legitimate actions of labor organizations in their struggle for industrial benefit," he declared, "or under the guise of protecting property rights unwarrantably to invade the fundamental rights of the individual." Yet such injunctions grew daily and with them the indignation of "large numbers of our citizens." Roosevelt then hurled a thunderbolt at the "ultra-conservatives" who objected to any reform of procedure in labor cases. They would do well to remember, he warned, that "if the popular feeling does become strong many of those upon whom they rely to defend them will be the first to turn against them."[2]

On February 3, the day Chief Justice Fuller read his opinion in *Loewe,* Daniel Davenport returned Roosevelt's fire by calling on the president to include labor boycotters in his trust-busting campaigns. In March an AABA pamphlet pointedly reproduced a passage from Roosevelt's annual message of 1903, in which TR proclaimed his willingness to move against corporations, unions, or any other body that acted "in a spirit of arbitrary and tyrannous interference with the rights of others." Davenport's efforts and the sarcastic editorials of the New York *Sun* evidently drew blood. By summer, Roosevelt's protégé William Howard Taft was referring to James Beck as "one of those reactionaries that has attacked the President." When, in early 1912, a Philadelphia businessman sent Roosevelt an AABA leaflet criticizing the colonel's policies concerning organized labor, he angrily responded that the AABA was "influenced by as noxious a class spirit as any labor association" and that the group and its allies were "just as untrustworthy, just as much enemies to the republic as Mr. Debs' *Appeal to Reason.*" Once again, Davenport repaid the compliment. TR was an "adroit, brilliant, and I must say unscrupulous, intriguer," he declared before a congressional committee.[3]

The *Buck's Stove* case can be treated as a chapter in the development of the law of industrial disputes. The litigants, lawyers, and judges debated the legality of the closed shop and secondary boycotts, rehearsed old arguments against the issuance of injunctions in labor disputes, and added new ones about the impact of court orders on freedom of speech and the press. Doubts about whether the company could obtain an injunction under the Sherman Act—an issue that would reappear in the AABA's later cases and lobbying—probably led Davenport to base the suit on the common law. During the latter stages of the case many pages of legal briefs and court reports were consumed by discussions of whether the defendants were properly prosecuted for civil or criminal contempt or the applicability of a statute of limitations.

Yet these contributions to the law of industrial disputes were less significant than the case's impact on American political history. The *Buck's Stove* case was brought by a business executive, James Wallace Van Cleave (1849–1910), who was willing to jeopardize the finances of his business in order to organize proprietary capitalists into a disciplined political force, with himself at the head.[4] His opponents, AFL president Samuel Gompers, vice-president John Mitchell, and secretary Frank Morrison, conducted their side of the case with an eye to extending and strengthening their influence within the labor movement. Pursuing their aims within and without the national political parties, the two sides quickly adopted many of the electoral and extra-electoral strategies of pressure-group politics. Faced with urgently pressed and sharply conflicting demands, public officials refused to intervene decisively on one side or the other. They successfully avoided taking positions that would dim their or their patrons' electoral chances, much as contemporary public-choice theorists would predict.

The case did produce an alarming example of judicial bias in the open partisanship of Daniel Thew Wright, Gould's colleague on the Supreme Court of the District of Columbia. Far from typifying the judicial response to organized labor, Wright would be forced to resign to escape impeachment for his injudicious—even sordid—behavior. The judges of the intermediate appellate courts modified his orders and publicly rebuked his conduct. On the whole, they and at least some of the U.S. Supreme Court justices who reviewed the cases were as concerned with protecting the courts' reputation for nonpartisanship as they were with the merits of the case. Holmes might protest, "Idiots talk as if we were passing a political vote and had been free to send Gompers to prison in spite of the statute that we thought applicable," but he and his fellow justices in fact were influenced by a political consideration, of a sort: the concern of courts, like other political bodies, to preserve their legitimacy.[5]

Van Cleave

The dream of the United Hatters—of an industry flourishing under the guardianship of skilled workers—was realized in the stove industry by the end of the nineteenth century. After an initial period of belligerency, the Stove Founders' National Defense Association (SFNDA) adopted a "conference agreement" in 1891 and began bargaining with the dominant labor organization in the industry, the Iron Molders' Union. The frank aim of the stove manufacturers was to standardize labor costs throughout the industry and thus to stabilize prices. Although in 1900 only a quarter of the stove foundries in the country were members of the SFNDA, these included practically all of the largest firms, and the union agreed to hold the rest to the same wage rates and labor conditions.[6] Most of the leading stove manufacturers applauded the agreement for banishing "unfair" competition, but employers in competitive branches of the foundry industry had a different opinion. They saw the conference agreement as a corrupt pact between "a stove trust and a labor trust, . . . a restraint of trade in direct violation of the laws and sound public policy."[7]

The Buck's Stove and Range Company of St. Louis was a major firm in the stove industry and a long-time member of the SFNDA. The company's sales had grown rapidly after Van Cleave took the helm in 1888 and instituted an aggressive marketing program, which included the house organ *Buck's Shot,* distributed to merchants throughout the country. In 1906 sales stood at $1.25 million annually. The company's enormous factory sprawled over several city blocks and employed 745 workers. "In one of the foundries, which is nearly a thousand feet long," a business journalist reported, "one will see three hundred splendid, large-muscled men, stripped to their waists, at work under ideal conditions."[8]

"Tough, intelligent, opinionated," and ambitious, James Wallace Van Cleave, the company's president, drove himself and those around him at a hard pace.[9] "There are no drones in his hive," a close friend once declared. Like so many capitalists of his generation, Van Cleave was proud of an American ancestry stretching back to colonial times—in his case, to the founding of New Amsterdam. He also attributed his success to his sharp wits and a lifetime of ceaseless labor under the burden of enormous responsibilities. When he was only thirteen he fought with the Confederate army. Before he was twenty the death of his father left Van Cleave the principal provider for his mother and two sisters. He supported his family as a clerk and salesman for stove manufacturers in Louisville and St. Louis. In the early 1880s he built his own stove company into one of the largest in the South before leaving it for the presidency and part ownership of the Buck's Stove Company. Although originally a Democrat, Van Cleave joined the Republicans after the "free silver heresy" captured his party.[10]

When another self-made man, Dietrich Loewe, found himself at odds with organized labor, the hat manufacturer could convincingly describe himself as a person who just wanted to be left alone. In contrast, Van Cleave was an outspoken antiunion warrior. Before the summer of 1906 he hired a labor spy to sniff out opportunities to provoke the molders' union into rebelling against the conference agreement. In May 1906, he hoped the union's officials realized he considered them "an unscrupulous, irresponsible set of liars" when he brusquely refused to negotiate with their business agent. When the molders complained to the SFNDA, Van Cleave was delighted at the thought that he might have engineered a break with the union. ("Ha! Ha! That is funny, ain't it?" he wrote to the head of his detective agency.) Assuming the presidency of the NAM in May 1906, he continued the belligerent antiunionism of his predecessors. As he privately confessed, his public pronouncements were intended to leave Samuel Gompers "frothing at the mouth."[11]

The occasion for the AABA's lawsuit—its purported gravamen—arose during a drive by the metal polishers' union for a nine-hour workday. The union campaigned for shorter hours on two fronts. On the national level, its leaders bargained for the nine-hour day in negotiating the conference agreement with the SFNDA. As this proved unsuccessful, the union also proceeded on a firm-by-firm basis. For some months in 1905 one of Van Cleave's foremen permitted metal polishers to quit early, but when Van Cleave caught wind of the practice he moved to reestablish the ten-hour day. The company closed for repairs in the fall of 1905. When it reopened, Van Cleave explicitly obligated his metal polishers to work ten hours. The metal polishers did so until August 27, 1906, when, prompted by a letter from the national leadership, the members of the local union left work after nine hours. Van Cleave promptly fired the leaders of the local union, and the rest of the union metal polishers left soon thereafter.[12]

There matters stood until October, when Van Cleave had a stormy meeting with the metal polishers and representatives of St. Louis's central labor union. Van Cleave pointed out that his workers received good wages, a point the unionists conceded. He then reminded the delegation that the union had failed to have the nine-hour day written into the conference agreement. "If the Defense Association [would] agree to the nine hour day tomorrow, I would put our entire shop on a nine hour basis at once," he insisted. Until then, however, he refused to incur higher labor costs than his competitors.[13]

When the two sides met, the union's leaders had already asked the AFL to place the Buck's Stove Company on its "We Don't Patronize" list. Although no final decision had been made, Van Cleave knew that plans for a local boycott were underway, and he must have understood the threat in a parting comment of one trade unionist. "You must never forget the fact that your Association and your class of people are not buying your Stoves," the unionist warned. "They have steam heat, and the working men are using the Stoves." The boycott commenced at once on the local level. In November a special committee of the AFL's annual convention reported on the dispute, and the company appeared in the "We Don't Patronize" list in the May 1907 issue of the *American Federationist*.[14]

Canceled orders flooded the company throughout 1907. A retailer from Youngstown, Ohio, explained that although he had long been a loyal customer and was reluctant to switch lines, he could not "endanger the success of our entire business by arousing the antagonism and animosity of the labor unions." A storekeeper from an Illinois coal town felt no need to explain himself. "Of course I cannot ruin my business for your stoves," he wrote. Another merchant counseled, "Get right with the Union people and send your agent around and I will give him an order." And from Great Falls, Montana, a merchant wrote that his plans for a big season "were knocked in the head" by a delegation of local labor leaders. "We are rather up against a stump on Buck's Stoves and Ranges," he confessed.[15]

At first Van Cleave professed not to be troubled by the boycott. In January 1907 he wrote Charles W. Post, a Battle Creek cereal manufacturer and a fellow soldier in the open-shop movement, "I am not losing any sleep over it and our company is not losing any business." (In the same letter Van Cleave thanked Post for sending him a sample of "Elijah's Manna," which, he explained, he would try out on his dog before distributing to his subordinates.) By October, however, Van Cleave was terribly worried about the state of his personal finances and the demands of the majority stockholder, Frederic W. Gardner. He turned to Post for help, asking the cereal manufacturer to purchase some of his stock.[16]

Post did acquire a stake in the company and took an active interest in its affairs. What he discovered alarmed him. "I am satisfied that more harm has been done the Stove company than you realize," he wrote to Van Cleave in early 1908. "You are right straight up against it in this labor union contest, and you must face the facts as they are." Post encouraged Van Cleave to learn from his own experience with timid retailers:

When I found a grocer driven to exclude the goods from his shelves because of the threats of labor union committees, I at times took space in the local papers and said that if the customers wanted Postum and Grape-Nuts and found that his grocer did not keep them, that in itself could be taken as evidence that that particular grocer was dominated by the labor unions, and I suggested that the customer transfer his business to the other grocer down the street, who was not dominated by labor trusts.

Post urged Van Cleave to pick a locale where a retailer had given up the fight, advertise that fact, and install his own sales force to sell directly to consumers. "It is the province and duty of every manufacturer, when he is attacked unfairly, to turn this attack into a big advertisement and make money out of it," he counseled.[17]

In the summer of 1908 Van Cleave finally conceded to Post, "You might be right when you say the business had been harmed by the Boycott," although he also claimed sales were off throughout the industry. "The very bottom seems to have dropped out of our business," Van Cleave confided to another manufacturer in the fall. "Just how much of this is due to the cowardly boycott of Gompers and his associate is hard to tell. . . . I am frank to say that I am at sea when we attempt to analyze it," he confessed.[18]

These private worries, expressed with difficulty even to comrades in the open-shop movement, contrast markedly with Van Cleave's ambitious plans and pronouncements as president of the NAM. Early in 1907 he forced out the independent and secretive secretary Marshall Cushing and replaced him with James A. Emery, who had established a reputation for forceful and effective advocacy of the open-shop cause as counsel to the Citizens Industrial Alliance of Grand Rapids. In May, the annual convention authorized Van Cleave to raise a war chest of $1.5 million over three years to "free this country from industrial oppression" through lobbying and other educational campaigns. On August 19, after many months of planning, Van Cleave met with Daniel Davenport and other leaders of the open-shop movement in Washington to found the National Council for Industrial Defense (NCID) to coordinate lobbying against the "vicious class legislation" of organized labor. Van Cleave hoped the new association would establish the NAM's hegemony over the movement, but when the other groups insisted on their independence the NCID became little more than the staging ground for Emery's lobbying efforts.[19]

The date and venue of the meeting were convenient, for Van Cleave and Davenport had other business in Washington on August 19, 1907. On that date Davenport filed a bill of complaint in the Supreme Court of the District of Columbia to enjoin the AFL and its officers from conducting a boycott against the Buck's Stove and Range Company. Although Davenport alleged a conspiracy in restraint of interstate business, he ultimately grounded the case on the common law rather than the Sherman Act. Justice Gould's temporary injunction, issued December 17, 1907, closely tracked an injunction Davenport had earlier won in a branch of the *Loewe* litigation. Gould agreed that trade unionists could deny their own patronage to dealers who handled Buck's Stoves, but he enjoined the defendants "from publishing or otherwise circulating, whether in writing or orally, any statements or notice of any kind or character whatsoever, calling attention of the complainant's customers, or of dealers, or tradesmen, or the public, to any boycott against the complainant, its business or its product." Knowledgeable commentators recognized the injunction was part of Van Cleave's general campaign to establish the NAM's political preeminence, and they were convinced Gould's injunction would bring new members into the association.[20]

Labor's Inherent Rights

Viewed from the perspective of Samuel Gompers and the other business unionists of the AFL's Executive Council, Van Cleave's suit was not a completely unwelcome event. Since the 1890s Gompers had protested decisions attacking workers' right to strike or patronize whomever they pleased. He insisted that workers could exercise that right for any reason or without reason at all, and that they could do so singly or in concert.[21]

Gompers's protests grew more emphatic with the rise of the open-shop lawyers, whom he dubbed "legal tools and hirelings in the pay of Parryized capital." "Can any right be more fundamental, more 'inalienable,' than the right to dispose of your patronage as you please?" Gompers demanded. Davenport might try to abolish the "We Don't Patronize" list, Gompers warned in 1903, but his efforts would only give a ring of "impecunious shysters a little business at the expense of foolish, misguided, and incapable employers."[22]

A lawsuit by one of Davenport's legal associates seems to have convinced Gompers that something more than brave words in the *American Federationist* was required and precipitated the AFL's new departure in national politics in early 1906. In October 1905, not long after the Illinois Supreme Court affirmed Frances Adams's controversial decision in *Christensen*, James Wilkerson sought to enjoin the peaceful picketing of Chicago printers on strike for the eight-hour day. Although even the newspapers most critical of the printers' demands conceded that the pickets were orderly, Judge Jesse Holdom granted the employers' request for a ban on all strike-related activity. The injunction and subsequent contempt proceedings prompted Gompers to thunder against the unconstitutional orders of "Holdom and capitalistic tools like him," to call for legislation ending "the injunction outrage," and to urge workers "to defeat every bigoted, ignorant or class-serving judge, and every legislator who is not willing to pledge himself to oppose the destruction of liberty and the acquiescence of legislatures, national and state, in judicial tyranny and judicial insolence."[23]

On March 21, 1906, Gompers convened a meeting of the presidents of all affiliated unions to reconsider the federation's political program. The result was "Labor's Bill of Grievances," a call for a variety of legislative and executive measures, including the abolition of the labor injunction. The response from legislative leaders and President Roosevelt was not heartening. Speaker Joseph Cannon, who had opposed the AFL's earlier legislative initiatives, rebuked an AFL delegation. "Union labor is not the whole shooting match," Cannon scolded. "There are the workmen to be considered who refuse to wear the shackles of unionism." Roosevelt's response was hardly more encouraging. Although sometimes abused, he acknowledged, the injunction power was "absolutely necessary." Roosevelt noted that his trust-busting campaign had never taken on organized labor, but he also warned the trade unionists not to draw the wrong conclusion. "Understand me, gentlemen, if I ever thought it necessary, if I ever thought a combination of laborers were doing wrong, I would apply for an injunction against them just as quickly as against so many capitalists."[24]

Although the AFL had long urged unionists to cast their votes for the friends of organized labor and against its enemies, in the wake of the Bill of Grievances the Executive Council actively enlisted its local affiliates in an unprecedented intervention in the congressional elections of 1906.

Maine's second congressional district was a major battleground, as Samuel Gompers personally campaigned to oust Charles E. Littlefield, who had used his position on the House Judiciary Committee to block anti-injunction legislation. Littlefield carried the district, thanks in part to the speeches of William Howard Taft and Speaker Cannon.[25]

Thus, when Davenport commenced the *Buck's Stove* case in the summer of 1907, Samuel Gompers had already committed the AFL to a political campaign to abolish the labor injunction. Just as Van Cleave saw his suit as an opportunity to conduct antiunion politics by other means, so Gompers realized that the lawsuit could serve as a vehicle for political mobilization. Gompers may genuinely have hoped that the case would end in a complete judicial vindication of his position, a ruling that wiped out "all injunctions against labor organizations . . . at one stroke." Yet from the start he also calculated that a judicial defeat might galvanize supporters and ultimately lead to a victory in Congress. "I have insisted that the defense should be a challenge of the right of the courts to issue injunctions of this character," he reported to the Executive Council. "If we are enjoined from doing the things we have the lawful right to do, and we perform them, the injunction to the contrary notwithstanding, it will have the effect of riveting attention to the outrageous procedure on the part of the courts in the issuance of these unwarranted injunctions, and do more than anything else can to secure either a favorable decision from the courts or relief at the hands of Congress." In November the Executive Council approved Gompers's plans by authorizing a one-cent levy on the rank and file of the affiliates.[26]

To produce the test case he envisioned, Gompers needed lawyers who shared his absolutist understanding of "labor's inherent rights." One candidate was Thomas Spelling, a lawyer with the Interstate Commerce Commission and a leading authority on injunctions, who had advised Gompers on legal matters since 1906. Spelling played a modest role in the early stages of the *Buck's Stove* case, but he was dropped from the litigation team in 1908 for reasons that remain unclear.[27] From the start, another Washington lawyer, Jackson H. Ralston (1857–1945), assisted by his partner Frederick L. Siddons, enjoyed a larger share of Gompers's confidence. Once a union printer, Ralston had litigated on behalf of organized labor as early as 1888, when he obtained a writ of habeas corpus to free musicians denied a jury in their trial for criminal conspiracy. More recently, he had represented the AFL before congressional committees considering anti-injunction legislation he helped draft.[28]

Gompers must have found Ralston's absolutist view of the law congenial. In 1904 Ralston told John J. Jenkins, chair of the House Judiciary Committee, that a person had "a legal right to purchase from whomever one chooses," even though it starved a person to death. As he later declared of free speech, "A constitutional right, as I understand it, is an absolute and a sacred thing."[29] Yet even Ralston proved too circumspect when he and Siddons advised Gompers against violating the injunction lest it prejudice the courts against his case. "The difficulty is to have lawyers take the bold position before the courts," Gompers complained to Andrew Furuseth, president of the International Seamen's Union. Lawyers were for the most part "men who are either in the employ of some form of corporation or hope to get a retainer from that source." Moreover, any lawyer who coveted a judgeship "aims to be so circumspect that in the effort not to offend . . . they become politically subservient." Gompers allowed that Ralston, Siddons, and Spelling were honorable men, but he despaired of finding "counsel that stand eminently in the public eye" who would give him the advice he wanted to hear.[30]

Finding a lawyer of national reputation to complete the litigation team was thus a major concern of the AFL leaders. Some consideration was given to George Turner, U.S. senator for the state of Washington from 1897 to 1903. More substantial attempts were made to interest Richard Olney in the job. As Grover Cleveland's attorney general Olney had overseen the prosecution of Eugene Debs, but the corporation lawyer was nonetheless an outspoken defender of the business unionism of the railroad brotherhoods and AFL affiliates. He reviewed the case but ultimately declined Gompers's offer, troubled by some issues it presented.[31]

Only after Gould issued his injunction did Gompers find the man he wanted in Alton B. Parker. The author of *National Protective Association v. Cumming* had resigned his judgeship to run, quite unspectacularly, as the Democratic standard-bearer in the 1904 presidential campaign. After his defeat he went into private practice in New York City. His selection as president of the American Bar Association in 1906 may well have satisfied Gompers that Parker would bring sufficient legal stature to the defendants' cause.[32]

Gompers first met with Parker in January 1908. After assuring Gompers that his initial consultation would be free, Parker outlined an absolutist and a priori defense of the AFL leaders that was consistent with both the jurisprudence of the *Cumming* decision and Gompers's own view of the law. Parker assured the labor leader that he believed the AFL could lawfully place Van Cleave on an unfair list. (In fact, he would later defend the boycott as deducible through "the severe rules of logic" from *Cumming*.)[33] He nonetheless advised Gompers to drop Buck's Stove from the "We Don't Patronize" list while continuing to speak out against Van Cleave. The criticism would violate the injunction, but in a way that would dissociate the case from the boycott and present "a clean-cut issue of the liberty of the press."[34]

Gompers may have satisfied himself that this strategy entailed no real compromise of his constitutional views or political aspirations. Nonetheless, it shifted the focus of the dispute from the legality of distributor-targeted secondary boycotts to the freedom of speech and of the press. In July, when President Gompers, Vice-President John Mitchell, and Secretary Frank Morrison were held in contempt for speaking out against Van Cleave, Gompers even trumpeted his compliance with the injunction insofar as it prohibited speech that set in action the mechanics of secondary boycotts:

> We obeyed the terms of the injunction and removed the Van Cleave Buck's Stove and Range Company of St. Louis from the "We Don't Patronize List" published in the *American Federationist*. What else would the court have us do? . . .
>
> We cannot bring ourselves to believe that the court will hold we have been in contempt of its order. To so hold would indeed be the severest blow to freedom of the press and freedom of speech, and the sooner the country shall definitely know it the better.[35]

Gompers's turn to free speech and free press was not without its dangers, for it opened him to the charge of turning his back on a powerful symbol of class solidarity. In fact, some unionists thought him foolhardy for appealing to individual rights in a polity dominated by capitalists. A carpenters' local in Oregon, for example, refused to contribute to the suit on the grounds that it would produce "a bad case of social deference."[36] But such views were exceptional. Many more labor radicals were moved by Gompers's defense of his "inherent right as a man" and citizen to speak out against an enemy of labor. Mahlon Barnes, a socialist nemesis of Gompers within the cigar makers' union, pledged his support to Gompers, for example. The socialist Victor Berger called upon every labor newspaper to print the "We Don't Patronize" list, and the San Francisco syndicalist Olaf A. Tveitmoe congratulated Gompers "upon your good fight for human freedom and constitutional rights." In AFL conventions before the war Gompers regularly faced strong challenges from socialists, but a wild demonstration ensued when his name was placed in nomination in November 1909, and he was reelected unanimously.[37]

While the turn to free speech helped strengthen Gompers's position within the labor movement, it also permitted the construction of a coalition between the AFL and prominent liberal reformers. The liberals wanted to foster good unions, "the kind of union which in contributing to the interest of its members contributes also to the general economic interest."[38] They considered trade unions an invaluable check on overreaching by employers, but they insisted that all groups in society must respect the common welfare. Most felt distributor-targeted secondary boycotts and sympathetic strikes that crossed industrial lines went beyond the legitimate interest of trade unionists and should be punished under the common law.[39] But although few would acknowledge a natural right to wield collective economic power, arguments from freedom of speech and of the press would have far greater appeal. As a cartoon from *The Survey,* a magazine of social reform, suggests, injunctions like Gould's pushed the balance between capital and labor too far in the former's favor and threatened to inaugurate a reign of industrial despotism under which all would suffer.

The possibility of cross-class collaboration presented itself in two events that made the *Buck's Stove* case a household name. The first was the 1908 presidential campaign in which Samuel Gompers all but enlisted the AFL in the cause of the Democrat William Jennings Bryan in his struggle with the "injunction judge" William Howard Taft. The second was the remarkable conduct of the Daniel Thew Wright, the trial judge whose sentencing of Gompers, Mitchell, and Morrison for contempt scandalized not only liberal reformers but also other members of the federal judiciary.

PRESIDENTIAL POLITICS, 1908

Coming just two months after Gould's injunction, the Supreme Court's decision in *Loewe* convinced Gompers that the very existence of the AFL was in jeopardy. "The more thought I gave it," he wrote to the members of the Executive Council, "the broader its scope and character appeared in its inimical attitude toward even the most innocent and heretofore lawful action of the trade unions and labor organizations of the country."[40] As in 1906, Gompers convened a conference of labor leaders in Washington. This time, however, the resulting document, "Protest to Congress," was limited to the single issue of the Sherman Act's application to organized labor. When neither Congress nor Roosevelt proved responsive, Gompers readied the AFL to enter the presidential campaign on the Democratic side.

Presidential politics intertwined with the *Buck's Stove* case throughout the summer and early fall of 1908. Gompers lobbied the platform committee of the Republican National Convention in June. He was greeted there by Van Cleave, Emery, and an avalanche of antilabor telegrams from the rank and file of the open-shop movement. The mildly reformist plank that Roosevelt and Taft pushed through pleased neither Gompers nor the open-shop leaders. Gompers called the proposal "a flimsy, tricky evasion of the issue"; Davenport thought it "quite wishy-washy." In Denver the following month, the delegates to the Democratic National Convention (who included Ralston and Parker) were more forthcoming. This time, the lobbying of the employers was in vain, thanks to Parker's efforts as a member of the platform committee.[41]

On July 20, soon after the Democrats adjourned, Davenport petitioned to have Gompers, Mitchell, and Morrison found in contempt of court, and the three were ordered to appear in early September to show cause why they should not be punished. The prospect that Gompers might be jailed just weeks before election day alarmed Roosevelt. "That injunction contempt case ought under no circumstances be tried until after the election," he directed Taft on August 24. "It really begins to look to me as if Van Cleave wanted you defeated."[42]

Taft followed Roosevelt's counsel and asked his postmaster general George Meyer and another official to reach Beck through the Wall Street lawyer William Nelson Cromwell. Beck and Davenport had earlier insisted that any delay would be fatal to their case, but on August 27 Meyer could write to Taft, "You need not trouble yourself any further about the contempt proceedings in the American Stove Company case. I have received assurances today which indicate the case will be postponed."[43] Sure enough, at the hearing on September 10, Davenport asked Justice Gould for more time to take testimony. Parker wanted to proceed at once, but Gould granted Davenport's motion and allowed sixty days for the taking of testimony, thereby placing the next court date after election day.[44]

On October 13 the daily newspapers carried an open letter from Gompers that all but endorsed Bryan. The move was controversial within the labor movement. Some preferred Republican or Socialist candidates. Others saw Gompers's move as a troubling break with the practices of the party period. "Voting with regard to one's separate interest is not an evil in itself, so long as the welfare of the whole be not ignored," allowed Henry White of the United Garment Workers. But no group had the right to seek "special advantages through their ability to influence votes." This would put "the obligations of sect or class or division before the demands of citizenship."[45]

Gompers's attempt to deliver "the laboring men of America . . . like chattels to Mr. Bryan" also elicited a strong response from Roosevelt in the form of an open letter to Senator Philander C. Knox. Roosevelt repeatedly contrasted Taft's unequivocal condemnation of the "oppressive, unjust, and immoral" secondary boycott with Bryan's apparent sympathy for AFL-backed legislation to abolish the labor injunction. Roosevelt's appeal to the "earnest-minded, thinking people, who are sincerely interested in the steady advance and legitimate aspirations of labor" received wide notice—not least among the open-shop movement. Van Cleave congratulated Roosevelt for his "splendid" letter, and Davenport would later count it a major factor in the Democrats' defeat.[46]

Taft's victory elated the open-shop leaders. Van Cleave predicted that Gompers would be overthrown at the AFL's annual meeting, held in Denver just after election day. "Then, after he is down and out, the decision for contempt of court in the Buck's Stove and Range Company's case will be rendered . . . and will enable him, I hope, to spend some days, weeks or months in peaceful seclusion, breaking rocks, or at some other honorable profession."[47] As the AFL met, Roosevelt mended fences with labor by inviting trade unionists who had backed Taft, government officials, the social gospeler and editor Lyman Abbott, and Supreme Court justices Holmes and Moody to a "bully" dinner at the White House. Holmes used the occasion to disabuse any trade unionist who might mistake him for a partisan of labor. "I said to one of them who had been spouting about the judges," he recalled twenty years later, "What you want is favor not justice; but when I am on my job I don't care what you want or what Roosevelt wants." Holmes repeated the remark to Roosevelt himself, as he "didn't like to say it behind his back and not to his face."[48]

With the election over, one might have thought Roosevelt's presidency would end without the *Buck's Stove* case again capturing the attention of the nation's most prominent political actors. On December 23, however, the case reached its climax with the sentencing of the AFL leaders in a District of Columbia courtroom. A year earlier, Gould's injunction had moved Roosevelt to call for the reform of the labor injunction lest workers lose their confidence in the state. Now, Justice Daniel Thew Wright's performance awakened the same concern among a wide segment of the middle class.

"The Supremacy of Law"

Wright found his way to the District of Columbia judiciary from the same legal and political community that produced William Howard Taft. Both men graduated from the Cincinnati Law School: Taft in 1880 after college at Yale; Wright in 1885 without having first taken an undergraduate degree. While still a law student Wright demonstrated his devotion to the rule of law by volunteering for duty in an artillery battery that helped suppress the Cincinnati Court House Riot of 1884. He served as city solicitor and mayor of a Cincinnati suburb and assistant prosecuting attorney for Hamilton County before being elected judge of the court of common pleas in 1890.[49] Although a participant in a fusion movement opposed to the local Republican machine, Wright subsequently threw in his lot with Taft's nemesis, Joseph Benson Foraker, who represented Ohio and the Standard Oil Company in the U.S. Senate from 1897 to 1909. With Foraker's backing, Roosevelt appointed Wright to the District of Columbia Supreme Court in November 1903. "The local practitioners have been prejudiced in his favor by the reports they have had of his ability and his sterling character as a man," reported the Washington *Post*. The paper added, however, "None of the members of the District court bench is personally acquainted with Judge Wright."[50]

Wright's performance over the next eleven years could not have been more at odds with his advance billing. During impeachment hearings in the summer of 1914, attorney after attorney testified to the judge's unbecoming conduct. Some simply spoke of Wright's arbitrary rulings, backed by threats of contempt citations for the attorney who objected too strenuously. Others recalled occasions when Wright falsified trial records to protect himself from appellate review, the day Wright wore a gun in court, and the many times he demanded and received bribes. Still others charged him with setting aside the divorce decree of a friend who wanted to stop paying alimony, with having an affair with a woman whose divorce suit was pending before him, with appointing to receiverships only those lawyers who "kicked back" a portion of their fees, and with soliciting contributions from the bar on behalf of a crony caught embezzling funds. No wonder Attorney General Bonaparte wrote Roosevelt that "Judge Wright *does* sometimes act arbitrarily, and he has embarrassed the Department on several occasions by such action."[51]

Wright's conduct off the bench was just as shocking. It was said he never paid his bills, safe in the knowledge that no merchant would risk his enmity. (One banker who tried to collect on Wright's $500 note found himself on jury duty in the judge's court for weeks at a time.) He was known to frequent some of the city's most notorious establishments. Wright scandalized at least one student at the Georgetown Law School by teaching the subject of criminal sexuality "with more or less hilarity." An anonymous report, passed along to Gompers by Congressman George Norris, involved Wright and Justice Gould. Wright, it was said, participated in a late-night interrogation of a young woman who apparently stole $1,500 from a bedroom bureau when Gould brought her to his home while his wife was away.[52]

Such was the man before whom Gompers, Mitchell, and Morrison appeared on December 23 to learn whether they would be held in contempt of court. Wright ordered the three men to sit in chairs placed directly in front of the bench. For the next two hours and twenty minutes the judge read his opinion, termed by a newspaperman "one of the most scathing arraignments that ever came from the bench in this city." Wright detailed the occasions on which the trade unionists drew attention to the boycott in violation of the injunction. Wright found particularly galling Gompers's suggestion that his opponents "Go to —— with your injunctions," a phrase the labor leader rendered under oath as "Go ahead with your injunctions." ("I have seen that in classic works," Gompers explained in response to Davenport's questioning.) Wright was also irked by a notice published in several labor newspapers. The notice declared, "It is unlawful for the American Federation of Labor and its members and sympathizers to boycott the Buck's Stove and Range Company," but with the last seven words printed in bold capitals, thereby conveying a quite different message than the sentence as a whole.[53]

"Everywhere, all over, within the court and out," Wright fumed, "utter, rampant, insolent defiance is heralded and proclaimed; unrefined insult, coarse affront, vulgar indignity measures the litigants' conception of the tribunal's due wherein his cause still pends." To Wright, the case presented an example of "studied, determined, defiant conduct, precipitated in the open light of day, between the decrees of a tribunal ordained by the Government of the Federal Union, and of the tribunals of another federation, grown up in the land." It offered a choice "between the supremacy of law over the rabble or its prostration under the feet of the disordered throng."[54]

Wright was no more willing to see mob rule triumph in 1908 than he was during the Court House Riot of 1884, and he was just as eager to chastise miscreants who fell into his grasp. Before doing so he asked the defendants if they had anything to say for themselves. The three men stood—Gompers in the middle, Mitchell on his left, and Morrison to his right. Although Wright would later claim "they looked so saucy that I made up my mind to soak the sons of b——s," eyewitnesses thought only Mitchell seemed composed.[55] Gompers stepped a pace forward and stood for a full minute in the crowded, silent courtroom. "Your honor," he began, "I am not conscious at any time during my life of having violated any law of the country or of the State in which I live. I would not consciously violate a law now or at any time during my whole life." With great emotion he invoked freedom of speech and of the press in support of his cause. He concluded, "I may say, your honor, that this is a struggle of the working people of the country—a struggle for rights. The labor movement does not undertake to presume to be a higher tribunal than the courts or the other branches of the government of our country."[56]

Convinced that a jail term was needed to "vindicate the orderly power of judicial tribunals, and to establish over this litigation the supremacy of Law," Wright announced his sentences: six months for Morrison, nine for Mitchell, a year for Gompers. Gompers wept as he heard his sentence; his wife and daughter were also visibly affected. The three labor leaders then left the court, free on bail pending their appeal.[57]

Beck haled the decision as the "death knell" of the boycott and the most important labor decision since *Debs*. Fred Boocock of the AABA applauded Wright for applying the law to the facts of the case with "undeviating courage" and patriotism. John Spooner's characterization of the AABA as "a liberty league" never seemed more appropriate, Boocock declared.[58]

Some observers shared the open-shop leaders' enthusiasm for Wright's harangue. The Detroit *Free Press,* for example, called it "an admirably written document of almost Blackstonian clearness, vigor and precision of statement."[59] But many were alarmed by Wright's scathing tone. *The Outlook* immediately wired Roosevelt for information and then editorialized, "The undue heat of Mr. Gompers in a political campaign, a heat for which some excuse may be found in the fact he was campaigning, excited a like quality in Judge Wright, for whose passion the same excuse cannot be found." Editor Lyman Abbott wrote to Roosevelt that Wright's decision, although "probably correct" in law, was "unpardonably bad in spirit. It was as full of passion as Gompers' speeches and editorials." The Boston *Herald* ran the patrician Robert Treat Paine's protest against Wright's "astounding decision" across its front page. Seth Low, then president of the National Civic Federation (NCF), could not second the AFL's "natural right" to boycott, but he deplored the proceedings for being "as dangerous as the boycott itself." An associate of Low's in the NCF deplored "the unfortunate violence of expression which disfigured the contempt decree of Justice Wright." She counseled that "time and brains and infinite patience" were needed if the problem of the boycott was to be solved.[60]

Roosevelt asked the Department of Justice for a report as calls for a presidential pardon flooded the White House. Bonaparte advised Roosevelt that as president he possessed the power to pardon the labor leaders, a point that Davenport had disputed.[61] The attorney general also called the sentences *"very much* too severe"—on the same order as the $29 million fine Judge Kenesaw Mountain Landis had recently levied against the Standard Oil Company. Still, the attorney general counseled against any immediate action. "The Executive has no proper concern until the Courts have finished with it," Bonaparte claimed. If the defendants abandoned their appeal, their application for executive clemency should receive careful consideration. Until then, however, it would be inappropriate for Roosevelt to act, "especially since, in all human probability, another President will have to deal practically with the question."[62]

Roosevelt followed his attorney general's advice. "I feel that Landis helped the big corrupt corporations by imposing what the average man regarded as an excessive fine," he wrote to Abbott, "and I feel Judge Wright performed the same service for the worst leaders of labor."[63] But Gompers wanted no part of a presidential pardon. "If my fellows have suffered for the exercise of the rights to which they are entitled under the laws and Constitution of our country," he wrote to a sympathetic lawyer on December 30, "I can give no good reason why I should flinch from the consequences of my assertion and maintenance of my rights as a citizen and as a man." Gompers's enemies might get their pound of flesh, he declared, but they would find no "yellow streak" in it.[64]

ENDGAME

The denouement of the *Buck's Stove* case was played out over the next five years as federal appellate courts attempted to limit the damage of Wright's actions. In the process, they betrayed growing doubts over the continuing validity of the universalism and individualism of Wright's address in a plural society.

Ralston had appealed Gould's injunction in December 1908. In March 1909, by a 2-1 vote, the court of appeals affirmed, but only after modifying the terms of the order. Justice Charles Robb's opinion for the majority condemned the boycott in terms borrowed from the opinions of the Great Upheaval. To accept Parker's arguments on behalf of the boycott, Robb explained, was "to give legal support and standing to an engine of harm and oppression utterly at variance with the spirit and theory of our institutions, place the weak at the mercy of the strong, foster monopoly, permit an unwarranted interference with the natural course of trade, and deprive the citizen of the freedom guaranteed him by the Constitution." But Robb also ruled that Gould's order went too far in prohibiting the defendants from making any references to the dispute when only speech in direct furtherance of the secondary boycott could be enjoined. Justice Josiah Van Orsdel wrote separately to denounce Gould's injunction as an act of "judicial tyranny," but only Chief Justice Seth Shepard (1847–1917) dissented. The Texas Democrat fully endorsed Parker's a priori defense of the boycott and the free-speech rights of the defendants.[65]

The trade unionists' appeal of the contempt case came before the court of appeals in April. Gompers was thrilled by Parker's "magnificent" argument and printed it in full in the *American Federationist*.[66] In November the court announced its decision. Once again Van Orsdel and Robb voted to affirm over Shepard's dissent. Although the majority concluded that "the higher principle" of the supremacy of law required that Wright's order be upheld, it also praised Gompers, Mitchell, and Morrison as "distinguished citizens, leaders in a great cause for the improvement and uplift of their fellow men, with a larger following, probably, than was ever marshaled under single leadership in any philanthropic movement." The most the majority would say for the other side was that "the fairness or unfairness of the Buck's Stove & Range Company and the larger organization to which it belongs . . . are not matters to be here considered."[67]

The injunction and contempt proceedings were then joined for a further appeal to the U.S. Supreme Court. While the appeals were pending, however, the case took an unexpected turn. Van Cleave died suddenly in May 1910, and control of the company passed to Frederic Gardner. In June, Gardner went before the board of the AABA to plead that the firm could no longer afford the 40 percent decline in revenues produced by the boycott. On July 19 he settled the dispute. Gardner promised that the company would "withdraw its attorneys from any case pending in the courts" against the AFL or its affiliates, and the AFL agreed to publish the fact of the settlement and urge workers to patronize the firm.[68]

The open-shop leaders were disgusted. Post, for one, heaped invective on Gardner. The "little pinhead" was "trying to trot in a race where muskrats like him have no business." Post tried to block the settlement with a shareholder's suit. This harried Gardner and Gompers for several years but had no lasting effect. The AABA publicly resolved to push on as before, and its lawyers prepared to argue the injunction and contempt cases before the Supreme Court. In private, however, the open-shop lawyers acknowledged that a "body blow" had been dealt the movement.[69]

The lawyers' concern arose from the doctrine of mootness. Courts could only render decisions when the results would have some practical effect on an existing controversy. The settlement certainly mooted the appeal of the injunction, the proceeding that most directly placed the merits of the case before the court. With this soapbox taken away, the litigants would find it harder to make their denunciations and defenses of the boycott heard. Further, if Wright's order were considered a civil contempt—that is, a phase of Van Cleave's original suit for injunction—the contempt proceeding would be mooted as well. The great test case both sides wanted would evaporate just as it reached the Supreme Court.

Gompers did not realize the consequences of the settlement until early October, when he met with Ralston and other labor lawyers to discuss Post's suit. Mortified at the possibility that workers might think he had lost his nerve, Gompers asked the metal polishers and Gardner to accept a modification of the agreement in a belated attempt to have "the principles for which we have been so long contending" come before the court. At a conference shortly before oral argument in December 1910, Gompers's lawyers told him they were ethically obliged to acknowledge the settlement. It was "a course against which my whole nature revolted and against which I emphatically protested," he assured the Executive Council.[70]

The three defendants directed their lawyers to state frankly "the present relations between the company and organized labor without attaching great importance to the agreement and then endeavor with all your power and ability to prevail upon the court to hear the arguments and to consider and decide all the questions contained in the appeals." While feeling "considerable satisfaction in the dissenting opinion of Chief Justice Shepard," the defendants nonetheless were convinced that the modified injunction denied them and other unionists their constitutional and inherent rights. "We cannot even seemingly give our assent to the provisions of the injunction as modified by the court," they explained. This would violate "the duty we owe to our fellow workers and to our fellow citizens, as well as to our own self-respect."[71]

The Supreme Court justices disappointed the AFL's and AABA's hopes for a ringing judicial endorsement of their positions. After hearing out Ralston and the AABA's local co-counsel J. J. Darlington, Justice Horace Lurton stopped Davenport and confirmed that the dispute had been settled. Argument then continued, but only on the appeal of the contempt case.[72] Davenport awaited the Court's decision with less than complete confidence in the outcome. Observing to James Emery that Congress had abolished Washington's jail, the AABA lawyer suggested that President Taft would have to invite the defendants to the White House "should the Supreme Court be so behind the times as to hold them to have been properly convicted or sentenced."[73]

Taft was spared his house guests. On May 15, 1911, the Court issued its opinion unanimously reversing the contempt decree. Justice Joseph R. Lamar disposed of the case on a question "more or less technical," but did so in a way that favored Gompers and his codefendants rather more than the AABA. He declared labor unions a natural and legitimate part of modern life. "Society itself is an organization and does not object to organizations for social, religious, business and all legal purposes. The law, therefore, recognizes the right of workingmen to unite and to invite others to join their ranks, thereby making available the strength, influence and power that come from such association." But while affirming that organized labor could lawfully possess the "vast power" that Davenport and Beck deplored, Lamar also stressed that the state must reign above all groups to prevent the sacrifice of individual rights. Had Wright ordered the jail terms after a criminal trial to vindicate the dignity of his own court, Lamar wrote, the convictions would have to be affirmed. But Wright had imposed the punishments in a civil suit at the behest of a private party, and so his judgment had to be reversed, albeit "without prejudice to Wright's power and right . . . to punish by a proper proceeding, contempt, if any, committed against it."[74]

Lamar presented his conclusion as a simple matter of requiring that proper procedures be followed, but close readers saw in it an unspoken snub to Wright and a caution to other judges. By ordering a criminal punishment in a civil suit, Lamar implied, Wright had betrayed himself. His mixing of public and private procedure was a metaphor for the open partisanship he displayed in the case. Wright's "flagrant error occurred in a species of proceedings nowadays regarded with such jealousy that it will hardly be able to survive a great many blunders," a law journal editorialized. "It will not be strange if the court's oversight of grave technical errors in a proceeding for imprisonment of its own foes is attributed by hostile critics to the blindness of rage."[75]

If Wright and the AABA took Lamar's point, they gave no indication. On May 16, the day after Lamar's opinion was announced, Wright appointed a committee to investigate whether a criminal proceeding was in order. Wright's choices for the committee—Daniel Davenport, James Beck, J. J. Darlington, and Clarence R. Wilson (the U.S. attorney for the District of Columbia)—hardly embodied the sharp distinction between private and public interests Lamar envisioned.[76] On June 12 the committee recommended that a new contempt citation be issued unless the defendants apologized to Wright. Gompers, Mitchell, and Morrison refused to confess error, but they were also ready to end the litigation. They authorized their lawyers to plead the statute of limitations as a bar to further proceedings.[77]

Wright refused the plea and a trial ensued. In June 1912, as AFL and open-shop lobbyists again laid siege to the Democratic national convention, Wright reimposed the harsh sentences of his original order in another forceful opinion. "It will be as clear to any laymen as to a lawyer," James Emery predicted, "and should cut a decided figure in the approaching campaign, in which it will undoubtedly receive considerable criticism."[78]

Another year passed before the court of appeals decided the ensuing appeal. Over Shepard's dissent, Van Orsdel and Robb ruled that Wright could lawfully hold the labor leaders in contempt, but that the severity of his sentences (which exceeded those imposed on Debs and his associates in 1894) amounted to an abuse of discretion. The majority settled on much lighter punishments: thirty days in jail for Gompers, $500 fines for Mitchell and Morrison. "The sentence is now so far reduced that the court practically is rebuked," the *New York Times* observed. In 1908 the newspaper had supported Wright, but now it welcomed the opportunity the appeal gave the public to reconsider its position on the case. "To speak candidly," the *Times* confided, "there is danger that the courts will be used for private purposes, as the Legislature has been, unless a halt be called."[79] The New York *Globe* was less restrained and more sarcastic in its criticism of Wright. In spite of "the continuous shoutings of the mild and impartial judge that they should be instantly clapped into jail," the "wild and truculent trio" had been at large throughout the proceedings. "Something has always intervened. . . . It is most discouraging to a judge who is aflame with holy zeal against labor unions."[80]

Both sides mounted appeals to the Supreme Court. After twice hearing oral arguments, it finally decided the case in May 1914 in an opinion by Justice Holmes holding that the statute of limitations barred the criminal contempt proceeding. Neither side could find the result thoroughly satisfying. Gompers and his codefendants at last were rid of the case, but Holmes had dismissed Parker's constitutional arguments with the remark that the statute of limitations was the "only real defence."[81] Davenport belabored the fact that Holmes did not say that Gompers was innocent of the criminal contempt. "Everyone must agree that guilty criminals who claim such immunity should have the benefit of it, and be no longer subject for their crimes. The declaration by the highest court of the land as to the heinous nature of their conduct may perhaps deter them from its repetition, and others from imitating them."[82]

Although the *Buck's Stove* case consumed hundreds of pages in the law reports, the lasting significance of the case lies beyond the courts. From the start, neither Van Cleave nor Gompers valued the case solely or even primarily for the chance it presented to break new doctrinal ground on the legality of the secondary boycott or the labor injunction. Each side was far more concerned with using the litigation to cement their constituencies behind their leadership and to win allies who would prove useful when the battleground shifted to Congress. These concerns influenced the AFL's decision about whether to raise the mootness issue or the statute of limitations. They also help explain the litigants' preference for an a priori, natural-rights jurisprudence when that position had been abandoned by leading legal academics and the younger and more scholarly members of the judiciary. Mixing the language of the courtroom with the language of the stump, natural-rights jurisprudence served the litigants' dual purpose, and it was the native tongue of the lawyer-politicians arrayed on either side of the dispute.

The political nature of the case is also clear in the response of the federal judiciary and the federal executive. Justice Wright was, of course, an eager and aggressive partisan, but this most injudicious judge was not representative of the bench as a whole. Most of the appellate judges who heard the case rejected the Victorian theory of the labor union as enjoying no authority greater than the sum of its members' rights. Yet they also insisted that these new centers of collective economic power be subject to law and the commonweal. When some narrow basis for disposing of the case arose, they adopted it rather than court controversy. Emery warned Post that the popular "criticism of labor injunctions" would impel federal judges to comb the pleadings in his shareholder's suit for procedural errors. To like effect, a lawyer complained to Harvard president Charles Eliot that because judges often saw "a political aspect" in labor cases, they were tempted to "avoid offending—to decide the particular case on some technical ground" rather than give broader issues "the courageous treatment they demand."[83]

Federal executive officials were just as reluctant to offend voters whose support was no longer a given after the decline of party loyalties and the rise of issue-focussed politics. Roosevelt seized the opportunity to cast himself and, by implication, his supporters as progressive reformers battling both "the corrupt and lawless labor leader" and "the corrupt and law-less capitalist." At the same time, he and Taft did what it took to ensure that their "embarrassing friend Mr. Van Cleave" (as Taft dubbed him) did not send the Republican party down to defeat.[84] When it came to orga-nized labor, the Republican presidents spoke loudly but carried a small stick. They favored inaction over action—in working for the postponement of the contempt proceedings, in ducking the pardon issue, and in ignor-ing the demands for antitrust prosecutions of the AFL that regularly is-sued from the open-shop camp.

The *Buck's Stove* case thus ended in a judicial and political stalemate. Of the two sides, the AABA had the greater cause for concern. First, as the dispute proceeded, the AFL found common ground with managers, law-yers, and other defenders of the large business corporation who gathered under the auspices of the NCF. When the Supreme Court announced its first decision in *Loewe,* a circle of managers, lawyers, and economists or-ganized by the NCF was mounting a sustained attempt to revise the anti-trust laws (chapter 9). The prospect of enlisting the labor vote and a grow-ing "labor bloc" in Congress made the AFL an attractive ally, particularly since the federation did not seem inclined to organize the new immigrants in the work force of the large firms.[85] An alliance with the AABA and the NAM, whose constituents considered themselves menaced by the large firms, held no comparable promise.

Just as ominous for the AABA were the AFL's close ties to the Demo-cratic party, which was firmly in control of the national government in May 1914. When Davenport commenced the *Buck's Stove* case almost seven years earlier, the House was secure under Joseph Cannon's tutelage, the Senate was the domain of such sober Republicans as Joseph Foraker and Nelson Aldrich, and President Roosevelt had not yet revealed himself as "a trim-mer" who paid too much attention to Samuel Gompers.[86] When Holm-es's decision finally ended the dispute, James Maher, the officer who de-livered the United Hatters' ultimatum to Loewe, was a Democratic congressman from Brooklyn. John Moffitt, the union president who or-dered the Loewe boycott, was a commissioner of conciliation in the newly established Department of Labor. The AFL was mounting a promising campaign to exempt organized labor from the antitrust laws and to limit injunctions in labor disputes. And an investigation was underway into the conduct of Justice Daniel Thew Wright, who would resign in October to escape impeachment. To replace him, President Woodrow Wilson would name Frederick L. Siddons, co-counsel with Jackson Ralston and Alton Parker in the *Buck's Stove* case.[87]

The family of Charles H. Merritt, possibly taken in 1915 at the fiftieth anniversary of his wedding to Luana Kniffen. Walter Gordon Merritt is standing at the far left. (Courtesy of the Danbury Scott-Fanton Museum and Historical Society)

Residence of Charles H. Merritt, 350 Main St., Danbury, Connecticut. (Courtesy of the Danbury Scott-Fanton Museum and Historical Society)

Dietrich Eduard Loewe, ca. 1916. (Courtesy of the State Historical Society of Wisconsin)

Rear view of the factory of Dietrich Eduard Loewe, around the 1890s. (Courtesy of Danbury Scott-Fanton Museum and Historical Society)

The leadership of the United Hatters in 1904. Treasurer James P. Maher, who negotiated directly with Dietrich Loewe, is standing to the left. Martin Lawlor, a defendant in the suit, stands to Maher's right. President John A. Moffitt is seated on the right.

Daniel Davenport, general counsel, American Anti-Boycott Association, ca. 1915. (Courtesy of the State Historical Society of Wisconsin)

The Labor Trust, 1906, according to the Citizen's Industrial Association of America, Charles W. Post, president, from *The Square Deal,* February 1906. (Courtesy of the State Historical Society of Wisconsin)

The Honorable Daniel Thew Wright,
associate justice of the Supreme Court
of the District of Columbia. (Courtesy
of the Library of Congress)

The defendants in *Buck's Stove & Range Company v. Gompers*, 1909.
John Mitchell and Samuel Gompers are seated. Frank Morrison
is standing. (Courtesy of the Bettman Archive)

Alton Brooks Parker, 1904, chief judge of the
New York Court of Appeals, Democratic
presidential candidate in 1904, and counsel to
the American Federation of Labor in *Buck's
Stove & Range Company v. Gompers*. (Courtesy of the Bettman Archive)

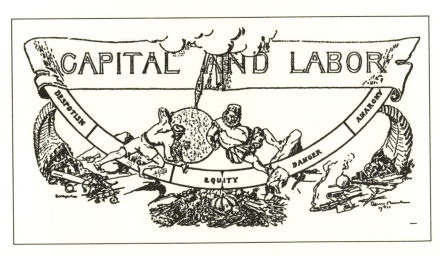

Liberal reformers (such as those who encountered this cartoon in *The Survey* for
February 7, 1914) favored an equitable balance between the despotism of unchecked
capital and the anarchy of unrestrained labor. (Courtesy of the Library of the
Department of Labor)

ANNOUNCEMENT

It is unlawful for the American Federation of Labor and its members and sympathizers to

BOYCOTT

THE BUCK'S STOVE & RANGE CO.

"Justice Gould in the Equity Court of the District of Columbia, on December 17th, handed down a decision granting the company a temporary injunction preventing the Federation from publishing the fact that the

BUCK'S STOVE & RANGE CO.

is on the

....UNFAIR LIST OF ORGANIZED LABOR....

The Letter of the Law. Notice from the St. Louis *Labor*, February 1908, reproduced in the AABA's pamphlet edition of Justice Daniel Thew Wright's opinion, delivered December 1908. (Courtesy of the Library of the Department of Labor)

Walter Gordon Merritt, associate counsel, American Anti-Boycott Association, ca. 1914. (Courtesy of the State Historical Society of Wisconsin)

Congress: Let Him Find Out What's
In It.

The Clayton Act as viewed by the open-shop press, from the *American Employer*, June 1914. (Courtesy of the State Historical Society of Wisconsin)

EIGHT

Labor Incorporated

After all, our legal theories will and must be judged by their applicability to the facts they endeavour to resume. It is clear enough that unless we treat the personality of our group persons as real and apply the fact of reality throughout the whole realm of law, what we call justice will, in truth, be no more than a chaotic and illogical muddle.

—Harold J. Laski (1916)

While the leaders of the employers' and labor movement squared off in the *Buck's Stove* case, a quieter drama with humbler participants was played out in the Danbury hatters' case. After deciding in February 1908 that the United Hatters' boycott of Dietrich Loewe's distributors was actionable under the Sherman Anti-Trust Act, the U.S. Supreme Court remanded the case to the federal district court for trial, which commenced in October 1909. The presiding judge was James P. Platt, a far more temperate man than Daniel Thew Wright.[1] In place of the belligerent James Van Cleave sat Dietrich Loewe, an "ideal plaintiff" in his lawyers' estimation, "who had himself been a workman at the bench" and had never "lost sympathy or consideration for the working people who had been less successful than he."[2] Loewe was represented by Daniel Davenport and his young co-counsel Walter Gordon Merritt; James Beck was too busy with his corporate clients to try the case.

But the greatest contrast with the *Buck's Stove* case may have been provided by the defendants. Samuel Gompers, John Mitchell, and Frank Morrison were among the most eminent figures in the American labor movement. When Beck and Davenport described the threesome as the masters of a million minds, many observers outside the labor movement nodded in agreement. The elderly defendants called to the witness stand in *Loewe* were far less imposing figures. Consider, for example, William Humphries. Born in Ireland in 1840, Humphries had come with his parents to the United States at the age of nine. He had worked in the hatting industry since 1854, interrupting his labors only to "wear the blue" of the Union army. The hat finisher had taken little interest in the boycotts ordered by the leaders of the national union. "I am willing to acquiesce in the matter," he testified, "because I didn't take any part in electing them." Indeed, Humphries had taken little part in *any* aspect of union affairs. He "didn't know the national officers . . . either by sight or by name." He rarely read the United Hatters' *Journal.* "I couldn't see very good," Humphries explained, "and I hadn't time to do it." As an honorary member of his local union since his fiftieth birthday, Humphries was excused from appearing at its meetings. In fact, he almost never attended them.[3]

To an uninstructed member of the general public, the idea that this unexceptional working man was somehow responsible for the acts of a distant leadership must have been surprising. Certainly Humphries himself thought the idea incredible. "I never was a party to a conspiracy to interfere with Mr. Loewe or anybody else," he protested. "I never was a party to any conspiracy of any kind."[4]

But a suit against William Humphries made perfect sense to Daniel Davenport. The lawyer's upbringing taught him to think of individuals, not groups, as the fundamental units in the American polity. To be sure, individuals could voluntarily associate to advance their mutual aims, but unless they incorporated they remained personally liable for their collective actions. Further, as a voluntary association, the United Hatters could not be sued in its collective capacity and name under the common law.[5] Under Davenport's voluntarist theory of the trade union, a suit against Humphries and his fellows placed responsibility where it belonged: on the individual. As members of the union, they were obligated to police the conduct of their agents—the national leadership—or suffer the consequences.[6]

Samuel Gompers was quick to assign a different motive to Davenport. As in the *Buck's Stove* case, he charged, Davenport was invoking the individual liberty of employers in order to suppress the individual liberty of workers. His aim was "to strike terror and fright into the heart and mind of every man and woman who was a member of a labor organization by making them believe they could be mulcted in threefold damages, with the hope they would thereby withdraw from the organization and disband the movement." Davenport, "like a ghoul," had proclaimed the verdict a new declaration of independence. Gompers agreed—if by independence Davenport meant "the independence of the tyrant to do as he will."[7]

Many observers of the latter years of the Danbury hatters' case saw a different lesson in William Humphries's plight. To many institutional economists, progressive lawyers, and social commentators, the trade union was not the product of the free contracts of autonomous, rights-bearing individuals but a distinct and natural entity that the law should recognize even when not incorporated formally. The group was a natural phenomenon, existing prior to the individual; it shaped individual preferences as much as it aggregated them. These observers were satisfied with neither Davenport's nor Gompers's account of the trade union, because both overlooked what they took as fundamental, the pluralism of American society. The law needed to acknowledge the collective power of the trade union, the observers held, which far exceeded the sum of the rights of its individual members. The incorporation of trade unions or its equivalent was the only way to ensure that collective responsibility followed collective power in a plural society.

The Trials of Loewe

Lasting from October 1909 to February 1910, the trial over which Judge Platt presided was as tedious and time-consuming as he feared it would be when he sustained the defendants' demurrer in December 1906. Davenport and Merritt introduced evidence of the boycott and its effects on Loewe's finances, but the bulk of their energies was devoted to establishing that the individual defendants knew or reasonably should have known of the boycott, so that their continued membership in the union was an implicit authorization or ratification of the campaign against Loewe. The lawyers for the hatters—John Beach, John Light, and Robert DeForest (Davenport's erstwhile comrade in Bridgeport's Democratic party)—countered with testimony from 175 of the defendants that they had no personal knowledge of the boycott. They also relied on DeForest's closing argument, in which he denounced the AABA as a secret cabal and wept over the condition of the hatters.[8]

When Davenport rose to address the jury, he reached what was for him, a veteran trial lawyer, the climactic moment in the case. His closing argument was something of a coda to his career as a genteel lawyer-politician. He made short work of DeForest, in the process revealing his contempt for a politician who had bartered principle for political office by staying in the Democratic party after 1896. DeForest had turned "on a little of his artificial water works for you this morning," Davenport told the jury. The speech reminded Davenport of the many DeForest had given "when he was on the stump running for Congress—these poor workingmen and the cruel oppressions they were under, received at the hand of capitalists. Oh, how familiar that sounded to me! It got rather stale, though, in the Fourth Congressional District before he retired from public life."[9]

Then Davenport presented his own portrayal of the Danbury hatters' case in a republican jeremiad that invited the jury to resist the corrupting innovation of the hatters' combination. Earlier, Walter Gordon Merritt had painted Loewe as an exemplar of the free-labor creed, a life "free from blemish" and devoted to building a patrimony for his four sons. Now Davenport gave Loewe a place in history. "Oh, if I had a few moments' time," Davenport told the jurors, "I would like to tell you the history of Danbury. I was born and raised fifteen miles below there and when a boy it was my privilege to talk with old men, who, as boys, had talked with old men who, as boys and young men, were in Danbury in Revolution. What patriotism was then displayed by the whole people!" Davenport then turned to the benighted conditions of present-day Danbury, where men were fined a thousand dollars for the "privilege" of going to work and where nonunion goods were forbidden by the central labor union. "Can you imagine that condition of affairs in good old Danbury, a town with its history?" Davenport marveled.[10]

Not content with linking Loewe to the heritage of the American Revolution, Davenport pushed further back in time, to the settlement of Connecticut by those who fled the political and religious tyranny of the Old World. He reminded the jury that the case was tried on the spot where, "271 years ago last week," settlers framed Connecticut's first constitution. "Gentlemen, it is a fact, though we cannot see them, that the invisible hosts are camped around this court room which brought into existence this beautiful heritage which we enjoy and which we hope to transmit to our children and our children's children." He urged them to consider, too, "the great host that would come after us, whose rights and whose interests are in the decision which you shall make in this case."[11]

At last Davenport came to his ultimate historical resting place, the Old Testament. As he grew to know Loewe, the lawyer told the jurors, he found himself thinking of the lamentations of Job:

> Oh, that I were as in months past, as in the days when God preserved me; when his candle shined upon my head, and when by his light I walked through darkness. When the Almighty was yet with me, when my children were about me; when I went out to the gate through the city, when I prepared my seat in the street! The young men saw me, and hid themselves; and the aged arose, and stood up, because I delivered the poor that cried, and the fatherless and him that had no one to help him. I was eyes to the blind, and feet was I to the lame. I was a father to the poor and the cause which I knew not I searched out. I caused the widow's heart to sing for joy, but now they that hate me without cause are more than the hairs of my head.

"The jury wept," Davenport's co-counsel reported.[12]

After Davenport had spoken, Judge Platt took the most difficult issue from the jury. Convinced the defendants' continued membership in the union established their liability as a matter of law, Platt directed the jury to find for Loewe on that point. He charged the jury with determining the damages Loewe suffered. After several hours of deliberation, the jury returned a verdict for Loewe of $74,000, which was trebled under the Sherman Act to $222,000.[13]

In the wake of the verdict, Gompers wrote John Moffitt, president of the United Hatters, that he expected no other result after the union's lawyers failed to present "the rights and principles involved" in the case to the Supreme Court. Gompers now set his sight on a legislative reversal of the decision, and to that end he urged Moffitt to prepare a statement on the verdict.[14]

The AABA offered to settle for $150,000 damages and $10,000 court and attorney fees, but the United Hatters decided on an appeal. The union dropped Light and DeForest and added Alton Parker and the Toledo lawyer Frank L. Mulholland. The United Hatters won a temporary victory in April 1911, when an intermediate appellate court reversed Platt's judgment on the grounds that the conflicting testimony on the defendants' personal knowledge of the boycott created a question of fact for the jury. In August 1912, Loewe and the surviving defendants endured a second lengthy trial. It ended in October 1912 with an even larger verdict for Loewe. Evidently, Davenport's rhetorical powers were undiminished; the jurors asked whether they could award Loewe an amount greater than he had sought. Before leaving the jury box, they sang the Doxology to give proper credit to the ultimate author of their judgment.[15]

The judges who decided the ensuing and final round of appeals were just as emphatic. "A soldier who with his regiment charges the enemy's line can hardly be heard to assert that he did not know a battle was in progress," declared the chief judge of the Second Circuit. Holmes thought the defendants "got all that they were entitled to ask in not being held chargeable with knowledge as a matter of law." Given the reportage of the boycott, it was "almost inconceivable" that they knew nothing of it and, in any case, as union members they were "bound to know the constitution of their societies."[16]

The St. Louis Labor called the result another "golden nail in the coffin of capitalism," but the mainstream press hailed Holmes's decision much as it had Fuller's. "The members of a union are liable for the acts of their officers and agents in the same way that a partnership or corporation is," the New York Times editorialized. "If unionists are held responsible for the acts of the unions they will be what they ought to be, law-abiding and beneficent organizations, entitled to the respect of all."[17]

Danbury's Dupes

Such confident pronouncements about the need to fix "definite responsibility somewhere upon somebody" gave way to second thoughts as Davenport and Merritt moved to collect the judgment.[18] The AABA's lawyers steadfastly insisted that contracts between the individual defendants and the United Hatters obligated the union to pay the judgment. They also pointed to a resolution of the AFL's Denver convention pledging "moral and such financial support as may be necessary in the pending contention." A levy of about $35 on each member of the United Hatters would satisfy the judgment, the AABA pointed out, and a tax on every member of the AFL would drop the individual contribution to just fifteen cents.[19] An open letter from Loewe emphasized his patience in collecting the judgment; behind the scenes, Davenport and Merritt made offers of settlement.[20]

The United Hatters and AFL raised funds for the relief of the individual defendants, but they denied that the money would go to Loewe and his lawyers. In July 1910, Gompers wrote Moffitt that the Denver resolution did not obligate the AFL to pay the judgment. After Holmes's decision Gompers told the press, "I feel awful in regard to how the men will take this when their homes are sold to pay this terrible judgment." (The *New York Times* retorted, "There is nothing to prevent those who feel that the boycott is a sacred right from chipping in a few cents a piece.")[21] In fact, the AFL raised the bulk of the funds needed to satisfy the judgment. In 1910 the AFL voted a two-cent assessment on the members of its affiliated unions. It later declared January 27, 1916 (Gompers's birthday) "Hatters' Day" and asked trade unionists to donate an hour's earnings to the cause.[22]

The leaders of the United Hatters adopted a similar course. In February 1915, they and Gompers petitioned Congress to satisfy the judgment on the theory that the Sherman Act had been erroneously applied to organized labor, as evidenced by the labor provisions of the Clayton Act, adopted in 1914. The unionists went away empty-handed. A resolve of the May 1915 convention denied that the union was legally obligated to pay the judgment, but it also authorized a 1 percent assessment on each member's earnings.[23]

Still, the two sides could not come to terms, and it seemed possible in the summer of 1917 that the AABA would foreclose its liens on the hatters' homes. The bad publicity this would generate was one force pressing the AABA to compromise; another was Loewe's creditors, for his firm had gone into receivership during the litigation. "The bankers' committee was at my elbow urging compromise," Merritt recalled, "but I did not wish to end what seemed to me to be a noble battle with an anticlimax of haggling."

Despite the bankers' "glowering glances of disapproval," he insisted on the full amount due. He received it on July 12. Of the $234,192 paid Loewe on that date, the AFL had raised $216,024.[24]

Behind the hemming and hawing of the labor leaders was their desire to avoid establishing in fact what did not exist in law: the corporate responsibility of a union for liabilities incurred by its officers. The New York *World* charged that the AFL and United Hatters were quite prepared to sacrifice "their dupes in Danbury" rather than recognize the principle that "labor organizations, like other combinations, may be held responsible for their acts."[25]

The AABA's insistence on holding the individual hatters liable, and the union's apparent willingness to see their homes go into foreclosure, troubled *The Outlook*'s editor, Lyman Abbott. He dispatched Lyman Beecher Stowe to Danbury in the summer of 1915 to report on the case. Stowe met some hatters who believed in unionism as staunchly as Loewe believed in the open shop. He asked one defendant, "a defiant little man upwards of sixty," if he believed the United Hatters would compensate him for his losses. "He fairly shouted at me," Stowe reported, "'Of course we'll be taken care of by the union. Guess you never belonged to a union, or you wouldn't ask such a question? Don't you know that's the whole idea—the whole philosophy of a unionism?'"[26]

But Stowe's conversations with other defendants revealed a rank and file alienated from its leadership. A "big, lethargic-looking German" told Stowe in imperfect English that he joined the union "to keep my job same as the others." At first he attended meetings of the union, but, he recalled, "I couldn't understand what they was talkin' about, so I finally says, 'I leave it to them as can talk and I won't go no more.' So when this trouble started I hadn't been near no meetin' for years, and I didn't know nothin' about the union." The hatter ignored the attachment of his home, because, as he figured it, "There ain't no law as can hold me responsible for things what I ain't never heard about." When Stowe explained that the law presumed that the individual defendants were principals who controlled the union's leadership, the hatter interrupted, "Well, then, if they presume that they presume just the opposite from what is the truth. Yes, we pay them, but we don't control them—they controls us!"

Another defendant had also stopped attending union meetings long before the start of the boycott. "I found that I could talk myself black in the face without anybody's paying attention. I found I had no real voice in their matters and that it was just a waste of time and breath." This hatter believed that the union was run by a "ring," and he had harsh words for then-president John Scully, whose "backing an' fillin' an' quibblin'" over settling the case was "very unmanly." "Why don't he take his medicine an' acknowledge we're beaten and try to come to terms so we can get out of it the best we can?" the hatter asked. Scully should have met regularly with the defendants; instead, the hatter complained, "He paid no more attention to us than if we was children. . . . We were never consulted about the boycott or about the trial, or about anything," he fumed.[27]

Stowe found that the defendants were enduring significant hardships as a result of the suit. A hatter who had vowed to ignore the attachment of his house finally asked to discuss the matter with local officials. He apologetically explained, "The old woman was worried about losin' her home an' wanted I should come round an' inquire." The attachments kept a second defendant, it was said, from raising the money needed to treat a tubercular daughter, who subsequently died.[28] Stowe might have come across the story of a third defendant, whose wife wrote the union that when her husband died after a year's illness, "Our savings vanished. . . . My only support was gone." She tried to lease the house, but the threat of foreclosure deterred renters. "I finally was obliged to offer it for less than half the rent as an inducement rather than close up the place."[29]

But perhaps the saddest tale involved Nathan Hoy, the man who followed William Humphries on the witness stand in the fall of 1912. Hoy was sixty-six when he testified. He had never worked for Loewe, he explained, although he had known the employer "just to speak" for twenty-five years. Like Humphries, he stopped going to union meetings well before the strike broke out. He denied that he was an active member of the United Hatters: "I never considered myself really a member of anything that I couldn't have my say in when there was a meeting going on." When Merritt asked why Hoy had taken no steps to defend himself after Loewe filed suit, the hatter replied that he had left the matter "entirely to those that caused the trouble. I hadn't caused the trouble."

Merritt then turned to the task of establishing that Hoy had personal knowledge of the boycott. He first asked Hoy if he recalled receiving the circular Loewe sent out threatening suit. Hoy could not, nor, he testified, could "the lady of the house." Merritt then inquired whether Hoy had seen Loewe's notice in the Danbury *News*. Once again, the old hatter was uncertain. "There is somebody that is connected with me that likes to get the paper first," he explained, "and if I get the paper first, it is stale news to her. Consequently, I sit down and smoke while she reads it to me."[30]

Five years later, the "somebody connected" to Hoy wrote the United Hatters for help in making repairs to her home. "Mr. Hoy having full confidence in your promises took your advice and let the property run down and I am left with it on my hands in a deplorable condition," Mrs. Hoy explained. Her house was the least of her troubles. Far greater was her loss of "the best of husbands through this attachment. The Dr says the worry and injustice was the first cause of the disease that resulted in his death."[31]

Stowe fully appreciated the hardships suffered by the "innocent, industrious, frugal, and elderly" workmen of Danbury. But the culprit eluded him. He recognized that Loewe was no corporate tyrant. In Danbury, Stowe reported, "business is still done in comparatively small units, so that the average employer knows his men personally, knows their families and their affairs, and calls them by their first name." Loewe himself seemed to be on good terms with the union men of the town, including the very men whose homes were under attachment. "Who is to blame?" Stowe asked. "What is to blame?"[32]

Stowe and his editor Abbott were not willing to vilify Loewe for insisting on the few departures from industrywide working conditions needed to keep his firm afloat. Further, although Abbott attacked the secondary boycott, both he and Stowe saw the hatters as honorable men whose suffering grew out of a condition they could not effectively alter, the legal status of their union. The solution to the predicament, the two believed, was for the law to treat unions as the corporate bodies they had in fact become. "Should not labor unions be incorporated so as to prevent suits against individual members," Stowe asked, "just as employers incorporate to protect their stockholders?"[33]

Unions, Markets, and Personality

Stowe's reflections on the Danbury hatters' case joined a debate on the incorporation of trade unions dating to the early 1880s. At that time business unionists favored legislation providing for voluntary incorporation to ensure that their growing organizations could own property, sue for breach of contract, or recover funds embezzled by wayward officials. The result was the O'Neill Act of 1886, which permitted trade unions to incorporate in the District of Columbia. Few unions took advantage of the statute, however, as many discovered that courts would permit labor leaders to sue on their own behalf or under legislation permitting suit by voluntary associations in their common name.[34]

In the interim, the AFL's leaders became increasingly concerned that incorporation would make it easier for antiunion employers to recover damages for strikes and boycotts. When incorporation again surfaced in congressional debates leading up to the passage of the Erdman Act of 1898, Gompers declared it "inimical to the interest of labor and destructive of labor and organizations." As he later elaborated, "When the whole history of jurisprudence has been against the laborer," it would be foolhardy for organized labor to make itself more amenable to suit. Moreover, it would upset the fundamental basis for trade unionism as Gompers understood it. Trade unions were "the free, basic and natural" outgrowth of modern industrial conditions. Their leaders merely expressed the spontaneous "judgment of each and all" of its members. Incorporation would create a distinct personality that owed its existence not to the workers but to the state. It would reduce unions to the mere agents of the state and those who controlled it.[35]

For all their differences, Daniel Davenport shared Gompers's ideal of the union as a private, voluntary association of autonomous, rights-bearing workers. In May 1915, at a hearing of the United States Commission on Industrial Relations, Davenport surprised the commissioners by opposing mandatory incorporation. He noted that immunity of unions and other unincorporated associations extended only to suits for damages. Labor injunctions, the preferred remedy of the employer, were always available, because equity courts allowed plaintiffs to name labor leaders as representatives of the entire union. Even in damage suits, Davenport pointed out, several states had enacted laws allowing suits against the union in its own name.[36] And under the common law of agency in all states individual members of the union were personally responsible for the acts of officers done within the scope of their duties, a point underscored by Holmes's recent decision. "The effect of incorporation would be to relieve the individual members from responsibility," Davenport explained, "but in doing that, of course, they would have to come under Government supervision." On this question Davenport "would come around to the same view" as Gompers. The employment relation was a private affair, and courts stepped in only when the natural rights of the parties had been infringed.[37]

Both Gompers and Davenport took for granted a rigid distinction between private voluntary associations and public corporate bodies. Both assumed individuals existed prior to, and subsequently constituted, civil society and the state. Private individuals could associate for their mutual benefit, but they had to respect the liberty of dissenters within their ranks. To permit a majority within a voluntary association to bind a dissenting minority would be to endow a private group with some of the sovereign's coercive power over its subjects. The association would become an *imperium in imperio*—a faction, in the language of civic humanism. In contrast, a majority of the members of an incorporated body could lawfully bind the minority. By obtaining a charter from the state, the association not only acquired a portion of the sovereign's power, but it also assumed the status of a public body and subjected itself to regulation in the public interest.[38]

The reception of German historicism into American social scientific and legal thought produced an alternate, organic theory of the group. The individuals of the new theorists were not the autonomous creators of society, but realized their identity as part of a preexisting group, institution, or "going concern."[39] The mores and interests of the group were not so much imposed on individuals as they were an inherent part of their nature. The judge who upheld the right to strike for the closed shop or otherwise treated trade unions as corporate bodies was not subverting the liberty of individual workers. The workers' liberty never extended to acts that jeopardized the collective interest of the group.

The new theorists never lost sight of the possibility that claims of group solidarity could mask the self-aggrandizement of the union's leadership—particularly after the sensational exposés of graft in the New York City building trades in 1904. Moreover, they were aware that the claims of the group could conflict with the overriding welfare of the public. Most, however, believed that the abuses of trade unionism were less significant than the evils of cut-throat competition in unorganized industries. They favored incorporation not so much to make unions more accountable as to affirm their legitimacy and to incorporate them into the body politic.

The historian Edward P. Cheyney produced an early and remarkable example of a historicist approach to trade unionism in 1889. The judges of the Great Upheaval condemned any labor combination for the closed shop as a violation of the liberty of contract of the nonunion worker. The judges analyzed the cases in the categorical terms of the *sic utere* maxim: Workers must not use their own rights so as to injure others. Cheyney, in contrast, thought the cases presented a question of degree, "what amount of pressure upon an individual workman by a combination of workmen" made the combination unlawful. The answer could not be deduced from first principles; it could only be settled from "a broad social point of view." He sought a balance between providing individuals "the utmost freedom of action" and ensuring that efforts to form trade unions not founder on "the passive resistance of a few who, from selfishness or obstinacy or even, more worthily, from a love of independence or a difference in judgment, refuse to combine with the great mass of those with whom their interests are identical."[40]

Historicist defenders of trade unions reprised and elaborated upon Cheyney's arguments during the rise of the open-shop movement. Edwin R. A. Seligman, a political scientist at Columbia University and an active participant in the work of the National Civic Federation (NCF), was a noteworthy example. Human life "is the life of man in society," Seligman wrote. "Individual existence moves within the framework of the social structure and is modified by it." Individual liberty was not the absolute right to do what one willed, considered in the abstract, but the freedom to serve the collective interest. What the open-shop leaders overlooked, according to Seligman, was that liberty was a means, rather than an end in itself. If granting individual workers the right to make their own contracts would advance the welfare of the whole, safeguarding the right of dissenting workers was appropriate. Too often, however, open-shop leaders like the

NAM's David Parry argued not for true freedom, but for "the subjection of the oppressed." In industries like the garment trades of New York City, "a certain sacrifice of that 'liberty of the individual' which Mr. Parry regards as of supreme importance" was necessary to promote the workers' collective interest in better wages and working conditions and the public interest in the intelligence and welfare of the citizenry.[41]

The economists, capitalists, and financiers associated with the NCF had a more specific vision of how treating trade unions as corporate bodies would advance the public good. These corporate liberals argued that the rise of concentrated, capital-intensive industries at the turn of the century made the classical model of competitive markets obsolete. That model might have described a commercial economy, in which capital was relatively mobile and could readily shift to meet new demands. But where capital was a fixed cost, industrialists preferred to keep their plants operating at a loss rather than incur the greater expense of halting or dismantling their operations. This led them to take steps to keep production stable by limiting access to needed raw materials, for example, or by setting their prices low enough to avoid attracting competition. By 1900 prominent economists like Arthur Hadley, Jeremiah Jenks, and Jenks's student Dana Durand converted the common sense of the capitalists into a theoretical defense of administered markets. The capitalists' control of the market promised to lessen the frequency and severity of depressions and stabilize the employment of capital and labor, "a progressive advance" over industrial conditions under proprietary capitalism.[42]

Economists who propagated this "new thinking" about markets found a role for trade unions—as a source of predictability and stability—that had no counterpart in classical economics. Cheyney glimpsed the rationale in 1889. In the long run, he wrote, trade unions have "been an element of stability, not of disturbance in industrial society." The tendency of trade unionism was to make "wages a fixed factor in the cost of production" and thereby limit the "variation, change, [and] disturbance" that characterized proprietary capitalism.[43]

A decade later, Jenks, Durand, John R. Commons, and other economists revised Cheyney's views in light of the rise of large, oligopolistic firms in several "trustified" industries. At first they ventured that the trusts might find it useful to recognize unions and pass along the cost of industrial peace to consumers. As late as 1900, Jenks, for example, still considered it an open question whether the great corporations had delivered "the death blow" to trade unions. The steel industry's war on the Amalgamated Association of Iron, Steel and Tin Workers the following year resolved the doubts of most observers. Thereafter, a cartel of a few industrialists organized around a strong union's control of skilled labor, such as the glass industry, increasingly seemed exceptional.[44]

The fate of the unions in concentrated, mass production industries did nothing to diminish the corporate liberals' enthusiasm for collective bargaining with employers who were too disorganized to taste the delights of administered markets. In industries where capitalists could not prevent the entry of new firms and skilled labor was a substantial component of production costs, trade agreements enforced by strong national unions could create the same control over supply that giant firms in concentrated industry enjoyed. If organized labor at least tacitly abandoned the goal of organizing the work force of the great corporations, corporate managers could join economists like Jenks, Commons, and Seligman in urging collective bargaining upon employers in competitive industries. Such an "entente" was midwifed by the NCF, which established a conciliation department in late 1900 to promote the stabilization of wages through trade agreements.[45]

This notion of the merits of trade unionism gave a distinctive cast to the corporate liberals' arguments in favor of incorporating trade unions. Although most commentators on incorporation dwelt upon the importance of making unions liable for their tortious conduct during strikes and boycotts, corporate liberals were concerned with making unions responsible for their collective bargaining agreements.[46] "While a labor contract might be enforced against the employer, who is usually a man of financial responsibility," the report of the United States Industrial Commission explained, "it cannot be so readily enforced against the workingmen." The responsibility of workers "might be greatly increased by the incorporation of labor organizations, while at the same time such incorporation would give those organizations a more satisfactory standing before the courts in forcing employers to live up to their agreements."[47]

Advocates of incorporation among corporate liberals met some opposition from those who doubted that combinations of employers and employees could be trusted with the power to set prices. In 1903 Harvard law professor Eugene Wambaugh called the incorporation of trade unions "unnecessary, inappropriate, and dangerous." Workers who once restrained "the vast power of combinations of capitalists" would be controlled by a handful of leaders and unite with employers to soak the consumer. "Unquestionably the alliance would mean an increase in wages," Wambaugh warned, "and unquestionably it would mean a still greater increase in prices."[48]

Notwithstanding such objections, corporate liberals struggled to find some way to create a contractual partner for disorganized capitalists without subjecting unions to the tort suits of industrial renegades like James Van Cleave. The Industrial Commission, for example, hoped for "some special form of incorporation which should restrict the liability of incorporated unions so that it should exist only as regards to contracts relating to conditions of labor." In the interim, however, trade unionists within the AFL opposed incorporation. Trade agreements must rest "merely upon honor," John Mitchell's lawyer maintained before the Anthracite Coal Strike Commission. This was sufficient, Gompers later added, because "there are few, exceedingly few, of the unions of labor . . . who violate the terms of their agreements. In truth, those who violate agreements between organized workmen and employers usually are the employers." The two men's objections effectively prevented incorporation from becoming the official policy of the NCF.[49]

INCORPORATION AND CITIZENSHIP

While Jenks, Hadley, and their associates were making a utilitarian case for the incorporation of trade unions, a group of reform-minded lawyers and law professors endorsed it on different and sometimes incompatible grounds. Like the economists, the lawyers rejected Davenport's and Gompers's voluntarist theory of the trade union, believed incorporation would encourage more employers to enter into trade agreements, and argued that the spread of industrywide collective bargaining would help eradicate intolerable working conditions in competitive industries. The lawyers differed from the economists in two respects. First, they were more concerned about making unions responsible for their torts. Second, they were more likely to see the ultimate value of trade unions as the uplift and assimilation of the immigrants whose long hours and "un-American" living standards kept them from becoming good citizens of the Republic. And they were just as concerned about the citizen-workers of United States Steel as they were about the toilers in the sweatshops of New York City's clothing trades.

The most prominent legal advocate of incorporation during the first decade of the twentieth century was Louis D. Brandeis, then a brilliant lawyer with a substantial clientele among Massachusetts's proprietary capitalists. In a public debate with Samuel Gompers in 1902, Brandeis surprised those who knew him only as a lawyer for employers and trade associations with his thoughtful and sincere praise of the labor movement. Trade unionism, Brandeis declared, subordinated "the interests of the individual to that of the class," a claim Davenport might have seconded. But what Davenport denounced, Brandeis celebrated as "essentially noble" and "the spirit of brotherhood—a near approach to altruism." Trade unions had occasionally sacrificed individuals to the greater good of the movement, Brandeis conceded, but they had also brought higher wages, improved working conditions, and checks on child labor, which more than offset the excesses of organized labor. "The trade unions have done this, not for the workmen alone," Brandeis lectured, "but for all of us; since the conditions under which so large a part of our fellow citizens work and live will determine, in great measure, the future of our country for good and evil."[50]

Brandeis's praise for strikers as "heroes of peace" was in sharp contrast with Harvard president Charles W. Eliot's widely noted defense of the strikebreaker as "a creditable type of nineteenth century hero."[51] Gompers himself was pleased by the lawyer's "splendid tribute" to the trade-union movement. But the two parted company over Brandeis's belief that incorporation was needed to make unions "more deliberate, less arbitrary, and more patient with the trammels of a civilized community." Make unions responsible members of the community, Brandeis claimed, and the employers' "deep-rooted sense of injustice, arising from the feeling that . . . the union holds a position of legal irresponsibility" would disappear. By becoming amenable to law, the labor leaders would remove a major obstacle to collective bargaining. They would also show they were "in full sympathy with the spirit of the people, whose political system rests upon the proposition that this is a government of law, and not of men."[52]

In the following years Brandeis would further elaborate his argument that the community needed unions "to raise the level of the citizen."[53] Through his work for a client in the shoe industry and the national and New England civic federations he learned to defend production-stabilizing agreements among small firms in much the same terms as the corporate liberals. "The great aim of the manufacturer must be to run his factory full all the time," Brandeis told the Boston Central Labor Union in 1905. "Many factories can only earn their profit if they do." But he also argued that steady employment would end the enforced idleness responsible for the bad habits and wastefulness of many workers.[54] Brandeis's efforts to publicize the "Protocols of Peace," a system of collective bargaining he helped establish in the garment industry of New York, similarly mixed the language of the corporate liberals with concern for the character and intelligence of the individual worker. "We can never secure real efficiency without a full development of the individual," he told readers of an early personnel journal. "We must remove not only the conscious discontent but give the working man that development of his powers which comes only from freedom and sharing in the responsibilities of business."[55]

Other influential legal theorists and reformers followed Brandeis in demanding that trade unions be treated as corporate bodies. In 1916, for example, the English political scientist Harold Laski wrote in the pages of *Harvard Law Review* that humans were "essentially . . . associative" animals, that their nature was largely determined by their group relationships, and that courts could safely treat voluntary associations like corporations if that was what social welfare required. Although British trade unionists denounced the *Taff Vale* decision of 1901, which made unincorporated trade unions suable under a statute granting them the right to register and own property, Laski considered the decision "a vital advance" over the common law because it ensured that unions would be responsible for their wrongs.[56]

Undoubtedly the most influential devotee of Brandeis was his protégé Felix Frankfurter. As head of the War Labor Policy Board, Frankfurter saw firsthand that economic planning required well-organized unions directed by a strong national executive. He was particularly impressed with Sidney Hillman, whose union, the Amalgamated Clothing Workers of America, had taken on the task of organizing central and southern European immigrants slighted by the AFL. When in 1920 an employer in Rochester, New York, enjoined the ACWA for mounting a strike for the closed shop, Frankfurter answered Hillman's call for help, "not for the sake of the Amalgamated, but because public issues are involved." To advertise the public benefits of industrial unionism, Frankfurter assembled a strong litigation team and drafted the labor economist Leo Wolman to prepare exhibits on working conditions in the clothing trades. Although the presiding judge refused to admit Wolman's work into evidence, Hillman's lengthy testimony established the many ways in which the Amalgamated had "guarded" the interests of the industry. Although the case was ultimately decided on a narrow ground, Frankfurter still looked back on the trial with satisfaction. "I believe that was the beginning of unions' realizing that union efforts aren't merely a parading with placards and such like, but . . . depended upon intelligent direction."[57]

Such activities established Frankfurter's reputation among the open-shop lawyers as a dangerous liberal with "advanced views on labor's place in the social organism." Yet neither Frankfurter's support of industrial unionism nor his later attacks on the labor injunction implied support for Gompers's voluntarism. Like most other progressives, Frankfurter rejected arguments for "collective laissez faire" just as strongly as he rejected the individualistic laissez-faire of liberty-of-contract judges. An advocate of social engineering through lawsuits and governmental agencies, he argued that the law must take the collective nature of trade unions as an established social fact, and he insisted that group rights, no less than individual rights, were subject to the overriding interest of the commonweal.[58]

Frankfurter spelled out his views in commentary on the Supreme Court's *Coronado Coal Company* decision of 1922. In an opinion joined by Brandeis and Holmes, Chief Justice William Howard Taft found that the United Mine Workers of America was a legal person under the federal antitrust laws and could be sued for damages for torts committed during a strike. Like Brandeis, Taft praised trade unions and thought their place within the American polity was secured beyond question. Yet he also believed that only suits against unions in their corporate capacity could provide an effective check on these powerful institutions.[59]

Before *Coronado* was announced, Frankfurter had gone out of his way to urge judges to see labor disputes as part of a "matrix of the industrial struggle," in which the conditions of employment in one firm might well undermine the standards of life for union members elsewhere.[60] But when Gompers denounced *Coronado* as the decisive victory of employers in their campaign for the incorporation of trade unions, Frankfurter defended it in the *New Republic*. By various interpretive devices, Frankfurter observed, state courts were already recognizing that the trade union was a collective entity responsible for its trade agreements and torts. Organized labor ought not resist this legal "adjustment to reality" simply because it subjected unions to the uncertainties of litigation. "That is a risk which every one runs." Organized labor should stop claiming to be beyond the reach of law. "Complete immunity for all conduct is too great an immunity to confer upon any group." The proper response to *Coronado,* according to Frankfurter, was "not to deny the fact that a trade union *is,* but to work out the legal scope of its activities."[61]

THE RESPONSIBLE GROUP

Thus, as *Loewe v. Lawlor* ground on toward its conclusion, observers became increasingly troubled by what they saw as a gap between legal theory, grounded in a voluntarist notion of the trade union, and a reality in which workers were organized into groups with corporate personalities of their own. To paraphrase Laski: What Davenport called justice, progressive reporters and editors like Stowe and Abbott, corporate liberals like Jenks, and legal reformers like Brandeis and Frankfurter considered a chaotic and illogical muddle. None of the reformers thought the solution to the confusion lay in Gompers's voluntarism, which, they believed, disingenuously denied that trade unions were corporate bodies legally accountable for their collective wrongs. Their solution was pluralist: Grant trade unions a legal status unknown to Victorian America, but regulate them in the public interest, as measured by the social consequences of their actions.[62]

In the decade after *Coronado,* state courts finally worked out common-law grounds for treating unions' leaders as the real parties to trade agreements.[63] Long before then, a pluralist theory of labor relations was influencing labor legislation and the common law of sympathetic strikes. The next chapter turns to the AFL's fight for an "exemption" from the federal antitrust laws. For all their heated exchanges in congressional hearings, Davenport and Gompers saw the issue as a matter of recognizing the inherent, a priori rights of individuals. Although each man found like-minded supporters within Congress, each also saw their arguments restated in pluralist and consequentialist terms. These figures took the collective power of trade unions for granted, but they differed sharply on the costs and benefits of AFL trade unionism and whether the courts were the best policymakers in the field of industrial disputes. The most prominent statements of the pluralist case for the trade union came from the political economist Henry R. Seager, who taught with Seligman at Columbia University, and the insurgent Senator Albert B. Cummins, who played a leading role in shaping the antitrust legislation of 1914. The most prominent statements of a pluralist and consequentialist case against the trade union came from an unexpected quarter—from within the AABA itself. As Daniel Davenport aired the old arguments against selfish factions and "class legislation" in Washington, back in New York his young associate Walter Gordon Merritt argued against the labor exemption from premises that had more in common with progressive reformers than the founders of the AABA.

NINE

Magna Carta

There is no question here whether labor unions should be regulated or not. Labor unions equally with any other large bodies of men should be kept subject to the whole people.

—Lyman Abbott (1914)

"Gentlemen, to-day, as has been the fact for more than five years, the organizations of working people exist at the whim, the fancy, or the mercy of any administration." With these words Samuel Gompers explained why, in December 1913, he was asking Congressman Henry Clayton's Judiciary Committee to exempt organized labor from the reach of the federal antitrust laws. When Woodrow Wilson signed the Clayton Act into law ten months later, Gompers hailed the measure as "the Magna Carta upon which the working people will rear their structure of industrial freedom." He especially praised section 6 of the statute, which announced that "the labor of a human being is not a commodity or article of commerce." By proclaiming the "absolute right of man to ownership of himself and his labor power," Gompers declared, Congress uttered the most important statement ever made by any legislative body in the history of the world.[1]

Daniel Davenport thought otherwise. Throughout the summer of 1914 he and James Emery had vigilantly lobbied against the bill. Davenport denounced the version adopted by the House on June 5, but he was confident that subsequent changes made by the Senate Judiciary Committee kept the bill from hampering the AABA's litigation under federal antitrust law. The Supreme Court gave tentative support to Davenport's views in dicta in an AABA-sponsored suit, *Paine Lumber Company v. Neal* (1917). Then, over a dissent by Justices Brandeis, Holmes, and John H. Clarke, a majority of the court unambiguously adopted Davenport's reading in another AABA case, *Duplex Printing Press Company v. Deering* (1921). "O Liberty, Liberty! how many crimes are committed in thy name," Gompers wailed. The AABA, in contrast, saw *Duplex* as a decisive rebuke to organized labor's efforts "to become a class apart, exempt from the legal restraints to which other citizens are subject."[2]

The spin-doctoring of Gompers and Davenport provides at best a starting point for understanding the "enigma" of the Clayton Act. Both men explained the statute in terms of the absolute rights of autonomous individuals. Gompers equated it with a great landmark of Anglo-American constitutionalism, and Davenport pilloried Gompers's congressional supporters for renouncing "the Jeffersonian maxim of equal rights for all and special privileges for none."[3]

Neither man was much disposed to see the Clayton Act as a typical example of interest-group politics. Since 1906 both sides had tested and perfected mechanisms for mobilizing their constituency and making their views known to key congressmen. In 1914 the result was what subsequent political theorists would have predicted.[4] Rather than risk alienating voters by taking a strong stand, the Senate Judiciary Committee produced an ambiguous statute that permitted both sides to claim victory. Who in fact won would be known only when the federal judiciary interpreted the act. In effect, Congress delegated the decision about organized labor's status under the antitrust laws to the courts.

Interpreting the Clayton Act as Gompers and Davenport did would also obscure the ways in which debate on the measure was a crossroads of old and new thinking about groups, the legislative process, and the regulatory state. The origins of that debate go back to February 1908, when Chief Justice Fuller's decision in *Loewe* galvanized Gompers into joining an NCF-sponsored movement to revise the Sherman Act. The "Hepburn Bill" ultimately failed of passage, but not before generating a revealing debate about the costs and benefits of administering markets through industry-wide collective bargaining agreements. In 1910 the insurgent Republicans' revolt against Speaker Joseph Cannon and the election of a Democratic majority and a "labor bloc" in the House upset the strict party discipline that kept the AFL's bills bottled up in committee. Thereafter, the pace of the debate and of lobbying by the AFL, AABA, and NAM quickened. The federal executive, too, became a target for lobbying, as first Taft and then Wilson neither attacked unions under the antitrust laws nor renounced their power to do so.

What emerged in the Senate debates on the labor provisions of the Clayton Act was nothing like a singular "intent" of the legislature. Senator William R. Hughes of New Jersey, a leader of the labor bloc, made sure of that. Even without Hughes's efforts, the senators took conflicting positions on the status of organized labor under the antitrust laws, the costs and benefits of industrywide collective bargaining, and the nature and legitimacy of labor boycotts. Notwithstanding these areas of difference, most senators agreed that trade unions and many forms of collective bargaining were in the public interest, that most forms of secondary boycotting and sympathetic strikes exceeded the proper limits of group interest, and that legislators were free to distinguish between business and labor combinations when empirical conditions warranted. In conceding the legitimacy of groups but insisting on their regulation, in seeking a middle way between the individual and the class, in rejecting a priori classification for consequentialism, Congress, like the common-law courts, helped fashion a pluralist law of industrial disputes.

The Outlawry of Organized Labor?

Fuller's decision in *Loewe v. Lawlor* crystallized Gompers's growing fears over the status of organized labor under the law. "The more thought I gave it," he wrote shortly after the decision was announced, "the broader its scope and character appeared." On February 24, 1908, he told a House committee that the implications of *Loewe* went far beyond the secondary boycott. Gompers noted that Chief Justice Fuller repeated Davenport's allegations that the United Hatters' sought to drive nonunion firms from the industry. Gompers asserted that Fuller intended to make the goal of industrywide collective bargaining unlawful under the Sherman Act's prohibition of conspiracies and combinations in restraint of trade. If having this goal was enough to make a labor combination unlawful, Gompers reasoned, then all AFL unions were in violation of the federal antitrust statute. Thus, as he told Senate President Charles Fairbanks and House Speaker Joseph Cannon the following month, "It is indeed true that under the decision our very organized existence is unlawful."[5]

Gompers's conclusion that *Loewe* outlawed organized labor was challenged immediately. "Our war has not been against labor organizations, but against the boycott," protested James Beck. Many newspaper editors followed the AABA lawyer. The Hartford *Daily Courant* called Gompers's reading of *Loewe* "a singular but apparently intentional perversion of fact." Why would Gompers intentionally misread the decision, making its holding more threatening to the labor movement than it really was? To build public support for legislation exempting organized labor from the Sherman Act, the newspapers concluded. In short, as the Buffalo *Commercial* maintained, "What Mr. Gompers means to do, under cover of this misrepresentation, is to justify the boycott as a means of punishing employers who do not accede to the demands of organized labor." Gompers sought not the legitimation of the collective power of organized labor, but the freedom to use and abuse that power as he saw fit.[6]

On the narrow question of the scope of the holding in *Loewe,* the AABA and the newspaper editors reached the better conclusion under the canons of judicial reasoning prevailing at the time. Fuller's discussion of the proposed United Hatters' campaign was not necessary to his reasoning, which turned on the lawfulness of the means the United Hatters used, the distributor-targeted secondary boycott. The headnotes to the case, drafted by the court reporter and approved by the justices, did not even mention the extent of collective bargaining in the hatting industry. The remarks that alarmed Gompers were mere dicta and not binding on subsequent courts.[7]

But Gompers's alarm becomes understandable when considered in light of contemporaneous common-law decisions, Gompers's lack of formal legal training, and his unwillingness to accept unwelcome advice from legal experts. ("I am not learned in the law," he once confessed, "that is, I am not a lawyer; but I do think there are some lawyers who are similarly situated.")[8] Recall that Gompers was very familiar with Judge Adams's controversial opinion in *Christensen v. Kellogg Switchboard and Supply* (1903), decided in part on the grounds that the closed shop was an unlawful purpose under the conspiracy doctrine. Recall as well that a sweeping injunction issued under the conspiracy doctrine by Judge Holdom in 1905 helped convince Gompers to lead the AFL into politics in 1906. Justice Gould's injunction in the *Buck's Stove* case brought the threat to Gompers's doorstep in December 1907. Now, in February 1908, *Loewe* had unambiguously held that the Sherman Act reached organized labor. By doing this, Gompers reasoned, the Supreme Court had federalized the conspiracy doctrine, made the AABA's case against industrywide collective bargaining the law of the land, and authorized the Department of Justice to proceed against labor unions anywhere in the country.

Gompers's reasoning was open to devastating objections in that it overlooked the antitrust doctrine of ancillary restraints and constitutional doctrine on the limits of the commerce power. Further, Gompers did not take account of the waning influence of the conspiracy doctrine and the growing acceptance of the consequentialist theory of intentional torts. In this, however, Gompers was indeed "similarly situated" with many lawyers, including Daniel Davenport and a state trial judge who ordered a national trade union dissolved under the common law of conspiracy just ten days before *Loewe* was announced.

Kealey v. Faulkner was brought in an Ohio court in late 1907 by a faction of the Amalgamated Window Glass Workers of America. Since the 1880s the various branches of the glass workers had won a series of industrywide closed-shop agreements that closely regulated the workplace. The

unions' control over skilled labor was so tight that they successfully limited the entry of new firms into the industry. The glass manufacturers' earlier attempts to establish a cartel on their own invariably broke down, but
prices, profits, and wages stayed high once the union enforced limitations
on production.[9]

The mechanization of important steps in the production process after
the turn of the century threatened to upset this peaceable kingdom. Production jumped, and prices and wages fell precipitously. In the midst of
the resulting chaos, cutters and flatteners, two of the four trades in the
industry, sought to wrest control of the Amalgamated from the blowers and
gatherers, who were most affected by the new machines. To bring the organization down, the cutters and flatteners asked an Ohio court to review
the Amalgamated's bylaws, which, their lawyers claimed, made the union
a menace to the public welfare.

George L. Phillips (1844–1921) was then in the midst of a long tenure
as judge of the court of common pleas. His guiding principle, according
to a eulogist, "was to do justly, and to love mercy, and to walk humbly with
his God." In an opinion given orally on December 26, 1907, Phillips reviewed the union's bylaws and found that they established a closed shop,
limited the number of glassworkers employed by a firm, regulated the pace
and methods of production, and compelled employers to hire union "boss
cutters." Measured against the requirements of "distributive justice," Phillips found the bylaws wanting. They violated the fundamental postulate that
every person "is perfectly free to bring his capital, or his labor, into the
market on such terms as he may deem best," he announced. Public policy
not only encouraged the formation of trade unions, but it also forbid them
from impairing employers' rights to conduct business as they saw fit. The
bylaws also placed individual workers in "complete servility" to the union's
leadership. "Every member of this body has surrendered his individuality,
and his industrial freedom, and is no longer a personal factor in the world,"
the judge concluded. "This is violative of fundamental personal rights, and
of public rights, and is therefore unlawful."[10]

Phillips then had to decide what relief, if any, to grant the cutters and
flatteners, erstwhile participants in the Amalgamated's monopoly. He ruled
that under the "clean hands" doctrine the rival faction was not entitled to
any relief. Then, citing another equity doctrine, the judge announced he
would proceed in the interest of the public and grant such relief as promoted the public good. On January 24, 1908, he decided that "fairness and
reason" required him to dissolve the union and distribute its funds to its
members.[11]

Gompers did not refer to *Kealey* in his public statements in the immediate aftermath of *Loewe*, but by December 1913 it had become his favorite

example of the danger that organized labor faced under anticonspiracy and antitrust laws.[12] Long before then Gompers had joined corporate liberals associated with the NCF in seeking legislation to revise the Sherman Act, which, as the justices reaffirmed in *Loewe*, proscribed "every" conspiracy in restraint of trade. The industrial freedom and unrestricted competition Phillips championed was, for Gompers, an apology for "gradgrinds, who are always trying to nibble at the wages and conditions of workmen." For the NCF leaders, it was a prescription for financial ruin and industrial chaos.[13]

THE QUARREL IN CONGRESS, 1908

Loewe was decided just as the NCF was finalizing legislation to loosen the strictures of the Sherman Act and to permit corporate managers to set and maintain reasonable prices and production levels in their industries. In 1907 Secretary Ralph Easley and President Seth Low brought together procorporation economists like Jeremiah Jenks and Arthur Hadley, prominent corporation lawyers like James Beck, Francis Lynde Stetson, and Victor Morawetz, and other figures in a series of conferences, luncheons, and drafting sessions. In early 1908 William P. Hepburn of Iowa introduced the result in the House. The bill required business corporations to register with the federal Bureau of Corporations and submit detailed information on its governance, structure, and finances. Registered corporations could then submit their contracts to the bureau for review. If the bureau found them to be "in unreasonable restraint of trade or commerce among the several States," it could declare that fact; otherwise, the federal executive would be barred from prosecuting the corporation for entering into an unlawful agreement. Trade unions could register with a much less detailed filing and also receive immunity for agreements submitted to the bureau and found not to restrain trade unreasonably.[14]

As the historian Martin Sklar observes, the measure was far less than the AFL leaders sought. "The exemption was not outright," Sklar notes, "but contingent upon registration, although a perfunctory one, and it still did not exempt 'unreasonable' or 'unfair' contracts or agreements, including the boycott."[15] Still Gompers, Mitchell, and Alton Parker cooperated with Easley, who did his best to be conciliatory. When it appeared that open-shop leaders would attend the NCF's conference on trusts in November 1907, for example, Easley passed on to Louis Brandeis the labor leaders' request that the reformer "wipe up the floor, so to speak, with Van Cleave, Parry and Post." But Easley never attempted to legalize the secondary boycott, well aware of the opposition the effort would generate from President Theodore Roosevelt and a majority of Congress. Given these political considerations, Gompers told Easley, the AFL leaders would publicly support the bill's provisions for business corporations but go further and ask for an outright exemption of labor unions. "In the end," Easley reported to an associate, "they will support our bill as the best that they can secure at this time."[16]

Hearings on the Hepburn bill opened in early April before a three-person subcommittee chaired by the AFL's nemesis, Charles E. Littlefield. Shorter hearings before a Senate committee commenced later that month. Davenport, James Emery, and George F. Monaghan of the National Founders' Association presented themselves in opposition to the measure and nominated Davenport their leader. Seth Low and Jeremiah Jenks took the most active role in defending the bill.

The hearings produced revealing testimony of the meaning of the *Loewe* decision, the nature of collective bargaining, and the extent to which Congress could legitimately differentiate among groups in its legislation. Gompers argued that *Loewe* did not simply prohibit distributor-targeted secondary boycotts but outlawed a fundamental aim of trade unionism. "The court in its decision takes . . . the successful cooperation of the employers with the employees to maintain industrial peace as the evidence that these combinations or agreements are in restraint of trade." Because all AFL unions sought to standardize hours, wages, and working conditions throughout their industries, all of them violated the Sherman Act as interpreted in *Loewe*. Davenport professed amazement at Gompers's "misconstruction and misconception" of the decision. "There is nothing in that decision that prevents laboring men . . . from bargaining collectively with their employers," Davenport maintained, "nothing that prevents them from making agreements, such as he mentioned, with the employers."[17]

Even Gompers's allies in the NCF sided with Davenport on this issue. At one point during testimony before the Senate committee, Low and Davenport jointly compiled reasons why the Sherman Act could not reach a trade agreement between an employer and a union. Low thought the commerce power could not support federal suits grounded on collective bargaining agreements. "So far as such contracts relate to employment it does not seem to me that they have anything to do with interstate trade and commerce," Low testified. "Certainly if manufacture is not interstate trade or commerce, as I believe was decided in the Knight case, the labor that enters into the process of manufacture can hardly be considered interstate trade or commerce." Davenport agreed with Low and added a second reason. Agreements between employers and their workers were not a direct restraints of trade, he observed. Any effect on competition was merely ancillary to the legitimate concerns of the parties. As such, it was unexceptionable under the common law of conspiracy and the Sherman Act so long as trade unionists employed no other means to stop trade.[18]

This exchanged puzzled the lawmakers: If trade agreements were already beyond the reach of the Sherman Act, why pass a bill to declare that fact? The "necessity for such action," Low explained, "lies in a psychological condition in the minds of organized labor all over the United States at the present moment. . . . Every legal friend I have takes exactly the position that Judge Davenport and Mr. Emery take." Nevertheless, the leaders of the labor movement were convinced that the right to strike, to combine, and to make trade agreements was in jeopardy, and no "assurance from the legal fraternity would make them believe otherwise."[19]

One lawmaker, Senator Knute Nelson, was convinced that Low misstated the aims of the labor leaders. They knew they had the right to strike or to combine to raise wages, Nelson maintained. What they really sought was the legalization of the closed shop and boycott. "They have now a right to combine for higher wages and to strike. Having these two rights, what others do they want, or what others ought we to give them?" he demanded. "The right to make trade agreements with their employers," Low replied.[20]

The incident revealed a fundamental confusion about the scope and nature of the normal trade agreement. If the agreement was merely a contract between a single employer and his employees, then all conceded it was lawful at common law and under the Sherman Act. But what if the agreement was part of an attempt to establish collective bargaining throughout an entire industry? If skilled labor formed a major portion of the costs of production, the union was directed by capable and aggressive leaders, and the industry protected from foreign firms, then the agreement could be a means of regulating prices and output. The union could bar the entry of new firms (as in the glass industry), drive out marginal producers (as in the hatting industry), or blockade a local market from the goods of nonunion producers (as in the construction industry). In such instances a defense based on the commerce power would not save the contracting parties from liability under the Sherman Act, because under the *Swift* line of decisions the direct object of the trade union and employers would be to restrain interstate trade. Nor could the anticompetitive consequences of the agreement be dismissed as merely ancillary to some legitimate aim of the parties. The prevention of competition was the very end sought.[21]

Thus, Gompers's claim that *Loewe* threatened to outlaw trade unions was persuasive only insofar as his audience understood the anticompetitive consequences of industrywide trade agreements. Gompers and Davenport each presented views on the subject but left the lawmakers with no clear view of its dimensions. Gompers condemned unrestricted competition in much the same terms as the corporate liberals of the NCF, albeit with greater emphasis on the plight of the workers. Without industrywide collective bargaining, Gompers claimed, "the greatest dissatisfaction" prevailed among employers and "the greatest misery and poverty" among their employees. Dietrich Loewe, he charged, was a menace to the stability of the hatting industry. If the United Hatters could not unionize Loewe's shop, Gompers asked, how could they expect the other manufacturers in the industry to pay decent wages? Faced with the choice of forcing unionization upon Loewe or seeing unionized employers defect, the hatters had to boycott Loewe. "It was a matter of self-defense."[22]

A younger or differently educated lawyer might have objected that the stability Gompers sought came at the consumer's expense. Davenport never made such consequentialist concerns the centerpiece of his argument. Instead he maintained that legalizing trade unions' reasonable restraints of trade would violate timeless moral and economic principles. He stood squarely against revising the Sherman Act ("the very Magna Charta of commercial freedom in this country"). Further, he attacked the leading example of administered markets in the Progressive Era when he paused in his testimony to denounce a recent public statement by Elbert Gary, chair of United States Steel. Gary deigned to usurp "the sovereign regulator of the industrial world," he complained. "The price which is to be fixed shall not be fixed by competition between those who desire to purchase," Davenport fumed, "nor shall it be fixed by competition between those who desire to sell, but it shall be fixed at the sweet will and determination, actuated by the best of motives, of course, of those who have control of the product." Bad as Gary was, Davenport continued, he was no worse than that "great labor trust manager, Mr. Gompers." Both men disrupted the natural workings of supply and demand.[23]

Although the Hepburn bill did not provide organized labor with an outright exemption from the federal antitrust law, Davenport and Gompers did discuss whether such a proposal would be constitutional under the Fourteenth Amendment. Davenport insisted that a labor exemption would be an unconstitutional piece of class legislation. A majority of the Fuller Court apparently agreed. In *Connolly v. Union Sewer Pipe Company* (1902), the Court, speaking through Justice John Marshall Harlan, struck down an Illinois antitrust statute because it exempted producers of agricultural commodities from its purview. According to Harlan, the legislation did not treat all similarly situated persons "'alike under like circumstances and considerations, both in the privileges conferred, and in the limitations imposed.'" Harlan conceded that legislatures could classify persons, businesses, and associations, but he insisted that these classifications must bear a "just and proper relation" to some natural difference between the two classes. Given the universalist premises of his genteel Victorian education, Harlan could see no difference between agricultural and other combinations that justified exempting the former from the discipline of the market while leaving the latter within its reach.[24]

Davenport took a similar tack during the hearings on the Hepburn bill.

Gompers argued that exempting labor would not grant trade unionists a special privilege. It would simply treat differently two unlike things: the products of industrialists, which were commodities and a fit subject for antitrust law, and labor, which was a human attribute, inseparable from the "breathing, respiring, body and heart and brain" of the worker. "We hear so much of this equality before the law!" he exclaimed. "Well, that is really all we want." But Davenport replied that Gompers only offered "fanciful" reasons for distinguishing between capital and labor. The right to work and the right to manage were essentially similar, not different. Both were species of property requiring equal treatment.[25]

The Hepburn bill languished in committee for the rest of 1908 and finally expired in early 1909, the victim of Roosevelt's indifference once he realized it could not serve as a vehicle for strengthening presidential control over the nation's business.[26] In the five years after the Hepburn hearings the labor exemption remained controversial, thanks to an upheaval in Congress and the adoption of a new strategy by labor's supporters: writing into federal appropriation bills a provision against expending funds for prosecutions of organized labor under the Sherman Act.

FLANK MOVEMENTS

As long as Joseph Cannon presided over the House and Nelson Aldrich governed the Senate, the AFL's bills to abolish labor injunctions and exempt organized labor from the antitrust laws stayed buried in committee. By early 1911, the open-shop lobbyists lost the exuberant confidence of their early battles. Emery still maintained his sense of humor, one observer noted, but it could not mask "the bitter consciousness of losing ground." In January, Emery complained about the chaotic condition of Congress to C. W. Post. The Republican party was "more hopelessly disorganized than the Democratic Party ever has been. It has lost even the binding power of self-interest. . . . Party lines are less binding and local conditions more compelling." He feared that even "the second coming of Roosevelt" would probably not prevent the election of a Democrat in 1912.[27]

Emery was reacting to a series of upheavals in Congress. The Payne-Aldrich tariff of 1909 had fractured Senate Republicans into an Old Guard and a group of able, articulate Progressives, including Robert La Follette of Wisconsin, Albert B. Cummins of Iowa, and William E. Borah of Idaho. In 1909–10, Progressive congressmen in the House worked to overthrow Cannon's control, scoring a major victory in March 1910. That fall, with the Republican party badly divided, the Democrats gained control of the House. An ominous development for the open-shop movement was the election of fifteen trade unionists to the House of Representatives, including the former UMW official William B. Wilson, the hatter James Maher, and the textile worker William R. Hughes.[28]

The resulting House of Representatives, as Davenport handicapped it in March 1911, seemed "well-nigh hopeless." In replying to Davenport, Emery was only slightly more optimistic. He predicted a good judiciary committee—at least, "as good as we could expect from your Democratic brethren"—but he conceded the Labor Committee would be hostile to the open-shop cause. (He was accurate: Wilson was appointed chair.) "But what can we do," Emery asked, "with the Denver platform and Gompers undoubtedly a powerful influence?"[29]

Davenport and Emery were right to be concerned. Between 1910 and 1914 organized labor scored a series of significant legislative victories. In the summer of 1913, for example, with the Senate and the presidency in Democratic hands, the open-shop lawyers could not prevent an investigation of lobbying against the Underwood tariff from broadening into a sensational and damaging exposé of the legislative practices of the NAM. (Jackson Ralston's efforts to use Congress's subpoena power to breach the secrecy of the AABA failed, however.)[30] The AFL could not muster support to push an outright exemption through Congress, but the "labor bloc" ultimately succeeded in enacting a proviso that forbid any use of funds appropriated for the Department of Justice for antitrust prosecutions of organized labor.

The AFL's purpose in seeking the rider was more to keep the labor exemption on the national political agenda than to block any actual or imminent campaign from the Department of Justice. Between the *Debs* indictments of the 1890s and December 1913, federal attorneys initiated proceedings under the Sherman Act against organized labor on only six occasions. In each case the litigation was initiated by a U.S. attorney without prior authorization from Washington. Four cases—two under Republican presidents, two under the Democrat Wilson—were terminated short of trial on orders from the Department of Justice. A fifth, an indictment of Florida longshoremen in November 1911, ended in a guilty plea and a four-hour confinement for the defendants.[31] The sixth was an injunction against Chicago's electrical workers, directed by the notorious labor grafter Mike Boyle. The case was commenced during the last days of the Taft administration by U.S. Attorney James Wilkerson, the one-time associate counsel of the AABA. Wilkerson's superiors in Washington urged him to find other grounds for the suit, then relented when he assured them the union would not contest a consent decree.[32]

The first attempt to pass the rider was in response to none of these suits. On June 21, 1910, New Jersey congressman William R. Hughes, a leader of the labor caucus, offered the rider as an amendment to the sundry civil appropriations bill. Although the proviso carried in the House, it failed in the Senate, and on June 23 the House accepted the Senate bill without the measure. The following Labor Day, with congressional elections looming, President Taft attacked the attempt to limit the discretion of his Department of Justice in antitrust matters. "I have not the slightest expectation that the money will ever be used for anything but the prosecution of corporations and business firms," Taft declared; still, he denounced the proviso as consistent with "neither justice, nor wisdom, nor good statesmanship."[33]

In February 1913, after the Democrats had captured the Senate, the proviso passed both houses of Congress. On March 4 Taft vetoed the bill, calling it "class legislation of the most vicious sort." The Senate failed to override, but the new Congress repassed the proviso in April and sent it to Woodrow Wilson for his approval.

As president of Princeton University, Woodrow Wilson was much like Harvard's Charles Eliot in his mistrust of trade unionism and public pronouncements on organized labor. One interview, published in the New York *World*, may have won him an invitation to address the AABA's annual banquet. He declined, but not before proclaiming himself "a fierce partizan of the Open Shop and of all things that make for individual liberty."[34] In 1907 Wilson deplored the AFL's campaign for a labor exemption, finding it intolerable "that any class should assert its exemption from the law." During his term as New Jersey's governor, however, Wilson's respect for the labor movement grew. It was further strengthened by the AFL's efforts on his behalf during the presidential campaign in 1912.[35]

The antitrust proviso reached Wilson at a crucial juncture in congressional debates over the tariff. Wilson may have reasoned that the appropriation bill would work no fundamental change in federal policy, for although Taft had vetoed the proviso, his Department of Justice had no established tradition of prosecuting organized labor under the Sherman Act. Further, going along with Congress would keep the Democrats united during the fight over the tariff. But when Wilson publicly implied he would sign the bill with the rider attached he provoked what historian Arthur Link has called a "virtually nation-wide outpouring" against the proviso. Surprised by the vehemence of the public reaction, Wilson looked for some compromise. He settled on a public statement terming the proviso "unjustifiable in character and in principle." He claimed he would veto the proviso if he could without rejecting the entire bill and insisted that in signing the bill he was not really limiting the discretion of the Department of Justice, which could use other funds should the occasion for an antitrust suit arise.[36]

As Wilson had the sundry civil appropriations bill under consideration, the issue of labor and the Sherman Act confronted him from a different direction, the bituminous coalfields of West Virginia and Colorado. Since the nineteenth century, employers in the geographically dispersed, labor-intensive, soft-coal industry had sought ways of limiting production. Invariably, however, the lack of barriers to entry and the threat of a Sherman Act prosecution stood in their way. At the end of the nineteenth century, however, operators in the so-called Central Competitive Field (CCF) of western Pennsylvania, Ohio, Indiana, and Illinois decided the UMW could serve as an alternate means of administering prices and output in the industry. Regularly undersold by the nonunion coal fields of West Virginia and the South, the CCF operators asked the UMW to regularize labor costs throughout the industry and end the competitive advantage enjoyed by their low-wage, nonunion competitors.[37]

When pressure from UMW organizers became too great, the nonunion coal operators fought back. In large part, the employers bypassed the civilities of the courtroom for the naked force of state militias or their own armies of private detectives. The resulting industrial warfare included one of the most shocking outrages of the Progressive Era, the widely noted Ludlow Massacre of 1914.[38] But the courts, too, played a role in the coal operators' strategy, and the Sherman Act in particular was an important basis for their litigation.

The leading case was *Hitchman Coal & Coke Co. v. Mitchell*, commenced by a West Virginia firm in October 1907 to enjoin an alleged conspiracy of UMW officials and CCF operators. In December 1912, Alston G. Dayton, a federal district judge, permanently enjoined the UMW from organizing the plaintiff's workers. Since 1898, the judge charged, the UMW had sought to "restrain and even destroy" West Virginia's coal industry for the benefit of the unionized fields. A union victory would deprive consumers of the right to purchase better coal at a lower cost than that offered by the CCF operators, in violation of both the common law and the Sherman Act.[39] On June 7, 1913, with the controversy over the antitrust proviso raging, a U.S. attorney, acting without authorization from Washington, had officials of the UMW in West Virginia indicted for conspiring with the CCF operators to "fix and control prices." Attorney General McReynolds called for a full report and promptly ordered the proceedings terminated. In December a U.S. attorney in Colorado, again acting on his own initiative, obtained another set of indictments against the UWM. Once again, Washington intervened, and the proceedings were terminated short of trial.[40]

The two sets of indictments were the subject of wide public comment. The *New York Times* thought the West Virginia case revealed "about as obnoxious a conspiracy in restraint of trade as could well be imagined." In contrast, the *Chicago Tribune* believed the Colorado proceedings ought to raise "doubts and questioning in the minds of the public. . . . Should a strong union be declared a monopoly of labor, it will mean the death of trade-unionism," the newspaper ventured. The result would be a deep chasm between capital and labor.[41]

THE NEW TERMS OF DEBATE

The most interesting discussion of the indictments occurred in *The Survey*, a leading journal of social reform, in January 1914, as the hearings that produced the Clayton Act were well underway. The case for exempting organized labor from the Sherman Act was presented by Henry Rogers Seager, a member of Columbia University's economics department. As an undergraduate at the University of Michigan, Seager studied with the prominent historicist economist Henry Carter Adams, who found in the socially constructed nature of human institutions a mandate for an activist state. Seager then commenced graduate studies at the Johns Hopkins University under Richard Ely, perhaps the most outspoken reformer among the professional economists of his day. From 1891 to 1893, Seager studied first at the font of historical economics, the University of Berlin, and then at the University of Halle, the center of marginalism in economic thought. He completed his education at the University of Pennsylvania under yet another heterodox economist, Simon Patten. Together with his colleague Edwin R. A. Seligman, Seager helped make Columbia a leading center of institutional economics.[42]

Seager first published major articles on the law and labor in late 1907, as the NCF's campaign for antitrust revision was coming to a head. Like other historicist economists, Seager urged that trusts and labor unions be accepted as natural and potentially beneficial developments. They should not be abolished even if they could be, he argued, but they should be regulated to ensure they did not abuse their power. Based largely on his reading of Great Upheaval labor cases, Seager concluded that the courts could not be trusted with the job of policing industrial combinations, because the legal mind was too preoccupied with precedents and traditions to give sufficient regard to the social consequences of industrial combination. (As he later wrote, "So long as American judges must, like Judge Dayton, look to the common law for guidance as to what is lawful and what is unlawful in trade disputes, the injunctions they issue must continue to seem ill adapted to contemporary conditions or contemporary opinions of right and wrong.") In place of the courts, Seager called for the creation of a federal commission to regulate the unions and their internal affairs. He applauded the British Trade Disputes Act of 1906 for freeing labor unions from civil conspiracy suits while requiring them to register and comply with a series of internal regulations.[43]

In the wake of the Colorado indictments, Seager restated these arguments with specific reference to the Sherman Act. As he noted, part of the NCF's aims in promoting the Hepburn Act had been realized with the Supreme Court's "Rule of Reason" cases. After *Standard Oil Company v. United States* (1911) and *American Tobacco Company v. United States* (1911), only "unreasonable" restraints of trade were in violation of the act.[44] Like Louis Brandeis, Seager believed that after the decisions courts would be more willing to conclude that a given labor combination had beneficial social consequences and was therefore a "reasonable" and lawful restraint.[45] The problem for Seager was that the decisions still left the making of antitrust policy to the judiciary, which he considered ill-equipped for the task. Why should the proper limits of labor combination emerge piecemeal through adjudication, Seager asked, when "certain principles of condemnation" were already known and could be embodied in legislation? Thus, if Gompers called for a labor exemption to put the nonviolent collective action of workers beyond the reach of the state, Seager urged it as a preliminary to transferring the regulation of labor unions to an expert administrative agency.[46]

Within weeks of the publication of Seager's article, *The Survey* carried a reply by Walter Gordon Merritt. At the time, Merritt was preparing several cases for the AABA under the antitrust act, including a suit against the UMW in Arkansas and another against New York City's carpenters for refusing to handle nonunion woodtrim. Merritt argued that Seager had erred in believing that labor combinations affected only the production of commodities and not their distribution. In fact, he charged, labor unions often joined with employers in order to "block the channels of interstate commerce to fill their own pocket books." In Manhattan, for example, a combination of carpenters, their employers, and local manufacturers had driven inexpensive nonunion woodtrim from the market. "Monopoly and inflated prices are thus assured," Merritt wrote, "while employer and employé divide the spoils." He also claimed that the UMW's campaign in West Virginia was inspired and probably financed by the CCF operators. In each case, contracts between organized labor and union manufacturers were the linchpin of a monopoly. "Were the law to legalize such combinations the public would be delivered to the mercy of the monopolist more completely than ever before," he warned.[47]

As Seager acknowledged in a reply, the two men shared much common ground. Both were willing to make the social consequences and not a priori rights the ultimate test for measuring the lawfulness of a labor combination. Both recognized that strong unions could abuse their power. (In the construction trades, Seager had written in 1907, "liberty spells license.") Both insisted that the state should prevent unions from becoming "close monopolies," although Seager thought "a federal labor commission, like the federal trade commission which President Wilson is advocating" was the best agency for curbing abuses. The principal difference between the two was their understanding of the normal aims and policies of labor unions. For Merritt, overreaching by organized labor was the rule; for Seager, the exception. The economist believed the public interest had much more to gain by promoting trade unions than by policing them under the antitrust laws.[48]

Seager's response to Merritt was published as the Wilson administration turned in earnest to the task of revising the antitrust laws. On January 20, the president called on Congress to pass legislation embodying "the best business judgment of America" on the limits of fair competition. For a time, Wilson was convinced that unfair business practices could be explicitly identified and prohibited by statute. This was the approach taken by the bill Henry Clayton's House Judiciary Committee had under consideration when Samuel Gompers testified in December 1913. Wilson also urged that a commission help create policy in the area. Proposals for both "weak" commissions, empowered to investigate and publicize but not to punish unfair business practices, and "strong" ones, authorized to approve or disapprove restraints of trade, had been debated in Congress with increasing seriousness after the Rule of Reason decisions. Nowhere was the discussion more thoughtful than in the Senate's Interstate Commerce Committee, where the Democrat Francis Newlands and the progressive Republican Albert Cummins played leading roles. In the spring of 1914, as Wilson came to doubt that unfair competition was as easily defined as he had thought, he focussed his attention on proposals for a trade commission. By summer he had lost interest in the Clayton bill and was devoting his energies to pushing a "strong" commission bill through Congress.[49]

Many members of Congress who discussed labor and the antitrust laws in hearings or debate on these measures simply trotted out the a priori, individualistic arguments of Gompers and Davenport. The Democrat Henry French Hollis of New Hampshire, for example, denounced as "unjust and pathetic" a law that classed the humble wage-earner with the Standard Oil Company and the Sugar Trust, while the Republican Porter James McCumber of North Dakota argued that a labor exemption would destroy "the very life principle of our Government—equality under the law."[50] The most knowledgeable and influential figures on both sides of the question approached the subject differently. They willingly conceded that trade unions legitimately exercised collective power and agreed that social consequences provided the standard for distinguishing between good and bad labor practices. Like Seager and Merritt, they differed over whether the benefits of strong, industrywide collective bargaining outweighed its costs.

Albert Cummins perhaps best articulated the progressive position on the labor exemption. His statements echoed the arguments of institutionalist economists like Seager and Seligman, and of progressive lawyers like Ernst Freund and Brandeis. Cummins showed that historicism and pluralism were no longer the sole property of an avant-garde of academics and reformers. Although stated in less formal and abstract terms, these ideas had joined the mainstream of public debate. In the realm of public policy, as in the wider culture of middle-class Americans, "the old, rigid certainties" of the nineteenth century had been thrown on the defensive.[51]

Cummins's support for a regulatory and accommodationist approach to industrial combination encouraged the corporate liberals of the NCF to consider him an ally. (He was certainly more promising than his fellow progressive, William E. Borah, an outspoken antitruster.)[52] But Cummins's ideas on the public benefits of collective bargaining were closer to Brandeis's than to Jeremiah Jenks's or Arthur Hadley's. Viewing American industry at a distance, from an agricultural state, he took in the main lines of recent economic developments and was not limited, as were Davenport and even Merritt, by disproportionate experience with industries in which proprietary capitalism still flourished. Like Brandeis, he was most concerned about the plight of the unskilled worker in concentrated industries. A "labor trust" was an impossibility under such conditions, Cummins decided. "There is no danger, is there," he asked Lyman Abbott in 1912, "that . . . any labor organization will ever be able to raise the price of labor above a fair or reasonable price?" When Abbott agreed, Cummins observed, "Inasmuch as we make our laws to protect the people against existing or impending evils, and inasmuch as we know there is no danger that the laboring man of this country will ever get what actually belongs to him, there is no use protecting against their organizations."[53]

During the Senate's debate of the Clayton Act in 1914 Cummins used data from the 1910 census to support his position that workers were, on average, too poorly paid to "discharge their duties as citizens. . . . There is a potential competition always confronting wageworkers that will inevitably reduce the compensation far below the point at which it should in equity and in good conscience rest," he maintained. The result was that "the men and women who constitute the bone, the sinew, the strength of the Republic" lacked the money to support their families and to train their children to be good citizens. The public interest demanded that government encourage combination among wage workers and remove any possibility of them being found conspiracies in restraint of trade.[54]

Cummins offered an equally pluralist and empirical response to McCumber's charge that a labor exemption would be class legislation. Legislation distinguishing among social groups was neither rare nor unconstitutional. In fact, "three-fourths of all the legislation adopted by Congress is class legislation." General laws, framed without regard for the social circumstances of preexisting groups, he pointed out, could not accomplish their goals.[55] Victorian jurists denounced class legislation for creating differences among individuals where none in fact existed. They believed workers and capitalists were equals unless and until legislation upset this condition. In contrast, Cummins, like the historicist jurists Freund, Roscoe Pound, and Holmes, took the existence of social groups as a given and would not fault legislatures for taking account of their differences. In August 1914 he could point to a recent decision of the Supreme Court upholding Missouri's antitrust statute, which all but reversed *Connolly*.[56]

Like the historicist jurists, too, Cummins believed the differences between labor and capital called for a different set of regulations and not outright immunity. "I do not believe in the secondary boycott," he declared on the Senate floor. "I do not believe labor unions or any other organizations ought to be permitted to combine together to injure or destroy an innocent man because he may have dealings with a person who is unfair to labor."[57] In a simple strike or a collective bargaining agreement, trade unionists squared off against their employers within a particular industry. The workers quite properly pursued the interests of their group, whose limits were set by the industry in which they labored. Secondary boycotts and sympathetic strikes crossed industrial lines; they went beyond the legitimate concerns of the group; they could be lawful only in a society organized on class lines, which American society, thankfully, was not.

If the senators thus heard from Cummins a pluralist defense of a labor exemption, they also heard a pluralist attack from Charles S. Thomas, a Bryan Democrat from Colorado. Thomas interpreted the ambiguous language of the Clayton bill as stopping short of complete immunity for organized labor under the antitrust laws. He was glad the bill established beyond any doubt that labor unions were not "per se organizations in restraint of trade." At last they would "start out upon the same plane and occupy the same position held and occupied by a corporation." But Thomas insisted that the Clayton bill would not and should not permit organized labor to use its economic power to disrupt markets for the goods they produced, whether through secondary boycotts or collective bargaining agreements. With references to Merritt's article in *The Survey,* Thomas attacked the CCF operators for joining with the UMW in an attempt to monopolize the industry. If the UMW's combination and that of the carpenters of New York City were immune from prosecution, Thomas warned, imitators would spring up in every industry, "snap [their] fingers in the face of the antitrust act and march forward to monopoly without regard to the power and dignity of the Government."[58]

Pressure Politics

As the senators debated, Gompers watched from the gallery. "Opposite me I saw Judge Davenport, who had been fighting vigorously against our labor measures," he later recalled. "I must confess that I felt a measure of sincere gratification as I realized that the justice of our cause was about to prevail despite the tireless opposition of vested interests."[59]

But was it? The AFL had originally sought stronger language for the bill but settled for a compromise with a president who publicly denied that the measure would legalize the secondary boycott. Lobbying on both sides of the issue had exceeded even the "unremitting vigilance and pressure" of the sundry civil appropriations bills.[60] And the senators themselves offered widely varying interpretations of the law. *Did* the Clayton Act place the unreasonable restraints of trade of organized labor beyond the reach of the antitrust laws? Under the circumstances, few observers could do better than the Washington correspondent of the New York *Tribune:* "No one can tell until the courts have passed upon the jumble of vague words into which the concession is cast."[61]

Gompers had himself to thank for the confusion. Throughout congressional consideration of the bill Gompers insisted that *Loewe* made the normal operations of trade unions unlawful under the antitrust laws, without bothering to engage the substantial legal consensus to the contrary. Further, in testimony before the House Judiciary Committee he made a mistake of law that would return to haunt him. Asked to name a case that dissolved a labor union under the Sherman Act, Gompers referred to the facts of *Kealey v. Faulkner.* Without identifying the case by name, he explicitly (and erroneously) claimed that the Sherman Act had provided the basis for the decision. "Their agreements with employers was cited as part of the conspiracy in restraint of trade, just as the Supreme Court held in the case of Loewe v. Lawlor," Gompers testified. The majority report of the House Judiciary Committee repeated Gompers's mistake and reprinted the colloquy in which it was made.[62] Gompers's allies in Congress restated his reading of *Loewe,* improbable though it was. When William Hughes, who had moved from the House to the Senate in 1913, repeated Gompers's claim, Thomas C. Spelling, the AFL's old attorney, protested to Senator Borah that no "truthful lawyer of any intelligence" could think *Loewe* outlawed trade unions.[63]

Even so, Woodrow Wilson found it useful to take Gompers's claim at face value. In negotiations with the AFL's representatives in April and May, Wilson and his congressional allies could argue that freeing trade unions from the threat of dissolution proceedings under the Sherman Act was a real change in the law. Having granted the AFL part of what they wanted, Wilson could then decline to go further and legalize the secondary boycott and the sympathetic strike. This would spare him further charges of favoritism to labor. Moreover, Wilson may genuinely have wished to preserve his power to bring suit against organized labor under the antitrust laws. His administration gave some consideration to such a suit in February, when members of the New York printing trades boycotted the publishing house of his ambassador to England.[64]

For their part, the AFL's leaders sought to write a clear labor exemption in section 7 of the House bill (renumbered section 6 in the enacted law).[65] In April they approved the following measure, which the Judiciary Committee reported to the House in on May 6: "That nothing contained in the antitrust laws shall be construed to forbid the existence and operation of fraternal, labor, consumers, agricultural, or horticultural organizations, orders, or associations . . . instituted for the purposes of mutual help, and not having capital stock or conducted for profit, or to forbid or restrain individual members of such orders or associations from carrying out the legitimate objects of such associations."[66] Soon thereafter, the AFL leaders, advised by Alton Parker, had second thoughts. Section 7 would certainly block suits to end the "existence and operation" of trade unions, but would it foreclose indictments or damage actions punishing trade unions for secondary boycotts?

To remove all doubt, labor-bloc congressmen asked Wilson and Attorney General James McReynolds for new language removing the ambiguity. At first the president rejected any changes, but in mid-May, after the AFL threatened to oppose the administration's entire antitrust program, a two-part compromise was reached. On June 1, Edwin Y. Webb, the new chair of the Judiciary Committee, moved that the following language would be appended to section 7: "nor shall such organizations, orders, or associations, or the members thereof, be held or construed to be illegal combinations or conspiracies in restraint of trade, under the antitrust laws."

On the same day, Webb also moved an amendment to section 18 (renumbered section 20 in the enacted law). As reported to the House, section 18 was a general limitation on the issuance of injunctions by federal courts and part of a long campaign by the AFL.[67] The section prohibited federal judges from enjoining workers who quit work or peacefully counseled others to quit work, who picketed peacefully, who ceased to patronize or peacefully counseled others to cease patronizing a party to a labor dispute, who gave or received strike benefits, who assembled peacefully and in a lawful manner, or who did "any act or thing which might lawfully be done in the absence of such dispute by any party thereto."[68]

In itself, this language said nothing about the legality of the named conduct under the antitrust laws; it merely addressed the courts' power to issue injunctions. The "Webb amendment" changed the bill by adding the following words to the end of section 18: "nor shall any of the acts specified in this paragraph be considered or held unlawful." This language went beyond questions of procedure. It transformed a limitation on a legal remedy, the injunction, into a revision of the substantive law of labor relations.[69]

In public and private statements Samuel Gompers insisted the two-part amendment was the outright exemption that organized labor sought. Not only Parker and Ralston but also other eminent legal authorities had been consulted, he wrote to Peter Brady, the secretary of New York City's Printing Trades Council. "If Labor at last is deceived as to the provisions of Section 7, there will be many others, some of high legal authority, who will be equally deceived." In contrast, Wilson and Webb claimed that the "so-called labor exemption" simply foreclosed the possibility that unions would be dissolved in restraint of trade. "Evidently, somebody is getting a gold brick," observed the Brooklyn *Standard Union*. "Is it the people who believe Mr. Gompers or the people who believe President Wilson?"[70]

Lobbying on both sides of the legislation was intense. Only 207 of the House's 435 members were present for the vote on the amendment to section 7. As the House considered the amendment to section 18 the following day, Congressman J. Hampton Moore, a Republican from Pennsylvania, caused a sensation when he shook his fist at Frank Morrison and declared, "I have not waited for a nod from the galleries to determine how I shall vote." Newspapers and news magazines fretted about "Labor's Influence over Congress," and the *Wall Street Journal* applauded Moore for telling "the cringing poltroons in the House of Representatives what their squalid dicker with the labor-union leaders really means."[71]

After the House passed the bill on June 5, trade unionists and employers filled the senators' mailboxes with resolutions and protests. The Senate Judiciary Committee, to which the House bill was referred, was urged to pass the House bill by members of the printing trades, the railroad brotherhoods, the brewery workers, carpenters, garment workers, and journeymen horseshoers. A mass meeting held in Cooper Union on June 10 restated Gompers's case for a complete exemption. "Organizations of workers are different in purpose and in nature from the trusts and monopolies which the Sherman Anti-Trust Law was intended to regulate," the gathering resolved, "in that these organizations control only the power to labor, a power inseparable from the personality and body of the individual worker himself." Gompers himself was active, calling the attention of trade unionists to individual senators "who are either indifferent or [in] manifest opposition to the attainment of labor's rights."[72]

The AABA and NAM were just as quick to muster their rank and file into the controversy. Congressmen E. R. Bathwick, representing Akron, discovered that the local chamber of commerce had "started a row" over his support of the Clayton bill and wrote to Gompers for help. (Gompers dismissed the group as one of the NAM's "catspaws.") Scores of manufacturers and business organizations wrote the Senate Judiciary Committee to condemn the bill. One proprietary capitalist called section 7 "particularly revolting, giving as it does immunity and freedom to one class as against all others." Another deplored the economic consequences of the bill. "One of the chief causes of high prices for commodities is the limiting of production by union efforts," the businessman lectured his senator, "and you politicians entirely ignore that which is one of the chief restraints of trade in existence today."[73]

Scattered among these angry protests were letters from businessmen who had tasted the fruits of industrial cooperation and who qualified their opposition in revealing ways. A union coal operator from Indiana opposed the exemption only because he feared that it would give free rein to "Anarchists and Socialists" among the miners. He stressed that he had once belonged to a union, that he successfully negotiated with union leaders, and that he believed in the union cause. "Labor and Capital must work together instead of trying to dictate to each other," the operator from the CCF counseled. In contrast, the president of the New England Coal Dealer's Association, whose control over the distribution of coal was jeopardized by an unrelated provision of the bill, was more opportunistic. "We urge upon you the elimination of Section #7 H.R. Bill #15657, which exempts Farmers and Labor Organizations," the merchant wrote. "If this is impossible, then we request that all Mercantile Organizations similar to our own, be included in the exemption."[74]

Throughout the spring and summer, Daniel Davenport was in Washington monitoring the legislative situation. He asked to appear before the House Judiciary Committee, was refused, and responded with an open letter attacking the anti-injunction provisions of the bill. After the vote in the House, Davenport lobbied the Senate Judiciary Committee to hold hearings on the "astonishing" Webb Amendment. Again he was rebuffed: The committee issued a compilation of earlier hearings on antitrust matters, including (as the assistant clerk pointedly noted) four at which Davenport had already testified.[75]

Undaunted, Davenport urged the Senate committee to adopt language to blunt the "revolutionary and destructive" thrust of the bill.[76] In its report submitted July 22, the Judiciary Committee, chaired by the Texas Democrat Charles A. Culberson, did just that by adding the words *lawfully* and *lawful* in sections 7 and 18. Thus, section 7, as amended, declared that the antitrust laws did not forbid the members of labor organizations from "lawfully carrying out the legitimate objects thereof." Section 18, already diluted with two "lawfuls" and a "lawfully" in the House version, received another "lawful" for good measure. The effect was that the bill's provisions applied only to conduct that was already lawful. Under the most plausible reading of the relevant language, the Clayton Act had been recast as a simple reaffirmation of the law, a bill to legalize lawful conduct.[77]

The result brought a howl of protest from Thomas Spelling, who still followed labor legislation closely, although not with the blessing of the AFL. "The Senate Committee has shot it all to pieces," he complained to Borah.[78] But Borah, a member of the Judiciary Committee, had no desire to legalize the secondary boycott. Although an outspoken proponent of labor legislation, this leading progressive senator was also a fierce critic of industrial combination. "It is not only the right, but in my opinion, the duty of labor to organize," Borah declared on the floor of the Senate. "I have no doubt that union labor has not only been of great value and benefit to the members of the organizations, but, indirectly, of benefit to those who are not members of the organization." Still, Borah would not vote for the Clayton bill if he thought it would exempt organized labor from the Sherman Act. Borah announced he would vote for the bill because he believed its only effect would be to remove the unlikely possibility of an attack upon the mere existence of a labor union. "In other words," he explained, "it removes a fear, possibly well grounded, but in my judgment unfounded in the law as it now exists. The section gives these organizations a status and permits them to lawfully carry out their legitimate purposes."[79]

Borah arrived at this position with the help of Daniel Davenport, who met with Borah on at least two occasions and provided him with extensive and detailed analyses of the Senate bill. On August 13, for example, Davenport explained why section 7, considered apart from section 18, would work no change in the law. He also denied that any federal court had ever declared the mere existence of labor unions to be an unlawful restraint of trade. The House Judiciary Committee had been misled by Gompers's reference to *Kealey*, Davenport charged, which Gompers, "with his usual inaccuracy," had stated was brought in a federal court under the Sherman Act rather than in "a *nisi prius* court in the State of Ohio under the common law of that State. . . . Without further investigation the Judiciary Committees of both the House and Senate . . . took their law from Mr. Gompers, and to quiet his apprehensions framed this section."[80]

Four days later Davenport sent Borah his analysis of section 18. Davenport argued that because the provision only addressed the "lawful" and "peaceful" conduct of workers, the Webb Amendment made no change in the liability of unions under the antitrust laws. The courts had never interfered in a labor case except to protect property rights from irreparable injury or to halt labor combinations for other unlawful purposes, and they would continue to do so if the bill became law. For this reason, the total exemption long sought by organized labor was "not promoted one bit by the Clayton Bill." Instead of being Labor's Magna Carta, it was "nothing but a humbug and sham."[81]

If Davenport had the ear of Senator Borah, Gompers found a sympathetic listener in Senator Cummins. At some point in August, Gompers suggested to Cummins that section 7 would be strengthened if it included a statement of the "fundamental" principle it embraced. This turned out to be none other than the essential difference between labor and tangible goods that Gompers had asserted during the hearings on the Hepburn bill. In June, Gompers had endorsed California's antitrust statute, which stated, "Labor whether skilled or unskilled is not a commodity within the meaning of this act." The amendment to section 7 that Cummins offered on September 1 similarly commenced, "The labor of a human being is not a commodity or article of commerce."[82]

Cummins certainly shared many of Gompers's views. It disturbed him, Cummins told his fellow senators, "to hear labor termed a commodity— to hear the power of a man or woman to exercise the strength of mind or body in the production of something useful to the human race confused with the product which is the result of its exercise." To specify circumstances in which labor unions were beyond the reach of the antitrust laws was simply to make a legislative declaration of "the essential character of things." Thus Cummins rejected the analogy that had made the "Labor Trust" a favorite epithet of open-shop lawyers.[83]

But Gompers suggested the amendment to put the nonviolent actions of labor combinations beyond the reach of the law. For Cummins it meant something quite different—that labor disputes required a distinct system of regulation, free from the threat of inappropriate analogies from the law of business conspiracies. He was no more willing to allow "one class to escape and another class to be bound" than Davenport was. Thus Cummins's amendment did not stop with Gompers's declaration, but went on to specify acts organized labor might lawfully take. He expressly denied that his amendment would legalize the secondary boycott, and he offered the facts of the Danbury hatters' case to explain why he did not consider it a "fair weapon" of industrial combat.[84]

Although Cummins's "code" received the votes of Borah and several other progressives, a majority of the Senate rejected it for the committee's version, with William Hughes's approval. In a conciliatory gesture, however, Senator Culberson moved that the first sentence of Cummins's amendment be added to section 7 ("I am anxious to please everybody," Culberson declared). It was adopted and remained in the legislation as sent to President Wilson on October 8.[85]

Wilson had remained a judicious distance from the debate over the labor provisions. For example, when his new attorney general Thomas W. Gregory fretted over the ambiguity of the Senate bill, Wilson replied that he shared Gregory's concerns but would not suggest alternatives to sections 7 and 18. "They have been gone over so often and worked at so conscientiously that I really feel we must risk them as they are." In an open letter congratulating Congress on the antitrust legislation he praised the labor provisions in terms that were well calculated to appeal to workers without committing the administration to the AFL's reading of the bill. "Incidentally, justice has been done to the laborer," Wilson said. "His labor is no longer to be treated as if it were merely an inanimate object of commerce disconnected from the fortunes and happiness of a living human being." Great as that change was, it was hardly more than a corollary of the underlying principle of the entire bill, "whose object is individual freedom and initiative as against any kind of private domination."[86]

GOLD BRICKS CONTAINING DYNAMITE

Under intense political pressure, then, Congress produced an ambiguous piece of legislation that permitted all sides to claim victory and left the politically costly job of establishing a clear meaning to the federal judiciary. Davenport, of course, quickly stated the case for treating the Clayton Act as having made no substantial change in the law. In the six years between the passage of the Clayton Act and the Supreme Court's definitive ruling on the labor provisions, most commentators concluded with Davenport that the statute did not give organized labor what they wanted. Edwin Witte, who wrote the minority report for the House Judiciary Committee as secretary to the progressive Republican John Nelson, argued that the labor sections were almost meaningless. ("I was in close touch with Judge Webb and others who framed the labor provisions of the Clayton Act," Witte later explained, "and believe their predominant motive was to please labor and yet make no change in the law.")[87] Other liberals, such as an anonymous writer in the *New Republic*, blamed "a pusillanimous Congressional committee of lawyers who were willing to draft a deceitful statute and shield themselves of the wrath of labor behind the Supreme Court of the United States." Spelling, the AFL's erstwhile legal advisor, agreed with Davenport's dismissal of the statute as being as worthless as "a treaty of neutrality with Belgium."[88]

The only legal authority of any eminence who took the position that the labor provisions legalized the secondary boycott was George W. Wickersham, Taft's attorney general, and even he believed that after the Supreme Court reached this conclusion it would then strike down the statute as unconstitutional class legislation. Taft, in contrast, believed the Supreme Court would treat it as "a mere declaratory statement of existing law in order to remove the unfounded fears of those petitioning for such a statement," rather than declare it unconstitutional under Wickersham's reading.[89]

As Taft predicted, a majority of the Supreme Court adopted his and Davenport's interpretation of the Clayton Act, in passing in *Paine Lumber Company v. Neal* (1917) and as the holding of *Duplex Printing Press Company v. Deering* (1921).[90] Felix Frankfurter criticized *Duplex:* "It is an elementary principle of statutory construction that *some* effect must be given to legislation—all effect, in fact, that the traffic of the language will bear."[91] But Holmes, who joined Justice Brandeis's dissent, thought it a harder case than Frankfurter implied. "Of course I liked your article," he wrote Frankfurter,

> but I am bound to admit that to anyone who allowed his personal preferences to affect his judgment there was a strong case for holding the Clayton Act to be a piece of legislative humbug—intended to sound promising and to do nothing. It seems to me, however, that, although it was not an unlikely conjecture that that was what was meant we were bound to assume the contrary and could not assume the contrary without coming to Brandeis's conclusions. But I don't think it a case for treating the majority opinion as bending the obvious to their wishes.

Whatever his "personal preferences," Holmes's "judgment" was that the historical forces represented by organized labor had made their presence felt in the legislature. Although Holmes was "not inclined to be severe on the opposite view," to deny this fact, as the majority did, was "a public misfortune."[92]

Had *Duplex* simply left organized labor where it was before the passage of the Clayton Act, the entire episode would have been a costly lesson in interest-group politics. In fact, the statute, as interpreted in *Duplex,* dramatically worsened labor's position under the law. Other sections of the Clayton Act authorized an injunction at the suit of a private party, a remedy not explicitly provided for in the original Sherman Act. The AFL's lobbyists had counted on section 18 to abolish the federal injunction in labor disputes, but once *Duplex* neutralized this provision the right of private parties to injunctions in such cases became clear. Although Davenport predicted the outcome in 1914, one of Borah's correspondents described the result best. The labor provisions were not just "gold bricks." They were "gold bricks containing dynamite."[93]

TEN

The Woodtrim War

The Danbury hatters' and *Buck's Stove* cases sharply curtailed secondary boycotts targeting the wholesalers and retailers of nonunion consumer goods. After February 1908 most labor newspapers dropped their "unfair lists," and most national trade unions gave up the practice of dispatching agents to organize boycotts in local consumer markets.[1] But the implications of the AABA's two great cases for other forms of "secondary pressure" were by no means clear. Foremost among these was the refusal by union workers to handle materials produced in nonunion firms. Although unions in the building trades had employed "materials" boycotts since the 1880s, at the founding of the AABA few state supreme courts had passed on their legality, and they had never been attacked under federal antitrust law.

The most prominent of the materials boycotts was conducted by the New York City locals of the United Brotherhood of Carpenters and Joiners against the products of open-shop lumber mills. Local carpenters notified the city's builders that they would handle only union woodtrim as early as 1896, and the campaign enjoyed the official support of the national union since 1904. By 1910, the New York carpenters had driven nonunion doors, sashes, and woodtrim from a "restricted district" encompassing Manhattan and the Bronx south of 177th Street. In March the Joint District Council of New York and Vicinity (JDC) broadened their objective to include the woodtrim manufacturers of Brooklyn.[2]

From 1910 to 1917 the AABA fought the carpenters' boycott with a barrage of injunction suits, contempt proceedings, damage actions, and criminal prosecutions. With Daniel Davenport dividing his time between Washington and Bridgeport, the bulk of the work fell to Walter Gordon Merritt in the AABA's Manhattan office. The experience bolstered the confidence of the young lawyer and complemented his efforts to fashion a pluralist and consumer-oriented platform for the AABA (chapter 11). The litigation, conducted in New York and federal courts, ended in dismissals of the AABA's suits, results that led one historian of the United Brotherhood to conclude, "The head of the Anti-Boycott Association went up in the Carpenters' trophy room."[3] Yet the courts that passed judgment on the "Woodtrim War" never endorsed the collective laissez-faire of the labor movement. A majority of the Supreme Court would have condemned the carpenter's boycott had not a procedural issue provided an alternate grounds for disposing of the case. The New York Court of Appeals upheld the boycott as a legitimate expression of group solidarity, but in doing so it followed other state courts in asserting the power to fix the limits of unions' privilege to inflict economic loss.

LUMBER BARONS AND LABOR BARONS

For most of the nineteenth century, the lumber industry was composed of a very large number of manufacturers who produced for local and regional markets. After 1890, however, technological change permitted some firms to boost their productivity and seek a national market for their goods. Among the industry leaders in 1911 was the Paine Lumber Company of Oshkosh, Wisconsin, with annual sales of $2.5 million, 90 percent of which went to out-of-state buyers. Four other Oshkosh lumber manufacturers, the Gould Manufacturing Company, the R. McMillen Company, the Lothman Cypress Company, and Morgan and Company, had annual sales of $450,000 to $1,250,000. Like Paine, they sold primarily to the firms outside their state.[4]

The rise of a national market led many manufacturers to form trade associations organized by region and product. The groups often attempted to limit competition by circulating price lists, boycotting manufacturers who sold directly to retailers or customers, and other strategies. Apologists for the trade associations haled this "spirit of healthy cooperation" as a great improvement over the intense rivalry of bygone days. Most government officials had a dimmer view of the "lumber trusts." In 1907 a wave of agitation in Missouri produced a suit to prevent price-fixing manufacturers from doing business in the state, and the United States Bureau of Corporations launched a three-year investigation of the lumber industry. In 1911 federal prosecutors sought an injunction against several eastern lumber distributors for violating the Sherman Act. The decree they obtained was ultimately upheld by the Supreme Court in *Eastern States Retail Lumber Dealers Association v. United States* (1914).[5]

These attempts at price fixing notwithstanding, leading lumber manufacturers often undersold local firms, burdened with higher wage bills and operating expenses. This was particularly true in and around New York City. Manhattan manufacturers were especially hard-pressed and faced the prospect of becoming mere jobbers of "western material." Such sales were also a substantial part of the business of several Brooklyn producers, including the AABA members Louis J. Bossert and Son and the Albro J. Newton Company. As woodtrim flooded the city, union leaders feared local lumberyards would fire the bulk of their employees, retaining only "a few, to handle the stuff."[6]

From its founding, the United Brotherhood of Carpenters and Joiners included within its ranks "outside" carpenters, who worked at construction sites, and "inside" carpenters, employed in lumber mills. Although the national leadership normally shared the craft outlook of the outside carpenters, millworkers were an important constituency, and their influence grew after the United Brotherhood absorbed the Amalgamated Wood Workers International Union between 1910 and 1912.[7] In some locales, carpenters moved from higher paying construction jobs into the mills and back again as conditions in the building industry warranted. In New York, for example, this migration produced "a continual wrangle" between outside and inside carpenters, much to the consternation of trade union officials. In contrast, where millworkers were primarily machine tenders, as in the big Oshkosh mills, the inside workers—often women and children—rarely joined the ranks of outside carpenters.[8]

The means to stem the flood of western materials came to hand in 1903, when, after years of graft and sympathetic strikes, employers in New York City's building trades formed an association and locked out their employees until they agreed to a scheme for arbitrating labor disputes. Under the General Arbitration Plan the Master Carpenters' Association agreed to employ only union workers, while the Building Trades Employers Association and the unions agreed to arbitrate their differences. The plan brought the building trades a measure of industrial peace. It also kept contractors from employing nonunion carpenters when erecting substantial buildings anywhere in Manhattan.[9]

With this victory won, the JDC next demanded that master carpenters use only union-made woodtrim on their jobs. In an agreement signed October 30, 1909, the master carpenters, eager to obtain "a firm condition under which we can do business," finally conceded. Fearful that marginal contractors would use cheaper woodtrim and underbid them, the master carpenters limited the scope of the agreement to Manhattan and the South Bronx, where the JDC was strong enough to police its terms.[10]

In January 1910 the JDC brought the local lumber manufacturers into the fold with the promise that if the bosses would employ only union workers, the carpenters would erect or install only union-made woodtrim. The JDC quickly made good on its pledge, so that "not a stick" of nonunion trim could be found in the restricted district. Further, the New York carpenters sometimes refused to handle union-made woodtrim produced outside of the metropolitan area when it undersold the local manufacturers. The sole object for the materials boycott, explained Eldridge Neal, secretary of the JDC, was "to keep our union men employed. . . . If the union mills were driven out of business, our men would be driven out of employment." Union-made western material was scarcely less of a threat to New York City's mills as nonunion woodtrim. "It would have the same tendency to put them out of business as the non-union material would."[11]

In 1912 the national leadership would sharply condemn such union boycotts of union products, but in the fall of 1910 they did not keep the United Brotherhood's General Convention from endorsing the JDC's campaign to extend the restricted district to Brooklyn. In September 1910 the carpenters called strikes on four different jobs using trim produced by the Albro J. Newton Company. In 1911 and 1912 the carpenters targeted other nonunion employers in Brooklyn and Queens, including Louis J. Bossert and Son, the Tisdale Lumber Company, and Parshelsky Brothers.[12]

THE AABA INTERVENES

The AABA's involvement in the these matters began in April 1910, when a JDC official called out four union carpenters at work on an organ casement at the Cathedral of St. John the Divine. The casement was the product of Irving and Casson, a "fancy" woodwork firm located in East Cambridge, Massachusetts, which had been the target of work stoppages by the United Brotherhood since 1906. The company's general manager for New York City turned to the AABA, whose associate counsel, Walter Gordon Merritt, quickly obtained a temporary restraining order from the federal district court. The sweeping order enjoined union officials not only from recommending that members strike, but also from informing any carpenter that Irving and Casson or its products were unfair. Alarmed, union officials devoted the greater part of an issue of the United Brotherhood's journal to the complaint, affidavits, and restraining order in the case. In July, Circuit Judge Henry Ward continued the order as an preliminary injunction but in a modified form. Strikes remained forbidden, but the union could inform its members that they were handling unfair material.[13]

The conflict escalated in the fall and winter of 1910–11. In September 1910 the carpenters struck jobs using material produced by the Newton firm, and Merritt responded with a temporary restraining order from Judge Frederick Crane of the New York Supreme Court for Brooklyn. On January 6, 1911, Crane's fellow judge Abel Blackmar issued a lengthy and widely noted opinion granting Newton a preliminary injunction.[14]

Meanwhile, Merritt made preparations for a second front in the federal courts on behalf of the large midwestern firms who found themselves barred from the New York market. In November 1910 Nathan Paine, vice president of the Paine Lumber Company, met with Merritt and agreed to drum up support among his fellow manufacturers. Later that month Paine wrote G. W. Dwelle, the secretary for two trade associations, that the merger of the Amalgamated Wood Workers and the United Brotherhood menaced employers throughout the industry. Now, Paine warned, even mills with nonunion work forces were threatened by a nationwide campaign of "outside" carpenters against their millwork. "This, to say the least, would be very embarrassing to any mill and in most cases would probably result in . . . compelling it to unionize." Paine noted that the United Brotherhood was negotiating with several factories "to the end that if the factories will unionize the unions will boycott and refuse to install the product of their neighboring non-union factories."[15]

Paine told Dwelle that the manufacturers' best hope was a lawsuit sponsored by the AABA. Merritt had "the utmost confidence in the attitude of the courts," the manufacturer reported, but the lawyer needed "as strong a representation of mill work interests behind them, as could be assembled." Although the expense might be great, Paine assured Dwelle, it would be borne by the AABA's entire membership "without any special charge" to any one firm. The lumber firms need only join the AABA for the duration of the suit and pay a $25 initiation fee and additional assessments that rarely ran to more than $25 a year.[16]

Dwelle gave the lawsuit his full support. "Are not all prominent manufacturers of mill work greatly interested in this matter and would it not be wise policy for all of them to cooperate therein?" Dwelle wrote the members of one of his trade associations. On February 14, 1911, Merritt presented the annual meeting of the group with "an interesting review of the work and aims of organized labor in relation to the wood working industry." He was followed by the AABA's secretary, who explained the privileges of membership in the organization. When a manufacturer asked whether any of his fellow members already belonged to the AABA, several volunteered that they did and others promised to join at once, as the litigation was "in the interest of all engaged in the millwork business."[17]

Foremost in the minds of the large national manufacturers was the desire to market their products in New York City at competitive prices. To be sure, some employers cast themselves as defenders of free labor or the consumer interest. "The influence that brought us to bring the action," Nathan Paine protested, was only "incidentally a matter of economy. We have been invited to join with union labor and advance prices to the consumer fifty per cent. but have declined." Yet the Pennsylvania manufacturer

George Wesley Crooks (one of the complainants in *Paine*) conceded he would have joined the United Brotherhood's combination had he been certain it would work outside New York City. Only 15 percent of his business went to that high-wage market, Crooks explained. For the other 85 percent, "We compete with mills that are paying a lower rate of wages than we are." If his firm adopted union wages and hours, "We would have to charge a whole lot more for our goods and lose the trade we have been twenty-five years building up." Although not averse to unionizing his plant, Crooks would do so only on an equal basis with the rest of the industry.[18]

In February 1911 Merritt filed *Paine Lumber Company v. Neal* in the federal district court in New York City on behalf of eight woodtrim manufacturers with factories in Wisconsin, Tennessee, and Pennsylvania. The complaint alleged that the defendants—twenty-three officers and agents of the United Brotherhood, five union lumber manufacturers, and over one hundred master carpenters and builders—had entered into a conspiracy in restraint of trade, contrary to the Sherman Act and the statutes and common law of the state of New York. The complainants sought a sweeping injunction in terms similar to Crane's temporary restraining order in *Newton*, as well as an order declaring unenforceable the ban on nonunion woodtrim in the agreement between the JDC and the master carpenters.[19]

THE CARPENTERS' COUNTEROFFENSIVE

The carpenters responded through their attorney, Charles Maitland Beattie. A boastful and boisterous man, Beattie argued their case with imagination and zeal, if something less than a profound command of the law.[20] In defending the JDC in *Irving*, Beattie used his answer to Merritt's complaint as a chance to counterattack. By supporting the suit, Beattie charged, the AABA violated New York laws against the "maintenance" of litigation. Here Beattie invoked the law of champerty, which prohibited a stranger to a lawsuit from agreeing to finance the litigation in exchange for a share of any proceeds recovered. Beattie then invoked the equitable doctrine of "clean hands," which directed equity courts not to grant relief to parties whose prior conduct violated conscience or good faith. Because an injunction could only be obtained from equity courts, this "novel defense in avoidance" would "strike at the existence" of the AABA, Beattie boasted to Samuel Gompers. If generally accepted, it would limit the AABA to damage actions in common-law courts—a poor alternative to injunctive relief.[21]

Judge Ward rejected Beattie's argument on the grounds that the AABA had no contractual right to recover any funds the Irving and Casson might obtain. "The only connection the association has with the claim is to prosecute it for the benefit of the complainants at its own expense," Ward wrote. "Exactly the same thing is being done for the defendants by the United Brotherhood and Joint District Council." Undaunted, Beattie decided to attack the AABA through legislative means. Noting that section 280 of the New York Penal Code forbid corporations from practicing law, Beattie drafted an amendment to extend the prohibition to voluntary associations. The amendment did not specifically refer to the AABA, and it sailed through the legislature on unanimous votes. Its effective date was September 1, 1911.[22]

In the spring and summer of 1911, Merritt and Beattie gathered evidence for trials in *Irving, Newton* and *Paine.* In early October the carpenters called strikes on several jobs over material supplied by Louis J. Bossert and Son, and Merritt responded with a temporary restraining order on Bossert's behalf. In November, Merritt initiated contempt proceedings against carpenters who refused to handle Paine's material, but the district judge discontinued the action when Beattie announced he would advise his clients to resume work at the disputed job. In the same month Beattie commenced *Savage v. Potter,* an injunction suit against the AABA under the recently amended section 280, and Beattie and Merritt again squared off in a hearing on Merritt's motion for a preliminary injunction in the *Bossert* case.[23]

Between December 1911 and May 1912 the carpenters suffered a series of alarming legal setbacks when Bossert and two other lumber manufacturers, Parshelsky Brothers and the Tisdale Lumber Company, obtained preliminary injunctions against the JDC. Each time the presiding judge ruled that Blackmar's opinion in *Newton,* as affirmed by the Appellate Division, governed the case before them. This infuriated the carpenters. "If you wished to get an injunction against the workingmen under similar conditions," they declared in their national convention, "you do not need to go to the Supreme Court, but apply to the American Anti-Boycott Association, which will prepare the paper for you and then they will compel the judge to sign it."[24]

At a spirited meeting in June 1912 union officials charged the AABA with violating section 280 and, in a reference to the *Eastern States* case, accused the Brooklyn manufacturers of being "members of a gigantic lumber trust. . . . We are enjoined as a property right into slavery," the carpenters protested, "for the benefit of a few lumber kings who have tried for years to control the trade in a combination, in violation of the Sherman anti-trust law." The AABA's lawyers had said not a word about the *manufacturers'* boycott, the gathering pointedly noted, for if they did they "would soon lose their meal ticket." Before adjourning the carpenters called for a citywide protest against the AABA and its injunctions.[25]

This occurred on an astonishing scale on the evening of October 26, two days before *Savage* went to trial. Twenty-three thousand workers from virtually every branch of the building trades, accompanied by twenty bands, marched from Fifth Avenue and 58th Street to Cooper Union. Each parader wore a badge giving the name of his union and the inscription "Square Deal," every other marcher waived an American flag, and many carried banners declaring "We Demand Our Rights" and "Equality Before the Law." Amid this outpouring of Americanism, the socialist New York *Call* spotted some heartening signs of radicalism. The red flag was well-represented, and, the paper reported, many bands played the Marseillaise.[26]

At Cooper Union the overflow crowd heard addresses from leaders of the United Brotherhood, an official of the AFL's Metal Trades Department, and Samuel Gompers, who, as the *New York Tribune* noted, spoke "in the shadow of the jail for contempt of the court's injunction in the Buck's Stove and Range boycott case." The members of New York's building trades—notorious for their independence—gave Gompers only a lukewarm welcome when he appeared on stage, halfway through another speaker's address. Several times "a fighting minority" of hecklers interrupted Gompers's speech, and when he asked his audience's leave to read from some judicial opinions, several voices shouted, "No." Gompers shrugged and started to fold up his papers when others called for him to continue with cheers of "Go on," "Read them," "Sing your song," and "Never mind him, Sammy." For his part Gompers scolded the New York carpenters for not protesting against injunctions until they themselves had been enjoined. But after this sparring Gompers warmed to his subject, and "the stream of his impetuous and stormy eloquence carried nearly everybody along with it."[27]

The legal skirmishing continued for another five years. *Savage* stalemated when the presiding judge held that the AABA violated section 280 but also ruled that this criminal statute gave the United Brotherhood no basis for relief in a civil court. In January 1916, the JDC had Merritt arrested under the statute. ("It was time for the worm to turn," Beattie explained.) Once again, the result disappointed the carpenters: after trial in November a panel of judges dismissed the complaint by a 2-1 vote. Merritt kept up the pressure with various legal feints. Bossert's preliminary injunction was made permanent in May 1913. A damage action on Bossert's behalf soon followed. In 1914 and 1915 Merritt initiated contempt proceedings against union officials under the Bossert injunction, and his complaint commenced a criminal action against the same officials in June 1915.[28]

None of this litigation broke the carpenters' boycott. "The lawyers in New York cannot do anything," Parshelsky Brothers wrote to one of the *Paine* complainants. "It seems that the temporary injunction that you got out is of no use as these people pay no attention to same."[29] Two reasons account for the ineffectiveness of the injunctions. The first was a problem of proof. The terms of the injunctions required Merritt to show that union officials actually *ordered* carpenters to stop work. Proof that officials had merely informed workers that they were handling nonunion woodtrim was not sufficient, because none of the injunctions prohibited this speech, and carpenters uniformly testified that they quit voluntarily once they learned the nature of the material. A second reason went to the merits of the dispute. Some judges argued that even an order to quit work on pain of expulsion from the union did not amount to the "compulsion" that the injunction prohibited. An opinion to this effect in one phase of the *Bossert* case by Judge Crane delighted union officials, and they trotted it out whenever the AABA referred to Blackmar's opinion in *Newton*.[30]

At length, Merritt and Beattie agreed to appeal one of the federal cases and two of the New York suits to the highest court in each jurisdiction.[31] *Paine* was the vehicle for the federal appeals. After depositions in New York, Pennsylvania, Tennessee, Indiana, and Wisconsin, the federal district court finally dismissed the complaint in November 1913. Judge Julius Mayer ruled that although the carpenters' boycott violated the Sherman Act, the only remedies the statute gave private parties were damage suits and criminal prosecutions, so that it could not be the basis for the injunctive relief Merritt sought. The U.S Circuit Court affirmed in April 1914 in a per curiam opinion. The circuit court agreed that private parties could not obtain injunctions under the Sherman Act, but it offered no opinion as to whether the boycott violated the antitrust laws. Merritt and Beattie first argued *Paine* before the Supreme Court in May 1915, but when Charles E. Hughes's resignation left the justices evenly divided, the case was restored to the docket for reargument. The Court finally announced its decision in June 1917. By a 5-4 margin the Court affirmed in an opinion written by Oliver Wendell Holmes, Jr., on the procedural ground adopted by the lower courts.[32]

Of the New York cases, Merritt and Beattie decided to appeal *Bossert* and *Newton*. Like *Paine*, the cases progressed slowly through the courts. Permanent injunctions were granted in *Newton* in May 1912 and in *Bossert* in April 1913. In November 1914, the appellate division affirmed the trial courts. Both sides appealed: the carpenters to remove the taint of illegality from their boycott; the AABA to obtain more effective injunctions. In October 1917, the court of appeals reversed the lower courts and dismissed the complaints, holding that the carpenters' boycott did not violate New York's conspiracy laws.[33]

SOLIDARITY AND JUSTIFICATION

Like litigation over the closed shop, the Woodtrim War presented judges with the task of defining the legal limits of group solidarity. Their efforts can best be understood in the larger context of law writing and litigation on secondary pressure in the building trades. All jurisdictions agreed that workers in a particular trade could justifiably unite to inflict economic loss on an actual or potential employer, but they differed once other trades and other businesses were brought into the dispute. Could electricians, for example, ask the local building trades council to call out all construction workers if a nonunion electrical contractor was hired for a particular job? Or could they refuse to work for a building owner who purchased materials from a firm that supplied materials to the offending contractor? Nineteenth-century courts would consider either strike a coercive interference with the electrical contractor's right to manage. By the time the New York Court of Appeals handed down its decision in *Bossert*, however, leading state supreme courts had concluded that such actions were legitimate exercises of the workers' right of "competition" and hence justifiable acts of economic warfare.

Although attempts to organize workers across the construction industry antedate the Great Upheaval, lasting building trades councils (BTCs) emerged in New York, Chicago, and San Francisco only after the depression of the 1890s. In New York, for example, six construction unions organized a Board of Delegates in 1884, but factional warfare plagued the body until March 1902, when the United Board of Building Trades brought twenty-two skilled and fifteen unskilled trades into an effective union. In San Francisco a permanent BTC was organized in 1896 and became a potent force in municipal politics under the leadership of the carpenter P. H. McCarthy, who in 1900 presided over a strike by the local building trades that closed San Francisco to nonunion woodtrim. Seventy-one local BTCs were in existence by 1906, and the number reached 372 in 1926.[34]

From the start, the BTC was intended as "a war agency." "It prevented the employer from defeating one craft at a time," an industrial relations scholar wrote in 1930, and it made "the sympathetic strike a weapon to be feared." It also fostered solidarity across the building trades. In 1912, Solomon Blum, a labor economist trained at Johns Hopkins, thought the building trades comprised the largest "sympathetic group" in the labor movement founded on a "community of interest" in opposition to nonunion labor.[35]

The judges who first confronted the job actions of the BTCs often relied on two late-nineteenth-century cases decided on analogous facts. The first was William Howard Taft's opinion in *Moores & Co. v. Bricklayers' Union No. 1* (1890), which was brought by a supplier to Cincinnati's building trades against bricklayers who refused to handle the firm's lime because the firm sold to nonunion general contractors. Taft decided the case within the framework provided by Sir Charles Bowen's opinion in *Mogul Steamship Co. v.*

McGregor, Gow & Co. (1889). In particular, he asked whether the bricklayers could claim "competition" as a justification for their actions. He concluded they could not. Between the striking bricklayers and the supplier Moores, Taft decided, there was "no competition or possible contractual relation . . . where their interest were naturally opposed." Taft thus limited the term *competition* to the rivalry between employees and employers with whom they at least potentially shared a "contractual relation." Although the supplier Moores and the general contractors were themselves joined in a contractual relationship, Taft did not consider this sufficient reason for the bricklayers to treat the supplier as an enemy. So long as Moores and the contractors were distinct business enterprises, their mutual interest in open-shop conditions did not justify the loss the workers inflicted.[36]

A second leading case, *Hopkins v. Oxley Stave Co.* (1897), involved a boycott of machine-hooped barrels produced by means of a labor-saving device. Judge Amos M. Thayer of the Eighth Circuit Court of Appeals enjoined the coopers' union from asking other labor groups to refrain from handling or purchasing commodities packed in the plaintiff's barrels. Unlike Taft, Thayer analyzed the case in terms of the conspiracy doctrine, but he still found occasion to discuss Bowen's opinion in *Mogul*. Like Taft, he distinguished the English case on the grounds that it involved "no more than lawful competition in trade," while the coopers' campaign was "a species of intimidation" that denied Oxley Stave "the right to manage its business according to the dictates of its own judgment" and denied "the public at large the benefits to be derived from a labor-saving machine." Thayer's attempt to limit the scope of the word *competition* provoked a sharp dissent. Judge Henry Clay Caldwell turned to the *Century Dictionary* to define competition as an "endeavor to gain what another is endeavoring to gain at the same time." The coopers' boycott, Caldwell claimed, fell well within that definition and was not actionable.[37]

In both cases, the prevailing opinions denied that concerted refusals to handle goods by those not actually or potentially the employees of the targeted employer constituted "competition." To borrow from Holmes, the judges were not convinced that this form of collective action were "worth more to society than it costs."[38] The legal historian Herbert Hovenkamp has suggested that the reason for their doubts lay in their understanding that the only true competition was the "horizontal" rivalry between the sellers or between the buyers of the same good, an understanding he attributes to the triumph of neoclassical economic thought at the turn of the twentieth century. Henceforth judges would no longer count the "vertical" rivalry of sellers and buyers of the same good (such as labor), because it produced none of the benefits neoclassical economic theory ascribed to perfect competition.[39]

In fact, judges never limited themselves to so strict a usage of the term *competition*. For example, they regularly used it to describe the loss inflicted in a simple strike over hours, wages, and working conditions, even though it was an act of "vertical" and not "horizontal" rivalry. The term was more important to the judges for what it connoted than what it denoted. First, it connoted the absence of malice in fact. Competitors sought some end other than the infliction of harm for its own sake. They were endeavoring with another for the same object (in Caldwell's formulation) or engaging in the "free struggle for life" (in Holmes's better-known expression). That an employer was hurt in the process was "gratifying but incidental."[40] Thus, judges sometimes called workers' conduct competition in order to distinguish it from loss inflicted out of actual malice, a class of intentionally inflicted loss that was never justifiable.

Second, competition connoted a permissible act of economic rivalry. Taft and Thayer assumed that the only permissible form of economic pressure was that which workers brought to bear against entities with whom they shared or might share a contractual relation of employment. Such economic pressure could be collective, so long as the united workers were arrayed against an actual or potential employer. As Taft later wrote,[41]

> Union was essential to give laborers opportunity to deal on equality with their employer. They united to exert influence upon him and to leave him in a body in order by this inconvenience to induce him to make better terms with them. They were withholding their labor of economic value to make them pay what they thought it was worth. . . . The strike became a lawful instrument in a lawful economic struggle or competition between employer and employees as to the share or division between them of the joint product of labor and capital.

Taft thus acknowledged that workers could "exert influence upon" employers by denying them their labor and still engage in an act of "lawful economic struggle or competition." Taft's younger contemporaries in the legal realist movement saw such acknowledgements as a confession that competition was itself a form of coercion, so that judges could no longer base their reasoning on the distinction between the two.[42] But Taft clung to the distinction. Economic pressure looking toward the division of the "joint product of labor and capital" of employers and their actual or potential employees was "lawful economic struggle or competition." Economic pressure that did not was coercion and unjustifiable.

In *Moores*, Taft thought the Cincinnati bricklayers had no valid dispute with the supplier, because any harm they inflicted upon Moores would not reduce the "joint product" of the bricklayers' labor and Moores's capital. For the same reason Thayer could see no connection between the packinghouse worker who refused to handle a machine-hooped barrel and Oxley Stave. Such orthodox judges, then, took the organization of capital as the starting point for their analysis. If organized labor's targets were organized as separate firms, the judges would not permit them to be grouped together. The judges saw no logical stopping point between affirming such sympathetic strikes and endorsing class war.

The twentieth-century building trades cases presented jurists with opportunities to revise the orthodox view on facts involving closely allied businessmen and closely allied unions. Perhaps the earliest attempt was a 1902 article by the treatise writer Frederick Hale Cooke. Like orthodox jurists, Cooke insisted that workers' collective action must be reasonably related to their industrial situation. But where orthodox jurists limited the class of permissible targets to actual or potential employers, Cooke would accept the infliction of economic loss by a broader group of workers against a broader group of businessmen if that action was "the natural incident and outgrowth" of existing industrial conditions.[43]

Cooke thought his formula was more generous to workers than the orthodox view. He criticized *Moores* and *Hopkins* for their "more or less distinct failure to give effect to the doctrine of solidarity of interest as justifying a boycott." Further, he argued that jurisdictional disputes among rival unions were justified, notwithstanding the contrary precedent of *Plant v. Woods* (1900). "Of such injuries," he wrote, "the universal, inevitable result of the struggle for existence, the law can take no account."[44] On the other hand, Boston iron workers who induced a strike by a jewelry manufacturing concern in San Francisco would be engaging in "purely wanton" conduct, because "it is not easy to conceive of the Boston iron workers as having any relation to the San Francisco jeweler or his employees, such as to furnish a basis for the legality of their boycott." Cooke never made clear what made the one dispute a natural outgrowth of industrial conditions and the other purely wanton conduct. What is clear is that Cooke thought his principle of deference to "natural" expressions of group solidarity was the basis for a general rethinking of the law to allow greater room for collective economic action, whether by workers, employers, financiers, or merchants.[45]

In 1907 the Harvard law professor Jeremiah Smith followed with a more comprehensive and influential treatment of the problem. Like Holmes, Smith believed combinations of workers were essential counterweights to combinations of capital, but, like Dicey, he was troubled by the danger unions posed to "insiders (the members)" and to "outsiders," whom Smith identified as "non-union workmen, employers, and the general public." To balance the two concerns Smith demanded that unions demonstrate some special justification for their intentionally inflicted damage. In particular, Smith would have them show (1) "some conflict of interest" between trade unionists and an actual or potential employer; (2) that the damaging act was "reasonably calculated to substantially advance" the trade unionists' interests; (3) that the damage to the plaintiff and the general public was proportionate to the benefit the trade unionists sought for themselves; and (4) that the trade unionists did not induce an "outsider" to exert pressure on the employer.[46]

Smith offered a series of examples to help define "the legitimate bounds of competition or of economic warfare" in labor disputes. For the most part he was as reluctant as any orthodox judge to accept claims of group solidarity for boycotts that worked through distinct business concerns. He decided, for example, that union carpenters could not refuse to handle the goods of a lumber dealer who sold to a nonunion contractor (facts analogous to the *Moores* case). He was also reluctant to accept "the principle of unionism" as justification when the members of distinct trades united against a single employer. For example, he concluded that union printers could not justifiably strike to protest the hiring of a nonunion carpenter to repair their employer's home. Even instances where the trades were more closely related failed to win his approval. Thus, union bricklayers could not refuse to handle the products of nonunion brickmakers.

Still, Smith recognized that his categories of "insiders" and "outsiders" could not be fixed through a process of a priori deduction, and he indicated some willingness to defer to the natural processes of group formation. "Undoubtedly there may be close questions as to where the line shall be drawn between certain occupations, to determine whether men pursuing them belong to the same trade or to different trades." To make his point he offered an example taken from the printing industry. Whether pressmen and compositors belonged to the same or distinct trades, he suggested, was a difficult question, but one which could safely be left to the finder of fact. Smith did not explain why these unions provided a difficult case when his other examples did not, but it seems significant that pressmen and compositors, like the various members of the building trades, had organized themselves into local trades councils for the purposes of collective bargaining. Employers' acceptance of this arrangement may have inclined Smith to treat joint action by two crafts as an organic response to evolving industrial conditions, rather than an unnatural (and un-American) expression of class animus.[47]

In the following years other commentators would call for greater tolerance of secondary pressure "kept within reasonable limits."[48] At the same time the courts themselves pushed beyond Smith in cases involving collective action by allied unions in the building trades. Their rulings upheld organization beyond the bounds of a single craft, but of course stopped well short of endorsing the massing of the entire working class against a foe.

Often the judges indicated their approval by terming the collective action "competition," although the allied trades were neither the horizontal nor the vertical rivals of the proscribed employers.

One of the earliest of the twentieth-century cases was *Gray v. Building Trades Council,* decided by the Minnesota Supreme Court in 1903. *Gray* involved a dispute between an association of nonunion electrical contractors and local electricians' unions, backed by the Minneapolis BTC. On the authority of *Moores, Hopkins,* and other cases, the Minnesota court ruled that the BTC could not threaten building owners with a strike should they employ the plaintiffs. But the court went beyond the orthodox view by permitting the BTC to call out the members of all of its constituent unions wherever the nonunion electrical contractors were at work—just as long as it did not "threaten" to do so in advance. The court reached this conclusion even though most of the strikers belonged to other crafts and would never be employed as electricians. Under *Gray,* the "principle of trade unionism" thus served as justification for a strike by carpenters, masons, painters, and other construction workers when a nonunion electrician was employed on the same job. Small wonder, then, that Gompers hailed the decision as "a severe blow to Parryism and its legal juggling."[49]

Another landmark was *Booth & Brother v. Burgess* (1906), which involved a boycott by a New Jersey BTC of the products of Booth and Brother, a nonunion dealer and manufacturer of nonunion doors and woodtrim. Vice-Chancellor Eugene Stevenson ultimately enjoined the boycott on the ground that the participation of the members of the various building trades was coerced by the threat of expulsion from their union. Had Stevenson been convinced that the trade unionists participated as an act of "free combination," he would have refused to enjoin the boycott, for it would then be an authentic expression of mutual interest among construction workers. To be sure, Stevenson's depiction of the business agent Burgess as a man who, with a snap of his fingers, could force carpenters to drop their tools or suffer "expulsion . . . , social ostracism, and poverty" revealed a lingering concern over the power of the BTC. But even Stevenson conceded that the BTC could exercise coercion in cases where the relationship between the construction workers and the lumber dealers' employees was more direct.[50]

A second case decided in 1906 showed even greater deference to labor unions on the issue of the proper limits of group solidarity. This time, however, the union wished to exclude a class of workers rather than assert solidarity with them. *Pickett v. Walsh* involved a dispute between the bricklayers' union and a group of brick and stone pointers, skilled at cleaning brick and stone faces with acid and applying finish to the mortar. Builders generally preferred dealing with the pointers because they worked as independent contractors (thus limiting the builders' liability), were more expert at the job, and did the work at lower cost. The masons demanded that general contractors hire them to clean and point or else face a strike on other job sites where bricklayers were employed. They called strikes on several jobs for which the firm of L. P. Soule and Son were general contractors, because Soule had been general contractor for the erection of Boston's Ford Building, whose owner had hired pointers to finish the structure.

Justice William Loring of the Massachusetts Supreme Judicial Court had no difficulty concluding that the job action against Soule was an unjustifiable interference with the contractor's business. "It is a refusal to work for A [Soule], with whom the strikers have no dispute, because A works for B [the owners of the Ford Building], with whom the strikers have a dispute, for the purpose of forcing A to force B to yield to the strikers' demands. . . . That passes beyond a case of competition where the owner of the Ford Building is left to choose between two competitors." On this issue, Loring broke no new ground and kept Massachusetts committed to the orthodox position, which insisted that general contractors and building owners be treated as distinct entities.[51]

The remarkable phase of Loring's opinion involved his conclusion that the masons were justified in demanding that general contractors hire them, even though it would drive the pointers from the workplace. Strictly speaking, the holding was consistent with the orthodox view, for masons and general contractors were joined in the very contractual relationship Loring could not find between masons and Soule's customers. But in light of the *Plant* decision, *Pickett* was a significant reversal of Massachusetts law. Loring acknowledged, much as the *Plant* court did, that the bricklayers' actions surely amounted to "coercion and compulsion." Although mindful of the pointers' plight, Loring would not intervene in the natural competition among the masons, the pointers, and the contractors. "The case at bar is an instance where the evils which are or may be incident to competition bear very harshly on those interested," Loring wrote. Contractors would be denied the services of pointers who did "better work with less liability at a smaller cost," and the consequences for the pointers were "disastrous." "In spite of such evils," Loring concluded, "competition is necessary to the welfare of the community."[52]

An even stronger recognition of collective ordering in the workplace came in *Parkinson v. Building Trades Council of Santa Clara* (1908). In *Parkinson*, California's supreme court refused to enjoin a BTC for boycotting the materials supplied by a lumberyard that employed a nonunion tinner in its plumbing and tinning shop. The case was doubly problematic for an orthodox judge. First, the members of the BTC targeted not only the owner of the lumberyard but also builders who used their wares, thus conflating businesses that orthodox courts would consider distinct. Second, the members of all BTC unions joined in the boycott, even though only union tinners were denied employment in the plaintiff's lumberyard. On similar facts Vice-Chancellor Stevenson found for the employer, but the California court refused to intervene absent some statutory basis for the suit. Although framed in the outdated language of the conspiracy doctrine, the decision defended the BTC's posting of unfair notices:

> The contractors were working in harmony with the unions (as indeed the plaintiff had previously done) and fair dealing required that the council, representing and acting for the unions, should protect such contractors from any loss they might incur if left in ignorance of the action taken. If they had not sent the notices some of those contractors who felt constrained to stop dealing with plaintiff when informed that it had been declared unfair might have purchased material which they could not have used.

The *Parkinson* court assumed the law should defer to the private ordering of the building trades by the BTC and, having made that assumption, thought it "fair dealing" for the BTC to notify contractors that the plaintiff's supplies were "materials which they could not have used." What an orthodox judge would have denounced as an unlawful interference with the general contractor's right to manage, the California court considered simply the disclosure of "a fact . . . essential to his freedom of contract."[53]

Although courts and commentators balked at affirming *Parkinson* in its entirety, most subsequent courts continued its general policy of deference to organizing through BTCs.[54] In 1910 the Florida Supreme Court turned down the appeal of a general contractor targeted by Tampa's BTC for employing nonunion labor. In February 1917, in a suit brought on behalf of an AABA member, Minnesota's highest court also refused to enjoin the members of St. Paul's building trades at the request of a nonunion general contractor. Union teamsters refused to handle sand excavated by the plaintiff, union men refused to work with the plaintiff's scaffolding and steam shovel when hired out to other contractors, and two of the plaintiff's customers were labeled unfair for using the plaintiff's services; still, the plaintiff obtained no relief. "It is best that we give to both employer and employé a broad field of action," the court explained.[55]

A final case came from the same Connecticut Supreme Court which in *Glidden* condemned a printers' boycott in some of the sternest language of the Great Upheaval. The Cohn and Roth Electric Company, an electrical contractor, sought an injunction against the Hartford BTC when it discovered no member of an affiliated union would work on jobs on which its materials and nonunion workers were employed. The court was not at all troubled by the massing of the building trades against the electrical contractor, for whatever injury the plaintiff suffered was but "a consequence of trade competition." Like the *Parkinson* court, the Connecticut justices saw nothing wrong in the BTC's notifying general contractors that the Cohn firm was unfair. "It did not take away the free choice from the contractor or owner; it possessed him of the facts which might affect his decision." Even the plaintiff's showing that on one occasion the BTC halted work on five buildings being erected by a builder because the plaintiff had been hired on one of the jobs was not enough to convince the appellate court that the trial judge had abused his discretion in refusing to enjoin the BTC.[56]

Thus, most of the state supreme courts who passed judgment on cases involving secondary pressure by members of building trades unions found justification for the actions in the defense of the closed shop throughout the building trades. In most cases the judges were not particularly troubled by the fact that some or all of the striking workers had no contractual relations with the subcontractor, general contractor, or materialman who was the ultimate target of the dispute. None of the judges fully spelled out the considerations of social advantage behind their decisions; most thought it sufficient to call the workers' conduct a species of competition. A few judges noted that collective bargaining, the closed shop, and the BTC had brought "harmony" to the construction industry. If they were troubled that industrial peace came at too high a cost to the consuming public, they did not reveal it in their opinions.

Judges were most likely to balk when they became convinced that the allied trades were not joined in some system of collective bargaining that struck them as a natural response to evolving industrial conditions. In such cases the judges found not a legitimate expression of group solidarity but a dangerous display of class spirit. They decided the strikers' interests were too remote and that their acts were coercive and lacked the justification of "lawful economic struggle or competition."

"The Ordinary Action of a Labor Union"

The litigation generated by the Woodtrim War presented judges with much the same issue as the BTC cases. Was the refusal to handle woodtrim produced in nonunion mills or handled by nonunion dealers justified by the carpenters' community of interest with the millworkers, or was it an unjustifiable interference by the employees of one industry with the distribution of goods produced in another? Were the New York carpenters in competition with the employees of the Brooklyn and western mills, or did the two groups of workers have as little to do with one another as

Cooke's Boston ironworkers and San Francisco jewelry makers? *Paine*, the federal branch of the Woodtrim War, presented the justices of the United States Supreme Court with a dispute that contrasted the proud "Labor Barons" of New York City's building trades with the women and children who tended the milling machines of the upper midwest. On these facts a majority of the Court was prepared to rule against the carpenters but ultimately held for the United Brotherhood on procedural grounds. In *Bossert* evidence that the millworkers and outside carpenters participated in the same labor market led the New York judges to uphold the materials boycott. In so doing, however, the judges strengthened their power to distinguish lawful from unlawful uses of secondary pressure, a move that led some commentators to question whether judges were capable of acting as knowledgeable regulators of industrial strife.

If the judges of the Woodtrim War were just as reticent as their brethren in the BTC cases on the social consequences of their decisions, this was not for lack of the assistance of counsel. Each side offered reasons drawn from public policy in debating whether the materials boycott should be justified. Before the U.S. Supreme Court, for example, Merritt argued that although a strike by the employees of the woodtrim manufacturers would be justified as one of "the ordinary methods of legitimate competition," *Paine* was no ordinary labor case. Rather, it was an attempt to monopolize the New York City market for "the higher priced products of union mills." Already Manhattan was "as completely deprived of the benefits of trade and competition in open shop work as if it was surrounded by a fleet of hostile battleships."[57]

In reply, Charles Beattie snorted at the idea that Merritt's clients were the protectors of the consuming public when they included members of the lumber trust prosecuted in the *Eastern States* case. He also offered an affirmative justification for the carpenters' actions. Under the heading "Peace from Chaos in Manhattan," he detailed how the JDC's agreements with master carpenters and lumber mills brought order to New York City's construction industry. And in his answer to Merritt's complaint he defended the carpenters' boycott as a way of ending the intolerable working conditions prevailing in the western mills, where women and children labored at low wages on dangerous machinery. Whenever the defendants referred to wood products as unfair, Beattie explained, they had in mind these deplorable conditions just as much as the nonunion origin of the products.[58]

Beattie's view of the matter prevailed in the trial court in *Paine*. Judge Julius Mayer found no common-law basis for the suit. The carpenters were merely attempting to "better their condition in a continuing economic struggle" through the nationwide unionization of their trade, the judge wrote.[59] On appeal, Justice Holmes agreed but could not convince a majority of his brethren to join him. After Alton Parker's opinion in *Cumming*, Holmes wrote, "We shall not believe that the ordinary action of a labor union" is unlawful in New York until instructed otherwise by its highest court.[60] The justice stated his position more fully in an unpublished draft of his opinion. "The only restraint of trade attempted was such restraint as follows from the members of labor unions refusing to work with non-union men or upon materials made by non-union men, for the sole purpose of strengthening the union," Holmes wrote. "The refusal to work in the stated conditions is the principle upon which labor unions are based."[61] *Paine* was thus an easy case for a judge convinced (as he wrote in *Vegelahn*) "that free competition means combination" and that it would be futile to oppose the "ever increasing might and scope of combination."[62]

In contrast, Justice Mahlon Pitney took the orthodox view. "There is no relation of employer and employee, either present or prospective, between the parties in this case." Under the circumstances it was fallacious to say that the carpenters acted to strengthen their union. "A member of a labor union may refuse to work with non-union men, but this does not entitle him to threaten manufacturers for whom he is not working, and with whom he has no concern, with loss of trade and a closing of the channels of interstate commerce against their products if they do not conduct their business in a manner satisfactory to him." The combination Holmes considered a natural outgrowth of industrial history, Pitney considered an unjustifiable attack on a distinct group of employers, the nonunion mills.[63]

Although the carpenters escaped liability in *Paine,* the case was an evil portent for organized labor. A majority of the court ruled that private parties could not obtain an injunction under the Sherman Act, but a majority also apparently concluded that the Clayton Act corrected the omission, notwithstanding the "labor exemption" provisions in the legislation. (This aspect of the opinion led Merritt to rank *Paine* with *Debs* and *Loewe* as one of the greatest labor cases in American history.)[64] In 1921 the Supreme Court would remove all doubt in *Duplex Printing Press Co. v. Deering,* a case Merritt brought on behalf of an AABA member when machinists in New York City refused to install a printing press built in a nonunion plant in Battle Creek, Michigan. Once again, Justice Pitney concluded that the strikers' acts had "nothing to do with the conduct or management of the factory" of the plaintiff. Louis Brandeis, in an opinion joined by Holmes, thought the California, Minnesota, Connecticut, and state supreme courts displayed a "better appreciation of the facts of industry" in their BTC cases.[65]

The New York litigation proceeded under the common law, without the procedural drawbacks of the Sherman Act. Once again, the question of whether carpenters and millworkers shared a common interest divided the justices. When Abel Blackmar (1852–1931) decided to continue the preliminary injunction in *Newton,* he viewed the case in terms of the conspiracy doctrine, much as Daniel Davenport might have. Loss occasioned by business competition was mere *damnum absque injuria,* Blackmar observed, but the carpenter's boycott was altogether different. It was "a concerted attack upon the trade of a merchant or manufacturer by inducing or coercing his customers to cease dealing with him."[66]

Eighteen months later, Frederick Evan Crane (1869–1947) reached the opposite conclusion on the quite similar facts of the *Bossert* case. Elevated to the court of appeals in 1917, Crane differed from Blackmar in finding justification for the carpenters' acts in their mutual membership with the mill-workers in the United Brotherhood. If the carpenters had struck against "material not made by members of their own union," Crane suggested, an injunction against the boycott would be appropriate. Here the carpenters were procuring employment for their fellow members. If, under *Cumming,* that aim was sufficient justification for a strike for the closed shop, it was also sufficient for the carpenters' refusal to handle nonunion woodtrim. "One is the competition of labor and the other is the competition of manufacture. If the actions in one case are legal, so must be those in the other."[67]

When *Newton* and *Bossert* reached the Court of Appeals in 1917, Crane's view of the situation prevailed. Justice Emory Chase stressed that the court's holding was limited by the facts found below: that the outside and inside carpenters competed for the same jobs and were joined in the same union, that the carpenters bore no personal ill will toward the open-shop manufacturers, and that the plaintiff's mill was in actual competition with the unionized mills of Manhattan. On these facts, Chase wrote, the carpenters were within the bounds of "reasonable business competition." At the same time, Chase reserved for the Court of Appeals the right to determine as a matter of law whether a strike or boycott was "reasonably and directly calculated" to advance the lawful objectives of a union.[68]

The New York justices thus found justification for the carpenters' boycott when a majority of their counterparts on the United States Supreme Court did not. Although Chase's opinion leaves unclear many aspects of his reasoning, it seems likely that the close proximity of the carpenters and millworkers in *Bossert* and their mutual membership in the same locals of the United Brotherhood convinced the New York judges that the combination represented an authentic, voluntary, and organic group. The fact that, as a trial judge in *Bossert* observed, Manhattan's large builders found "certain mutual advantages" in the carpenters' proposals may have disposed the appellate judges to view the Woodtrim War as a passing phase in a general movement toward industrial cooperation.[69] If so, the New York cases represent another example of the advance of pluralist thought in the law of industrial disputes.

The judges' willingness to defer to groups of workers had its limits, and for the New York Court of Appeals the limit was reached in another case Walter Gordon Merritt argued on behalf of an AABA member, *Auburn Draying Co. v. Wardwell* (1919). In 1913 the Central Labor Union of Auburn launched a mass boycott of a nonunion trucking company. That the court considered this no ordinary labor case was obvious from the first sentence of Justice Collin's opinion: "This is a contest between the plaintiff and the labor unions of the city of Auburn, New York." Collin emphasized the breadth of the boycott. "Dealers, ice deliverers, bakers, butchers, builders, plumbers and contractors" all discontinued business with the plaintiff to avoid trouble with the city's unions. Given the breadth of working-class participation it was not surprising Collin found a "clear and inescapable distinction" between *Bossert* and *Auburn Draying*. If anything, the opinion was remarkable for its measured tone, handed down as New York and the nation were convulsed with fear of working-class radicalism during the Red Scare of 1919.[70]

The Woodtrim War commenced when the jurisprudence of the Great Upheaval still had substantial advocates among American jurists. When *Paine* and *Bossert* finally brought the litigation to a close, the consequentialist approach to the law of industrial disputes pioneered by Holmes had captured the law schools and was gaining judicial adherents. The difference between the old labor jurisprudence and the new is perhaps best captured in the legal realist Walter Wheeler Cook's comment on *Bossert*. Like his hero Holmes ("No man can consider himself to have a respectable opinion on this subject unless he has faced and settled with the dissenting opinion in *Vegelahn*"), Cook urged a course of judicial acquiescence to the peaceful development of powerful trade unions. The difficulty with *Bossert* for Cook was not its outcome, but Chase's pretense that he arrived at it through "a simple process of deductive reasoning" from *Cumming*. In this Chase was "following the fashion which still prevails in the majority of judicial opinions." What Cook wanted to see was less emphasis upon the interests of the parties and more upon the interests of "the community as a whole." Having said this (and volunteering that conflicting views of "sound economic and social policy" separated Holmes and Pitney in *Paine*), Cook doubted whether judges, unaided by the legislature, could give ample scope to collective bargaining and simultaneously protect the interests of all concerned.[71]

As Cook's comment suggests, by the time of the United States' entry into World War I, the leading edge of American legal thought had left the founding faiths of the AABA far behind. Daniel Davenport considered the common law of strikes and boycotts a guarantor of individual liberty; Cook's generation of legal reformers believed it a seriously flawed way of regulating the combinations that had become the fundamental constituents of American industrial life. Davenport could scarcely imagine a public interest apart from the vindication of the private rights of employers and employees; the legal reformers considered the common good an expansive concept, including the consumer's interest in reasonably priced goods and the state's interest in welfare of its worker-citizens. Davenport equated the interests of proprietary capitalists with the interest of all; the legal reformers tended to see them as industrial Neanderthals and preferred the more enlightened policies of the managers of the new business corporations.

Had the official policy of the AABA remained untouched by the new thinking on American industry, society, and law, it would not have survived World War I as an influential advocate of the business side of the law of industrial disputes. What was needed was a lawyer who could continue to make capital's case after the common law of strikes and boycotts had been demoted to one among many possible schemes for regulating industrial strife. As it happened, one was close at hand. By 1917 Walter Gordon Merritt had worked out the main lines of a program that owed much to the influence of progressive reform and the corporate liberals' defense of managerial capitalism. After his father's death in April 1918, Merritt moved swiftly to commit the AABA to his new vision. Rechristened the League for Industrial Rights (LIR), the group would set sail for the uncharted waters of the corporatist political economy of interwar America.

ELEVEN

Merritt

The League aims to be the progressive wing of
the employers' movement.

—LIR (1920)

Some of Walter Gordon Merritt's earliest memories were of his father and
industrial strife. "My father lived on Main Street in Danbury, Connecticut, where I was born," he wrote in his autobiography, "and at the north
end of that street was his hat factory." Born January 4, 1880, the youngest
son in a family of at least six children, Gordon was deeply impressed by
the hat manufacturers' lockout of 1893–94, in which his father played a
leading role. By all accounts, the Danbury hatters responded to the lockout with remarkable orderliness, but the Merritt family still felt under siege
in their large, Italianate house. "All the children, including myself, were
instructed not to let father answer the door," Gordon recalled. Charles
Merritt employed a watchman (dubbed "Merritt's bodyguard" by the locals) and ordered his own sons to the ramparts. "I sat up all night with a
brother twelve years my senior," Gordon remembered, "while from a commanding window he guarded our home with a revolver."[1]

The family was only one realm in which the elder Merritt enjoyed authority and command. His experience with unionized conditions left him
convinced of the need for personal control of his hat firm. He preferred to
close C. H. Merritt and Son in 1905 after twenty-five years of operation rather
than accept the terms of the United Hatters. By that time the employer had
spun himself a web of other business interests, including the Clark Box
Company, the J. M. Ives Company (a dealer in home furnishings), the Danbury and Bethel Gas and Electric Light Company, and the local Chamber
of Commerce, of which he was a founder. He never held public office, pre-

ferring to make private use of his "strong personal influence upon men and affairs in relation to public matters." At least since 1875, when he was president of an association to raise a memorial to the town's Civil War dead, Merritt was also a leader of Danbury's civic and philanthropic life. He was president and the "guiding spirit" of the town library, organizer of the Danbury Home for Dependent Children, a "moving spirit" in the founding of the local Associated Charities, instrumental in bringing a state trade school to Danbury, and president of the Wooster Cemetery. As a Quaker, he never joined the First Congregational church, but he faithfully attended services, belonged to the church's governing body, and concerned himself "in nearly everything that pertained" to its welfare. Small wonder, then, that Merritt was eulogized as "a commanding and guiding figure in local affairs," "a man who had perhaps been more closely and more actively identified with a greater number of public and corporate interests in this city than any other Danburian of the present generation."[2]

With three elder brothers to assist their father in his ventures, Gordon was free to consider a career beyond business, if not beyond the reach of his father.[3] He attended a private school fifteen miles north of Danbury, where his tutors found him a good but not stunning student. "He learns naturally and knows how to apply himself," one wrote in support of Gordon's application to Harvard College in 1898. "I should say that he had an intelligent rather than an original mind."[4] At Harvard, Gordon encountered a curriculum organized along fundamentally different premises than the one that greeted Daniel Davenport at Yale three decades earlier. Davenport devoted long semesters to classic texts in the civic humanist tradition, but Merritt's only guided study of them was in Latin class at his preparatory school, where his marks were quite indifferent.[5] The recently professionalized social sciences of history, government, and economics claimed more of his attention. As Gordon became a more independent thinker and grew in professional stature, the mildly reformist and pluralist vision he encountered in these sources provided the foundation for a new departure for the AABA under his leadership. Well into adulthood, however, the greatest influence on his thought would be his father.

HARVARD COLLEGE

If the lecture notes of students in his classes are a reliable guide, Merritt was provided with the tools for charting a mildly reformist course through a society composed of permanent classes, an economy in which the truisms of classical economics no longer held, and a polity and public culture ruled by the political boss and the yellow journalist. Doubtless some of the lessons Merritt took with him were imparted in courses not examined here. Surely Silas Macvane, Albert Bushnell Hart, and Charles Gross taught Merritt to view societies as undergoing fundamental change in any one of the seven courses on political history and constitutional law that he took under their aegis.[6] But Merritt's courses with two men most directly foreshadowed his mature writings on labor law. Both economist Frank W. Taussig and the Social Gospeler Francis Greenwood Peabody viewed their disciplines as the study of organic, evolutionary process, emphasized empirical verification, and called for the reform of American institutions to accommodate industrial and social change.[7]

In his nineteenth-century scholarship, Taussig strove to find middle ground between traditional economists, such as William Dunbar (his senior colleague at Harvard) and historical economists such as Richard T. Ely, Henry Carter Adams, and Edmund James. He declined to join the American Economics Association, formed by critics of "the Sumner crowd" in 1885, but he also shared their historicist approach to economic problems. His contribution to a published debate between the two groups, as the historian Mary Furner has noted, criticized not only "the exaggerated laissez faire tinge of a generation ago" but also rejected James's call for the state-directed cartelization of the economy.[8] Still, Taussig took combination, whether of capital or industry, to be inevitable and natural. "The history of labor organizations in the present century indicates that they will probably continue to grow in numbers and strength, and to secure a larger and larger share of attention in the management of industrial operations," he claimed in a review of a railroad strike in 1886. He attacked the classical version of the wages fund. "Nothing in the nature of a predetermined and rigid wages fund can be found," Taussig declared in 1896, because wages could grow with improvements in productivity. He even saw no reason to conclude that gains won by unionized workers always came at the expense of unorganized workers. "In concrete life it happens very rarely, probably never, that a specific rise in wages, secured by the strike or trades-union pressure or simple agreement, can be shown to bring offsetting loss in the wages of those concerned." His textbook, first published in 1911, argued that the anticompetitive tendencies of trade unions were rarely of permanent importance, that employers' objections to the standard wage were overstated, that unions of unskilled workers increased "the sum of human welfare" by improving the lot of the most needy in society, and that the prevailing system of partly open and partly closed shops was "not unsatisfactory" in that it prevented either unions or employers from pressing an advantage too far.[9]

The same lessons were taught in the two courses Merritt took under Taussig's aegis, "Outlines of Economics" and "The Economic History of the United States." Davenport's text, Arthur Latham Perry's *Elements of*

Political Economy, was in the same moral philosophic tradition as Adam Smith. In contrast, Merritt's lecturers attacked the classical economists' faith in unregulated competition and used Smith as something of a whipping boy. "In the United States the principle of laissez-faire has never been followed," Taussig told students in his economic history class, "for the Government has interfered to assist in production by protecting manufactures and by developing transportation facilities." A lecturer in the Outlines course taught that unregulated competition meant "the survival of the unfit" with an example involving a ten-firm shoe industry. The students were asked to suppose that nine of the ten firms paid fair wages but that the owner of the tenth was "a hustler" who paid workers inadequately for long hours under unsanitary conditions. "This unrighteous man inherits the world," the students were instructed. "He would control the market and compel the other nine to adopt the same standard or go out of business."[10]

The solution (and the natural course of American industry) was greater concentration of industry under the watchful supervision of an activist state. In the economic history course, Taussig assigned his students leading exemplars of the "new thinking" on industrial concentration by Carroll D. Wright, David Ames Wells, Jeremiah Jenks, George Gunton, and other corporate liberals.[11] He argued that the Sherman Act should be replaced with new measures to legalize and regulate trusts. "They are a feature of our economic life which will continue and must therefore be handled," he explained.[12]

On the specific issue of labor and trade unionism the lecturers took a remarkably tolerant and pluralist stance. The Outlines course restated Taussig's critique of the wages fund. The assigned text, John Stuart Mill's *Principles of Political Economy,* erred in asserting that rising wages invariably meant falling profits, the students were warned. "Modern textbooks say wages depend on the product of a community." With its efficient work force and abundant natural resources, the United States had seen both high wages and high profits.[13] Strikes for higher wages or improved working conditions were legitimate attempts by workers to win a share of the wealth they helped create.

The lectures also inculcated a vision of the American social and political order that was directly at odds with the one William Graham Sumner imparted to Yale College's class of 1873. By 1900, it seems, the United States had not escaped the social stratification of class-riven Europe after all. "Custom, habit, language, race tend to keep a man in the social state in which he was born and bred. A few poor boys always do rise out of their early environment, but they are in the main exceptions." To be sure, the Harvard professors invited their pupils to snicker at labor leaders, who tended to be among "the most gaseous and light-headed" members of the working class. But they also explained that the trade-union movement was "an attempt by workingmen to improve their condition by accepting the facts of modern civilization," namely, the existence of "a permanent working class." Like the trusts, they should not be opposed as an illegitimate and undesirable conspiracy against trade, "as some employers even now say," but accepted and made to conduct their affairs in a "business-like way."[14]

Finally, the Harvard students received a quite different view of political life than did Davenport and his classmates. By words and example, Sumner and Noah Porter urged the class of 1873 to take back the governance of public affairs from the ignorant and venal politicians of the Gilded Age. Students in Taussig's economic history course were encouraged to think the situation hopeless and that the "best men" had long since fled public life. "In politics, to get a following a man must now build up a ring and leave the swaying of public opinion to newspapers." Of course, "the law still attracts talent, but such men no longer use law as a stepping stone to politics. They now go [in]to the service of great corporations."[15]

With the public realm so unpromising, a Harvard undergraduate might well ask whether it was possible for him to serve the common welfare at all. Merritt found an answer in a course he took during his last full year at Harvard, "The Ethics of the Social Questions," taught by the Unitarian clergyman Francis Greenwood Peabody.[16] The son of an early leader of the Unitarian movement, Peabody had been graduated from Harvard College in 1869 and the Harvard Divinity School in 1872. He found the rationalism and abstraction of his formal instruction stultifying ("the fresh breeze of modern thought rarely penetrated the lecture rooms") but he was thrilled by an extracurricular course of lectures in philosophy taught to recent graduates of the college. He took particular interest in the "spiritualized evolutionism" of the historian John Fiske, and he resolved to study historicism at its font, in Germany. As the historian Sydney Ahlstrom wrote, "The combination of post-Kantian philosophy, experientially oriented theology, comparative religion, and historical emphasis" Peabody encountered at the University of Halle became a touchstone for his later religious thought.[17]

Peabody's social ethics course was his great innovation as a teacher. As he explained in 1884, the course (then nicknamed "Drainage, Drunkenness, and Divorce") was an attempt to bridge the chasm between the abstract study and the practical application of ethical ideals. "It seemed to me possible to approach the theory of ethics inductively, through the analysis of great moral movements, which could be easily characterized and from which principles could be deduced." He encouraged his students to prepare written reports based on their personal observation of some charitable institution or reform movement and then used the results to "draw out" general ethical principles. "The results of the examination showed that the students felt a living interest in the subjects treated," he claimed. "I think they will be more public-spirited as citizens and more discreet as reformers by even this slight opportunity for research."[18]

In the 1900–1901 school year Peabody took up several topics, including the family, charity, and temperance, but he devoted the greatest part of the course to the "various phases of the Labor Question."[19] Although no class notes survive for the year Merritt was enrolled, a set from early 1893 and Peabody's *Jesus Christ and the Social Question* (1900) provide considerable insight into the likely content of the lectures.

As in Taussig's economics courses, the inadequacy of "the old Political Economics" in an era of industrial combination was a major theme.[20] Peabody rejected the wages fund as "the parent of socialism," because it taught workers that revolution was the only way they could acquire a greater share of the profits of industry. It may have sufficed in "'a world with no weapon but deductive logic,'" but as combination supplanted free competition something more was required to address the labor problem, "a knowledge of life."[21] Given "the amazing expansion of modern industrial methods," unions were simply appropriating to their own ends the principle of organization that industrialists had worked out. If anything, trade unionists deserved a wider berth than capitalists. "It is almost impossible to hold the men's organization together, but easily six men get together and fix the price of all the coal in the United States."[22]

Like Taussig, Peabody assumed American society was no longer classless and governable by a simple process of deduction from universal codes of moral conduct. He did hold that all people should govern themselves in accordance with the moral example of Jesus Christ, but he also believed the implications of those lessons would vary with social position. According to Peabody, Christ himself took diversity of social condition "as a natural feature of human life."[23] Further, by the early 1890s Peabody had already started to envision a public interest in labor strife distinct from that of the combatants. Speaking of the same railroad strike Taussig had reviewed in 1886, Peabody claimed that the workers had lost about $900,000 and the railroad $13 million, but that the loss to the public was far greater still. By 1904, at least, he had fully elaborated this position. "The great, long-suffering, tax-paying multitude of consumers pays in the end the cost of industrial warfare in higher prices, derangement of business, personal inconvenience and domestic distress. The people carry both the employer and the employed on their backs." These circumstances gave the public a great interest in industrial peace, he maintained, and it justified their stance as "the dispassionate observer who is at the same time the final judge."[24]

This concern with the public interest in the labor problem might have led Peabody to socialism, and it may well explain his measured portrayal of socialist thought. Socialism escaped the wastefulness of free competition, he allowed; its vision of social equality possessed "a beautiful tranquility"; its simplicity promised to deliver Americans from the soulless materialism of Gilded Age capitalism. But Peabody believed socialism was impossible because the "competitive spirit is a piece of human nature." In any event, socialism failed at the only question Peabody believed mattered: "Will it make better men?" The industrial army of the socialists would produce a general "leveling down, not a leveling up," a society without individuality, without domestic privacy, and with very little domestic morality. It would be "stifling in effect."[25]

Judged by the proper standard—"the production of personality, the making of men"—capitalism reformed in the spirit of ethical idealism was a far superior system. Like Christ's teachings, it made "moral fibre hard and strong" and taught foresight, self-respect, frugality, truth, honor, and fidelity. The business world was not inherently immoral. On the contrary, considered as a whole, it was "a vast and complex movement of social service." It discerned real needs and supplied real benefits; its denizens demanded "the most scrupulous conformity" to its distinctive moral code. "What then becomes the duty of the follower of Jesus in his relation to the industrial world?" Peabody asked. "His duty is, not to deny himself this way of expressing the spirit of service, or to permit himself scepticism concerning the possibility of such expression, but to give himself with confidence and joy to his business affairs as to that opportunity for Christian life which lies nearest to his hands."[26]

What could Harvard undergraduates take away from the teachings of Taussig and Peabody? Certainly the premise that society underwent fundamental change, and the corollary that a relatively novel social practice might well be a functional response to natural industrial developments. The maxims of their fathers, grounded in the timeless, prepolitical rights of individuals, might well be outdated. ("Anyone who believes that labor unions can be got rid of or ought to be gotten rid of is about fifty years behind the times," one student dutifully wrote during a lecture in Peabody's class.)[27] They knew to look for large social forces and social consequences, as well as individual character, in judging their world. They did not regard the regeneration of the nation's political life as a pressing concern, but felt free to embark on a career in business or the professions without anxiety, secure in the knowledge that they were advancing the ethical ideal of service by meeting the material needs of society. And they learned to look for opportunities for intelligent philanthropy—"wise generosity," Peabody called it—to help the less fortunate. Using the horrors of the sweatshop and the tenement (Peabody discussed Jacob Riis's *How the Other Half Lives* with his classes), the Harvard instructors reminded their charges that they were part of an organically interdependent whole. "It is not every man for himself and devil take the hindmost," one learned in the Outlines course, because unregulated competition led to the "social and moral degeneration" of the entire nation. "The strong can't keep themselves strong without getting equal advantages for the weak."[28]

In short, Harvard College, circa 1900, provided its students with a quite serviceable set of beliefs as they set off to construct the corporate and liberal capitalism of twentieth-century America. In time, Walter Gordon Merritt would draw upon these beliefs in launching a new departure for the AABA. During his Harvard education and its immediate aftermath, however, Gordon's thinking was subject to a more powerful influence.

FIRST STEPS

In later life, Merritt sometimes described his early career as something other than the product of his freely willed decisions. "At the outset of my professional life, I was catapulted into the midst of the labor question," he wrote to his Harvard classmates in 1929. Twenty-five years later, to the same readership, he described his life-long involvement in labor relations as starting "by accident." In fact, Merritt's activities at the outset of his career were no accident, but he may well have felt them to have been governed by a force he could not resist. Charles Merritt's influence is readily discernible in his son's thoughts and career decisions. Only in 1910, when he helped Davenport try the Danbury hatters' case, did the younger Merritt acquire the self-assurance to make his own contributions to the labor jurisprudence of the employers' movement.[29]

Dietrich Loewe was already negotiating with the United Hatters in November 1900, the fall of Gordon's junior year. According to an account Gordon wrote in 1925, at some point in 1901, while still an undergraduate, he accompanied Loewe and Charles Merritt on the fateful walk in the hills near Danbury during which they hit upon the idea of the AABA. His father started organizing the AABA at once, and by the summer of 1902 he had engaged Daniel Davenport as general executive agent. Gordon was also a part of his father's plans. As he explained in his autobiography, "The union activities placed my father's business in such a precarious state that I abbreviated my college and law school education." Although he received his baccalaureate degree with his class at the 1902 commencement, Gordon left Harvard in 1901 to start studies toward the LL.B. at the New York Law School, a degree he obtained in 1903.[30]

Well before he received his law degree, Merritt was at work assisting his father in founding the AABA, which was more consuming than anything his law teachers offered him. (Merritt was somewhat apologetic about his law training. He inscribed a copy of his autobiography to the son of his law partner, "with admiration—I hope not envy"—a reference to the son's education at the Yale Law School.)[31] During the summer of 1902, at his father's request and under his close supervision, Gordon produced his first substantial essay on the law of strikes and boycotts, "The Neglected Side of Trade Unionism: The Boycott." Decades later he recalled "sitting on the front veranda of the home on Main Street and reading mediocre passages to my father, who was ever the patient listener." *The Outlook*'s rejection of the essay brought a sharp letter of reproof from the elder Merritt, who had it printed privately as a pamphlet. Excerpts finally appeared in an October issue of *Literary Digest,* alongside reportage of the Anthracite Coal Strike. Samuel Gompers discovered the pamphlet in time to deride the "precious document" in the November issue of the *American Federationist.* "We beg to say plainly and distinctly to Mr. Merritt and his fellow-sympathizers," the labor leader declared, "that the American Federation of Labor will never abandon the boycott and that the threats against the Federation are idle, impudent and impotent."[32]

The pamphlet owed more to the mindset of a Victorian-era proprietary capitalist than to the nascent corporate liberalism of turn-of-the-century Harvard. Merritt's premise was that because the general public only turned its attention to labor affairs during strikes, few citizens were aware of "the ceaseless gnawing of the silent boycott." He begged readers not to regard a boycott as simply the sum of the wholly voluntary decisions of individual consumers. Rather, "it is literally a reign of terror" directed at merchants by that "gigantic engine of tyranny," the American Federation of Labor. Without proclaiming unionization evil in itself, in 1902 Merritt displayed none of the open-mindedness toward unions modeled by his Harvard professors. Certainly their critique of laissez-faire economics had not penetrated deeply. The boycott was "a glaringly unjust conspiracy by which a part of that fair return from wages which economic laws have given to all labor is taken from [the nonunion worker] and appropriated to fatten the pocketbook of the union man," Merritt declared. "Remove the illegal boycott . . . , and matters will adjust themselves by natural laws."[33]

Other turn-of-the-century observers of the new unionism dwelt upon its consequences for the "unorganized public." For example, with prices rising, the muckraker Ray Stannard Baker could safely assume the "professional man, the lecturer, the writer, the artist, the farmer, [and] the salaried government employee" believed that organized labor and organized capital had grown wealthier at the expense of "the man-on-a-salary and most of the great middle class," who were paying more for the necessities of life. In 1904 Peabody himself fretted over the prospect that collective bargaining would soak "the innocent third party, the lookers-on, the consumers, the people." And the *Literary Digest* highlighted the cost of the boycott to consumers by quoting Merritt's description of the boycott as "a monstrous conspiracy to put up prices" in the opening sentence of its summary of his essay.[34]

In the original, however, Merritt mentioned this aspect of the United Hatters' boycott almost as an afterthought: "The consumer too bears an unjust burden inasmuch as the boycott often deprives him of the opportunity to purchasing the cheaper article." The old language of free labor was far more important to his argument. The boycott denied employers "their inalienable right to the unimpeded pursuit of a livelihood," he declared, and even if nonpartisans believed capitalists could take care of themselves, the plight of nonunion workers should arouse them to strong protest. "The free and independent man finds it nearly impossible to obtain and keep a position in a town containing a strong union faction, and his ability to earn subsistence for himself, his wife and children is impaired." In short, "those inalienable rights that Jefferson declared to be self-evident have been placed in jeopardy."[35]

If the bulk of Merritt's "Neglected Side" might have been written in the midst of the Great Upheaval, in one respect it was sensitive to developments since the 1880s, and this was in the one area where the young law student had stronger claims to expertise than his father. With only one year of legal education behind him, Gordon had already devoted considerable study to the law of strikes and boycotts. He knew to analyze the boycott as an intentional tort rather than in terms of the old conspiracy doctrine. Further, he raised and rejected the argument that the boycott could be justified as a form of competition in the same a priori manner of William Howard Taft's opinion in *Moores*. The boycott represented the destruction of true competition, Merritt wrote, and an attack on "all the forces of economic laws."[36]

Over the next eight years, Gordon not only continued to assist his father but also acquired the expertise in labor law that would ultimately give him an independent identity and authority within the AABA. After leaving Harvard in 1901, he lived in his father's house on Main Street in Danbury at least through 1906. His father probably arranged his first law job, a position with Granville Whittlesey (1864–1934). Whittlesey, a member of one of Danbury's oldest families and an active participant in local Republican politics, moved his law practice to William Street in Manhattan in 1901.[37] The nature and extent of Merritt's work with Whittlesey is not clear from the surviving records, but it seems always to have had a rival in his work for the AABA. The one identifiable case in which the two men collaborated was the United Hatters' suit against Charles Merritt for imitating the union label.[38] And throughout Gordon's association with Whittlesey the AABA office was located in the same building and was joined to the young lawyer's through a connecting door.

Other evidence suggests that Merritt had made his father's cause his own. In August 1903, having just graduated from law school, Gordon helped obtain the pretrial attachments of property that would win the Danbury hatters' case instant celebrity. "I remember very well my agitation," he later wrote, "when my father drove me in a buggy to the town clerk's office to examine the real estate titles of homes of the members of the union." According to Merritt, his father turned to him and said, "Son, you seem to be trembling. Is it excitement?" Merritt confessed that it was. The following year, emboldened by one of Charles Eliot's broadsides against the closed shop, Gordon explained the AABA's purposes to his former college president. When Eliot wrote back to object to the requirement that the group's membership be kept confidential, Gordon's reply indicated that he and his father spoke with one voice on the matter.[39]

Finally, Gordon's work for the AABA kept him in his father's shadow. His official title from the founding of the group until at least May 1910 was "special assistant to the chairman" (that is, his father). His principal work in the New York office—gathering, digesting, and indexing a substantial collection of pleadings, briefs, opinions, employment contracts, and articles on labor law—won him no mention in the published proceedings of annual meetings and banquets in 1904, 1907, and early 1908. As late as November 1908, an AABA pamphlet referred to him only as "one of the Legal Staff." In the estimation of James W. Van Cleave, the twenty-nine-year-old lawyer was still just "a grown up boy" in April 1909.[40]

Yet all this time Gordon worked to develop a philosophy of the law of industrial disputes. Published in several forms between June 1908 and January 1909, the writings showed considerable progress away from the labor jurisprudence of his father's generation. While reaffirming the fundamental nature of individual rights to American statecraft, Merritt focussed his energies on the "irresistable" development of industrial combination and the "change of attitude" it had forced upon the judiciary. Convinced that the rights of combinations of employers and workers were not "absolute or unqualified," he set out to show how they should be regulated in the public interest.[41]

Merritt approached the issue of justification and excuse from the premise that all employers and workers possessed certain individual rights, such as the "natural flow of labor" and "natural opportunities of seeking and obtaining employment." The "pressure of social and industrial conditions" had forced the courts to qualify those rights in one important respect. Workers could combine to strike to obtain higher wages, shorter hours, and improved working conditions. Although well established, the right was "an anomaly in our law" in that capitalists could not analogously combine to fix prices and in that it licensed the intentional infliction of grave economic loss. "In what other way did a civilized country ever give legal sanction to such a measure for the destruction of property, and interference with its legitimate use?" Merritt demanded. "It would seem as if the capitalist or employer had more reason to complain," given this "notable dispensation in favor of labor."[42]

Merritt believed that the exception to the general rule should be confined as strictly as possible. Workers' privilege to inflict economic loss upon their employer should be "limited to that which inseparably grows out of their right to quit work and deprive him of the services of a large number of people." A series of examples revealed just how restrictive the young lawyer believed his standard to be. Like Smith and Taft, Merritt would condemn strikes against employers with whom workers had "no connection." Of course this included the American Railway Union's boycott of Pullman cars in 1894, and it also included the very sympathetic strikes in the building trades that the courts were just starting to tolerate. But Merritt's conception of a true "connection" between an employer and employee was even more limited than Taft's. Even a strike by union workers throughout an industry in support of the employees of one factory was illegal unless the cause was "common to all engaged" in the walkout. In the face of growing precedent to the contrary, Merritt still maintained that strikes to oust nonunion workers were illegal. In an early statement of his views he also condemned strikes timed "to inflict the greatest possible injury to property" (as Loewe believed his had been), but he later acknowledged that his authority for the proposition was weak. Finally, Merritt declared unlawful strikes to break or induce the breach of contracts, a principle that would play a large role in his later labor jurisprudence. [43]

Merritt, of course, was not the first to boil the law of strikes down to a small number of general propositions. What was more novel was his belief that the common-law rules could be restated or modified by legislation in the public interest. When Davenport spoke of the common law of labor disputes, he assumed that it was a system of timeless, natural rights. For that reason he was delighted by Justice John Marshall Harlan's statement in *Adair v. United States* (1908) that the employer's freedom to make nonunion contracts could not be abridged by statute. Merritt, in contrast, believed that the legislature was free to "limit, modify, regulate or abolish the right to strike."[44]

Merritt's gradual recognition of an overriding public interest in labor disputes was also evident in his discussion of injunctive relief. Most previous defenders of the labor injunction defended the remedy as the means by which courts did corrective justice between two private parties. "The writ of injunction is not an act of legislation," U.S. Supreme Court Justice David Brewer wrote three years after *In re Debs*. "It only enforces rights which the constitution and the law have heretofore declared sacred. It is as old as the struggle of the English-speaking people for liberty, and it has been used to protect and not to govern."[45] Davenport had similarly spoken of the labor injunction as the guardian of individual liberty. In 1908, however, his junior in the AABA spoke of the injunction as "a weapon of the whole people," a device by which society protected itself from the "hasty outrages by any person whatsoever, rich or poor, idle or industrious, organized or unorganized."[46] In 1904, Davenport joined Samuel Gompers in condemning the compulsory arbitration of labor disputes. In 1908, Merritt called the injunction *"merely* a forced arbitration" of a labor dispute in "the common welfare."[47]

Within five years Merritt would be taking much longer strides away from the founding faiths of the AABA. With his new title of associate counsel, he received the authority to direct litigation on his own, once it had the approval of his father and the rest of the general executive board. Although holding Daniel Davenport in high esteem and seeking his advice on many matters, Merritt nonetheless committed the AABA to a program the older lawyer could not personally endorse. Davenport remained general counsel until his death in 1931, but by 1917, with his father in his seventy-fourth year, Walter Gordon Merritt effectively controlled the AABA.

Associate Counsel

"Perhaps the most distinctive part of my life," Merritt wrote his classmates on the occasion of their fiftieth reunion, "is the fact that I started early in my legal profession to major in the subject of labor relations by trying the celebrated Danbury Hatters case in 1910." In fact, the first trial of Loewe's case, commencing in Hartford in October 1909, was a rite of passage for the young lawyer. Merritt's closing argument, delivered in February 1910 (a month after his thirtieth birthday), so impressed the legal bibliographer Frederick Hicks that he printed it with Davenport's in a collection of jury speeches. Davenport himself acknowledged Merritt's new stature in his summation before the Hartford jury. "He has taken the laboring oar in this case and developed the facts . . . and the law bearing on those facts in a manner it seems to me remarkable in one so young," the AABA's general counsel declared. "I am sure my brethren on the other side . . . will unite with me in welcoming to the ranks of the profession this able and honorable young man."[48]

Other professional events made 1910 a watershed year for Merritt, most notably the start of his war with the carpenters that May. At least as significant was a personal rite of passage, Merritt's marriage in July to Isabel Kilbourne Hooker (1881–1963), to whom he became engaged during the trial of the hatters' case. Granddaughter and namesake of the suffragist Isabella Hooker, Isabel was a venturesome and (in the opinion of one who knew her) "adoring" wife.[49] On one occasion, probably the Lawrence textile strike of 1919, she sat in the audience during a stormy public debate and struck up a conversation with a socialist in order to get his reactions to her husband's speech.[50] (Isabel also shared Gordon's love of the wilderness and joined him on pack trains along the Continental Divide and, in their seventies, a two-week canoe trip in Quebec.)[51] They lived in an apartment on Park Avenue in Manhattan, a train ride away from Danbury and Charles Merritt.

In this period, too, Merritt became active in civic life. Although he identified himself as a Republican, he took no active part in electoral politics. Like other members of the college-educated, urban middle classes, he preferred to work for reform through civic organizations, such as the Reform Club and the Century Association, and through private charities.[52] His lengthy service (definitely including the years 1911–21) as secretary and member of the board of managers of New York City's best-known settlement, Greenwich House, brought him into regular contact with a host of progressive reformers eager to enlist an active state in the cause of social control. Others who served with Merritt or were otherwise active in Greenwich House included FDR's future secretary of labor, Frances Perkins (who, like Merritt, generally preferred labor legislation to union organizing), the Columbia economist Henry R. Seager (with whom Merritt quarreled over the labor exemption), and Seager's colleague Edwin R. A. Seligman.[53]

Merritt's maturation is discernible as well in his growing stature within the AABA. Questioned by Charles Beattie in 1912, Merritt explained he "would not think of starting a case without conferring with" Daniel Davenport. Once the litigation had Davenport's and his father's approval, however, it was Merritt's to direct. To be sure, in the one case for which the AABA's records survive, an antitrust suit against the United Mine Workers over a violent strike in Arkansas in 1915, Merritt repeatedly sought Davenport's advice on significant legal matters. Oversight of the lawyers who prepared and argued the case was clearly his responsibility, however, and he discharged it confidently—even brusquely—on matters ranging from establishing federal jurisdiction to the conduct of depositions to dealing with a shady witness.[54]

In 1913 Merritt withdrew from his partnership with Granville Whittlesey and joined a former state senator of some prominence and another law-

yer in a new firm at 135 Broadway.[55] The AABA's office followed him to
the new building. With it came a substantial caseload, as a partial reconstruction of Merritt's work for the AABA in 1916 makes clear. In February he directed the filing of the complaint in the injunction suit of the Justin
Seubert Company, a cigar-making concern in Syracuse, New York. On May
7 he was in Minneapolis for the trial of the George J. Grant Construction
Company's suit against the local building trades council. (While there, the
Minnesota Labor Review reported, Merritt cheered a meeting of the "de-
moralized organized slavers" of the Citizens' Industrial Alliance with tales
of "the distress which it had been possible for his organization to bring to
the old Hatters of Danbury.") He arrived in Syracuse late on the evening
of May 16 for the *Seubert* trial and took an active role in its conduct.[56] In
June he was involved in negotiations to collect the judgment in the Danbury hatters' case and oversaw the filing of the complaint of several Boston lumber companies that were being boycotted by the city's carpenters.
In July Merritt's name was on the bill of complaint filed in federal district
court by an Indianapolis lawyer on behalf of an AABA member.[57] Merritt
devoted August and September to an extended tour of national parks in
the American West. Upon his return he settled into the Arkansas coal suit;
it would claim well over eighty hours of his time before the end of the year.[58]
He and Davenport reargued the *Paine* case before the U.S. Supreme Court
in October. Less than two months later the two were back before the Supreme Court to argue a case involving the interest on the deposits attached
in Loewe's suit. In December Merritt argued *Grant* before the Supreme
Court of Minnesota and *Auburn Draying* before an intermediate appellate
court in Rochester. He may also have consulted with Chicago prosecutors
as they prepared for an early January trial of the labor grafter Michael Boyle,
and he probably readied himself for the trial of the Duplex Printing Company case, which commenced on January 16.[59]

This caseload gave Merritt increased confidence in his grasp of the law
of industrial disputes, and he became more self-confident in his writing on
the subject. With pieces in *The Outlook*, the *North American Review*, *The
Survey*, and Henry Holt's *Unpopular Review*, Merritt presented his ideas
to a far broader audience than the readership of the AABA's pamphlets.
Merritt's mature work rejected both the Victorian individualism of Davenport and his father and the collective laissez-faire of Gompers for a third
position, which historian Mary Furner has dubbed "democratic statism."[60]
Pluralist in his acknowledgment that workers had to be treated on a collective basis, Merritt nonetheless insisted that combinations of workers and
employers be regulated to ensure that "the sovereign right of the consumer" reigned supreme. Dissatisfied with the "old-time notion that competition is the life of trade," he saw in the federal antitrust legislation of 1914

"a new era of competition, in which the requirements of the law more nearly conform to what the moral judgment of mankind regards as fair and just." The "truly constructive" and "liberal" views Merritt expressed after 1910, although fundamentally incompatible with the principles of the AABA's founders, would become the basis for his reorganization of the group after his father's death.[61]

Merritt's early writings on the law of industrial disputes simply reviewed common-law decisions, without explicitly calling for statutory reform. In 1910, however, he used the occasion of a railroad strike in Georgia and a transit strike in Philadelphia to demand the passage of legislation to outlaw strikes against railroads and public utilities and to fix the terms of employment in those industries. Merritt denied the proposal represented a "step toward in Socialism." The rates of railroads and utilities were already regulated, Merritt observed; his proposal simply extended to employees the same obligation to serve the public under which their employers labored.[62]

As his litigation against the carpenters developed, Merritt advanced a more expansive legislative agenda. In 1912, for example, he acknowledged that trade unions did real service in redressing the ills their members suffered. For this reason he thought "nothing could be fairer" than a statute prohibiting combinations of employers from discriminating against union labor, notwithstanding the seeming roadblock of the *Adair* case, which Daniel Davenport cherished as a landmark of industrial freedom.[63] He applauded the railroad brotherhoods, much as he would applaud Sidney Hillman's Amalgamated Clothing Workers in the 1920s. Most important, he called for greater regulation of the labor contract, including many of the reforms advocated by the American Association for Labor Legislation and the National Child Labor Committee.[64]

In April 1914 Merritt elaborated his views before the NMTA. He acknowledged that many in his audience were irritated by "the vast amount of socialistic legislation covering nearly every phase of the workingman's contract." He himself objected to proposals for minimum wage laws and unemployment insurance on grounds Francis Peabody might have offered: their potential to "stunt the growth of individual character, responsibility and self-reliance among workers" and to discourage them from developing "individual foresight and thrift to meet the vicissitudes of life." Merritt nonetheless approved of a wide range of legislation, including laws governing the payment of wages (struck down in leading decisions of laissez-faire jurisprudence), the employment of women and children, the reportage of industrial accidents, and workmen's compensation. He asked his audience to be open-minded about laws mandating the provision of health insurance and pensions. And he went out of his way to urge this fiercely open-shop group to lobby on behalf of a law to forbid combinations of employers from discriminating against union labor. No less than his Harvard teachers, Merritt appreciated the social costs of unregulated competition, and he urged the NMTA members to back protective legislation as the best way to punish the "small group of unscrupulous employers" whose abuses were destroying their reputation for "fair dealing and civic responsibility."[65]

Merritt's testimony before the U.S. Commission on Industrial Relations in May and a set of recommendations sent to the commission in November contained his specific proposals for recasting the law of industrial disputes. "With the increasing tendency toward combination on the part of labor," Merritt explained, "the state must extend its intervention even as it has done in its treatment of capital."[66] He made four specific proposals. First, he restated his call for compulsory arbitration on public utilities, where the public inconvenience of strikes was greatest. Second, for industries not affected with a public interest he urged the statutory adoption of his earlier writings on the limits of justification in labor disputes. Strikes over wages in private industry would remain lawful, Merritt explained, but beyond that labor disputes should "as far as possible, be regulated by the State, and the field of industrial warfare thereby narrowed," if necessary under the superintendence of specialized "industrial courts." He specifically proposed the outlawry of strikes against open-shop products, other sympathetic strikes, and strikes called without "a free and unrestrained ballot" by the affected workers.[67] Third, Merritt called for procedures by which employers could file labor agreements with the courts, which would be empowered to enjoin any attempt to strike against their terms. Finally, he called for a statute to correct the "dangerous immunity" of trade unions by making unions and other voluntary association suable at common law in their own name.[68]

In May 1915, the commission heard conflicting testimony from Daniel Davenport. Armed with a pamphlet version of Merritt's recommendations, Chairman Frank P. Walsh quizzed the AABA's general counsel on his associate's proposals. At first Davenport declined to address their merits. He was "nothing but a practicing lawyer," Davenport protested, more interested in enforcing the fundamental principles of the *Adair* decision than in promoting law reform. When Walsh persisted, Davenport confessed that he saw no need to change the law. "I am that fossilized gentleman who thinks that existing laws are sufficient to deal with all these matters," he explained. Even on the issue of incorporation, Davenport "would come around to the same view" as his nemesis Samuel Gompers.[69]

When a majority of the commissioners opted for the collective laissez-faire of the AFL, Merritt protested vehemently. "Instead of narrowing the field of industrial warfare by state intervention and supervision wherever practicable the policy is to be hands off," he fumed. "Might shall be right."[70] But the lawyer was already developing an alternate way of writing his program into law. In maintaining the AABA's legal clearinghouse, Merritt collected a variety of employment agreements, including those which obliged employees to observe "the Open Shop principle."[71] Other contracts went further. These affirmatively antiunion, "yellow-dog" contracts obligated workers not to join unions during their term of employment. Under law dating back to the nineteenth century, either kind of contract created property rights that employers could enforce against outsiders by injunction.[72]

Although some commentators believed union organizing in the face of such contracts could be held justified under the general theory of intentional torts, Merritt was convinced that the courts would enjoin strikes against properly tailored agreements.[73] He found "great possibilities" in a Connecticut decision of 1914 that enforced a penal bond among manufacturers pledged to maintain the open shop. In 1915 he commended a model contract to the NAM's rank and file as a "means of formulating a definite labor policy so entitled to protection that it may not be lawfully assailed or tampered with by organized labor through any means, however lawful in themselves." Joined to the labor injunction, these contracts could serve as a judicial equivalent to Merritt's legislative proposals, an affirmative statement of public policy in labor disputes, albeit one originating in the private ordering of the parties.[74]

Merritt's model contract grew over time. In 1915 it obligated the parties to "strictly adhere to the Open Shop plan." In early 1917 it did this and required notice before strikes, lockouts, quittings, or discharges. The 1919 version further obligated signers not to strike or lockout without first making "a sincere endeavor" to adjust the difficulty without resort to outsiders.[75] At no point, however, did the AABA endorse yellow-dog contracts. When solicited in 1916 to argue *Hitchman Coal and Coke Company v. Mitchell* (1917), an injunction suit based on a yellow-dog contract, Merritt (as he recalled) "immediately expressed my positive disapproval of such use of property rights to suppress unionism. Frankness naturally eliminated the possibility of my being retained." Such steadfastness to his ethical ideals became a point of pride for Merritt, part of his conviction that he had been his own man in representing the AABA. In serving the group, he insisted, he was "honestly seeking what one believes to be right."[76]

Merritt's contemporaries outside the employers' movement overlooked or dismissed his rejection of explicit antiunionism. In 1925, for example, a young labor lawyer attributed the recent spread of yellow-dog contracts to Merritt's organization. While noting that "no labor hater in good standing" could embrace all of Merritt's proposals, Gompers denounced them as "a new labor slaving device."[77] Still Merritt expected "nothing but abuse . . . for his heresies" from members of the employers' movement, who would never concede, as Merritt now did, that unions were "one of the agencies of human betterment."[78]

A full statement of his views before the New York State Bankers' Association in January 1918 apparently brought Merritt the enmity he expected. Since the United States' entry into World War I the previous April, Merritt declared, "our expanded patriotism and the war-swollen power of government" showed how employers, workers, and the state could collaborate in the "constructive and liberal" reform of industrial relations. "Little progress can be made toward industrial peace," Merritt said, "when the National Manufacturers and kindred organizations . . . denounce labor leaders as serpents" and the AFL returned the compliment. In place of "personal resentment, distrust and suspicion," Merritt offered a program based on (1) "union responsibility" for labor's torts and breaches of collective bargaining agreements; (2) "union recognition," with its "golden opportunities for promoting harmony and cooperation"; (3) collective bargaining to give workers a say in "that part of the government of industry which concerns their welfare"; and (4) the open shop. Merritt urged his audience to cross "the threshold of a new epoch with a sense of social faith and social duty" and with deference to "the State, as the agency of the people," to which all owed loyalty and obedience.[79]

The League for Industrial Rights

According to Merritt, the employers' reaction to his speech was as vehement as he predicted. "In March 1918 a fairly formidable employers' movement was organized to reduce me to innocuous desuetude," he wrote in his autobiography. But one might also have expected opposition closer to home. Charles Hart Merritt maintained his formal status as chair of the AABA throughout 1917 and early 1918 as his son became increasingly bold in his criticism of proprietary capitalists. Neither age nor infirmity explains the elder Merritt's silence: his obituary claimed he was in "remarkable physical and intellectual strength for one of his advanced age," literally "dying in the harness." Doubtless his day-to-day oversight of the AABA diminished in the fifteen years since its founding. As early as April 1917, for example, the AABA's vice chairman Walter Wood (like Merritt, a Republican, a businessmen, and a Quaker but more experienced in finance and large industry) was making decisions on the conduct of AABA litigation in the elder Merritt's stead. Further, Gordon mentioned neither his father nor Daniel Davenport in his reminiscence of eleventh-hour negotiations over the satisfaction of Loewe's judgment in July 1917. Still, the father contributed brief introductions to AABA bulletins within months of his death on April 4, 1918, and he almost surely apprised himself of his son's actions.[80]

Some evidence suggests that Charles's silence contained a measure of approval, that the warrior of the turn-of-the-century open-shop movement had moderated his views sufficiently to acquiesce in his son's opinions. At his death, friends told the Danbury *News* that "with advancing age his broadness and capacity for understanding others increased rather than diminished and that as a man of seventy he became more tolerant and more receptive of the ideas of others than he was as a young man." In particular, the *News* quoted "a man who knew him more intimately, perhaps, than any other person" to the effect that the elder's views on labor organizations and collective bargaining had "become modified in the last few years."[81]

If Charles Merritt in fact came to accept trade unionism before his death, than perhaps his change in heart originated in a change in his experience as a businessman. At the founding of the AABA, the elder Merritt's main business concern was C. H. Merritt and Son, the firm he owned and personally managed and whose goods he sold at prices set by a competitive market. After the closing of his hat company, he focused his formidable energy on the Danbury and Bethel Gas and Electric Lighting Company. As president and general manager he may well have identified closely with the firm, but he could not overlook the fact that he was an officer of a public corporation, enjoying a monopoly over its market and subject to the rate-making power of the state's public services commission. Moreover, after 1912 the Danbury utility was acquired by Cities Services, one of the largest holding companies in the electric power industry. As a testament to his business acumen, Merritt was kept on to run the local company. In performing his duties he may well have gained an introduction to the "broad-gauged" world of finance capitalism.[82]

In any event, Charles Merritt's death is the place to end a history of the American Anti-Boycott Association. Before 1918 was out, his son had polled the membership on his proposals and proposed a new name for the organization, the League for Industrial Rights. "Our members have long since outgrown the suggested limitations of its name and is extending its work into additional fields," the AABA's *Bulletin* explained. In May 1919 a new constitution formally adopted the new name and pledged that the League "shall be conducted without prejudice to labor, organized or unorganized, in its legitimate activities for economic and social betterment."[83] Over the next two years Merritt vigorously campaigned for his reforms before business and civic groups across the country, Woodrow Wilson's two industrial conferences, and state legislatures, as well as in the pages of leading trade journals and the League's own monthly, *Law and Labor*.[84]

During these years a second open-shop movement found a willing voice in the National Association of Manufacturers, but Merritt attacked the new antiunionism, even at the cost of alienating longtime supporters of the AABA.[85] Down to the dissolution of the League in 1940 and beyond, Merritt called for an expanded state role in the regulation of labor disputes, the adoption of employee representation plans and other corporate personnel policies, and a healthy rivalry between those plans and national trade unions, whose legitimacy he willingly conceded.[86] He attacked sympathetic strikes in two more landmark cases, *Bedford v. Journeymen Stone Cutters' Association* (1927) and *Allen Bradley Co. v. Local Union No. 3* (1945), but these suits owed no more to Victorian labor jurisprudence than did Thurman Arnold's antitrust prosecutions of the building trades during the New Deal.[87] He opposed anti-injunction bills in the 1920s and 1930s not, as Davenport had, as class legislation, but because it handcuffed the state while leaving unions with "a power for good or ill far beyond the aggregate powers" of their members.[88] He opposed the National Labor Relations Act of 1935 not because it interfered with liberty of contract, but because it failed to prohibit the unfair practices of organized labor and outlawed all company unions, whether adopted in good faith or otherwise.[89]

The passage of the Taft-Hartley Act in 1947 left Merritt satisfied with the main lines of federal labor policy. In that year Max Zaritsky, president of the hatters' union, sent him a copy of the check with which the United Hatters had paid off Loewe's judgment. "Each of us has learned something in the last thirty years," Zaritsky wrote. "I choose to believe that there is more responsibility and more sanity on both sides of the fence—if a fence there is—than was the case at the time." In the 1950s, some of his clients, including the Hat Corporation of America, thought Merritt was altogether too close to his union counterparts. Several canceled their retainers on the ground that Merritt was not tough enough in negotiations.[90]

By that time Merritt could count General Motors, General Electric, Westinghouse, Union Carbide, Nabisco, and AT&T among his clients, and he had fully reconciled himself to life in a society organized into large interest groups superintended by a democratic state.[91] "If unions were to accept a reasonable degree of regulation so that their conduct would more fully conform to democratic ideals," this child of the open-shop movement wrote in 1951, "I would not be averse to the idea that such dynamic functional groups should exercise broad powers of self-government subject to overriding laws to protect the public." In an undated fragment, prompted by a passage in Adolf A. Berle's *Twentieth Century Capitalist Revolution* (1954), Merritt argued that the corporation, too, "will be permitted to run with the ball as long as society as a whole believes it is doing a good job, but regulation after regulation . . . will see to it that it does not override the sanctions of society." And in a 1957 article he celebrated the fact that the welfare state had steered a middle course between "unalloyed Christian idealism and unalloyed free enterprise" on grounds that Francis Peabody would have approved: neither was a sound "social structure for imperfect man."[92]

Considered apart from the person who spoke them, such sentiments are scarcely worth noting, for they were but drops in an ocean of self-congratulation in postwar America. (Merritt's schoolteacher was right: Gordon was not a particularly original thinker.) But considered in the context of Merritt's life, they show that pluralism in American law and politics originated not in some postwar consensus or even the triumph of the New Deal. Its origins stretch back to the early encounters of American judges, lawyers, and legislators with national trade unionism. By the end of the Progressive Era these lawmakers had already set the terms upon which the labor trust would be welcomed into the body politic, and they had done so over the vigorous objections of the founding fathers of the American Anti-Boycott Association.

Notes

INTRODUCTION

1. Darrow quote from U.S. Senate, *Industrial Relations*, 11:10792; Livingston, "The Social Analysis of Economic History and Theory," 93.

2. Williston, "Freedom of Contract," 366.

3. Hofstadter, *The Age of Reform from Bryan to F.D.R.*, 241. For the phrase "collective laissez faire," see Fink, "Labor, Liberty, and the Law," 915–16.

4. Sollors, *Beyond Ethnicity*, 13.

5. Witte, *The Government in Labor Disputes*; Perlman, *The Theory of the Movement*, and "Foreword," in Karson, *American Labor Unions and Politics, 1900–1918*, vi; Wellington, *Labor and the Legal Process*, 7–26; see Tomlins, "The New Deal, Collective Bargaining, and the Triumph of Industrial Pluralism," 19–34; Ernst, "Common Laborers?" 59–100.

6. Klare, "Labor Law as Ideology," 450–82; Atleson, *Values and Assumptions in American Labor Law*.

7. Stone, "The Post-War Paradigm," 1509–80; Tomlins, *State and the Unions*. In the 1970s and 1980s several scholars writing from a libertarian perspective studied the era of the injunction judges. Like the industrial pluralists, they tended to attribute Victorian beliefs to the early-twentieth-century judges, although they praised what the industrial pluralists deplored. The scholars were not trained as professional historians, and they displayed so little interest in understanding the past on its own terms that their work had little impact. It remains a historiographic dead end. Petro, "Injunctions and Labor Disputes: 1880–1932," 341–76; Epstein, "A Common Law of Labor Relations?" 1357–408; Poulson, "Criminal Conspiracy, Injunctions and Damage Suits in Labor Law," 212–27; Dickman, *Industrial Democracy in America*.

8. The list could be longer. Higham, "Multiculturalism and Universalism," 195–219, and "Rejoinder," 255.

9. An exception is Keller's chapter on labor law in *Regulating a New Economy*. In arguing that class is a less useful guide than a perspective drawn from the pluralist tradition, this book is consistent with Keller's. It differs from his in making some of the assumptions of traditional pluralist theory a subject for investigation.

10. "Collective actors should never be assumed as premises," writes the legal sociologist Joel Rogers, "but only regarded as possible outcomes." Rogers, "Divide and Conquer," 3n.6. For an example showing how planned litigation could help build a social movement, see Tushnet, *The NAACP's Legal Strategy against Segregated Education, 1925–1950.*

11. Skocpol, "Political Response to Capitalist Crisis," 155–201. For an excellent example of the methodological eclecticism of recent work, see Barenberg, "The Political Economy of the Wagner Act," 1379–496.

12. James, "On a Certain Blindness in Human Beings," 269; Kloppenberg, *Uncertain Victory,* 11. For the revival of pragmatic thought among law professors, see "Symposium on the Renaissance of Pragmatism in American Legal Thought," 1569–853.

13. Bentley, *The Processes of Government* (1908), quoted in Ross, *Origins,* 334; see Holt, *Congressional Insurgents.* On the danger of dating the advent of pluralism in political thought with Bentley's book, see Rodgers, *Contested Truths,* 185, 195.

14. Rodgers, "In Search of Progressivism," 116; McCormick, *The Party Period and Public Policy.*

15. Scranton, *Figured Tapestry,* 2.

16. Lamoreaux, *The Great Merger Movement;* Vatter, *The Drive to Industrial Maturity,* 170–71; Livingston, *Origins of the Federal Reserve System,* 55–57; Scranton, "Diversity in Diversity," 27–90.

17. Lippmann, *Drift and Mastery,* 42.

18. Gordon, *New Deals,* 87–88.

19. Sklar, *The Corporate Reconstruction.*

20. Cochran and Miller, *The Age of Enterprise,* 240–41.

21. Hoxie, *Trade Unionism in the United States,* 30.

Chapter 1: Origins

1. U.S. Senate, *Control of Corporations,* 1154–55, 1181, 1180. See Strum, *Brandeis,* 150–51.

2. U.S. Senate, *Control of Corporations,* 1981, 2054–55, 1995, 1155, 2000.

3. Kolko, *The Triumph of Conservatism;* Weinstein, *The Corporate Ideal in the Liberal State, 1900–1918;* Sklar, *The Corporate Reconstruction;* Livingston, *Origins of the Federal Reserve System.*

4. Bensman, *Practice of Solidarity,* 34–41.

5. *Hat Review* 27 (Jan. 1900): 27–28; *American Hatter* 30 (March 1901): 58; Scranton and Licht, *Work Sights,* 155–70; Licht, "Studying Work," 62–63.

6. Bensman, *Practice of Solidarity,* 35, 39; Bureau of the Census, *Statistics of Manufacturers, 1900,* 1:537; "Hatting in Connecticut," 18; New Jersey Bureau of Statistics, *Twenty-fifth Annual Report,* 15. These conditions persisted into the 1930s, when the industrial planners of the National Recovery Administration concluded that efforts to organize such "an essentially individualistic industry" would be futile. Dewhurst and Stewart, "Hat Industry," 327; see also Green, *The Headwear Workers.*

7. *Hat Review* 30 (March 1903): 42; 27 (May 1900): 38; see also 28 (July 1901): 26 and 31 (Oct. 1903): 11.

8. "Advance in Hat Prices," 39.

9. *Hat Review* 29 (Aug. 1901): 65; "The Hat Trust," 50. For a price-fixing agreement among Danbury's leading stiff-hat firms, see *American Hatter* 32 (March 1903): 18. On the merger movement, see Lamoreaux, *The Great Merger Movement*.

10. *American Hatter* 30 (Sept. 1900): 45.

11. New York Bureau of Labor Statistics, *Fourth Annual Report*, 723.

12. Dulles and Dubofsky, *Labor in America*, 142–45; Hoxie, "The Principle of Uniformity," 714–17.

13. Connecticut Bureau of Labor Statistics, *Sixth Annual Report*, 131, 133. Tweedy's complaint that manufacturers received inadequate return on their capital was a common lament in the Gilded Age, as Livingston makes clear in "The Social Analysis of Economic History and Theory," 74–77.

14. Connecticut Bureau of Labor Statistics, *Sixth Annual Report*, 134, 135, 137; see also Bensman, "Artisan Culture," 224–35.

15. Bensman, *Practice of Solidarity*, 155–57, 171–78; Connecticut Bureau of Labor Statistics, *Sixth Annual Report*, 139–49, 163; "Explanatory Circular Issued by the Members of the Fur Hat Manufacturers' Association of Danbury, Conn.," Nov. 20, 1893, box HRD-17, United Hatters of North America Papers; Bensman, "Artisan Culture," 342–59.

16. See generally, Bensman, *Practice of Solidarity*, 185–89, 198–201; Robinson, *Spotlight on a Union*, 78–79.

17. *American Hatter* 30 (Sept. 1900): 28, 45, 48; 30 (Nov. 1900): 41; *Hat Review* 28 (Sept. 1900): 62; United Hatters of North America Proceedings, 1900, 1903, in Record at 17, 33–36, Lawlor v. Loewe, 235 U.S. 522 (1915).

18. That month another prominent Danbury firm, E. A. Mallory & Sons, went fair after negotiations over the fate of "a number of employees who were under the ban of the union." Danbury *Evening News,* Nov. 9, 1900, in Record at 1120, *Lawlor,* 235 U.S. 522 (1915).

19. Record at 978–99, *Lawlor,* 235 U.S. 522 (1915); Robinson, *Spotlight on a Union,* 81–82.

20. Bensman, *Practice of Solidarity,* 202; Record at 39–43, 459–60, 1095, *Lawlor,* 235 U.S. 522 (1915); Danbury *Evening News,* April 9, 1902, ibid., 1120; South Norwalk *Evening Sentinel,* June 2, 1902, ibid., 1138; Thomas McNally, interview with Stephen A. Collins, Jan. 14, 1964, Side 4, Scott-Fanton Museum Library, Danbury, Conn.

21. In the hatters' version of the meeting, Loewe declared that "if he died he would never come to the trade." Record at 1017–22, *Lawlor,* 235 U.S. 522 (1915); *Journal of the United Hatters* 4 (Sept. 1902): 12–14; *American Hatter* 30 (Nov. 1901): 1.

22. American Anti-Boycott Association [hereafter cited as AABA], *Million against One;* AABA, *Application,* 33; AABA, *"A Liberty League,"* 5, 27; Record at 1021, *Lawlor,* 235 U.S. 522 (1915).

23. New York *Post,* Sept. 16, 1903, in "Legal Fight against the Boycott," 31; see also *Four Cities and Towns of Connecticut,* 18.

24. Danbury *News-Times,* Sept. 12, 1935; *Commemorative Biographical Record of Fairfield County,* 664–65; Osborn, *Men of Mark in Connecticut,* 5:481.

25. Connecticut, 11:280, 12:442, R. G. Dun & Co. Collection, Baker Library,

Harvard University Graduate School of Business Administration; Osborn, *Men of Mark in Connecticut*, 483.

26. Ives, "Connecticut in the Manufacturing World," 641–42.

27. Record at 976, 981, 1068–74, 1077, *Lawlor*, 235 U.S. 522 (1915). By way of contrast, for the fiscal year ending November 30, 1899, the Stetson firm reported net profits of $384,830. In that year, Loewe's profits amounted to a mere $12,000. *Hat Review* 27 (Jan. 1900): 27–28. At the time of the strike, Loewe had $130,000 invested in the firm (some of it borrowed). In contrast, the Roelof firm announced an initial capitalization of $2 million when it incorporated in 1903. Record at 976, *Lawlor*, 235 U.S. 522 (1915); *American Hatter* 32 (Jan. 1903): 44.

28. Record at 981, *Lawlor*, 235 U.S. 522 (1915).

29. Dietrich E. Loewe to National Officers of the United Hatters of North America, April 22, 1901, reprinted in "Hundreds of Unionists Haled to Court," 5–6; Record at 984, *Lawlor*, 235 U.S. 522 (1915). Loewe later testified that the actual author of this letter was his fellow hat manufacturer Charles H. Merritt, who worked from memoranda Loewe had prepared. Ibid., 1093–94.

30. Record at 1017, 1019, *Lawlor*, 235 U.S. 522 (1915).

31. Thomas D. Stokes to D. E. Loewe, Dec. 2, 1902, in Record at 516, *Lawlor*, 235 U.S. 522 (1915).

32. Stokes to Loewe, Jan. 20, 1903, in Record at 525–26, *Lawlor*, 235 U.S. 522 (1915). Stokes was by no means unusual in this reversal. The chief of Connecticut's Bureau of Labor Statistics, reviewing boycotting by hatters in 1885, concluded, "The wholesale house is no longer the natural ally of the capitalist." Even when a manufacturer was prepared to fight, his wholesalers could "desert him at the critical moment." Connecticut Bureau of Labor Statistics, *First Annual Report*, 37.

33. Record at 1068–74, *Lawlor*, 235 U.S. 522 (1915); United Hatters of North America, *Proceedings of the Convention*, 20.

34. Record at 1025–26, *Lawlor*, 235 U.S. 522 (1915); Merritt, *Destination Unknown*, 8; Alexander Moss White to Charles Hart Merritt, Nov. 13, 1895 (typescript copy in the possession of Mary Shawah Merritt, New Fairfield, Conn.); *Danbury Evening News*, April 4, 1918; "Charles H. Merritt," 98; Connecticut, 10:816, 881, R. G. Dun & Co. Collection.

35. Record at 73, 75–77, Lawlor v. Merritt, 78 Conn. 630 (1906), Connecticut State Library, Hartford.

36. Record at 73, 77–78, 79, Lawlor v. Merritt, 78 Conn. 630 (1906); *American Hatter* 30 (Feb. 1901): 5; *United Mine Workers Journal*, Oct. 1, 1926, 7; *Hat Review* 28 (March 1900): 44.

37. Lawlor v. Merritt, 78 Conn. 630, 63 A. 639 (1906). The leading case of *Weener v. Brayton*, 152 Mass. 101, 25 N.E. 46 (1890), had determined that the common law of trademarks protected only the marks individual businessmen used to identify their products. After *Weener*, Massachusetts, Connecticut, and many other states passed statutes to give union labels similar protection. In *Tracy v. Banker*, 170 Mass. 266, 49 N.E. 1308 (1898), Oliver Wendell Holmes, Jr., held that Massachusetts's statute gave the cigar makers' union a protectable property interest in its label. The *Merritt* court interpreted a similar statute quite differently. The act only protect-

ed the marks of the actual producer of the goods to which they were attached, the court decided. Because hats were produced not by the hatters' union, but by "some manufacturer for whom its members work," the statute gave the union label no more protection than it had under the common law. *Merritt*, 78 Conn. at 633, 63 A. at 640; see Edwards, "The Labor Legislation of Connecticut," 191–98.

The court's reasoning was in no way compelled by canons of statutory interpretation; indeed, it violated several. Quite possibly the Connecticut judges were influenced by a defense raised by Walter Gordon Merritt but rejected by the trial judge and by Holmes in *Tracy:* that the union label was (in Merritt's words) "a weapon of boycott." Record at 36, 79, Lawlor v. Merritt, 78 Conn. 630 (1906); Defendant's Brief at 6–7, ibid. Although the *Merritt* court did not mention the defense, the judges may have been influenced by it nonetheless, particularly in light of the publicity attending the filing of *Loewe v. Lawlor.*

38. "United Hatters vs. C. H. Merritt & Son," 41–42; "Hat Chat," 71. An informant to R. G. Dun and Company estimated Merritt's worth as surpassing $100,000 in 1887. Connecticut, 10:1077, R. G. Dun & Co. Collection. After closing his factory, Merritt devoted his energies to other business interests, such as a gas and electric company with which he had been connected since 1872, and to religious and charitable organizations. Danbury *Evening News*, April 4, 1918.

39. Merritt, *History of the League for Industrial Rights*, 4–5, 9–13; Circular Letter, Feb. 17, 1902, reprinted in "The Question of To-Day," 65–66.

40. AABA, Constitution, box 298, Charles W. Eliot Papers.

41. The language is from Judge Peter Oxenbridge Thacher's jury charge in *Commonwealth v. Hunt* (1840), as quoted in Nelles, "Commonwealth v. Hunt," 1146–47.

42. Tomlins insightfully discussed the republican critique of trade unionism in *State and the Unions*, 36–52. His more recent and extensive study of the labor conspiracy cases argues that although the antebellum prosecutions were considered a policing of a "public realm of constitutional law and democratic politics," post-Civil War cases were thought of as arising in "a private realm of 'industrial relations.'" *Law, Labor and Ideology in the Early Republic*, 130.

43. For entrées into this literature, see Hawley, *The Great War and the Search for a Modern Order*, 6–9; McCormick, *The Party Period and Public Policy*, 313–15; Rodgers, "In Search of Progressivism," 119–21.

44. Merritt, "Employers' Associations," 880–81; see also AABA, *"A Liberty League,"* 7. Merritt settled on "the wily and sometimes unscrupulous purchaser"— that is, wholesalers—as the source of ill will among business rivals. Merritt, "Employers' Associations," 881.

45. Merritt, "List of Objections and Responses for Not Joining," pamphlet in box 298, Charles W. Eliot Papers; Blackstone, *Commentaries on the Laws of England*, 1:135; Guthrie, "The Constitutionality of the Sherman Anti-Trust Act of 1890," 93. See also Hovenkamp, "The Sherman Act and the Classical Theory of Competition," 1023–24.

46. "The Trusts Not the Employers," 323–24. The editor concluded by approvingly quoting from an antitrust speech of Louis Brandeis.

47. AABA, *"A Liberty League,"* 6.

CHAPTER 2: DAVENPORT

1. Yale College, *History of the Yale Class of 1873*, 86.
2. Kloppenberg, "The Virtues of Liberalism," 9–33; Howe, "Victorian Culture in America," 3–28.
3. For the quoted language, see Persons, *The Decline of American Gentility*, 247, see also 297; Haber, *The Quest for Authority and Honor*, 67–87, 130–32, 161–68, 206–39.
4. Persons, *The Decline of American Gentility*, 58.
5. Waldo, ed., *History of Bridgeport*, 2:30–31; Persons, *The Decline of American Gentility*, 3, 56–59.
6. Waldo, ed., *History of Bridgeport*, 2:30.
7. Ibid.; Loomis and Calhoun, *Judicial and Civil History*, 278; Dell, *Lincoln and the War Democrats*, 85, 153; Silbey, *A Respectable Minority*, 56–59.
8. Porter, *Address at the Inauguration of Noah Porter*, 45–46; see also Porter, *American Colleges and the American Public*, 95–96, and Stevenson, *Scholarly Means*, 50–66.
9. Cmeil, *Democratic Eloquence*, 58.
10. Davenport, *Address of Daniel Davenport*. On Davenport's work for the antiregulatory group, see Wiebe, *Businessmen and Reform*, 51–54.
11. Wood, *The Creation of the American Republic, 1776–1787*, 49.
12. Porter, *American Colleges and the American Public*, 45; Porter, "Classical Study and Instruction," ibid.; see Persons, *The Decline of American Gentility*, 179–202; Veysey, *The Emergence of the American University*, 22–27, 30–36, 50–51.
13. Howe, "Classical Education and Political Culture in Nineteenth-Century America," 9–10.
14. Cicero, *De Officiis*, 53, 87; see Ferguson, *Law and Letters in American Culture*, 72–78; Botein, "Cicero as Role Model for Early American Lawyers," 313–21.
15. Ross, "The Liberal Tradition Revisited," 123.
16. Tocqueville quoted in Bercovitch, *American Jeremiad*, 167n.
17. Bercovitch, *American Jeremiad*, 143–44; Ross, *Origins*, 22–30; Grossberg, "Institutionalizing Masculinity," 133–51.
18. Meyer, *Instructed Conscience*, 23–24, 35–36, 154; Ahlstrom, "The Scottish Philosophy and American Theology," 257–72. Stevenson, in *Scholarly Means*, 31–37, 69–73, and James in "Philosophy of Noah Porter," 111–43, have emphasized Porter's revision of the field in light of English romanticism and German idealism. This is not significant for my point here, which is to identify moral philosophy as one source of Davenport's universalist ethics.
19. Porter, "Conquest over the World" (June 23, 1873), in *Fifteen Years in the Chapel of Yale College*, 111; see James, "Philosophy of Noah Porter," 142–43, 145.
20. Porter, *Intellectual Science*, 1, 556, 33, 54; see James, "Philosophy of Noah Porter," 43.
21. Porter, *Intellectual Science*, 60, 520–21, 421; Porter, *Moral Science*, 149; see Meyer, *Instructed Conscience*, 154; Smith, *Professors and Public Ethics*, 36–38; Persons, *American Minds*, 192.
22. Porter, *Moral Science*, 234–35.

23. Porter, "Conquest over the World," 99, 109, 105, 106–7.

24. McNulty, *The Origins and Development of Labor Economics*, 160–63.

25. Daniel Davenport to Charles W. Eliot, Dec. 19, 1904, box 297, Charles W. Eliot Papers; New York *World*, Dec. 19, 1904; Davenport, *The Two Hundredth Anniversary*, 15–16; Yale University, *Fourth Supplement to the History of the Yale Class of 1873*, 648–49.

26. Curtis, *Sumner*, 14–21.

27. Persons, *The Decline of American Gentility*, 191–94; Sumner, "The Responsibility of the Individual for Public Opinion" (1870), quoted in Starr, *Sumner*, 141–43.

28. Starr, *Sumner*, 375, 322.

29. Keller, *Reminiscences (Mainly Personal) of William Graham Sumner*, 3; Henry DeForest Baldwin (class of 1885), in Sumner, *Challenge of Facts*, 432.

30. Barber, "The Fortunes of Political Economy in an Environment of Academic Conservatism: Yale University," in *Breaking the Academic Mould*, 143; Fine, *Laissez Faire*, 80.

31. Quoted in Persons, *American Minds*, 196, from whom I borrow the term *clerical economics*.

32. On Wayland and his influence, see Meyer, *Instructed Conscience*, 13–16, and Hovenkamp, *Enterprise*, 74–77.

33. Ross, *Origins*, 77–78; Perry, *Elements*, 150; Dorfman, *The Economic Mind in American Civilization, 1606–1865*, 2:980–82.

34. Curtis, *Sumner*, 59; Starr, *Sumner*, 379.

35. Perry, *Elements*, 140–41; Sumner, "Industrial War" (1886), reprinted in Sumner, *Challenge of Facts*, 97–98.

36. Perry, *Elements*, 149; Sumner, "The Abolition of Poverty" (1887), quoted in Fine, *Laissez Faire*, 82–83; see also Sumner, "Wages," in Sumner, *Essays*, 57.

37. For able and accessible discussions of the wages fund, see Dickman, *Industrial Democracy in America*, 39–42, 127–46; Hovenkamp, *Enterprise*, 193–98.

38. Perry, *Elements*, 139, 134, 138, 144, 136.

39. Sumner, "Protective Taxes and Wages," 275, 271; Sumner, "Strikes and Industrial Organization" (1887), in Sumner, *Essays*, 2:39–40. Because no notes survive from Sumner's earliest courses on political economy, I am left to infer his position on the wages fund from later work. This seems consistent with Sumner's disparagement of "the simple old wages fund doctrine that wages are paid out of capital" in "Cairnes's Political Economy," 9. See Bellomy, "Iconoclast," 278–79, 317–19.

40. Sumner, "Protective Taxes and Wages," 274.

41. Sumner, "Wages," 56, "Strikes and Industrial Organization," 41–42, and "Industrial War," 99, 100; see also Sumner, *What Social Classes Owe*, 80–83.

42. U.S. House Committee on the Judiciary, *Hearings on House Bill 19745*, 244–45. I discuss the Hepburn bill in chapter 9. James May relates the "real value" test of antitrust law to classical economics in "Antitrust Practice and Procedure in the Formative Era," 561–84.

43. U.S. House Committee on the Judiciary, *Hearings on House Bill 19745*, 294, 296, 297, 298. Davenport found the article in a popular encyclopedia edited by John

J. Lalor, *Cyclopedia of Political Science, Political Economy, and the Political History of the United States*, 1:539–47.

44. Sumner, *What Social Classes Owe*, 23, 24, 8–9, 11; Sumner, "Industrial War," 101. On German political philosophy and Sumner's reaction to it, see Kloppenberg, *Uncertain Victory*, 177–79, 396; Bellomy, "Iconoclast," 286.

45. U.S. House Committee on the Judiciary, *Hearings on House Bill 19745*, 307. In distinguishing between Lockean laissez-faire jurists like Field and historicist jurists like Thomas Cooley I follow Rodgers, *Contested Truths*, 152–54. Rodgers's book is also the immediate source of my point about how the former combined eighteenth-century natural rights talk with the rhetoric of the nineteenth-century antislavery movement.

46. Porter, *Moral Science*, 396–97, 490–93; see generally Rodgers, *Contested Truths*, 112–43. Novak has found the moral philosophers' notion of the social nature of man in the influential antebellum legal writings of Nathaniel Chipman, James Kent, Zephaniah Swift, and James Wilson. *Intellectual Origins of the State Police Power*, 29–42.

47. Lieber, *On Civil Liberty and Self-Government*, 25, 40n.2; Hallam, *Constitutional History of England*. On Lieber's political philosophy, see Freidel, *Francis Lieber*, 144–70, 266–74; Ross, *Origins*, 37–42.

48. Sumner, *What Social Classes Owe*, 30; Sumner, "The Boon of Nature" (1887), quoted in Fine, *Laissez Faire*, 81; Sumner to David Ames Wells, June 6, 1881, quoted in ibid., 131n.16.

49. Bellomy, "Iconoclast," 255–57.

50. For samples of Davenport's historical research, see the summary of his brief in Flynn v. Morgan, 55 Conn. 130 (1887), and Davenport, *New Milford*.

51. McNeill, ed., *The Labor Movement*, 489; New York Bureau of Labor Statistics, *Third Annual Report*, 133–34; Ely, *The Labor Movement in America*, 297–98.

52. Thus, Henry May wrote that Victorian Americans found in Spencer's work "a new version of the unfolding moral law." *The End of American Innocence*, 12.

53. Sumner, *What Social Classes Owe*, 24; Fine, *Laissez Faire*, 81, 84.

54. In a careful and thoughtful article, Siegel has found teleological historicism (which he calls "historism") in the works of John N. Pomeroy, Thomas M. Cooley, and Christopher G. Tiedeman. See "Historism," 1431–547. For an earlier discussion of Cooley's historicism, see Jones, "Cooley," 762–63. On Tiedeman, consult Mayer, "The Jurisprudence of Christopher G. Tiedeman," 93–161.

55. Jones, "Cooley," 767–77; Fine, *Laissez Faire*, 128–29.

56. Holmes, *The Common Law*, 167; Lochner v. New York, 198 U.S. 45, 75 (1905) (Holmes, J., dissenting); see Siegel, "Historism," 1546–47.

57. Daniel Davenport to W. O. Burr, Dec. 6, 1909, Yale University Archives; Act of Aug. 12, 1909, ch. 209, 1909 Conn. Pub. Acts 1135; Buck v. Bell, 274 U.S. 200, 207 (1927).

58. Sumner, "Introductory Lecture to Courses in Political and Social Science" (1873), in Sumner, *Challenge of Facts*, 402–3.

59. Ibid.

60. See, for example, the testimony of Henry R. Seager in U.S. Senate, *Industrial Relations*, 11:10558–59.

61. Gordon, "'The Ideal and the Actual in the Law,'" 62 (emphasis deleted).

62. Waldo, ed., *History of Bridgeport*, 2:30–31; Yale College, *Biographical Record*, 42; Loomis and Calhoun, *Judicial and Civil History*, 586; *Who Was Who*, 1:962.

63. O'Hara, "Obituary Sketch"; Waldo, ed., *History of Bridgeport*, 2:675–76; Bryce, *The American Commonwealth*, 2:498–99. Davenport and O'Hara were partners from 1882 to 1899. In the latter year Davenport formed a partnership with a younger lawyer, Elmore S. Banks, that lasted until 1908. "Elmore Sherman Banks," in Osborn, *Men of Mark in Connecticut*, 1:263–64.

64. This was the verdict of Justice George W. Wheeler, who once campaigned for Grover Cleveland with Davenport and O'Hara. Wheeler reported that Davenport was the favorite of Chief Justice Simeon Baldwin, who knew him from Democratic political activities. O'Hara, "Obituary Sketch," 743–44; Daniel Davenport to Simeon E. Baldwin, Dec. 24, 1891, Simeon E. Baldwin Papers.

65. Merritt, *Destination Unknown*, 17; Yale College, *Quindecennial Record of the Class of 1873*, 15, Yale University Archives; O'Hara, "Obituary Sketch," 746; Clark v. Beers, 61 Conn. 87 (1891); Matzko, "'The Best Men of the Bar,'" 75–96. Davenport was president of Bridgeport's bar association in 1893–94. Bridgeport *Post*, Sept. 15, 1894.

66. "Address delivered by Algernon Sydney Sullivan at the Laying of the Corner Stone of the Consolidated Stock and Petroleum Exchange, New York City, Sept. 8, 1887," in Holmes, *Algernon Sydney Sullivan*, 233–37; see Lisagor and Lipsius, *A Law unto Itself*, 15–38.

67. Ideally, conclusions about Davenport's practice would be based on his office files or the manuscript records of the trial courts of Fairfield County. Inquiries with Davenport's descendants suggest the former have not survived. A time-consuming search of the latter would, I think, be unlikely to change my account significantly. The bar's agreement that Davenport was a remarkable courtroom advocate but weak on office work suggests that Bridgeport's industrialists looked elsewhere for their routine legal transactions. Further, one would expect appellate records to overstate the number of business concerns among Davenport's clients, as these would seem disproportionately likely to possess the resources to mount appeals.

68. Hartford *Times*, Jan. 10, 1902; Wilson v. Waterville School District, 44 Conn. 157 (1876); Cook v. Morris, 66 Conn. 196, 33 A. 594 (1895); Turney v. Bridgeport, 55 Conn. 412, 12 A. 520 (1887); Smith's Appeal, 65 Conn. 135, 31 A. 529 (1894); Rogers Silver Plate Co. v. Jennings, 67 Conn. 400, 35 A. 281 (1895); Beach v. Travelers Insurance Co., 73 Conn. 118, 46 A. 867 (1900); Baldwin v. Miles, 58 Conn. 496, 20 A. 618 (1890). On Bridgeport's industry, see *History of Bridgeport*, ed. Waldo, 1:153–92.

69. Lindsay v. Gunning, 59 Conn. 296, 22 A. 310 (1890); Roraback v. Pennsylvania Co., 58 Conn. 292, 20 A. 465 (1890).

70. Davenport cited Roraback's political influence in seeking to remove the case to the federal courts. Record at 20–21, *In re Pennsylvania Co.*, 137 U.S. 451 (1890). On the political influence of Alberto Roraback and his brother Henry, see "Alberto T. Roraback," in Osborn, *Men of Mark in Connecticut*, 2:15–17; Baney, *Yankees and the City*, 182–83.

71. Oral Argument, Dec. 15, 1890, 38, 40, New York & Northern Railway Co. v. New York & New England Railroad Co., Formal Docket No. 268, RG 134, Records of the Interstate Commerce Commission, National Archives, Suitland, Maryland; see Niven, *Connecticut for the Union*, 402–4.

72. Hearing, Sept. 22, 1890, 111–28, New York & Northern v. New York & New England, Formal Docket No. 268; Deposition, Oct. 11, 1890, 245–46, ibid.; Oral Argument, Dec. 15, 1890, 64, ibid.

73. Hearing, Sept. 19, 1890, 66–68, 105, ibid.; Oral Argument, Dec. 15, 1890, 49, 39, 44, ibid. On the political influence of the New York, New Haven & Hartford, see Heath, "Politics and Steady Habits," 48–49. Davenport lost the case. New York & Northern Railway v. New York & New England Railroad, 4 I.C.C. Rep. 702 (1891).

74. In re William Clark, 65 Conn. 17, 31 A. 522 (1894); Smith's Appeal, 65 Conn. 135, 31 A. 529 (1894); Maisenbacker v. Society Concordia, 71 Conn. 369, 42 A. 67 (1899).

75. U.S. House Committee on Labor, *Eight Hours*, 58th Cong., 1904, 24.

76. State ex rel. Harty v. Kirk, 46 Conn. 395 (1878); Gregory v. City of Bridgeport, 52 Conn. 40 (1884); State ex rel. Rylands v. Pinkerman, 63 Conn. 176, 28 A. 110 (1893); O'Flaherty v. Bridgeport, 64 Conn. 159, 29 A. 466 (1894); Coughlin v. McElroy, 72 Conn. 99, 43 A. 854 (1899); State ex rel. Williams v. Kennelly, 75 Conn. 704, 55 A. 555 (1903); Wooster v. Mullins, 64 Conn. 340, 30 A. 144 (1894); *Register and Manual of the State of Connecticut* (Hartford, 1901), 471. Davenport also represented a Democratic candidate for selectman in neighboring New Milford. Buck v. Barnes, 75 Conn. 460, 53 A. 1012 (1903).

77. O'Hara, "Obituary Sketch," 742; City of Bridgeport, *Municipal Register*, 1878: 175, 1886: 233.

78. Niven, "The Time of the Whirlwind," 448, 453, 561. The percentage of first- and second-generation immigrants in Bridgeport's population grew from 60 percent in 1890 to 68 percent in 1900. U.S. Census Office, *Compendium of the Eleventh Census*, 542, 670–71; U.S. Census Office, *Twelfth Census of the United States*, vol. 1, pt. 1, 866. Before 1900, Northern Europe provided the overwhelming majority of the city's immigrants. In 1900, a quarter of the city's residents had at least one parent born in Ireland, whereas only 3 percent had at least one Italian-born parent, and only 1 percent had at least one Russian-born parent. Ibid., 874–75, 883, 891, 899; see McSeveney, *Politics of Depression*, 31.

79. McFarland, "Breakdown of Deadlock," 381. Under Connecticut's scheme of apportionment, the town of Union, with 428 inhabitants in 1900, had the same number of delegates to Connecticut's house of representatives as New Haven, a city of 108,027 residents. Ford, "Rural Domination," 222.

80. Quoted in Kloppenberg, *Uncertain Victory*, 363; see McFarland, "Breakdown of Deadlock," 381–85.

81. McFarland, "Breakdown of Deadlock," 385–97.

82. "Robert E. DeForest," in *Representative Men of Connecticut, 1861–1894*, 421–23.

83. Heath, "Politics and Steady Habits," 41, 44, 51, 62, 68; McSeveney, *Politics of Depression*, 118–27, 190–96; Buenker, "Progressivism in Connecticut," 99–100.

84. Brooks Adams to Grover Cleveland, Oct. 23, 1884, quoted in Blodgett, "A New Look at the Gilded Age," 106; Wilson, "Mr. Cleveland as President," 289; White, "Cleveland," 324–25. The Wilson and White quotations are from Kelley's splendid chapter on Cleveland, "The Democrat as Social Moralist," in *Transatlantic Persuasion,* 295–96.

85. O'Hara, "Obituary Sketch," 742; Kelley, *Transatlantic Persuasion,* 307; U.S. House Committee on Labor, *Eight Hours,* 58th Cong., 1904, 22.

86. Daniel Davenport to Board of Public Works of the City of Bridgeport, June 27, 1894, in *Municipal Register of the City of Bridgeport for 1895* (Bridgeport, 1895), 473–75.

87. Bridgeport *Evening Post,* Sept. 11, 1894; Waldo, ed., *History of Bridgeport,* 2:676; Davenport to Common Council, Sept. 15, 1894, in *Municipal Register,* 478–80; Bridgeport *Evening Post,* Sept. 15, 1894. As president of the common council, O'Hara temporarily held the office while the real mayor was out of town.

88. Davenport to Common Council, Sept. 20, 1894, in *Municipal Register,* 481–82; Bridgeport *Evening Post,* Sept. 21, 1894.

89. Bridgeport *Evening Post,* Sept. 18, 22, 1894; Daniel Davenport to Common Council, June 27, 1895, in *Municipal Register,* 485–92.

90. For parallel developments in New York, consult McCormick, *From Realignment to Reform.*

91. Bridgeport *Evening Post,* Sept. 17, 1894. O'Hara never again held public office. Waldo, ed., *History of Bridgeport,* 2:676.

92. Bridgeport *Morning Telegram,* Sept. 19, 1898.

93. O'Hara, "Obituary Sketch," 742; Hartford *Courant,* July 6, 1908; U.S. House Committee on Labor, *Eight Hours,* 58th Cong., 1904, 24; *National Cyclopedia of American Biography,* 18:412. Davenport played no discernible role in the State Democratic Convention held in Bridgeport in 1898. Bridgeport *Morning Telegram,* Sept. 21, 22, 1898.

94. Davenport's opponent was Allan W. Paige, who, as counsel to the Bridgeport Traction Company, had publicly attacked Davenport in 1894. Bridgeport *Morning Telegram-Union,* Oct. 29, Nov. 1, 4, 1901; Howe, "Connecticut's Labor Mayors," 1259–64; Bridgeport *Evening Post,* Sept. 17, 1894.

95. Heath, "Politics and Steady Habits," 112, 123, 127, 129; *New York Times,* Oct. 5, 1894; Clark, "Connecticut Convention," 150; Ford, "Rural Domination," 226; Putnam, "What's the Matter with New England," 271.

96. Connecticut Constitutional Convention, "Resolution File No. 1–155," Nos. 61, 107, 108, 121, Library of Congress (call number JC3325 1902 A3) [hereafter cited as Convention Files]; "Stenographic Record of the Debates of the Constitutional Convention of the State on Connecticut, January 1, 1902 to May 15, 1902," 2326, 526–27, 178, Connecticut State Archives, Hartford.

97. "Stenographic Record," 79; Hartford *Times,* Jan. 9, 1902. The measure lost, 110 to 3. Ford, "Rural Domination," 232.

Davenport also introduced the resolve of Bridgeport's electrical workers asking that "eight hours constitute a legal day's work." Convention Files, File No. 119. I doubt he would have given the resolution even this pro forma support were it not possible to satisfy it with a "declaratory" bill making eight hours a legal day's work only when the parties to the employment contract had not specified otherwise. See Brandeis, "Labor Legislation," 3:541. Another measure introduced by Davenport was similarly ambiguous: "The rights of labor shall have just protection through laws calculated to secure to the laborer the proper rewards for his services, and to promote the industrial welfare of the State." Convention Files, File No. 121.

98. Hartford *Daily Courant*, Jan. 10, 1902; O'Hara, "Obituary Sketch," 745.

99. Hartford *Daily Courant*, Jan. 10, 1902.

100. Clark, "Connecticut Convention," 154–55, 158, 161; Perry, "Constitutional Convention of 1902," 1:481; *Journal of the Constitutional Convention of Connecticut*, 114, 116. Before a gathering in Hartford two days before the referendum, Davenport declared "unworthy of his ancestry" any Connecticut citizen who would vote for the proposed constitution, in light of the hardships the settlers endured for "equality in the system of representation." Hartford *Courant*, June 16, 1902, quoted in Baney, *Yankees and the City*, 164.

101. AABA, *"A Liberty League,"* 6.

102. Allison, "The Rise and Probable Decline of Private Corporations," 256.

103. Holmes, "Path of the Law," in *Collected Legal Papers*, 184. In the same spirit, Hovenkamp argues Holmes rightly denied that the Fourteenth Amendment enacted Spencer's *Social Statics*. "In fact," Hovenkamp writes, "it enacted Francis Wayland's *Elements of Political Economy*." Hovenkamp, *Enterprise*, 101.

104. Holmes, "Path of the Law," in *Collected Legal Papers*, 184. As Holmes protested in his *Lochner* dissent, "This case is decided upon an economic theory which a large part of the country does not entertain." *Lochner v. New York*, 198 U.S. 45, 75 (1905).

105. O'Hara, "Obituary Sketch," 745, 746, 744–45; "George Wakeman Wheeler," 350–51.

106. O'Hara, "Obituary Sketch," 745. The quoted language is from John Dewey, "The Discrediting of Idealism," *New Republic*, Oct. 8, 1919, 285–87, quoted in Kloppenberg, *Uncertain Victory*, 372.

Chapter 3: A Liberty League

1. AABA, *"A Liberty League,"* 50–51. On Spooner, see Parker, "The Business of Politics," 39–53.

2. U.S. House Committee on Labor, *Eight Hours*, 60th Cong., 1908, 643–44.

3. The seminal work on interest-group formation is Olson, *Logic*. For an accessible summary of the subsequent literature, consult McLean, *Public Choice*.

4. National Association of Manufacturers, *Proceedings of the Ninth Annual Convention*.

5. The key work here is that of McCormick: *From Realignment to Reform* and *The Party Period and Public Policy*. See also Rodgers, "In Search of Progressivism," 114–21.

6. Wolman, *The Growth of American Trade Unions*, 33; Stockton, *Closed Shop*, 40, 43; U.S. Commissioner of Labor, *Twenty-First Annual Report*, 56–57; Van Tine, *The Making of the Labor Bureaucrat*, 66–78.

7. U.S. Anthracite Coal Commission, "Report," 518; Dulles and Dubofsky, *Labor in America*, 179–84; Greenberg, *Roosevelt and Labor*, 91–182.

8. U.S. House Committee on the Judiciary, *Injunctions*, 284–85; *Who's Who in America, 1903–1905*, 1616.

9. Greenberg, *Roosevelt and Labor*, 183–223; *Weekly Bulletin of the Clothing Trades*, July 29, 1904, quoted in Stockton, *Closed Shop*, 53n.4.

10. Perlman and Taft, *History of Labor*, 129–37; Bonnett, *Employers' Associations*, 22–24; Wiebe, *Businessmen and Reform*, 25–27.

11. See McLean, *Public Choice*, 66–67; Miller, "Public Choice at the Dawn of the Special Interest State," 85–86, 93–101.

12. "Proceedings of the Fifth Annual Convention," 542, 591. One consequence of Davenport's piggybacking was noted by a contemporary observer of the open-shop movement: the AABA had as members "more representative association leaders than any other association, not excepting the National Association of Manufacturers." Bonnett, *Employers' Associations*, 471.

13. Daniel Davenport to James A. Emery, March 25, 1911, Emery to Davenport, March 27, 1911, in U.S. House Select Committee, *Charges against Members*, 1:66–68.

14. Cochran and Miller, *The Age of Enterprise*, 240–41; Watts, *Order against Chaos*, 153; see also Greene, "'Strike at the Ballot Box,'" 152–58.

15. National Association of Manufacturers, *Proceedings of the Ninth Annual Convention*, 184–85.

16. J. W. Van Cleave to Daniel Davenport, May 22, 1908, in U.S. Senate Committee on the Judiciary, *Maintenance of a Lobby: Appendix*, 2:1649.

17. J. W. Van Cleave to Ferdinand C. Schwedtman, April 12, 1909, in U.S. Senate Committee on the Judiciary, *Maintenance of a Lobby: Appendix*, 3:2790–91.

18. James A. Emery to Ferdinand C. Schwedtman, April 9, 1909, in U.S. Senate, *Maintenance of a Lobby: Appendix*, 3:2778.

19. Boocock, *Law and Reason*.

20. Walter Drew to John Kirby, March 9, 1911, Drew to F. J. Lucius, Feb. 14, 1911, Drew to Herman Frederic Lee, March 9, 1911, box 1, Walter W. Drew Papers.

21. Lee to Drew, March 13, 1911, Drew to Lee, March 14, 17, 1911, box 1, Walter W. Drew Papers.

22. AABA, *Reason for Existence*; see also Davenport, "The Boycott and How It Can Be Destroyed," 54–55; Boocock, *The Abuses of Organized Labor*, 6, 12; Fine, "The National Erectors' Association," 5–41.

23. AABA, *Convention Number, February Bulletin*; Feinstein, *Stamford in the Gilded Age*, 19–20.

24. Leonor F. Loree to Elihu Root, July 18, 1912, box 93, Elihu Root Papers; Witte, *The Government in Labor Disputes*, 113; Petro, "Injunctions and Labor Disputes: 1880–1932," 431.

25. Witte, *The Government in Labor Disputes*, 85–96; Frankfurter and Greene, *The Labor Injunction*, 53–81; Hurvitz, "American Labor Law," 333–44; Forbath, *Law and the Shaping of the American Labor Movement*, 59–97.

26. W. B. Cowles to American Anti-Boycott Association, July 25, 1907, in U.S. Senate, *Maintenance of a Lobby: Appendix*, 1:1020–21.

27. For a list of cases, consult Ernst, "The Lawyers and the Labor Trust," 350–51.

28. Another problem was that before 1914, federal antitrust law (the most promising basis for federal intervention in the proprietors' labor disputes) did not clearly authorize the issuance of an injunction in the suit of a private party. Employers rarely found the alternative, a suit for damages, adequate in a labor setting—unless they were supported by the AABA. Witte, *The Government in Labor Disputes*, 134–51.

29. In contrast, the earliest examples of planned litigation on a national scale were the Singer Manufacturing Company's campaign to overturn state laws barring it from developing a chain of retail outlets for its sewing machines and the "Big-Four" meat-packers' attack on state regulatory barriers to the marketing of its refrigerated beef. McCurdy, "American Law and the Marketing Structure of the Large Corporation," 632–49.

30. Record at 991, Paine Lumber Co. v. Neal, 244 U.S. 459 (1917). The AABA's policy was to build a $250,000 surplus by levying members at the rate of $1 for every $1,000 of their monthly payroll (up to a sum of $500) no more than six times a year. The group also accepted donations from any person, firm, or association "in whatever sums their interest or generosity may suggest." Transcript at 90, 92, Savage v. Potter, 159 A.D. 729, 145 N.Y.S. 78 (1913), vol. 2,836, Case No. 527, Library of the Association of the Bar of the City of New York, New York City.

31. These are Daniel Davenport's somewhat off-hand estimates, made during testimony before a federal commission. U.S. Senate, *Industrial Relations*, 11:10662. Davenport estimated the total expense of the *Christensen* case (chapter 5) at between $5,000 and $6,000. He placed the contribution of each individual member at between thirty and forty dollars. *Square Deal* 1 (Dec. 1905): 23.

32. Galanter, "Why the 'Haves' Come Out Ahead," 95–160.

33. Martin, *Law of Labor Unions*. A handful of less satisfactory works, lacking Martin's extensive formulary appendix, had appeared earlier. Further, parts of the field had received chapter-length treatments in nineteenth-century treatises on related subjects, like trusts and injunctions.

34. *Law and Labor* 1 (April 1919): 16; see U.S. Senate, *Industrial Relations*, 11:10662.

35. Keller, *In Defense of Yesterday*, 42–52, 55–56, 63–65, 67, 72–75; "James M. Beck's Promotion," 206.

36. AABA, *November Bulletin;* Walter Gordon Merritt to James B. McDonough, March 12, 1920, Walter Gordon Merritt Papers, Duke University; "Would Have Killed This Lawyer," 1–2.

37. AABA, *Bulletin,* Jan. 29, 1908; see Transcript at 38, *Savage,* 159 A.D. 729, 145 N.Y.S. 78 (1913).

38. Loewe v. Lawlor, 208 U.S. 274 (1908). Similarly, a nonunion hat manufacturer would benefit from the weakened state of the United Hatters as it defended itself against Loewe's suit, even though he never contributed a penny to the AABA.

39. McLean, *Public Choice,* 11–12, 62–65.

40. Stigler, "Free Riders and Collective Action," 360. This reasoning assumes the existence of a competitive market for the selective benefit. Favorable tax policies, governmental regulation, and monopoly power have sometimes sheltered interest groups from the competition of more conventional producers. Olson, *Logic,* 132–59.

41. McLean, *Public Choice*, 66.

42. Hanson, "The Political Economy of Group Membership," 79–80, 94, 81–82.

43. "Proceedings of the Fifth Annual Convention," 544; AABA, *Reason for Existence*; AABA, *Convention Number, February Bulletin*, 5, 13.

44. AABA, *Bulletin*, March 1, 1916, 9–10, Sept. 27, 1915; *Law and Labor* 2 (Jan. 1920): 2.

45. AABA, *Convention Number, February Bulletin*; AABA, *Bulletin*, March 22, 1911; Walter Gordon Merritt to Daniel Davenport, Oct. 17, 1916, Walter Gordon Merritt Papers, Duke University.

46. Walter Gordon Merritt to Henry S. Drinker, Oct. 21, 1916, Walter Gordon Merritt Papers, Duke University; Transcript at 9–11, 25–26, *Savage*, 159 A.D. 729, 145 N.Y.S. 78 (1913).

47. AABA to Justin Seubert, Inc., Oct. 8, 1915, Exhibit 75, "Defendant's Brief," folder 512, box 7, Paul F. Brissenden Papers. In 1912 Walter Gordon Merritt could recall only one occasion, soon after the founding of the AABA, when its lawyers gave advice to a non-member. Transcript at 29, *Savage*, 159 A.D. 729, 145 N.Y.S. 78 (1913).

48. Syracuse *Post Standard*, May 17, 1916; AABA, *Reason for Existence*. With the exception of a file on the Pennsylvania Mining Company case, surviving in the Walter Gordon Merritt Papers, Duke University, I have been unable to locate the internal records of the group, described in 1912 as back correspondence and a card catalog of members. Transcript at 42–43, *Savage*, 159 A.D. 729, 145 N.Y.S. 78 (1913). As a result, my count of AABA-sponsored cases is approximate, based on the AABA's *Bulletin* and a search of computerized databases of state and federal judicial decisions.

49. *National Cyclopedia of American Biography*, 38:34–35; AABA, *Convention Number, February Bulletin*.

50. B. S. Atwood to G. G. Huebner, Sept. 19, 1904, reel 12, *American Bureau of Industrial Research*; AABA, *Convention Number, February Bulletin*, 14.

Although the sources do not exist for a systematic description of the AABA's membership, Patterson and Atwood would appear to be representative of the rank and file. No charter member was (in Walter Gordon Merritt's words) "a so-called trust or any of the small group of the largest industrial organizations," and railroads never joined. At least two very large firms were members: the Yale & Towne Manufacturing Company, a giant in the hardware industry, and the Buck's Stove and Range Company, which was capitalized at almost $1 million and had annual sales of $1.25 million. The men who ran those firms, Henry R. Towne and James W. Van Cleave, had a proprietor's sense of responsibility for the business that made them see demands for the closed shop as intolerable challenges to their personal responsibility for their concerns. Most of the identifiable members were drawn from competitive industries in which proprietorships and partnerships were common: hatting, clothing, cigar making, metal fabricating and machining, lumber wholesaling, baking, and boxmaking. By early 1904 the one hundred charter firms had grown to approximately 250, with an aggregate payroll of $85 million; by May 1914 more than five hundred firms had joined; in the following year the AABA had nearly six hundred member firms and another three hundred contributing individuals and associations. Merritt, *History of the League for Industrial Rights,* 10–11; Feinstein, *Stamford in the Gilded Age,* 14–16; U.S. House Committee on the Judiciary, *Hearings on Trust Legislation,* 1:518. Record at 3, 4, Gompers v. Buck's Stove & Range Co., 221 U.S. 418 (1911); Walter Gordon Merritt to Charles W. Eliot, Feb. 14, 1904, Charles W. Eliot Papers; U.S. Senate, *Industrial Relations,* 11:10651; AABA, *Davenport Testimonial.*

51. Link, *Wilson: The Road to the White House,* 127; William Howard Taft to Henry B. Sargent, Dec. 23, 1913, reel 521, William Howard Taft Papers; *New York Times,* March 8, 1924; Program, Annual Banquet, League for Industrial Rights, March 4, 1926, in the possession of Mary Shawah Merritt, New Fairfield, Conn.; "Respectability Screens Anti-Union Assaults," 259–60, 320. The AABA was not unique in discovering that a good banquet helped assure the stability of an interest group. The Metal Manufacturers' Association of Philadelphia devoted as much as one-fifth of its annual income to banquets, usually a much greater amount than it spent on strikebreaking. Harris, "Getting It Together," 122.

52. *New York Times,* March 17, 1929.

53. AABA, *Convention Number, February Bulletin.*

54. Davenport, "For the Open Shop," 9–10.

55. Bercovitch, *American Jeremiad,* 132.

56. Davenport, "For the Open Shop," 9.

57. Lincoln, "Address Before the Young Men's Lyceum of Springfield, Illinois," in *Collected Works,* 1:108

58. Davenport, "For the Open Shop," 9; National Association of Manufacturers, *Proceedings of the Tenth Annual Convention,* 72; Citizens Industrial Association of America, "The Third Annual Convention," 24.

59. Davenport, "For the Open Shop," 11, 10. Bercovitch writes that the American jeremiad "united nationality and universality, civic and spiritual selfhood, secular and redemptive history, the country's past and paradise to be, in a single, synthetic ideal." *American Jeremiad,* 176.

60. Davenport, "For the Open Shop," 10, 11.

61. Ibid., 11.

62. National Association of Manufacturers, *Proceedings of the Tenth Annual Convention,* 72–73; see Hartog, "Mrs. Packard on Dependency," 79–103.

63. Davenport, "The Anti-Boycott Movement," 677.

64. National Association of Manufacturers, *Proceedings of the Ninth Annual Convention,* 191.

65. Davenport, "For the Open Shop," 10.

66. "Proceedings of the Fifth Annual Convention," 543.

67. Bercovitch, *American Jeremiad,* 136.

68. Theodore Roosevelt to Thomas Robins, Jan. 12, 1912, in *The Letters of Theodore Roosevelt,* ed. Morison, 7:471–72.

Chapter 4: From Conspiracy to Tort

1. Quote from Sir Frederick Pollock from *Law Quarterly Review* 20 (Jan. 1904): 3; U.S. House Committee on the Judiciary, *Anti-Injunction Bill,* 185.

2. White, *Tort Law in America*, 20–62.

3. Pound, "Mechanical Jurisprudence," 609–10; Frankfurter, "The Law and the Law Schools," 539–40.

4. James, *Pragmatism* (1907), in *Writings, 1902–1910*, 510.

5. Dulles and Dubofsky, *Labor in America*, 90–156.

6. Burke, *History and Function of Central Labor Unions*, 27, 43, 82–83; Commons et al., *History of Labour*, 2:444.

7. "Boycotting," 394, 395. See also Commons et al., *History of Labour*, 2:22–23; Zieren, "The Boycott and Working-Class Solidarity in Toledo," 131–49.

8. Connecticut Bureau of Labor Statistics, *First Annual Report*, 37; Bensman, *Practice of Solidarity*, 118–20, 131–41, 151–52.

9. "Boycotting," 394–96; Wolman, *The Boycott in American Trade Unions*, 37, 91; Barnett, *The Printers*, 268–73; New York Bureau of Labor Statistics, *Fourth Annual Report*, 719.

10. May, *Protestant Churches*, 99–103; Ernst, "Free Labor," 24–27.

11. *Commonwealth v. Carlisle*, Brightly's N.P. 36, 39–40 (Pa. 1821); Wright, *The Law of Criminal Conspiracies and Agreements*, 110–11.

12. State v. Stewart, 59 Vt. 273, 9 A. 559, 560–63 (1887).

13. "Hon. Horace Henry Powers," in *Genealogical and Family History of the State of Vermont*, 1:691–92; Ullery, comp., *Men of Vermont*, 323; "H(orace) Henry Powers," 990.

14. *Representative Men of Connecticut*, 281–83; Burton, ed., *Men of Progress*, 309–10.

15. "Elisha Carpenter," 69 Conn. 732 (1897).

16. "Elisha Carpenter," 69 Conn. at 735.

17. State v. Glidden, 55 Conn. 46, 71, 75, 8 A. 890, 894, 896 (1887); see *Stewart*, 59 Vt. at 291, 9 A. at 569.

18. *Stewart*, 59 Vt. at 285, 9 A. at 566, 569; *Glidden*, 55 Conn. at 72–73, 8 A. at 894.

19. *Stewart*, 59 Vt. at 286, 9 A. at 567; *Glidden*, 55 Conn. at 71, 74, 8 A. at 894, 895.

20. *Stewart*, 59 Vt. at 285, 9 A. at 566. Similarly, Carpenter thought it strange, "in this day and this free country—a country in which law interferes so little with the individual—that it should be necessary to announce from the bench that every man may carry on his business as he pleases, may do what he will with his own so long as he does nothing unlawful, and acts with due regard to the rights of others." *Glidden*, 55 Conn. at 71–72, 8 A. at 894.

21. *Stewart*, 59 Vt. at 289, 9 A. at 568.

22. *Glidden*, 55 Conn. at 72, 8 A. at 894.

23. McNeill, ed., *The Labor Movement*, 489.

24. *Stewart*, 59 Vt. at 285–86, 9 A. at 566. The Virginia Supreme Court made the same point more compactly: "Freedom, individual and associated, is the boon and the boasted policy and *peculium* of our country; but it is liberty regulated by law; and the motto of the law is: '*sic utere tuo ut alienum non laedas.*'" Crump v. Commonwealth, 84 Va. 927, 946, 6 S.E. 620, 630 (1888).

25. On the first known (although often overlooked) American labor injunction,

Mueller v. Grantz (N.Y. Sup. Ct. 1875), see folder 381, box 6, Paul F. Brissenden Papers, and the appendix to Merrihew, "Government by Injunction." The handful of labor injunctions issued during the Great Upheaval include Brushke v. Furniture Makers Union No. 1 (Super Ct. Cook Cnty., Ill., 1886), *Chicago Legal News* 18 (May 22, 1886): 614; New York, Lake Erie & Western R.R. v. Wenger, 17 *Weekly Law Bulletin* 306 (C.P. Cuyahoga Cnty, Ohio, 1887); Brace Brothers v. Evans, 5 Pa. C.C. 163 (C.P. Allegheny Cnty, 1888); Sherry v. Perkins, 147 Mass. 212, 17 N.E. 307 (1888); Thomas v. Musical Mutual Protective Union, 49 Hun 171, 2 N.Y.S. 195 (1888), *rev'd,* 121 N.Y. 45, 24 N.E. 24 (1890).

26. See Hurvitz, "American Labor Law," 333–44; McMurtrie, "Equity Jurisdiction," 1–15.

27. Toledo, Ann Arbor & North Michigan R.R. v. Pennsylvania Co., 54 F. 730 (C.C.N.D. Ohio, 1893); Thomas v. Cincinnati, New Orleans & Texas Pacific R.R., 62 F. 803 (C.C.S.D. Ohio, 1894); see Mason, "The Labor Decisions of Chief Justice Taft," 585–625.

28. In re Debs, 158 U.S. 564 (1895); Lewis, "Strikes and Courts of Equity," 1–2; Forbath, *Law and the Shaping of the American Labor Movement,* 59–97; Brissenden, "The Labor Injunction," 425, 426.

29. Vesey, *The Emergence of the American University,* 21–56, 87–97.

30. Stevens, *Law School,* 25–28, 95.

31. Langdell, *A Selection of Cases on the Law of Contracts,* vi–vii. On Langdell, see Kalman, *Legal Realism at Yale,* 10–14; Stevens, *Law School,* 35–72.

32. Hilliard, *The Law of Torts or Private Wrongs.* On the contracts treatises, see Atiyah, *The Rise and Fall of Freedom of Contract,* 682. On the writ system, see Friedman, *A History of American Law,* 56–58, 146–47, 391–98; Nelson, *Americanization of the Common Law,* 69–88.

33. Review of C. G. Addison, *The Law of Torts, American Law Review* 5 (Jan. 1871): 340–41, reprinted in *Justice Oliver Wendell Holmes,* ed. Shriver, 44–45. On Hilliard, Holmes, St. Green, and the other pioneers of tort law, see White, *Tort Law in America,* 3–19; Vandevelde, "History of Prima Facie Tort," 447–97; Horwitz, *The Transformation of American Law, 1870–1960,* 52–54.

34. Bigelow, *Elements of the Law of Torts,* 4, 5.

35. Pollock, *Law of Torts,* viii; Bishop, *Non-Contract Law,* iii–vi; Holmes, "Law in Science," reprinted in *Collected Legal Papers,* 222–23; Bigelow, *Law of Torts,* 8th ed., 3–69. Vandevelde establishes the significance of Holmes's, Pollock's, and Bigelow's work in "History of Prima Facie Tort," 457–70.

36. *Stewart,* 59 Vt. at 289, 9 A. at 568; Mason, "The Legal Aspect of the Strike and Boycott," 278; Rockel, "Boycotting," 149–50.

37. Cooley, *Torts,* 2d ed., 143.

38. Frank W. Morancy, in *American Law Review* 34 (May-June 1900): 468.

39. Heywood v. Tillson, 75 Me. 225 (1883); Payne v. W. Atl. R.R., 81 Tenn. 507 (1884); Bohn Mfg. Co. v. Hollis, 54 Minn. 223, 55 N.W. 1119 (1893); Macauley v. Tierney, 19 R.I. 255, 33 A. 1 (1895).

40. Holmes, *The Common Law,* 104.

41. As the epigraph suggests, the judges' tendency to use "malice" to describe the desire to promote (say) secondary boycotts as well as to inflict harm as an end

in itself caused the law writers considerable consternation. Many made peace with the judges' usage by distinguishing between "malice in fact" (actual ill-will) and "malice in law" (other impermissible motives).

42. Pollock, *Law of Torts*, 354, 106, 100.

43. Ibid., 100, 103.

44. Ibid., 209–10, 352–53. In this connection Pollock discussed the leading case of Lumley v. Gye, 2 Ellis & Blackburn 216, 118 Eng. Rep. 749 (1853).

45. Eddy, *The Law of Combinations*, 1:416; Martin, "Conspiracy," in *Cyclopedia of Law and Procedure*, 8:650.

46. Bigelow, *Elements of the Law of Torts*, 92–93; Pollock, *Law of Torts*, 208; Cooley, *Torts*, 2d ed., 142–45; Bishop, *Non-Contract Law*, 150; Cooke, *Law of Combinations*, 14–15.

47. Pollock, *Law of Torts*, 7th ed., 320–21.

48. Bigelow, *Law of Torts*, 8th ed., 24, 237–66. The Columbia law professor Francis M. Burdick was unusual in thinking the old reasons required him to devote a section to conspiracy in his torts treatise, first published in 1905. Burdick, *The Law of Torts*, 474–82, and "Conspiracy as a Crime," 229–47.

49. Walker v. Cronin, 107 Mass. 555, 562 (1871); Mogul Steamship Co. v. McGregor, Gow & Co., [1889] 23 Q.B.D. 598, aff'd, [1892] A.C. 25. On *Walker* and its American antecedents, see Vandevelde, "Prima Facie Tort," 452–54, 477–78.

50. *Mogul* 23 Q.B.D. at 612.

51. Id. at 613.

52. Pollock, *Law of Torts*, 7th ed., 319–20; Quinn v. Leatham, [1901] A.C. 495.

53. Holmes, "Privilege, Malice, and Intent," reprinted in *Collected Legal Papers*, 117–37; see Holmes to Pollock, June 26, 1894, in *Holmes-Pollock Letters*, ed. Howe, 1:54.

54. Ames, "How Far an Act," 411–22; Freund, "Malice and Unlawful Interference," 449–65; Huffcut, "Interference with Contracts and Business in New York," 423–43; Lewis, "The Closed Market," 444–51; Smith, "Crucial Issues in Labor Litigation," 429–55; Wyman, "The Law as to the Boycott," 208–15; see also Walton, "Motive as an Element in Tort," 501–19. For representative student work, see Ballard, "Injunction," 340–44, "Right of Labor Unions," 66–68; Hamburg, "Torts," 133–36.

55. Moores & Co. v. Bricklayers Union No. 1, 23 *Weekly Law Bulletin* 48, 50 (Ohio Super. Ct. 1890).

56. Id. at 50.

57. Id. at 52–53. On Sumner's influence, see Pringle, *William Howard Taft*, 1:34. For Taft's view of wages and competition, see Taft, "The Right of Private Property," 220–22. Taft reaffirmed the position he took in *Moores* in *The Anti-Trust Act and the Supreme Court*.

58. For another example, see McClennen, "Some of the Rights of Traders and Laborers," 237–54.

59. Holmes, "Path of the Law," in *Collected Legal Papers*, 179, 170, 172.

60. Holmes, *The Common Law*, 163, 38, 36.

61. Holmes, "Privilege, Malice, and Intent," 119; Aikens v. Wisconsin, 195 U.S. 194, 204 (1904). See Kelley, "Holmes on the Supreme Judicial Court," in *The History of the Law in Massachusetts*, 299–324.

62. Holmes, "Privilege, Malice, and Intent," in *Collected Legal Papers*, 129, 130–31, 122–23, 120. See also Holmes, "Law in Science," ibid., 240–42.

63. Holmes, "Privilege, Malice, and Intent," 129, 120–21, 124–25. See also *Aikens*, 195 U.S. at 204.

64. Vegelahn v. Guntner, 167 Mass. 92, 106, 107–9, 44 N.E. 1077, 1080, 1081 (1896) (Holmes, J., dissenting).

65. Plant v. Woods, 176 Mass. 492, 504–5, 57 N.E. 1011, 1015–16 (1900) (Holmes, J., dissenting).

66. *Vegelahn*, 167 Mass. at 106, 44 N.E. at 1080–81; Holmes, "Path of the Law," in *Collected Legal Papears*, 187.

67. Holmes, "Law in Science," ibid., 239, 225, 242.

68. Rodgers, "In Search of Progressivism," 124–26.

69. Stoner, "The Influence of Social and Economic Ideals," 471; Wyman, "The Maintenance of the Open Shop," 22.

70. Pound, "Law in Books and Law in Action," 12–36, and "The Scope and Purpose of Sociological Jurisprudence," 513. On the tension between "organicism" and "instrumentalism" in Pound's thought, see Wigdor, *Roscoe Pound*, 207–32, 255–71.

71. Ross, *Origins*, 247–53.

72. Harriman, "Melville M. Bigelow," 157–67; Church, "The Development of the Social Sciences," 175–219.

73. Bigelow, *Law of Torts*, 8th ed., iii–iv, 24, 33, 251n.2; Bigelow, "The Extension of Legal Education," 9–12. Bigelow regards "your dissenting judgement in *Vegelahn v. Guntner* . . . as fighting against the stars in their courses," Pollock wrote Holmes on Oct. 9, 1908. "It isn't so easy as he thinks to see which way the world is going." In *Holmes-Pollock Letters*, ed. Howe, 1:142.

74. *Dictionary of American Biography*, supp. 4: 490–92. For Patton's views on social control, see Ross, *Origins*, 197.

75. Lewis, "A Protest against Administering Criminal Law by Injunction," and "Strikes and Courts of Equity," 1–12.

76. Lewis, "Closed Market," 449–51; see also Lewis, "Some Leading English Cases," 160.

77. Kraines, *The World and Ideas of Ernst Freund*, 2; Freund, "Historical Jurisprudence in Germany," 468–86.

78. Freund, "Malice and Unlawful Interference," 463–65; Freund, "Recent Illinois Decisions," 46; see also Freund, *The Police Power*, 325.

79. Leonard, comp., *Who's Who in Jurisprudence*, 192; Baltimore *Morning Sun*, Aug. 17, 1973. Bryan wrote his thesis, *The Development of the English Law of Conspiracy*, under the direction of the political scientist W. W. Willoughby.

80. Bryan, "Proper Bounds of the Use," 300.

81. Kocourek, "Labor Unions," 324.

82. U.S. Commission on Industrial Relations, *Final Report*, 136–37, 377, 324. Bryan advised Edwin E. Witte, the researcher principally responsible for the commission's unpublished reports on labor law. Witte to Bryan, July 30, 1914, box 1, Edwin E. Witte Papers, State Historical Society of Wisconsin. On the commission, see Adams, *Age of Industrial Violence*.

83. *Vegelahn*, 167 Mass. at 106, 44 N.E. at 1080 (Holmes, J., dissenting).

CHAPTER 5: THE LABOR TRUST

1. Dicey, *Lectures on the Relation between Law and Public Opinion*, 468; Davenport, "Employers, Union Men," 2.

2. Rodgers, "In Search of Progressivism," 123–24, 119–20; Cooper, *The Pivotal Decades*, 85, 43–44; Sklar, *The Corporate Reconstruction*, 43–85, 184–90.

3. Hofstadter, *The Paranoid Style*, 199–200.

4. Seligman, *Principles of Economics*, 171. Rabban has shown how this insistence that individual liberty be in the service of some ultimate, collective end confined progressives' understanding of free expression in "The Free Speech League," 47–114.

5. "The Open Shop," 6.

6. Gompers, "A Damage Suit," 1039. Forbath has subtly explored the antistatist voluntarism of the AFL from its founding to the New Deal in *Law and the Shaping of the American Labor Movement*.

7. Farmers' Loan & Trust Co. v. Northern Pacific, 60 F. 803 (C.C.E.D. Wis. 1894); Vegelahn v. Guntner, 167 Mass. 92, 44 N.E. 1077 (1896); Erdman v. Mitchell, 207 Pa. 79, 56 A. 327 (1903); Casey v. Cincinnati Typographical Union, 45 F. 135 (C.C.S.D. Ohio 1891); Hopkins v. Oxley Stave Co., 83 F. 912 (8th Cir. 1897); Gray v. Building Trades Council, 91 Minn. 171, 97 N.W. 663 (1903). The pressures of building a majority often forced judges who preferred Bowen's formula to muddy their analysis with quotations from the older conspiracy cases. E.g., Old Dominion Steam-Ship Co. v. McKenna, 30 F. 48 (C.C.S.D.N.Y. 1887); Coeur d'Alene Consol. & Mining Co. v. Miners' Union of Wardner, 51 F. 260 (C.C.D. Idaho 1892); Lucke v. Clothing Cutters & Trimmers' Assembly, 77 Md. 396, 26 A. 505 (1893).

8. Clemmitt v. Watson, 14 Ind. App. 38, 42 N.E. 367 (1895); Foster v. Retail Clerks' Int'l Protective Ass'n, 39 Misc. 48, 78 N.Y.S. 860 (1902). On judicial reluctance to embrace the new utilitarian jurisprudence, see Stoner, "The Influence of Social and Economic Ideals," 468–69.

9. Curran v. Galen, 152 N.Y. 33, 46 N.E. 297 (1897).

10. Id. at 36–39, 46 N.E. at 298–99.

11. Davenport, "Employers, Union Men," 2.

12. *Curran*, 152 N.Y. at 37, 46 N.E. at 298.

13. Ernest F. Eidlitz to Otto M. Eidlitz, April 19, 1900, box 1, Marc Eidlitz & Son Papers. Some commentators offered a less nuanced reading of *Curran*. Beach, *A Treatise on the Law of Monopolies*, 344–45; Eddy, *The Law of Combinations*, 1:435.

14. National Protective Association of Steam Fitters v. Cumming, 170 N.Y. 314, 336–49, 63 N.E. 369, 375–80 (1902) (Vann, J., dissenting); *Who Was Who in America*, 1:1271; "Judge Irving G. Vann," 611.

15. *Dictionary of American Biography*, 7:212–14; Rogers, *American Bar Leaders*, 140–45.

16. *Cumming*, 170 N.Y. at 320–34, 63 N.E. at 369–74; Lewis, "Modern American Cases," 496; see also Wyman, "The Maintenance of the Open Shop," 29.

17. *Who Was Who in America*, 1:479.

18. *Cumming*, 170 N.Y. at 335, 334, 63 N.E. at 375 (Gray, J., concurring).

19. Id. at 335, 334.

20. The two most important predecessors of Parker's opinion were less of an obstacle because they came in a dissent, Hopkins v. Oxley Stave Company, 83 F. 912 (8th Cir. 1897) (Caldwell, C. J., dissenting), and from a weak bench, Clemmitt v. Watson, 14 Ind. App. 38, 42 N.E. 367 (1895) (Gavin, J.).

Appointed to the federal district court by Lincoln after heroic service in the Civil War (as well as the Republican convention of 1860), Henry Clay Caldwell (1832–1915) was raised on the midwestern frontier, far from the influence of genteel culture. He came to the bench with only a common-school education and no patience for close legal argument. Watson, "Henry Clay Caldwell," ed. Scott, 111–24; "Hon. Henry Clay Caldwell," 282–86. Although a Harvard graduate, Frank E. Gavin (1854–1936), like Parker, remained an active participant in the Democratic Party long after its departure from the sound principles of Grover Cleveland. Indianapolis *News,* Nov. 2, 1936, 13; Taylor, *Biographical Sketches,* 197–99; Dunn, *Greater Indianapolis,* 2:1125–26. In a nonjudicial capacity Gavin once proclaimed the vaguely historicist belief that "church and state and people are upon the upgrade, moving onward to a better and higher civilization." Gavin, "The Mutability of Social Institutions," 131.

21. *Square Deal* 1 (Dec. 1905): 23.

22. Christensen v. Kellogg Switchboard and Supply, Co., 110 Ill. App. 61, 66–67 (1903); Myers, "Policing," 433–59.

23. Hard, "A History of the Kellogg Strike," 25; *Chicago Daily Tribune,* July 21, 1903.

24. Chicago *Journal,* reprinted in *Bulletin of the National Metal Trades Association* 2 (Sept. 1903): 731.

25. *Chicago Tribune,* July 23–24, 1903; Illinois Bureau of Labor Statistics, *Eighth Annual Report,* 41; Myers, "Policing," 441–42.

26. For the terms of the injunction, see Christensen v. Kellogg Switchboard & Supply Co., 110 Ill. App. 61, 66–67 (1903). Holdom's remarks were made before a meeting of the Citizens Industrial Association of America in November 1905, at which Davenport also appeared. Holdom, *Legal and Historical Progress of Trade Unions,* 8.

27. *Christensen,* 110 Ill. App. at 73.

28. Darrow and Masters, *Brief and Argument,* 41, 45, 44–45, 47, 75–76 (deposited in U.S. Department of Labor Library, Washington, D.C.).

29. In later years Wilkerson's firm served as the AABA's "district counsel" in Chicago. As a federal district judge, Wilkerson would issue a sweeping and controversial injunction, reminiscent of Holdom's, during the railroad shopcrafts strike of 1922. Walter Gordon Merritt to Walter Drew, Feb. 23, 1922, "Legislation, 1922–1923," box 10, Walter W. Drew Papers; Bernstein, *The Lean Years,* 211–12.

30. AABA, *Jacob Christensen, et al.,* 168–69, 228, 169.

31. Ibid., 228, 180, 229.

32. *Christensen,* 110 Ill. App. at 70–71, 74, 72, 75.

33. "War on Boycotters," 738; Christensen v. People, 114 Ill. App. 40, 53–54, 55–57 (1904).

34. Holdom, "Some Comments," 553.

35. "Is the Closed Shop Illegal and Criminal?" 1–6, 10; "The Law of the 'Closed Shop,'" 46–47.

36. *Christensen,* 114 Ill. App. at 64–66.

37. *Christensen,* 114 Ill. App. at 70–71, *affirmed,* O'Brien v. People, 216 Ill. 354, 75 N.E. 108 (1905).

38. *Square Deal* 1 (Dec. 1905): 23.

39. "The Closed Shop," 334, 337, 329.

40. "Judicial Jumble on the 'Open Shop,'" 585.

41. "Is the Closed Shop Illegal and Criminal?" 2.

42. *Square Deal* 1 (Dec. 1905): 23.

43. Milwaukee Custom Tailors' Union v. Marnitz Tailoring Co., *Milwaukee Sentinel,* July 14, 1904, 4.

44. Id.; Jacobs v. Cohen, 99 A.D. 481, 485, 90 N.Y.S. 854 (1904); Berry v. Donovan, 188 Mass. 353, 74 N.E. 603 (1905). Knowlton was a Republican and a member of Yale College's Class of 1860. *Dictionary of American Biography,* 5:473–74.

45. Louis D. Brandeis to Hayes Robbins, Sept. 25, 1905, in *Letters of Louis D. Brandeis,* 1:361.

46. State v. Stockford, 77 Conn. 277, 58 A. 769 (1904); State v. Van Pelt, 136 N.C. 460, 49 S.E. 177 (1904).

47. Jacobs v. Cohen, 183 N.Y. 207, 210, 76 N.E. 5, 6 (1905). A seventh judge did not participate in the case.

48. Id. at 217, 219, 76 N.E. at 8, 9 (Vann, J., dissenting).

49. Id. at 214–15, 76 N.E. at 8.

50. Id. at 211, 76 N.E. at 7.

51. Gray made the remark in a decision upholding a contract between business rivals in which one obtained the other's promise not to run a competing steamship line. Leslie v. Lorillard, 110 N.Y. 519, 534, 18 N.E. 363, 366 (1888).

52. Martin, *Law of Labor Unions,* 217.

53. Horwitz, *The Transformation of American Law,* 10–11, 17–19.

54. Tomlins, *State and the Unions,* 36–52.

55. *Jacobs,* 183 N.Y. at 212, 76 N.E. at 7.

56. AABA, *Quarterly Bulletin: February 1906.* Davenport had earlier argued that the Due Process Clause protected "the right of a man to run his own business, the right and freedom of making contracts . . . , and the right of a man to use his hands, his skill, his strength in support of himself and his family." *Bulletin of the National Metal Trades Association* 2 (July 1903): 541.

Just months before the *Jacobs* decision, labor leaders considered appealing *Berry v. Donovan* to the U.S. Supreme Court—quite possibly to test their own reading of the Fourteenth Amendment—but decided not to after concluding their failure to raise a federal question before the Massachusetts courts would be fatal. AABA, *November Bulletin.*

57. AABA, *Quarterly Bulletin: February 1906.* Boocock similarly attributed the prolabor outcome in Bender v. Local Union No. 118, Bakery & Confectionery Workers' Int'l Union, 34 Wash. L. Rptr. 574 (D.C. 1906), to the weak record produced by lawyers unaffiliated with the AABA. AABA, *"A Liberty League,"* 12–13.

58. The bulk of the cases studied in this and the preceding chapter were suits brought by nonunion workers and employers under conspiracy or intentional tort. In such cases, trade unionists put the righteousness or social utility of their con-

duct at issue by raising the defense of justification. In contrast, *Jacobs* was brought by trade unionists to enforce a contract. It was the employer who raised a defense turning on the utility of closed-shop unionism by arguing that the contracts violated public policy and were therefore unenforceable, leaving the parties where the employer's breach placed them. Whether the same standard of illegality should govern in tort and contract was one large question *Jacobs* left unresolved. See Labatt, *Master and Servant*, 8:8542.

59. AABA, *Morals and Law*, 29; "Strike Injunctions and Picketing in Illinois," 241; Martin, *Law of Labor Unions*, 211; Clark, *The Law of the Employment*, 240–46; Groat, *Attitude of American Courts*, 168.

60. Kemp v. Division No. 241, 255 Ill. 213, 99 N.E. 389 (1912).

61. *Kemp*, 255 Ill. at 258, 99 N.E. at 405 (Cartwright, J., et al., dissenting).

62. *Kemp*, 255 Ill. at 226, 227–28, 99 N.E. at 392. The opinions for the majority read *Christensen* as Brandeis had, as a precedent against violent picketing. Adams's harsh words for the closed shop thus were mere dicta. Id. at 233–34, 99 N.E. at 397; id. at 248, 99 N.E. at 405 (Carter, J., concurring).

63. Crossley, "Orrin Nelson Carter," 371–72; Tuley, "Compulsory Arbitration," 77–144.

64. Crossley, "Orrin Nelson Carter," 372–73; Carter, "Address," 869, 876, 881.

65. Carter cited Holmes's opinion in *Aikens v. Wisconsin*, 195 U.S. 194 (1904), Pollock's treatise, and Smith's "Crucial Issues," 262. *Kemp*, 255 Ill. at 240, 99 N.E. at 399 (Carter, J., concurring). He also relied upon Ames, "How Far an Act," 411–22.

66. Moores & Co. v. Bricklayers' Union No. 1, 23 *Weekly Law Bulletin* 48, 50, 52–53 (Ohio Super. Ct. 1890).

67. *Kemp*, 255 Ill. at 237, 248, 99 N.E. at 398, 403, quoting Rideout v. Knox, 148 Mass. 368, 372, 19 N.E. 390 (1889) (Holmes, J.). Carter cited Bigelow's opening essay in *Centralization and the Law*, 7, for the proposition that judges should consider "the rights of the public 'as a distinct entity'" in deciding labor cases. He cited Tuttle v. Buck, 107 Minn. 145, 119 N.W. 946 (1909), a landmark of historicist jurisprudence, in support of the claim that "the law of evolution" applies to the regulation of industrial organizations. *Kemp*, 255 Ill. 242–43, 235, 99 N.E. at 400, 398 (Carter, J., concurring).

68. *Kemp*, 255 at 242, 99 N.E. at 400 (Carter, J., concurring); cf. Smith, "Crucial Issues," 361–62.

69. *Kemp*, 255 at 243, 99 N.E. at 400 (Carter, J., concurring); cf. Smith, "Crucial Issues," 428–51.

70. *Kemp*, 255 Ill. at 255, 99 N.E. at 405 (Carter, J., concurring).

71. AABA, *July Bulletin*, July 27, 1914; Merritt, *Destination Unknown*, 93–95; Anon. to Martin Lawlor, April 23, 1912, box HRD-20, United Hatters of North America Papers; Ralph Wheeler, "Charge of the Court," Connors v. Connolly (Super. Ct., Fairfield Cnty., 1912), 13, enclosed in ibid.

72. *Dictionary of American Biography*, 8:187–88.

73. Connors v. Connolly, 86 Conn. 641, 656–57, 86 A. 600, 606 (1913).

74. Id. at 652, 86 A. at 604; AABA, *July Bulletin*, July 27, 1914.

75. State v. Glidden, 55 Conn. 46, 72, 8 A. 890, 894 (1887).

76. *Connors,* 86 Conn. at 655, 647, 649–651, 86 A. at 602–4.

77. Labatt, *Master and Servant,* 8:8543.

78. U.S. Senate, *Industrial Relations,* 11:10654–55.

79. Hoxie, *Trade Unionism in the United States,* 30.

80. Kocourek, "Labor Unions," 324.

81. "Is the Closed Shop Illegal and Criminal?" 3.

82. Smith, "Crucial Issues," 352.

83. *Kemp,* 255 Ill. at 242, 99 N.E. at 400 (Carter, J., concurring).

84. Holmes, "Privilege, Malice, and Intent," in *Collected Legal Papers,* 120.

85. Pickett v. Walsh, 192 Mass. 572, 78 N.E. 753 (1906); Green, "Labor's Fighting Legionaries," 234.

86. Wigmore, "Boycott," 322.

87. See, for example, "The Legality of the Closed Shop," 217.

88. Milwaukee *Sentinel,* July 14, 1904, 4. For an entrée into the growing literature on industrial pluralism, see Atleson, "Wartime Labor Regulation."

89. Tarleton, "Some Reflections," 65; Green, "Labor's Fighting Legionaries," 239.

Chapter 6: The Liberty of the Trader

1. "Hundreds of Unionists Haled to Court," 5–6; Record at 719–24, 1025–26, 1093–94, *Lawlor v. Loewe,* 235 U.S. 522 (1915).

2. AABA, *Application,* 87–88. This pamphlet publishes the oral argument in the first appeal to the United State Supreme Court, *Loewe v. Lawlor,* 208 U.S. 274 (1908).

3. AABA, *Million against One.* The complaint has been published in *Pamphlets in American History: Labor.* Wherever possible, I cite the long and more accessible excerpt in *Loewe,* 208 U.S. at 284–96n.1.

4. In fact, Davenport originally commenced a separate suit under the common law in the Connecticut courts "as an anchor to the windward," but he later dropped the proceeding. Merritt, *History of the League for Industrial Rights,* 26.

5. AABA, *Million against One,* 1.

6. For sharply conflicting readings of the legislative history, see Mason, *Organized Labor and the Law,* 132–42, and Berman, *Labor and the Sherman Act,* 3–54. See also Thorelli, *Federal Anti-Trust Policy,* 231–32.

7. Hattam, "Courts and the Question of Class," 44–70; Eggert, *Railroad Labor Disputes,* 152–202; Thorelli, *Federal Anti-Trust Policy,* 440–41, 448–51, 478–80, 482; In re Debs, 158 U.S. 564, 600 (1895).

8. United States v. E. C. Knight Co., 156 U.S. 1, 17, 12 (1895); see McCurdy, "The *Knight* Sugar Decision," 304–42.

9. Hopkins v. United States, 171 U.S. 578 (1898); Anderson v. United States, 171 U.S. 604, 615–16 (1898); Addyston Pipe & Steel Co. v. United States, 175 U.S. 211, 240 (1899); see Thorelli, *Federal Anti-Trust Policy,* 462–70.

10. Complaint, in *Loewe,* 208 U.S. at 285, 290, 296; AABA, *Application,* 83. At oral argument Davenport stated Loewe's sales amounted to $10,000 in Connecticut and to $400,000 in other states. Ibid., 88.

11. Complaint, *Loewe,* 208 U.S. at 284, 289, 288, 286–87.

12. Ulman, *Rise of the National Trade Union;* Taft, *The A. F. of L.;* Montgomery, *Fall of the House of Labor,* 290–302; Greene, "'Strike at the Ballot Box,'" 171, 174–82, 188–89.

13. Witte, *The Government in Labor Disputes,* 142, 144–45. The contradiction between open-shop rhetoric and legal theory was evident in Davenport's description of Gompers in the complaint. The lawyer called Gompers the "chief agent" in the conspiracy against Loewe. "Chief" bore connotations of Gompers's de facto authority; "agent" denoted his de jure status.

14. Complaint, in Record, *Lawlor v. Loewe,* 235 U.S. 522 (1915); New York *Sun,* Sept. 23, 1903; see *New York Times,* Sept. 13, Oct. 5, 1903; New York *Tribune,* Nov. 12, 1903; "The Legal Status of the Boycott," 22–23; "The Question of To-Day," 61–68.

15. AABA, *Extracts from Addresses,* 9; Loewe v. Lawlor, 148 F. 924 (C.C.D. Conn. 1906). The issues raised by the demurrer could only be carried to a higher court after a verdict or other final disposition in the case. Sustaining the demurrer resulted in a final judgment; had Platt overruled the demurrer, the United Hatters could not have appealed his decision.

16. King, *Melville Weston Fuller,* 18–26, 41–60, 77–85, 99–113, 234; McCurdy, "Fuller, Melville W.," 2:813–16.

17. Montague & Co. v. Lowry, 193 U.S. 38, 47–48 (1904); Swift & Co. v. United States, 196 U.S. 375 (1905).

18. *Swift,* 196 U.S. at 397; see Thorelli, *Federal Anti-Trust Policy,* 425–28, 475–77.

19. The ninth justice, William Moody, was no more promising for the United Hatters. As Roosevelt's attorney general, Moody had successfully argued the government's case in *Swift.*

20. Holmes to Frederick Pollock, [Sept.] 23, 1902, in *Holmes-Pollock Letters,* ed. Howe, 1:106.

21. In contrast, Davenport's attempt at spellbinding oratory played poorly, far from the jury boxes of Connecticut's courtrooms. His folksy rendition of the Court's antitrust decisions, for example, was too much for Justice Moody. "I should like to know in what cases any of those things have been held," Moody protested at one point. AABA, *Application,* 86.

22. Moody asked Beck whether the Sherman Act merely nationalized the common law of conspiracy (which many believed permitted "reasonable" restraints of trade) or went further. "According as that question is decided, this case, possibly, might go." Beck replied that the Court's earlier decisions "certainly indicate that the application of the Sherman Antitrust law was much broader than the prohibition of restraints of trade that were unlawful at common law." Ibid., 18–19.

23. AABA, *Application,* 11; AABA, *"A Liberty League,"* 29, 27–28. In addition, Beck supported the National Civic Federation's proposal to revise the antitrust laws, introduced in Congress in early 1908 as the Hepburn bill. Sklar, *The Corporate Reconstruction,* 218n.53. Davenport led the opposition.

24. AABA, *Application,* 5, 8–9.

25. Ibid., 10, 34, 35, 27.

26. Ibid., 39, 48, 74, 72.

27. Holmes, "Privilege, Malice, and Intent," in *Collected Legal Papers,* 117; AABA, *Application,* 73.

28. AABA, *Application,* 47, 58, 64.

29. Gompers, "Labor Organizations Must Not Be Outlawed," 181. Thus, a better informed lawyer, Louis C. Jacoures, who advised unions in New York City's clothing trades, protested that Davenport might as well hold "the Masonic order, Knights of Columbus, B'Nai Brith or the Eagles" responsible as the AFL. "The Anti-Boycott Suit," 65.

30. AABA, *Application,* 40–41. Harlan's opinion in *Adair v. United States,* 208 U.S. 161 (1908), striking down a statute prohibiting employers from discriminating against union labor, would be announced on January 27, 1908. The case was argued less than two months before *Loewe.*

31. Holmes, "Path of the Law," in *Collected Legal Papers,* 184.

32. AABA, *Application,* 75–76. In his dissent in Northern Securities v. United States, 193 U.S. 197, 401 (1904), Holmes's first opinion involving the Sherman Act, the justice wrote, "What we have to do in this case is to find the meaning of some not very difficult words."

33. Holmes to Clara Stevens, Feb. 1, 1908, reel 25, in Holmes, *American Legal Manuscripts.* I am grateful to G. Edward White for identifying Clara Stevens as Holmes's correspondent.

34. Hitchman Coal & Coke Co. v. Mitchell, 245 U.S. 229 (1917) (Holmes, J., dissenting), reel 70, in Holmes, *American Legal Manuscripts;* see Holmes to Pollock, Oct. 26, 1919, *Holmes-Pollock Letters,* ed. Howe, 2:27–28.

35. Vegelahn v. Guntner, 167 Mass. 92, 108, 44 N.E. 1077, 1081 (1896) (Holmes, J., dissenting); Plant v. Woods, 176 Mass. 492, 505, 57 N.E. 1011, 1016 (1900) (Holmes, C. J., dissenting); Holmes to E. R. Thayer, Jan. 13, 1915, reel 26, in Holmes, *American Legal Manuscripts.*

36. Northern Securities v. United States, 193 U.S. 197, 401 (1904) (Holmes, J., dissenting); Holmes to Lewis Einstein, Feb. 10, 1908, in *Holmes-Einstein Letters,* 33–34; Holmes, "The Soldier's Faith" (1895), in *Occasional Speeches,* 76. Holmes often used martial metaphors in describing the role of the judge. See, for example, "Twenty Years in Retrospect," ibid., 157.

37. *Northern Securities,* 193 U.S. at 404–5 (Holmes, J., dissenting).

38. AABA, *"A Liberty League,"* 25.

39. *Loewe,* 208 U.S. at 297–99, 301, 292–96; cf. AABA, *Application,* 12; *Brief for Plaintiffs in Error* at 30–31, *Loewe,* 208 U.S. 274 (1908). On the advanced age of the Fuller Court, see Bickel, *The Judiciary and Responsible Government,* 3–4, 7–8.

40. New York *Journal of Commerce,* Feb. 5, 1908, in AABA, *Boycott and Public Opinion,* 18.

41. The following also are quoted from AABA, *Boycott and Public Opinion:* Albany *Telegram,* Feb. 9, 1908 (15); *New York Times,* Feb. 28, 1908 (15); Philadelphia *Public Ledger* (19); San Francisco *Chronicle,* Feb. 5, 1908 (6); and Boston *Transcript,* Feb. 4, 1908 (8).

CHAPTER 7: THE POLITICS OF LAW

1. Theodore Roosevelt to Kermit Roosevelt, Oct. 20, 1908, in *Letters,* 6:1304; Roosevelt to Charles Joseph Bonaparte, Dec. 23, 1907, ibid., 6:873; Roosevelt, "Fifth

Annual Message," Dec. 5, 1905, and "Sixth Annual Message," Dec. 3, 1906, both in *A Compilation of the Messages and Papers,* 16:6983, 16:7027; *New York Times,* Dec. 18, 1907, 2. Roosevelt also objected to an injunction issued by Judge Alston G. Dayton of West Virginia, subsequently reported in Hitchman Coal & Coke Co. v. Mitchell, 172 F. 963 (N.D. W. Va. 1909).

2. Roosevelt, "Special Message," Jan. 31, 1908, in *A Compilation of the Messages and Papers,* 16:7128–29.

3. Washington *Herald,* Feb. 4, 1908, and New York *Sun,* March 4, 14, 1908, both in Scrapbook, 1905–6, box 13, James Montgomery Beck Papers; AABA, *Boycott and Public Opinion,* 3–4; William Howard Taft to George von L. Meyer, Aug. 25, 1908, reel 246, William Howard Taft Papers; Roosevelt to Thomas Robins, Jan. 2, 1912, in *Letters,* 7:471–72; U.S. House Committee on the Judiciary, *Injunctions,* 263.

4. Wiebe, *Businessmen and Reform,* 29–30.

5. Holmes to Clara Stevens, June 14, 1904 [1914], reel 38, in Holmes, *American Legal Manuscripts;* cf. Bickel, *The Judiciary and Responsible Government,* 363–64.

6. Bonnett, *Employers' Associations,* 37–62; Barnett, "Report on the Agreement," 5–14; Bauder, "National Collective Bargaining," 464, 465–68, 475–76; Stockton, *The International Molders Union;* Hilbert, "Employers' Associations," 195.

7. "Stove Founders again Succumb," 12; "Stove Founders and Molders Union Agree," 7.

8. "Twenty Years in the Harness," 16; Clifford, "St. Louis's Pre-eminence," 413–14; Buck's Stove & Range Co. v. American Fed'n Labor, 36 Wash. L. Rep. 822, 822 (D.C. Sup. Ct. 1908).

9. Wiebe, *Businessmen and Reform,* 25.

10. "James Wallace Van Cleave," 12–13.

11. Van Cleave to J. K. Turner, May 28, 31, 1906, reel 61, *American Federation of Labor Records: The Gompers Era* [hereafter cited as *AFL Records*].

12. Laidler, *Boycotts,* 136; Helfand, "Labor and the Courts," 94–95.

13. AABA, *Buck's Stove and Range Company v. AFL,* 160, 165, 164.

14. Ibid., 161, 170, 19.

15. Ibid., 57–58, 60, 65, 67.

16. James W. Van Cleave to C. W. Post, Jan. 8, Oct. 19, 1907, box 1, Post Family Papers. On Post, see McLaughlin, "The Second Battle of Battle Creek," 323–39.

17. Post to Van Cleave, Jan. 13, 1908, box 1, Post Family Papers. "Merchants don't always buy thru love of manufacturers," Post later wrote Van Cleave on Sept. 11, 1908, "I have heard of cases where they buy for other reasons, and it is a pretty good plan for a manufacturer to be known among merchants as having the ability to take care of himself." Ibid.

18. Van Cleave to Post, Aug. 4, Sept. 1, 1908, ibid.; Van Cleave to H. E. Miles, Oct. 22, 1908, in U.S. Senate Committee on the Judiciary, *Maintenance of a Lobby: Appendix,* 2:2554.

19. Wiebe, *Businessmen and Reform,* 28–30.

20. Helfand, "Labor and the Courts," 96–98; Kennedy, "An Important Labor Injunction," 104.

21. "The Boycott as a Legitimate Weapon," 193, 194.

22. Gompers, "A Damage Suit," 1038–39.

23. O'Brien v. People, 216 Ill. 354, 75 N.E. 108 (1905); "Another Important Chicago Decision," 25–26; Barnes v. Chicago Typographical Union, 232 Ill. 424, 83 N.E. 940 (1908); "The Injunction in Labor Disputes Must Go," 228–30. See Karson, *American Labor Unions and Politics, 1900–1918*, 37–41.

24. Karson, *American Labor Unions and Politics, 1900–1918*, 42–43; Cannon quoted ibid., 43; *New York Times*, March 22, 1906. See Greenberg, *Roosevelt and Labor*, 399.

25. Cunniff, "Labor in Politics," 8130–35; Greene, "'Strike at the Ballot Box,'" 165–92; AABA, *Coercion of Congress*.

After resigning from Congress in September 1908, Littlefield practiced law in New York City. He maintained close ties to the AABA until his death in 1915. *Biographical Directory of the United States Congress, 1774–1989*, 1378; U.S. House Select Committee, *Charges against Members*, 2769.

26. "The Buck's Stove Case," 603; Gompers to Executive Council, Sept. 20, 1907, reel 115, Gompers Letterbooks, Library of Congress; Executive Council Minutes, Nov. 11, 1907, 5, 7, reel 3, *AFL Records*.

27. Spelling represented the AFL before Congress in the spring of 1906 on anti-injunction legislation. That summer he briefed Gompers on injunctions in the campaign against Littlefield. In 1907 he prepared a brief for Justice Gould's court in *Buck's Stove* and an amicus brief in *Loewe* for the AFL. U.S. House Committee on the Judiciary, *Anti-Injunction and Restraining Orders*, 144; Thomas Spelling to Gompers, June 2, 1906, reel 61, *AFL Records;* Thomas Carl Spelling, *The Right to Boycott. . . . Points, Authorities and Arguments of Thomas Carl Spelling, Attorney for the Defendants, on Application of Temporary Injunction* (Sup. Ct. D.C. Oct. Term 1907); *Brief of Thomas Carl Spelling on Behalf [of] the A. F. of L.*, Loewe v. Lawlor, 208 U.S. 274 (1908).

28. U.S. Senate, *Control of Corporations*, 1991; Callan v. Wilson, 127 U.S. 540 (1888); U.S. House Committee on the Judiciary, *Report on a Hearing*, 64; U.S. House Committee on the Judiciary, *Anti-Injunction Bill*, 186; AABA, *Arguments in Contempt Proceedings*, 149.

29. U.S. House Committee on the Judiciary, *Anti-Injunction Bill*, 186.

30. Samuel Gompers to Andrew Furuseth, Sept. 21, 1907, reel 116, Gompers Letterbooks.

31. Executive Council Minutes, Nov. 24, 1907, 6, reel 3, *AFL Records;* Richard Olney to John Mitchell, Aug. 22, 1907, John Mitchell Papers; Eggert, "Richard Olney," 386–88, 408–11, 430–31; Richard Olney, Amicus Brief, Platt v. Philadelphia & Reading R.R. (1894), in *Injunction Data Filed by Samuel Gompers*, 21–25; Olney, "Discrimination against Union Labor," 161–67.

32. Rogers, *American Bar Leaders*, 144–46; Gompers to Alton B. Parker, April 12, 1909, reel 135, Gompers Letterbooks.

33. Brief on Behalf of the American Federation of Labor at 33–52, Buck's Stove & Range Co. v. American Fed'n Labor, 219 U.S. 581 (1911).

34. Gompers to Executive Council, Jan. 10, 1908, reel 23, *AFL Records*.

35. "Van Cleave Hales Us," 615.

36. Gompers in National Civic Federation, *A Discussion of the Boycott Problem*, 6; Committee of the Local Union, United Brotherhood of Carpenters and Join-

ers of America No. 1777, North Bend, Oregon to Frank Morrison, Feb. 19, 1908, reel 19, *AFL Records*.

37. Mandel, *Gompers*, 275, 278; *Current Literature* 46 (Feb. 1909): 130; O. A. Tveitmoe to Gompers, Jan. 16, 1911, in Executive Council Minutes, Jan. 17, 1911, reel 3, *AFL Records*. For an important reassessment of the free-speech fights of Industrial Workers of the World, see Rabban, "The IWW Free Speech Fights."

38. Croly, *The Promise of American Life*, 387.

39. Tobin, *Organize or Perish*, 58–59; Martin, "Labor Unions and the Boycott," 1046–48.

40. Gompers to Executive Council, Feb. 17, 1908, Gompers Letterbooks. I will return to Gompers's fear that *Loewe* had outlawed organized labor—a concern Bonaparte termed "theoretical rather than practical"—in chapter 9. Bonaparte to Roosevelt, March 17, 1908, quoted in Sklar, *The Corporate Reconstruction*, 237.

41. Karson, *American Labor Unions and Politics, 1900–1918*, 57–59; U.S. House Committee on the Judiciary, *Injunctions*, 1912, 42; Greenberg, *Roosevelt and Labor*, 361; Leonard, comp., *Who's Who in Jurisprudence*, 1170; *New York Times*, July 8, 11, 1908; *Official Report of the Proceedings of the Democratic National Convention*, 30.

42. Record at 508, 159–73, Gompers v. Buck's Stove & Range Co., 33 App. D.C. 83 (1909) [hereafter cited as Record, *Gompers* (App. D.C. 1909)]; Roosevelt to Taft, Aug. 24, 1908, in *Letters*, 6:1196.

43. All in the William Howard Taft Papers: William Howard Taft to George von L. Meyer, Aug. 25, 1908, reel 246; F. C. Nunemacher to Taft, Aug. 24, 1908, reel 92; and Meyer to Taft, Aug. 27, 1908.

44. Washington *Post*, Sept. 10, 1908. Just how Davenport's change of heart was engineered is uncertain. On July 28 Daniel Thew Wright had offered Taft his help in the upcoming campaign in Ohio. Perhaps someone in Republican circles thought to ask Wright to ask Gould to postpone the hearing. Gould and Wright were cronies, a fact known to the Washington bar. Daniel Thew Wright to Taft, July 28, 1908, reel 89, William Howard Taft Papers; U.S. House Committee on the Judiciary, *Daniel Thew Wright*, 1010, 1192–92. Cf. Wiebe, *Businessmen and Reform*, 114.

45. Greene, "'Strike at the Ballot Box,'" 186–88; White, "The Labor Unions in the Presidential Campaign," 381.

46. Roosevelt to Philander Chase Knox, Oct. 21, 1908, in *Letters*, 6:1313, 1309, 1306; James W. Van Cleave to Roosevelt, Oct. 22, 1908, in U.S. Senate Committee on the Judiciary, *Maintenance of a Lobby: Appendix*, 2:2254; U.S. House Committee on the Judiciary, *Injunctions*, 276–77.

47. Van Cleave to John Kirby, Nov. 7, 1908, U.S. Senate Committee on the Judiciary, *Maintenance of a Lobby: Exhibits*, 3:341–12.

48. Washington *Star*, Nov. 18, 1908; Washington *Post*, Nov. 18, 1908; Holmes to Einstein, April 1, 1928, in *Holmes-Einstein Letters*, 279.

49. *National Cyclopedia of American Biography*, 32:241–42; Tunison, *The Cincinnati Riot*; Pringle, *William Howard Taft*, 1:83–87, 93–94.

50. Joseph Benson Foraker to Theodore Roosevelt, July 28, Aug. 29, 1903, Joseph Benton Foraker Papers; Washington *Post*, Nov. 6, 1903.

51. U.S. House Committee on the Judiciary, *Daniel Thew Wright*, 7–8, 1198, 2101–6.

52. Ibid., 2106; "First Year Law: 6:30, Nov. 5, [1911]," enclosed in Harry M. Clabaugh to Rev. Auguste J. Duarte, Nov. 16, 1911, box: Law School, 1871–1933, Georgetown University Archives; Anon. to George W. Norris, Aug. 7, 1912, enclosed in Gompers to John A. Maguire et al., August 8, 1912, reel 75, *AFL Records.*

53. Washington *Post,* Dec. 24, 1908; Record at 390–91, *Gompers* (App. D.C. 1909); *Buck's Stove,* 36 Wash. L. Rep. at 835–36.

54. *Buck's Stove,* 36 Wash. L. Rep. at 842.

55. Washington *Post,* Dec. 24, 1908; Gompers, Memo, Feb. 15, 1912, reel 74, *AFL Records.* Wright's impressions come to us as triple hearsay: from one Washington lawyer to another to Gompers, who wrote it down as soon as he heard it.

Mitchell would continue to view the case more coolly than Gompers. Gompers wrote in the *American Federationist* that "the flashing eyes, the twitching lips, the contemptuous frown of Justice Wright but poorly concealed a volcano of surging, relentless hatred." Mitchell thought this portrait "overdrawn." Better to let the judge's own words convict him, he counseled Gompers, than to distract readers with another display of emotion. Gompers, "Justice Wright's Denial," 130; Mitchell to Gompers, Jan. 18, 1909, reel 17, John Mitchell Papers.

56. Washington *Post,* Dec. 24, 1908.

57. *Buck's Stove,* 36 Wash. L. Rep. at 843; Washington *Post,* Dec. 24, 1908.

58. New York *Tribune,* Dec. 24, 1908, in box 13, James Montgomery Beck Papers; cover letter of F. R. Boocock, Jan. 22, 1909, reel 70, *AFL Records.*

59. Detroit *Free Press,* Dec. 24, 1908. See also the editorials collected in AABA, *Decision of Justice Wright in Contempt Proceedings,* 66–76.

60. Telegram, Lawrence F. Abbott to William Loeb, Jr., Dec. 24, 1908, reel 87, Theodore Roosevelt Papers; Lyman Abbott to Roosevelt, Dec. 27, 1908, reel 67, ibid.; "The Conviction of Labor Leaders," 6; Boston *American,* Dec. 27, 1908; Low, "The Contempt Cases," 13; Sweet, "A Great Plea," 15. See also "Right to Restrain the Right," 207.

61. Telegram, Roosevelt to Department of Justice, Dec. 23, 1908, box 1, file nos. 144, 619–43, Department of Justice Papers, Record Group 60 [hereafter cited as DOJ Papers]; Hale, "Injunctions and Pardons," 195.

62. Bonaparte assured Roosevelt that he was "not in the least misled by any sympathy for the Gompers outfit, having a very poor opinion of that crowd." Bonaparte to Roosevelt, Dec. 25, 1908, reel 87, Theodore Roosevelt Papers.

63. Roosevelt to Lyman Abbott, Dec. 29, 1908, Theodore Roosevelt Papers; *New York Times,* Dec. 27, 1908.

64. Gompers to F. S. Monnett, Dec. 30, 1908, reel 131, Gompers Letterbooks; see also *New York Times,* Nov. 27, 1909.

65. Helfand, "Labor and the Courts," 102–5; American Fed'n Labor v. Buck's Stove & Range Co., 33 App. D.C. 83, 106–7, 109, 125 (1909).

66. Gompers to Parker, April 20, 1909, reel 135, Gompers Letterbooks; Gompers, "Justice Wright's Decision," 438–54.

67. Gompers v. Buck's Stove & Range Co., 33 App. D.C. 516, 577, 576 (1909).

68. Merritt, *History of the League for Industrial Rights,* 40–44; "Buck's Stove and Range Company's Agreement," 807–8.

69. Post to James A. Emery, Oct. 7, 1910, box 1, Post Family Papers; James A.

Emery to C. W. Post, Sept. 21, 1910, box 1, Post Family Papers; Post v. Buck's Stove & Range Co., 200 F. 918 (8th Cir. 1912); Walter Drew to James A. Emery, Aug. 11, 1910, box 22, Walter W. Drew Papers.

70. Gompers to Joseph F. Valentine, Oct. 10, 1910, reel 149, Gompers Letterbooks; Gompers to Executive Council, Dec. 29, 1910, reel 23, *AFL Records;* see also Gompers to C. Legien, Jan. 11, 1911, reel 152, Gompers Letterbooks.

71. Gompers, Mitchell and Morrison to Parker, Ralston and Mulholland, Dec. 28, 1910, reel 23, *AFL Records.*

72. James A. Emery to C. W. Post, Jan. 31, 1911, box 1, Post Family Papers; Gompers to Frederic W. Gardner, Feb. 25, 1911, reel 153, Gompers Letterbooks.

73. Davenport to Emery, March 25, 1911, U.S. House Select Committee, *Lobby Activities of the NAM,* 1:66.

74. Gompers v. Buck's Stove & Range Co., 221 U.S. 418, 452 (1911).

75. "Regrettable Error," 43.

76. Wilson served in his personal capacity and not as a representative of the Department of Justice, which maintained a policy of neutrality toward the dispute. Testimony at Wright's impeachment hearings suggested Wilson often accommodated Wright's demands. John W. Davis to William Velpeau Rooker, Nov. 22, 1913, and William R. Harr to William Howard Taft, Aug. 30, 1910, both in DOJ Papers; U.S. Senate Committee on the Judiciary, *Daniel Thew Wright,* 1049–50.

77. Helfand, "Labor and the Courts," 110–11.

78. Emery to Drew, June 24, 1912, and Drew to Members of the National Erectors Association, June 26, 1912, both in box 16, Walter W. Drew Papers; Hunter, *Labor in Politics,* 41–42.

79. Helfand, "Labor and the Courts," 110–11; Re Gompers, 40 App. D.C. 293, 333–37 (1913); *New York Times,* May 6, 1913; cf. *New York Times,* Dec. 25, 1908.

80. New York *Globe,* May 6, 1913.

81. Gompers v. United States, 233 U.S. 604, 607 (1914).

82. AABA, *Bulletin,* May 18, 1914.

83. Emery to Post, Sept. 21, 1910, box 1, Post Family Papers; Franklin G. Ferguson to Charles W. Eliot, Aug. 11, 1906, box 297, Charles W. Eliot Papers. Walter Gordon Merritt felt the same way a decade later. "Committee Hearing on Issuance of Injunctions," 194–95.

84. Roosevelt to Thomas Robins, Jan. 11, 1912, reel 371, Theodore Roosevelt Papers; *New York Times,* April 4, 1910.

85. Mink, *Old Labor and New Immigrants,* 161–203.

86. Van Cleave to Atherton Brownell, Dec. 7, 1907, U.S. Senate Committee on the Judiciary, *Maintenance of a Lobby: Appendix,* 1:1191.

87. Merritt, *Destination Unknown,* 22; Washington *Star,* Oct. 6, 21, 1914.

CHAPTER 8: LABOR INCORPORATED

1. Laski, "Personality of Associations," 424. Platt was also a classmate of Daniel Davenport's at Yale. Hicks, comp., *Famous Jury Speeches,* 530.

2. Merritt, "Brief Statement of Facts," in AABA, *Loewe Case,* 9–10.

3. Record at 1215–18, 1227, Lawlor v. Loewe, 235 U.S. 522 (1915); United States

Census of Individuals, 1900, vol. 3, E.D. 56, sheet 2, line 2, s.v. "William Humphries."

4. Record at 1220, *Lawlor*, 235 U.S. 522 (1915).

5. Equity courts, in contrast, would entertain suits against labor leaders in their capacity as representatives of trade unions. This, as well as timeliness, was another advantage of the labor injunction over the damage suit. Martin, *Law of Labor Unions*, 281–88.

6. AABA, *January Bulletin*, Jan. 20, 1915.

7. U.S. House Committee on Appropriations, *Danbury Hatters' Judgment*, 14; Samuel Gompers to John A. Moffitt, Feb. 5, 1910, reel 141, Gompers Letterbooks.

8. Lawlor v. Loewe, 187 F. 522 (2d Cir. 1911), *cert. den'd*, 223 U.S. 729 (1912); Hicks, comp., *Famous Jury Speeches*, 545.

9. Hicks, comp., *Famous Jury Speeches*, 543–44, 545.

10. Ibid., 548, 518, 525–26, 548.

11. Ibid., 549–50.

12. Ibid., 555–56; Merritt, *Destination Unknown*, 20.

13. AABA, *Loewe Case*, 69–73.

14. Samuel Gompers to John A. Moffitt, Feb. 5, 1910, reel 141, Gompers Letterbooks.

15. Danbury *Evening News*, March 8, 1910; Merritt, *Destination Unknown*, 20–21; Lawlor v. Loewe, 187 F. 522 (2d Cir. 1911), *cert. den'd*, 223 U.S. 729 (1912); Hartford *Courant*, Oct. 12, 1912. At the time of the second verdict, thirty-four of the original defendants had died, and two had gone insane. Ibid.

16. Lawlor v. Loewe, 209 F. 721, 728 (2d Cir. 1913); Lawlor v. Loewe, 235 U.S. 522, 535–36 (1915).

17. "Danbury Hatters Lose," 53–54; *New York Times*, Jan. 7, 1915; see also "Knocked into a Cocked Hat," 785–87.

18. Boston *Herald*, Jan. 19, 1915.

19. Danbury *Evening News*, April 22, 1915, reprinted in AABA, *Danbury Hatters' Case*, 1–2; AABA, *June Bulletin*; E. E. Witte, "Danbury Hatters' Case," 4, box 120, Edwin E. Witte Papers, State Historical Society of Wisconsin.

20. AABA, *Bulletin*, April 6, 1917; Walter Gordon Merritt and Daniel Davenport to Martin J. Cunningham and William F. Tammany, Oct. 20, 1915 (copy), box HRD-17, United Hatters of North America Papers.

21. Gompers to John A. Moffitt, July 16, 1910, reel 141, Gompers Letterbooks; "Union Men to Pay," 86; *New York Times*, Jan. 21, 1916.

22. The 1910 assessment raised $98,756. The first Hatters' Day and a second, held on June 15, 1916, raised another $164,509. A final reckoning placed the total cost of the suit to organized labor at $421,477. Robinson, *Spotlight on a Union*, 92–94.

23. This raised another $50,382. Robinson, *Spotlight on a Union*, 93; Stowe, "Paying the Penalty," 613

24. Merritt, *Destination Unknown*, 24; "Danbury Hatters Case Finally Settled," 19.

25. U.S. House Committee on Appropriations, *Danbury Hatters' Judgment*, 16; New York *World*, April 24, 1915, reprinted in AABA, *Danbury Hatters' Case*, 3.

26. Stowe, "Paying the Penalty," 612.

27. Ibid., 613–14.

28. Ibid., 612.

29. Catherine Hunt to Martin Lawlor, Sept. 3, 1917, box HRD-19, United Hatters of North America Papers.

30. Record at 1230–40, *Lawlor*, 235 U.S. 522 (1915).

31. Mrs. Nathan C. Hoy to Officers of the United Hatters of North America, July 11, 1917, box HRD-19, United Hatters of North America Papers.

32. Stowe, "Paying the Penalty," 615.

33. Ibid.; "An Illegal Boycott," 370–71.

34. Act of June 29, 1886, 24 Stat. 86; *Congressional Record*, 49th Cong. 1st sess. (June 11, 1886), 5565–66; Walter, "Incorporation of Labor Unions," 69. See Furner, "Republican Tradition and the New Liberalism," 208.

35. Gompers to AFL Executive Committee, Jan. 23, 1897, quoted in Tomlins, *State and the Unions*, 85; Boston *Globe*, Dec. 5, 1902; Gompers, *Labor and the Common Welfare*, 5, 6, 15; Gompers to Moffitt, Feb. 5, 1910, reel 141, Gompers Letterbooks.

36. These statutes did not abolish the plaintiff's right to proceed against the individual members of the society. Even if Connecticut had such a statute—and it did not—Davenport could have still sued the hatters individually. See Sturges, "Unincorporated Associations," 404.

37. U.S. Senate, *Industrial Relations*, 11:10653, 10665. Other lawyers were less satisfied with existing law. Several days after Davenport testified, Walter Drew, counsel for the National Erectors' Association, told the commission that the open-shop lawyers "do not present a united front" on the incorporation issue. "Mr. Davenport happened to bring an action up in Connecticut where the laws permit an attachment before suit, and also against a union where there was a large number of individuals owning their own homes and some of this world's goods," Drew explained. "This has made his action against the individual members of the union a good and valuable asset." He thought these conditions would not hold for most damage suits, and he was certain they would not for suits against the "roving" structural iron workers his clients employed. Ibid., 10,753, 10,759.

38. Tomlins, *State and the Unions*, 36–52; Hurst, *Legitimacy of the Business Corporation*.

39. The last term was favored by the labor economist John R. Commons. Harter, *Commons*, 271, 231–32.

40. Cheyney, "Decisions of the Courts," 272, 277. Similarly, Cheyney rejected the notion that the closed shop was incompatible with employers' right to manage their businesses. "The matter could hardly be more completely misstated than in the case of State v. Glidden," he claimed. The idea "that any aggressive action on the part of the employees is an undue interference with the private affairs of the employer . . . seems to be distinctly a survival from a period when the courts served largely to keep the employed class in subjection to the employing class." Ibid., 269–70.

41. Seligman, *Economic Interpretation of History*, 3; Seligman, "Liberty, Democracy," 9. On Seligman, see Ross, *Origins*, 101–2, 104, 186–87, 193–95; Barrow, "From Marx to Madison," 383–90.

42. Sklar, *The Corporate Reconstruction*, 61. See also Wunderlin, *New Industrial Order;* Furner, "Republican Tradition and the New Liberalism," 231.

43. Cheyney, "Decisions of the Courts," 267.

44. Civic Federation of Chicago, *Chicago Conference on Trusts*, 31–32; Jenks, "Trade Unions and Wages," 49–53; Perlman and Taft, *History of Labor*, 97–109; Atkinsen, "Trusts and Trade Unions," 193–223.

45. Mink describes the formation of "the NCF entente" in *Old Labor and New Immigrants*, 161–203. See also Wunderlin, *New Industrial Order*, 47–56; Ramirez, *When Workers Fight*.

46. Abbott, "Illegal Boycott," 370–71; Steffee, "The Taff Vale Case," 393.

47. United States Industrial Commission, *Final Report of the Industrial Commission*, 19:857–58.

48. Wambaugh, "Should Trade Unions Be Incorporated?" 264–65.

49. United States Industrial Commission, *Final Report*, 19:858; "The Legal Effects of a Trade Agreement," *In the Matter of the Arbitration between John Mitchell . . . and the Philadelphia and Reading Coal and Iron Company* ([1902?]), reel 5, John Mitchell Papers; "Incorporation of Trade Unions" ([1902?]), ibid.; Boston *Globe*, Dec. 5, 1902; Mink, *Old Labor and New Immigrants*, 178–79.

50. Brandeis, "Incorporation," 11. On Brandeis's labor litigation and views on trade unionism, see Strum, *Brandeis*, 94–113.

51. *Boston Globe*, Dec. 5, 1902. On Eliot, see Eliot, *American Contributions*, 12–13; Green, "The National Civic Federation," 111–13; Rodgers, *The Work Ethic in Industrial America*, 233–42.

52. Boston *Globe*, Dec. 5, 1902; Brandeis, "Incorporation," 12, 13, 14.

53. "The Employers and Trades Unions" (April 21, 1904), in Brandeis, *Business*, 19.

54. Boston *Post*, Feb. 6, 1905. NCF Secretary Ralph Easley subsequently published the speech in the *National Civic Federation Monthly Review*. Strum, *Brandeis*, 107.

55. Brandeis, "The Preferential Shop," 179.

56. Laski, "Personality of Associations," 404, 422. On *Taff Vale Railway v. Amalgamated Society of Railway Servants*, [1901] A.C. 426, and earlier legislation, see Klarman, "The Judges versus the Unions," 1487–602.

57. Parrish, *Felix Frankfurter*, 72–75, 107–14, 124–25; Frankfurter, *Felix Frankfurter Reminisces*, 171–73; Coolidge, "Michaels Stern & Co.," 761; Chenery, "War and Peace at Rochester," 185.

58. Walter Drew to O. P. Briggs, May 16, 1918, box 12, Walter W. Drew Papers. On Frankfurter and the drafting of the Norris-LaGuardia Act of 1932, see Ernst, "Common Laborers?" 78–79.

59. United Mine Workers of America v. Coronado Coal Co., 259 U.S. 344, 388–390 (1922); see Kutler, "Chief Justice Taft," 68–83.

60. "The 'Law' and Labor," 247.

61. *A. F. of L. Weekly News Letter*, June 10, 1922, quoted in Witte, *The Government in Labor Disputes*, 137n.1; Frankfurter, "The Coronado Case," 330. See also "The Coronado Coal Case," 59–65.

62. Several important reformers, most notably John R. Commons and the St.

Louis lawyer Frank P. Walsh, opposed the regulation of labor disputes. They denied what other progressives steadfastly insisted: that properly trained, unbiased officials could identify outcomes that best advanced the public interest. As Commons put it, "A man cannot represent society as a whole. If he claims to do this, he really means he wishes to have things as they are." "Discussion," *Publications of the American Economic Association: Economic Studies* 4 (April 1899): 111–13, quoted in Ross, *Origins*, 194. Commons's views would have great influence on labor law after 1932, but they made little headway in public policy before the terminal date of this study.

63. See Stone, "The Post-War Paradigm," 1518–21; Tomlins, *State and the Unions*, 83–91.

CHAPTER 9: MAGNA CARTA

1. Abbott, "Trust Laws and Labor," 334; U.S. House Committee on the Judiciary, *Trust Legislation*, 16; Gompers, "The Charter of Industrial Freedom," 971–72; Gompers to Executive Council, Sept. 3, 1914, quoted in Jones, "Enigma," 214.

2. Paine Lumber Co. v. Neal, 244 U.S. 459, 485 (1917); Duplex Printing Co. v. Deering, 254 U.S. 473–74 (1921); "The Duplex Case," 30, 31.

3. Daniel Davenport to William E. Borah, Aug. 10, 1914, box 10, William E. Borah Papers.

4. See Eskridge and Frickey, *Cases and Materials*, 48–49, 51–56, 57–59.

5. Samuel Gompers to Executive Council, Feb. 17, 1908, reel 120, Gompers Letterbooks; U.S. House Committee on the Judiciary, *Hearings on House Bill 19745*, 49; *Cong. Record*, 60 Cong., 1st sess., 1908, 3767.

6. Beck, "The Supreme Court and Organized Labor," 21; Hartford *Daily Courant*, Feb. 26, 1908, and Buffalo *Commercial*, Feb. 27, 1908, both in in AABA, *The Boycott and Public Opinion*, 10, 6–7.

7. Loewe v. Lawlor, 208 U.S. 274, 274–75 (1908).

8. National Civic Federation, *A Discussion of the Boycott Problem*, 6.

9. Lamoreaux, *The Great Merger Movement*, 100–101; Ulman, *The Rise of the National Trade Union*, 526–31; Davis, *The Development of the American Glass Industry*, 198–99; Scoville, *Revolution in Glassmaking*, 212–34.

10. "The Late Judge George L. Phillips," 570; Kealey v. Faulkner, 18 Ohio Dec. 498, 503, 505, 510 (C.P. Cuyahoga Cnty, 1907).

11. *Kealey*, 18 Ohio Dec. at 516, 517.

12. A notice of the case appeared in the union's journal, *Glass Worker* 5 (Feb. 1908): 11.

13. U.S. House Committee on Labor, *Eight Hours*, 60th Cong., 1908.

14. The definitive account of the movement for antitrust revision is Sklar, *The Corporate Reconstruction*, 203–85. The text of the Hepburn bill appears in U.S. House Committee on the Judiciary, *Hearings on House Bill 19745*, 3–6.

15. Sklar, *The Corporate Reconstruction*, 233.

16. Ralph Easley to Louis D. Brandeis, Sept. 4, 1907, and Easley to Edgar Addison Bancroft, March 21, 1908, both quoted by Sklar, *The Corporate Reconstruction*, 210–11, 256–57.

17. U.S. House Committee on the Judiciary, *Hearings on House Bill 19745*, 43, 45; U.S. House Committee on Labor, *Eight Hours*, 60th Cong., 1908, 641.

18. U.S. Senate Committee on the Judiciary, *Amendment of the Sherman Antitrust Law*, 15. On the *Knight* case, see chapter 6; on ancillary restraints in the early jurisprudence of the Sherman Act, see Carstensen, *The Content of the Hollow Core of Antitrust.*

19. U.S. Senate Committee on the Judiciary, *Amendment of the Sherman Antitrust Law*, 26.

20. Ibid., 26, 27. In the House, Jeremiah Jenks, under questioning from Davenport and Emery, expressly denied that the Hepburn bill would legalize the secondary boycott. U.S. House Committee on the Judiciary, *Hearings on House Bill 19745*, 7–8, 136–37, 147.

21. To be sure, the plaintiff who sued a trade union on these grounds would bear the heavy burden of proving the intent to restrain interstate trade. *Coronado Coal Company v. United Mine Workers* was in the federal courts from 1914 to 1927; the AABA-sponsored *Pennsylvania Mining Company v. United Mine Workers* took just as long to litigate and ended in the plaintiff's nonsuit. See Witte, *The Government in Labor Disputes*, 136–38, 140; Berman, *Labor and the Sherman Act*, 302–4.

22. U.S. Senate Committee on the Judiciary, *Amendment of the Sherman Antitrust Law*, 179; U.S. House Committee on the Judiciary, *Hearings on House Bill 19745*, 64. Compare the position taken by Philip S. Post, Jr., International Harvester's general counsel, in "Trusts and Trade Unions," 631–35.

23. U.S. House Committee on the Judiciary, *Hearings on House Bill 19745*, 233–34.

24. Connolly v. Union Sewer Pipe Company, 184 U.S. 540, 599 (1902), quoting *Hayes v. Missouri*, 113 U.S. 68, 71 (1879); *Connolly*, at 560–61, quoting Gulf, Colorado & Santa Fe R.R. v. Ellis, 165 U.S. 150, 165 (1897). See Benedict, "Laissez-Faire and Liberty," 307–8.

25. U.S. House Committee on the Judiciary, *Hearings on House Bill 19745*, 52, 227; U.S. Senate Committee on the Judiciary, *Amendment of the Sherman Antitrust Law*, 185.

26. Sklar, *The Corporate Reconstruction*, 282–83.

27. Wright, "Contest in Congress," 252; James A. Emery to C. W. Post, Jan. 31, 1911, box 1, Post Family Papers.

28. Wright, "Contest in Congress," 251–52; "Members of the Trade Union Group in Congress," 4; "The Labor Lobby in Washington," 84–87. On William Wilson, see Boemke, "Colorado Coal Strike," 90–95.

29. Davenport to Emery, March 25, 1911, and Emery to Davenport, March 27, 1911, both in U.S. House Select Committee, *Charges against the Members*, 1:66–68.

30. Link, *Wilson: The New Freedom*, 186–90; Steigerwalt, *The National Association of Manufacturers*, 138–49; Jackson H. Ralston to Lee S. Overman, July 19, 1913, and Overman to Ralston, July 21, 1913, both in box 91, U.S. Senate Committee on the Judiciary, Lobby Investigation, SEN 63A-F15187, Records of the United States Senate, Record Group 46, National Archives.

31. *Federal Antitrust Laws*, 81, 91, 92–93, 101, 102, 104, 105; U.S. House Committee on the Judiciary, *Hearings on House Bill 19745*, 56.

32. James Wilkerson to Attorney General, Jan. 25, 1913, J. A. Fowler to Wilkerson, Feb. 1, 1913, and Wilkerson to Fowler, July 30, 1913, all in Case File No. 164951, DOJ Papers, Record Group 60, National Archives.

33. *Cong. Record,* 63 Cong., 2d sess., 1910, 9540–41; *New York Times,* Sept. 6, 1910.

34. Boemke, "Colorado Coal Strike," 48–54; Kerny, *The Political Education of Woodrow Wilson,* 34.

35. Woodrow Wilson, "Credo," Aug. 6, 1907, quoted in Boemeke, "Colorado Coal Strike," 53 n.124.

36. Link, *Wilson: The New Freedom,* 266–69.

37. Vittoz, *New Deal Labor Policy,* 47–51; Moderwell, "The Bituminous Coal Industry," 569–70.

38. Gitelman, *Legacy of the Ludlow Massacre,* 1–31.

39. Hitchman Coal & Coke Co. v. Mitchell, 202 F. 512, 545 (N.D.W. Va. 1912). Although the district court held that the UMW had violated the Sherman Act as well as the common law of conspiracy, higher courts rejected the statute as a basis for decision, arguing that it had not been raised in the pleadings and did not authorize the granting of injunctions at the behest of private parties. Thus when the U.S. Supreme Court decided the case in 1917, it treated the case as turning on a common-law issue, whether the UMW had violated the plaintiff's rights created by his "yellow-dog" employment contracts. Mitchell v. Hitchman Coal & Coke, 214 F. 685, 713 (4th Cir. 1914), *reversed,* 245 U.S. 225 (1917).

40. Jones, "Wilson Administration," 134–37; Commerce Clearing House, *Federal Antitrust Laws,* 102, 104, 105.

41. "Indicting a Labor Trust," 1365–66; "Miners' Union as a 'Labor Trust,'" 1214–15.

42. Wesley C. Mitchell, "In Memory of Henry R. Seager," and Seager, "Economics at Berlin and Vienna," both in Seager, *Labor and Other Economic Essays,* ix–x, 1–29. On Adams, Ely, and their circle, consult Ross, *Origins,* 106–18; Furner, "The Republican Tradition," 182–91.

43. "Attitude of the State," (Sept. 1907), "The Legal Status of Trade Unions in the United Kingdom with Conclusions Applicable to Wage-Earners" (Dec. 1907), and "The Injunction" (Feb. 1914), all in Seager, *Labor and Other Economic Essays,* 102–4, 106, 124, 128–9, and 241.

44. Sklar, *The Corporate Reconstruction,* 146–54.

45. On Brandeis and the rule of reason in labor cases, see "How Far Have We Come on the Road to Industrial Democracy?" (1913), in *The Curse of Bigness,* 46. The U.S. Supreme Court later upheld collective bargaining in the glass industry as a reasonable restraint of trade on facts much like those Judge Phillips deplored in *Kealey.* National Association of Window Glass Manufacturers v. United States, 263 U.S. 403 (1923) (Holmes, J.).

46. Seager, "Trade Unions and the Law" (Jan. 1914), in Seager, *Labor and Other Economic Essays,* 233, 236–37.

47. Merritt, "Trade Union and the Law," 524–25.

48. Seager, "Attitude of the State," 95–96; Seager, "Trade Unions and the Law," 237–39; Merritt, *Labor Legislation,* 26.

49. Link, *Wilson: The New Freedom,* 423–44; Sklar, *The Corporate Reconstruction,* 309–32.

50. *Cong. Record,* 63d Cong., 2d sess., 1914, 13967–68, 13965.

51. May, *Protestant Churches,* 104; May, *End of American Innocence.*

52. Sklar, *The Corporate Reconstruction,* 287; Green, "The National Civic Federation," 214–15; Holt, *Congressional Insurgents,* 14.

53. U.S. Senate Committee on Interstate Commerce, *Hearings Pursuant,* 1724.

54. *Cong. Record,* 63d Cong., 2d sess., 1914, 13979.

55. Ibid.

56. International Harvester Co. v. Missouri, 234 U.S. 199 (1914). For the jurists, see Freund, *Police Power,* 142, 633–34, 753; Wigdor, *Pound,* 90–91; Ernst, "The Critical Tradition," 1052–53; see also Chomsky, "Progressive Judges," 425–26. Henry Seager relied in part on Freund's *Police Power* for the proposition that the constitutionality of legislation was a question of "industrial fact": whether the legislature "'carves out a class from the body of the people,' or simply recognizes the existence of a class already in being." "The Attitude of American Courts towards Restrictive Labor Laws" (1904), in Seager, *Labor and Other Economic Essays,* 59, quoting State v. Haun, 61 Kan. 146, 59 P. 340 (1899).

57. *Cong. Record,* 63d Cong., 2d sess., 1914, 13982.

58. Ibid., 14020–23. Thomas referred to Merritt as "a gentleman whom I do not know, with whose views I am not in full accord."

59. Gompers, *Seventy Years,* 297. Davenport's thoughts were elsewhere. "I wonder whether their long ministrations at the altar of humbug has not unfitted your democratic colleagues to realize their own hypocrisy," he wrote to Senator William E. Borah on August 18, 1914. "This thought occurred to me after listening for an afternoon in the Senate gallery to their heroics denouncing trusts and monopolies and declaring their deep sympathy for their unfortunate victims." Box 15, William E. Borah Papers.

60. Wright, "Contest in Congress," 256.

61. "Changing the Trust Law to Suit Labor," 1346; see also Wright, "Contest in Congress," 260.

62. U.S. House Committee on the Judiciary, *Trust Legislation,* 16–17; House Report No. 267, Pt. 1, 63d Cong., 2d sess. (May 6, 1914), in Kintner, ed., *Legislative History,* 2:1095.

63. New York *American,* May 28, 1914; Spelling to Borah, May 28, 1914, box 10, William E. Borah Papers.

64. The printers refused to handle the photoengraved material of Doubleday, Page and Company and several other firms that used it. When Wilson named Walter H. Page as ambassador to England, the printers sent a public resolve to that government, urging Page's nomination be rejected. A federal grand jury and Attorney General James C. McReynolds investigated the matter, but his assistant directed that no indictments be sought. Walter Gordon Merritt then filed an ultimately unsuccessful lawsuit on behalf of a member of the AABA that was similarly affected by the boycott. Link, *Wilson: The New Freedom,* 428–29; Jones, "Wilson Administration," 137–38n.65; *New York Times,* Feb. 17, 22, March 18, April 9, 10, 1914; Gill Engraving Co. v. Doerr, 214 F. 111 (S.D.N.Y. 1914); Edwin E. Witte, interview with Matthew J. Woll, president of the International Photo Engravers Union, March 11, 22, 1915, Edwin E. Witte Papers (U.S. Mss. 20A), State Historical Society of Wisconsin.

65. My account of the legislative history of the labor provisions of the Clayton Act draws on Jones, "Enigma," 207–14; Link, *Wilson: The New Freedom*, 429–31.

66. *New York Times*, April 15, 1914, quoted by Jones, "Enigma," 209.

67. Edwin E. Witte, "History of the Anti-Injunction Bills before Congress, 1893–1914" (June 1914), Edwin E. Witte Papers, Cornell University.

68. Kintner, ed., *Legislative History*, 2:1179.

69. Ibid., 2:1730, 1736.

70. Gompers to Peter J. Brady, June 19, 1914, reel 183, Gompers Letterbooks; Wilson to Charles R. Van Hise, July 13, 1914, quoted in Jones, "Enigma," 213; New York *American*, May 28, 1914; "Labor's Influence," 1423–24.

71. "Labor's Influence," 1423.

72. Resolution adopted unanimously at mass meeting, Cooper Union, June 10th 1914, enclosed in Peter J. Brady to Francis G. Newlands, June 15, 1914, Committee on the Judiciary (SEN 63A-F15), Records of the United States Senate; Gompers to "Organized Labor, Ohio," July 10, 1914, reel 184, Gompers Letterbooks.

73. E. R. Bathwick to Gompers, July 2, 1914, reel 77, *AFL Records;* also from *AFL Records:* Gompers to Bathwick, July 13, 1914, F. A. Bennett to Charles A. Culberson, June 9, 1914, and Letter of George F. Dominick, Jr., June 4, 1914; see also Alex Laughlin, Jr., to Borah, July 28, 1914, box 15, William E. Borah Papers.

74. J. C. Kolson to Culberson, June 13, 1914, and W. A. Clark to Culberson, June 1914, both in *AFL Records.*

75. AABA, *May Bulletin*, May 11, 1914; Davenport, "The Clayton Anti-Trust Bill," 581–84; Davenport to Francis G. Newlands, June 3, 1914, Davenport to Charles A. Culberson, June 18, 20, 1914, and A. J. Clopton to Davenport, June 19, 1914, all in Committee on the Judiciary (SEN 63A-F15), Records of the United States Senate, Record Group 46, National Archives.

76. AABA, *Bulletin*, June 12, 1914.

77. U.S. Senate Committee on the Judiciary, *Hearings Before Subcommittee;* Lorwin, *American Federation of Labor*, 122–23; "H.R. 15657 as reported by the Senate Committee on the Judiciary," in Kintner, ed., *Legislative History*, 2:1756, 1765.

78. Spelling to Borah, July 28, 1914, box 15, William E. Borah Papers.

79. Holt, *Congressional Insurgents*, 113–14; *Cong. Record*, 63d Cong., 2d sess., 1914, 13,918; see also Borah to Edward P. Wallace, Aug. 21, 1914, box 10, William E. Borah Papers.

80. Davenport to Borah, Aug. 13, 1914, box 10, William E. Borah Papers. In debate on August 17, Borah correctly identified *Kealey* as being "the case of a nisi prius court . . . under the common law and statutes of the State of Ohio." *Cong. Record*, 63d Cong., 2d sess., 1914, 13909.

81. Davenport to Borah, Aug. 17, 1914, box 10, William E. Borah Papers.

82. Gompers, *Seventy Years*, 296–97; Gompers to Peter J. Brady, June 19, 1914, reel 183, Gompers Letterbooks; *Cong. Record*, 63d Cong., 2d sess., 1914, 13983.

83. *Cong. Record*, 63d Cong., 2d sess., 1914, 13981, 14546–47.

84. Ibid., 13982–83.

85. Ibid., 14590–91.

86. Thomas Watt Gregory to Wilson, Sept. 11, 1914, in *The Papers of Woodrow Wilson*, 31:24–26; Wilson to Gregory, Sept. 14, 1914, ibid., 29; Wilson to Oscar W. Underwood, Oct. 17, 1914, *Cong. Record*, 63d Cong., 2d sess., 1914, A1187–88.

87. Davenport, "An Analysis of the Labor Sections," 46–55; Witte, "Section Twenty"; Edwin E. Witte to Alpheus T. Mason, March 3, 1933, box 1, Edwin E. Witte Papers, State Historical Society of Wisconsin; see also Witte, "The Clayton Bill," 360.

88. "Labor Is Not a Commodity," 114. Spelling agreed with Davenport's assessment during hearings of the U.S. Commission on Industrial Relations in May 1915. When Gompers testified before the commission several weeks later, he denounced Spelling as "a supposed friend" and denied the lawyer represented the AFL "in the slightest degree." U.S. Senate, *Industrial Relations*, 11:10720–23, 10854–55.

89. Wickersham, "Labor Legislation in the Clayton Act," 493–503; Taft to Wickersham, Oct. 31, Nov. 8, 1914, reel 527, William Howard Taft Papers; Taft, "Address of the President," 374–75.

90. Paine Lumber Co. v. Neal, 244 U.S. 459, 485 (1917); Duplex Printing Co. v. Deering, 254 U.S. 443, 473–74 (1921).

91. "The 'Law' and Labor," 246. But even Frankfurter thought the labor provisions of the Clayton Act "a shabbily drawn piece of legislation" that better lawyers than Gompers's would have never approved. Ibid., 248.

92. Holmes to Frankfurter, Jan. 30, 1921, reel 21, in Holmes, *American Legal Manuscripts*.

93. Davenport to Borah, Aug. 17, 1914, and "Brieflet on the New Deal with Labor, and Proper Treatment Thereof," both in box 10, William E. Borah Papers. Thomas Spelling may have been the author of this document.

Chapter 10: The Woodtrim War

1. Witte, "Injunctions in Labor Disputes," Appendix E: "Injunctions and Trade Union Boycotts," Feb. 27, 1915, 42–52.

2. *Carpenter* (Jan. 1896): 4, quoted in Wolman, *The Boycott in American Trade Unions*, 50; Record at 14–41, Paine Lumber Co. v. Neal, 244 U.S. 459 (1917); U.S. Senate, *Industrial Relations*, 2:1617–18.

3. Christie, *Empire in Wood*, 167.

4. James, "Restrictive Agreements," 116–18; Brown, *American Lumber Industry*, 235, 47–51; Record at 1596, 1599, 1759, 1762, 1834, 1836, 1874, 1876, 1895, 1897, Paine Lumber Co. v. Neal, 244 U.S. 459 (1917).

5. James, "Restrictive Agreements," 118–19; Brown, *American Lumber Industry*, 233, 235; Compton, *The Organization of the Lumber Industry*, 130–34, 141–42; Eastern States Retail Lumber Dealers Association v. United States, 234 U.S. 600 (1914).

6. Record at 2431, *Paine*, 244 U.S. 459 (1917).

7. The merger was completed for New York City in January 1910 and on a nationwide basis in April 1912. Galenson, *United Brotherhood of Carpenters*, 99–107.

8. Record at 2420, 2413, 2058, 2418, 2424, 2418, 1597–98, *Paine*, 244 U.S. 459 (1917).

9. Record at 2510–13, *Paine*, 244 U.S. 459 (1917); U.S. Senate, *Industrial Relations*, 2:1583–1600; Commons, "New York Building Trades," 409–36.

10. U.S. Senate, *Industrial Relations*, 2:1617–20. For the agreement, see Record at 83, *Paine*, 244 U.S. 459 (1917).

11. Record at 2430, 2432, *Paine*, 244 U.S. 459 (1917). Neal testified in a deposition in *Paine* in February 1913. Appearing before the U.S. Commission on Indus-

trial Relations in May 1914, John Rice, an organizer for the United Brotherhood, denied that the New York locals boycotted union-made material. U.S. Senate, *Industrial Relations*, 2:1640–41.

12. Christie, *Empire in Wood*, 162; Brief for Appellants at 29, *Paine*, 244 U.S. 459 (1917); United Brotherhood of Carpenters and Joiners of America, *Proceedings of the Sixteenth Biennial Convention*, 561; Bossert v. Dhuy, 166 A.D. 251, 151 N.Y.S. 877 (1914); Brief for Appellants at 40–41, *Paine*, 244 U.S. 459 (1917); Tisdale Lumber Co. v. Stock, Case No. 562, Paul F. Brissenden Papers; United Brotherhood of Carpenters and Joiners of America, *Proceedings of the Seventeenth Biennial Convention*, 445 [hereafter cited as United Brotherhood, 1912 Conv. Proc.].

13. *New York Times*, May 4, 1910; "Suit Entered against the United Brotherhood," 2–33; Irving v. Joint District Council, 180 F. 896 (C.C.S.D.N.Y. 1910); AABA, *Bulletin*, July 25, 1910; *Carpenter* 20 (Sept. 1910): 23–26.

14. Albro J. Newton Co. v. Erickson, Case No. 398, Paul F. Brissenden Papers; AABA, *Bulletin*, Oct. 1910; Albro J. Newton Co. v. Erickson, 70 Misc. 291, 126 N.Y.S. 949 (1911); New York *Call*, Jan. 7, 1911; *New York Times*, Jan. 7, 1911.

15. Record at 1624, *Paine*, 244 U.S. 459 (1917); Nathan Paine to G. W. Dwelle, Nov. 28, 1910, in United Brotherhood, 1912 Conv. Proc., 191–92.

16. Nathan Paine to G. W. Dwelle, Nov. 28, 1910, in United Brotherhood, 1912 Conv. Proc., 189–91.

17. Paine to Dwelle, Dec. 12, 1910, in United Brotherhood, 1912 Conv. Proc., 191; Record at 1610–16, *Paine*, 244 U.S. 459 (1917); Dwelle to Members of the Eastern Door, Sash and Blind Manufacturers' Association, Dec. 13, 1910, and Minutes of the Annual Meeting of the Eastern Door, Sash and Blind Manufacturers' Association Held in New York City, Feb. 14, 1911, both in United Brotherhood, 1912 Conv. Proc., 188–89, 173.

18. *Oshkosh Daily Northwestern*, March 9, 1911, in Record at 1713–14, *Paine*, 244 U.S. 459 (1917); Record at 980, 982, ibid.

19. Record at 51–58, *Paine*, 244 U.S. 459 (1917). The complainants were the Paine Lumber Company of Oshkosh; the Gould Manufacturing Company of Oshkosh; the R. McMillen Company of Oshkosh; Morgan and Company of Oshkosh; the Lothman Cypress Company of Missouri and Oshkosh; the Curtis and Yale Company of Clinton, Iowa, and Wausau, Wisconsin; W. D. Crooks and Son of Williamsport, Pennsylvania; and the Bristol Door and Lumber Company of Bristol, Virginia, and Bristol, Tennessee.

20. Beattie was the son of Scottish-born parents and a graduate of the College of the City of New York. He was a newspaper reporter before his admission to the bar in 1900. *New York Times*, Nov. 22, 1935.

21. Charles Maitland Beattie to Samuel Gompers, Oct. 19, 1910, reel 72, *AFL Records*.

22. Irving v. Neal, 209 F. 471, 475 (S.D.N.Y. 1913); Act of June 13, 1911, ch. 317, 1911 New York Laws 738; Beattie to Brissenden, Aug. 23, 1932, Tisdale Lumber Company v. Stock, Paul F. Brissenden Papers; United Brotherhood, 1912 Conv. Proc., 192, 805; New York, *Assembly Journal* 1 (1911): 891; New York, *Senate Journal* 1 (1911): 1365.

23. Bossert v. Dhuy, Case No. 60, Paul F. Brissenden Papers; Transcript at 102–

3, 58, Savage v. Potter, 159 A.D. 729, 145 N.Y.S. 78 (1913), vol. 2,836, Case No. 527, Library of the Association of the Bar of the City of New York, New York City.

24. United Brotherhood, 1912 Conv. Proc., 449–50. In early 1912 the carpenters lost other skirmishes. Twice Beattie unsuccessfully sought preliminary injunctions against the AABA in the *Savage* case. In May two organizers were tried on criminal contempt charges and the injunction in *Newton* was made permanent. Ibid., 444–47; Merritt, *Destination Unknown*, 51; *Carpenter* 32 (Feb. 1912): 14; Albro J. Newton Co. v. Erickson, Paul F. Brissenden Papers.

25. "Protest against Injunction," 33–35; see also *Carpenter* 31 (Aug. 1911): 15–16. The Newton and Bossert firms were defendants in the federal suit. Record at 5, Eastern States Retail Lumber Dealers' Association v. United States, 234 U.S. 600 (1914).

26. *New York Times*, Oct. 27, 1912; New York *Call*, Oct. 28, 1912.

27. *New York Times*, Oct. 27, 1912; New York *Tribune*, Oct. 27, 1912. See Christie, *Empire in Wood*, 202.

28. Record at 2834–56, *Paine*, 244 U.S. 459 (1917); Merritt, *Destination Unknown*, 52; Bossert v. Dhuy, Paul F. Brissenden Papers; *New York Times*, June 19, 1913; United Brotherhood of Carpenters and Joiners of America, *Proceedings of the Nineteenth General Convention*, 174–78.

29. Parshelsky Brothers to Harry Gould, July 2, 1911, in Record at 1936–37, *Paine*, 244 U.S. 459 (1917); see also ibid., 1713–14, 1731, 1805; Witte, "Injunctions in Labor Disputes," Appendix D: "Injunctions and the Outcome of Strikes," 19–21.

30. Bossert v. United Brotherhood of Carpenters, 77 Misc. 592, 137 N.Y.S. 321 (1912); see U.S. Senate, *Industrial Relations*, 2:1651–55.

31. "Report of General President Kirby," 18–19; Beattie to Brissenden, Aug. 23, 1932, Tisdale Lumber Company v. Stock, Paul F. Brissenden Papers.

32. Paine Lumber Co. v. Neal, 212 F. 259 (S.D.N.Y. 1913), aff'd, 214 F. 82 (2d Cir. 1914), aff'd, 244 U.S. 459 (1917).

33. Bossert v. Dhuy, 166 A.D. 251, 151 N.Y.S. 877 (1914), rev'd, 221 N.Y. 342, 117 N.E. 582 (1917); Newton v. Erickson, 165 A.D. 930, 151 N.Y.S. 881 (1914), rev'd, 221 N.Y. 632, 117 N.E. 1059 (1917).

34. Haber, *Industrial Relations*, 347, 402; Kazin, *Barons of Labor*, 36–39, 45–50. The settlement also barred woodtrim from even union mills "working contrary to the prescribed number of hours contained in this agreement." San Francisco *Chronicle*, Feb. 29, 1901, quoted in Kazin, *Barons of Labor*, 50.

35. Haber, *Industrial Relations*, 330; Blum, "Trade-Union Rules in the Building Trades," 295, 315, 316.

36. Moores & Co. v. Bricklayers Union No. 1, 23 *Weekly Law Bulletin* 48, 52–53 (Ohio Super. Ct. 1890). Taft would quote at length from *Moores* in a decision rendered during the American Railway Union's refusal to handle Pullman railroad cars. The boycotting employees, Taft wrote, "came into no natural relation with Pullman in handling the cars. He paid them no wages. He did not regulate their hours or in any way determine their services." Thomas v. Cincinnati, N.O. & T.P. Ry., 62 F. 803, 819–20, 818 (C.C.S.D. Ohio 1894).

37. Hopkins v. Oxley Stave Co., 83 F. 912, 920, 921 (Thayer, C. J.), 936 (Caldwell, J., dissenting) (1897).

38. Vegelahn v. Guntner, 167 Mass. 92, 106, 44 N.E 1077, 1080 (Holmes, J., dissenting).

39. Hovenkamp, *Enterprise,* 216–17; see also Hovenkamp, "Labor Conspiracies," 919–65. Hovenkamp, it seems to me, has relied too heavily on the jurisprudence of the Sherman Act and extrapolations from the neoclassical economist John Bates Clark's nineteenth-century writings. On one point in particular, Hovenkamp's approach has led him seriously astray. Clark did not condemn unions for enabling "workers to receive more than their social contribution," nor did he argue that "wages should be the product of individual bargaining rather than group pressure," nor was he "just as hostile to the unions as any hard-core classicist." Hovenkamp, *Enterprise,* 221–22. Clark defended "large and powerful" (but open) unions because they helped ensure that wage increases due to improved productivity in some establishments were "quickly shared by the general body of workers elsewhere employed." Clark, "Theory of Collective Bargaining," 25, 37–38.

40. *Vegelahn,* 167 Mass. at 107, 44 N.E. at 1081 (Holmes, J., dissenting); Gill Engraving Co. v. Doerr, 214 F. 111, 117 (S.D.N.Y. 1914).

41. American Steel Foundries v. Tri-City Central Trades Council, 257 U.S. 184, 209 (1921).

42. Hale, "Coercion and Distribution," 470–78.

43. Cooke, "Solidarity of Interest," 155; see also Cooke, *Law of Trade,* 30–31.

44. Cooke, "Solidarity of Interest," 158n., 155.

45. For example, he would also privilege loss inflicted by tradesmen who collectively refused to deal with the debtor of one of their number. This was justified by their common interest to protect themselves against dishonest debtors. Ibid., 155, 158.

46. Smith, "Crucial Issues," 349, 346, 358, 361–62.

47. Ibid., 434–35, 438–39, 441, 451, 436; Mendel, "Cooperative Unionism," 354–75.

48. Groat, *Attitude of American Courts,* 115. This is a published version of the thesis Groat wrote under the direction of Edwin R. A. Seligman and Henry Seager in Columbia's economics department. See also Bryan, "Proper Bounds," 293, 298–301; Shepard, "Boycotts," 166.

49. Gray v. Building Trades Council, 91 Minn. 171, 97 N.W. 663 (1903); "Invading Labor's Rights," 130.

50. Stevenson wrote that the carpenters and other members of the building trades had "absolutely no concern whatever" with the dispute between Booth and its employees. He would have reached a different result had he believed that the carpenters, at least, competed for the same jobs as Booth's employees. Booth & Bro. v. Burgess, 72 N.J. Eq. 181, 193–94, 195–96, 197, 65 A. 226, 231, 232, 233 (1906).

51. Pickett v. Walsh, 192 Mass. 572, 587, 78 N.E. 753, 760 (1906). Other examples of the orthodox view include Purvis v. Local No. 500, 214 Pa. 348, 63 A. 585 (1906); and Lohse Patent Door Co. v. Fuelle, 215 Mo. 421, 114 S.W. 997 (1908). The Massachusetts court reaffirmed its holding on this branch of the case in Burnham v. Dowd, 217 Mass. 351, 104 N.E. 841 (1914).

52. *Pickett,* at 580, 586, 584, 585, 586, 78 N.E. at 757, 759, 758, 759.

53. J. F. Parkinson Co. v. Building Trades Council of Santa Clara County, 154 Cal. 581, 600, 98 P. 1027, 1035 (1908).

54. See, for example, Edwin S. Oakes's summary of the law of secondary boycotts in Labatt, *Commentaries,* 7:8463–71n.2.

55. George J. Grant Constr. Co. v. St. Paul Building Trades Council, 136 Minn. 167, 172, 161 N.W. 520, 522 (1917); Jetton-Dekle Lumber Co. v. Mather, 53 Fla. 969, 43 So. 590 (1907). For Gompers's reaction to *Grant,* see "Labor's Rights Judicially Upheld," 295–97.

56. Cohn & Roth Elec. Co. v. Bricklayers, Masons & Plasters Local Union No. 1, 92 Conn. 161, 167–68, 165, 101 A. 659, 661, 660 (1917); see also Meier v. Speer, 96 Ark. 618, 132 S.W. 988 (1910).

57. Brief for Appellants at 68–69, *Paine,* 244 U.S. 459 (1917). For a fuller statement, see Merritt, "Closed Shop," 67–72.

58. Answer at 121–22, 124, *Paine,* 244 U.S. 459 (1917); Brief on Behalf of the Labor-Union Defendants-Appellees at 13–16, 108–11. For a statement of the carpenters' views, see Neal, "The 'Open' Shop," 618–29.

59. Paine Lumber Co. v. Neal, 212 F. 259, 263 (S.D.N.Y. 1913).

60. *Paine,* 244 U.S. at 471. The New York Court of Appeals had not yet decided *Bossert* when Holmes's opinion appeared.

61. Paine Lumber Co. v. Neal (October Term 1915), 3, reel 70, in Holmes, *American Legal Manuscripts.* The printed version of this draft (prepared in the 1915 term) commenced, "Mr. Justice Holmes delivered the opinion of the Court." At some point Holmes lined out the last six words and wrote "dissenting" in the margin. When the opinion was published in the 1916 term, it stood as the opinion of the court, but with this discussion dropped. *Paine,* 244 U.S. at 471. I assume the justice dropped the language to win a majority for his opinion and not because of any second thoughts about his initial view of the matter.

62. *Vegelahn,* 167 Mass. at 108, 44 N.E. at 1081 (Holmes, J., dissenting).

63. *Paine,* 244 U.S. at 484 (Pitney, J., dissenting).

64. Merritt, "Are the Present Aims?" 325–26.

65. Duplex Printing Press Co. v. Deering, 254 U.S. 443, 462 (1921); id. at 482 (Brandeis, J., dissenting); Holmes to Frankfurter, Jan. 30, 1921, reel 21, in Holmes, *American Legal Manuscripts.*

66. Albro J. Newton Co. v. Erickson, 70 Misc. 292, 296–97, 126 N.Y.S. 949, 952–53 (1911). On Blackmar, see Feehan, "Memorial of Abel Edward Blackmar," 358–59.

67. Bossert v. United Brotherhood of Carpenters and Joiners, 77 Misc. 592, 599, 137 N.Y.S. 321, 324 (1912). On Crane, see *National Cyclopedia of American Biography,* 36:475–76.

68. Bossert v. Dhuy, 221 N.Y. 342, 365–66, 117 N.E. 582, 586–87 (1917). Among Chase's authorities was Jeremiah Smith's article setting forth a similar standard for reviewing the reasonableness of the union's means and ends.

69. The opinion, which Judge Harrington Putnam issued in granting the permanent injunction in *Bossert,* was adopted by the appellate division in the appeal of the New York cases. Bossert v. Dhuy, 166 A.D. 251, 255, 151 N.Y.S. 877, 879–80 (1914).

70. Auburn Draying Co. v. Wardwell, 227 N.Y. 1, 124 N.E. 97 (1919); see AABA *Bulletin,* April 5, 1915; Murray, *Red Scare,* 98–102. Even the civil libertarian,

prounion legal realist Walter Nelles hinted his approval of *Auburn Draying*. Nelles and Mermin, "Holmes and Labor Law," 546–47.

71. Cook, "Boycotts on 'Non-Union Materials,'" 540 n.6, 540, 542. I am indebted to John Henry Schlegel for drawing my attention to this comment.

CHAPTER 11: MERRITT

1. Letter of Dec. 11, 1920, quoted in Bonnett, *Employers' Associations*, 452; Merritt, *Destination Unknown*, 7–8; Bensman, "Artisan Culture," 352–53.

2. "Charles H. Merritt," 98; Danbury *Evening News*, April 4, 1918; *Four Cities and Towns of Connecticut*, 27; Bailey, *History of Danbury, Conn.*, 427, 448, 455.

3. George W. Merritt, Charles's eldest, was partner with his father in C. H. Merritt & Son. Charles H. Merritt, Jr., was associated with the Clark Box Company and would serve as president after his father's death. *Danbury City Directory*, 1905: 143; *Danbury and Bethel Directory* 14 (1926): 464.

4. A. W. Colton to Richard Cobb, n.d. [Summer 1898], Student Folder: Walter Gordon Merritt, UAIII, 15.88.10, Harvard University Archives.

5. Merritt's grades at the Ridge School appear on his Harvard College transcript. Ibid.

6. Higham, *History*, 161.

7. Kaplan, "Taussig, James and Peabody," 315–31.

8. Ross, *Origins*, 110; Furner, "The Republican Tradition," 182–83; *Science*, supp., 7 (1886): 488–90, quoted in *The State and Social Investigation*, ed. Lacey and Furner, 191 n.36.

9. Taussig, "The Southwestern Strike of 1886," 220; Taussig, *Wages and Capital* (1896), quoted in Kaplan, "Taussig, James, and Peabody," 328–29; Taussig, *Principles of Economics*, 2:266–67, 273, 270, 276–77.

10. Notes, Economics 1 (1899–1900), first half year, 23, HUC 8899.321.89, and Unauthorized Professional Tutor's Outline, Economics 6 (1899–1900), 8, HUC 8898.321.89.6, both in Harvard University Archives. The notes for the introductory course are from the year in which Merritt was enrolled. My sources for Taussig's economic history course, an Unauthorized Professional Tutor's Outline and Topics and References in Economics 6, are from the year before Merritt took the course. On Harvard's economics department at the turn of the century, see Church, "The Development of the Social Sciences," 578–630.

11. Topics and References in Economics 6 (1899–1900), HUC 8900.121.6, Harvard University Archives; see Parrini and Sklar, "New Thinking about the Market," 559–78; Furner, "Knowing Capitalism," 249–51.

12. Unauthorized Outline, Economics 6, 9.

13. Notes, Economics 1, 10, 7.

14. Ibid., 8, 21, 24, 26–27.

15. Unauthorized Outline, Economics 6, 9.

16. It was the only course for which Merritt received an A while at Harvard. He received two of his five Bs in Economics 1 and 6.

17. Peabody, *Reminiscences of Present-Day Saints* (1927), 65, quoted in Herbst, "Peabody," 46–47, also see 47–52; Ahlstrom, "Peabody, Francis Greenwood," 518.

18. Sanborn, "The Social Sciences, Their Growth and Future," *Journal of Social Science* 21 (1886): 7–8, quoted in Dombrowski, *Early Days of Christian Socialism*, 69. In 1900, Peabody explicitly acknowledged the parallel between his pedagogy and the case method of legal education, then flourishing at the Harvard Law School. Dorn, "Social Gospel and Socialism," 86 n.12.

19. *Harvard University Catalogue, 1900–1901*, 384; An Outline of Lectures on the Ethics of the Social Questions, Philosophy 5 (1900–1901), HUC 8900.169.5, Harvard University Archives.

20. Ralph C. Larrabee, "Philosophy 5 Lectures by Prof. F. G. Peabody, 1892–93, Part II, February to June," HUC 8892.370.5.48. In 1884 Peabody explained that he taught the "insufficiency" of laissez-faire economics throughout his course and claimed students generally came around to his position. Sanborn, quoted in Herbst, "Peabody," 70.

21. Larrabee, "Philosophy 5 Lectures," 31, 25.

22. Peabody, *Jesus Christ and the Social Question*, 268; Larrabee, "Philosophy 5 Lectures," 32, 31.

23. Peabody, *Mornings in the College Chapel* (1896), quoted in Kaplan, "Taussig, James, and Peabody," 322.

24. Peabody, "The People," 193, 208–9.

25. Outline of Lectures, Philosophy 5, 8; Larrabee, "Philosophy 5 Lectures," 36, 42; see also Peabody, *Jesus Christ and the Social Question*, 281, and Dorn, "Social Gospel and Socialism," 86–87. On "character" and late-nineteenth-century Protestantism, see Fox, "The Culture of Liberal Protestant Progressivism," 639–60.

26. Peabody, *Jesus Christ and the Social Question*, 310, 313, 312–13, 317, 319, 321.

27. Larrabee, "Philosophy 5 Lectures," 45.

28. Ibid., 31; Notes, Economics 1, 26.

29. Harvard College Class of 1902, *Twenty-fifth Annual Report*, 456–47, and *Fiftieth Annual Report*, 450.

30. Merritt, *History of the League of Industrial Relations*, 4–5; Merritt, *Destination Unknown*, 8; Harvard College Class of 1902, *Twenty-fifth Annual Report*, 456.

31. Henry Gardner Ingraham, interview with author, Northport, N.Y., Jan. 5, 1987.

32. Walter Gordon Merritt to Charles W. Eliot, Nov. 16, 1902, box 297, Charles W. Eliot Papers; Merritt, *Destination Unknown*, 11; Merritt, "Boycott as a Conspiracy," 478–79; Gompers, "The A. F. of L.," 808–9. My references are to the full and relatively accessible reprint, Merritt, "Neglected Side," 140–150.

33. Merritt, "Neglected Side," 140, 144, 142, 149, 150.

34. Baker, "Capital and Labor Hunt Together," 463; Peabody, "The People," 195–96; Merritt, "Boycott as Conspiracy," 478.

35. Merritt, "Neglected Side," 149, 144, 146.

36. Ibid., 145.

37. Harvard College Class of 1902, *First Class Report*, 181; *Danbury City Directory*, 1906: 149; Danbury *News-Times*, March 20, 1934; Transcript at 16, Savage v. Potter, 159 A.D. 729, 145 N.Y.S. 78 (1913), vol. 2,836, Case No. 527, Library of the Association of the Bar of the City of New York, New York City.

38. Lawlor v. Merritt, 78 Conn. 630, 63 A. 639 (1906); Transcript at 4–5, *Savage*, 159 A.D. 729, 145 N.Y.S. 78 (1913).

39. Merritt, *Destination Unknown,* 17; Walter Gordon Merritt to Charles W. Eliot, Feb. 13, 1904, box 297, Charles W. Eliot Papers; Merritt to Eliot, Feb. 16, 1904, ibid. ("My father is Chairman of the General Executive Board of this organization, and as one of its most active members our name is pretty generally associated with the work, so I can say, as our personal views, we hope" the AABA could someday drop the restriction.)

40. Transcript at 4–5, *Savage,* 159 A.D. 729, 145 N.Y.S. 78 (1913); U.S. Senate, *Industrial Relations,* 11:10662; AABA: *Individual Agreements in the Open Shop, Convention Number: February Bulletin, Extracts from Addresses, "A Liberty League,"* and *Morals and Law;* J. W. Van Cleave to Ferdinand C. Schwedtman, April 12, 1909, in U.S. Senate Committee on the Judiciary, *Maintenance of a Lobby: Appendix,* 3:2790–91.

41. Merritt, "Labor's Criticism," 246; Merritt, "Law Governing Actions," in AABA, *Morals and Law,* 24, 30, 31.

42. Merritt, "Labor's Criticism," 247, 246; Merritt, "Law Governing Actions," 26. The treatise writer Arthur Jerome Eddy made the same point in 1901. See Hovenkamp, *Enterprise,* 211–12.

43. Merritt, "Law Governing Actions," 27–29; Thomas McNally, interview with Stephen A. Collins, side 4, Scott-Fanton Museum Library, Danbury, Conn., Jan. 14, 1964; cf. Merritt, *Limitations,* 24. Merritt completed this version of his article between October 24, 1908, and January 9, 1909, when it was received by the State Historical Society of Wisconsin.

44. Adair v. United States, 208 U.S. 161, 172 (1908); U.S. Senate Committee on the Judiciary, *Limiting Federal Injunctions,* 871, 866–67, 1064; Merritt, *Limitations,* 12.

45. Brewer, "Government by Injunction," 849; see also Rogers, "Government by Injunction," 110–12.

46. Merritt, "Law Governing Actions," 30–31. For an early (1893) and historicist call for the compulsory arbitration of labor disputes by a judicial officer "clothed with all the powers of a chancellor," see Gibbons, "Legislation for the Protection of Labor," 131–41. That injunctions were equivalent to administrative law was still a novel claim a decade later. Mack, "The Revival of Criminal Equity," 400–401, 399.

47. U.S. House Committee on Labor, *National Arbitration Bill,* 33, 61–62, 138, 30–31, 21; Merritt, "Law Governing Actions," 31 (emphasis supplied).

48. Harvard College Class of 1902, *Fiftieth Anniversary Report,* 450; Hicks, comp., *Famous American Jury Speeches,* 492–26, 528.

49. Merritt, *Destination Unknown,* 20. For the characterization of Isabel, I am indebted to Barbara Ingraham, who joined my interview of her husband. I am also grateful to Anne T. Margolis for help in placing Isabella within the Beecher and Hooker families and to Diana Royce for information on Isabel's birth and death and for a copy of her wedding announcement in the collections of the Stowe-Day Library, Hartford, Conn.

50. "After I had finished my talk," Gordon explained, "she turned to her companion and, in her friendly way, said, 'What do you think of Merritt?' 'Why,' he said, 'he is another one of those capitalistic dubs.' 'Well,' she said, 'since you have

been so frank with me, I think I ought to tell you I am the dub's wife. Now will you tell me what you mean by a "dub"?' 'Well,' he said, 'a dub is a man who believes that any good can come out of the present social order.'" (Merritt confessed he was willing to be "dubbed a dub.") Merritt, "Social Control," 3–4.

51. Harvard College Class of 1902, *Fiftieth Anniversary Report,* 450. After Isabel's death, Gordon married Mary N. Shawah in 1967, who resides on Great Hollow, Merritt's estate along the Connecticut–New York border north of Danbury. Danbury *News-Times,* Sept. 14, 1968; Mary Shawah Merritt, interview with author, New Fairfield, Conn., Jan. 13, 1987.

52. Harvard College Class of 1902, *Twenty-fifth Annual Report,* 458; see Skolnik, "Civic Group Progressivism," 411–39; Hammack, *Power and Society;* McCormick, *The Party Period and Public Policy,* 177, 280–86.

53. Merritt claimed to have held office in Greenwich House for twenty-five years. Harvard College Class of 1902, *Fiftieth Anniversary Report,* 451. I have verified his service for the years 1911 to 1921. Merritt to Theodore Roosevelt, May 8, 1911, reel 106, Theodore Roosevelt Papers; "The Cooperative Social Settlement Society of the City of New York," National Federation of Settlements Records (1921), reel 152, in *The Jane Addams Papers.* On Greenwich House, see Simkovitch, *Neighborhood;* Wandersee, "'I'd Rather Pass a Law,'" 9.

Merritt's later public-interest work would include service as a director of the Legal Aid Society of New York between 1921 and 1930 and membership in the American Civil Liberties Union until his resignation in 1959 over prayer in the schools. He wrote the ACLU's amicus brief in defense of New York's civil rights law in Railway Mail Ass'n v. Corsi, 326 U.S. 88 (1945). (William Hastie and Thurgood Marshall filed an amicus brief on the same side on behalf of the NAACP.) Legal Aid Society of New York, *Annual Report,* 1920: 3, 1928: 3; Merritt to American Civil Liberties Union, March 4, 1959, Walter Gordon Merritt Papers, Great Hollow.

54. Transcript at 27, *Savage,* 159 A.D. 729, 145 N.Y.S. 78 (1913); Merritt to Davenport, Oct. 17, 1916, Sept. 27, 1918, Jan. 7, 1922; Merritt to James K. Gearhart, Nov. 6, 1915, Merritt to McKennon, Aug. 13, Sept. 28, 1918, July 23, 1919, reel 1, Walter Gordon Merritt Papers, Duke University. An untitled, five-page document on reel 2 of the microfilmed version of the papers ("Docket, Pennsylvania Mining Co. v. United Mine Workers"), detailing Merritt's work on the case between 1915 and 1920, includes many conferences with Davenport.

Pennsylvania Mining Company v. United Mine Workers, 266 U.S. 630 (1924), originated in the same strike that produced the better-known *Coronado Coal* case. Merritt prepared the complaint for *Coronado,* but at an early stage the case was given to the Philadelphia lawyer Henry S. Drinker. The reason for the change in counsel is not clear. Henry S. Drinker to Merritt, Nov. 6, 1918, reel 1, Walter Gordon Merritt Papers, Duke University.

55. "Law Partnership Established," 44.

56. "Summons and Complaint," Feb. 14, 1916, Seubert v. Reiff, Case No. 512, box 7, Paul F. Brissenden Papers; *Minnesota Labor Review,* May 19, 1916; Syracuse *Post,* May 17–20, 23–26, 1916.

57. AABA, *Bulletin,* June 20, 1916; Edmund A. Whitman to Edwin E. Witte,

April 12, 1928, Edwin E. Witte Papers (U.S. Mss. 20A), State Historical Society of Wisconsin; Bill of Complaint, Hydraulic Press Brick Co. v. Kasten (Eq. No. 165) (D. In. 1916), National Archives and Records Administration, Great Lakes Regional Branch, Chicago.

58. Gearhart to Merritt, Sept. 5, 1916, McKennon to Merritt, Sept. 23, 1916, reel 1, Walter Gordon Merritt Papers, Duke University; Docket, Pennsylvania Mining Co. v. United Mine Workers, reel 2.

59. Paine Lumber Co. v. Neal, 244 U.S. 459 (1917); Savings Bank of Danbury v. Loewe, 242 U.S. 357 (1917); AABA, *Bulletin*, Feb. 1, 1917; Merritt, *Destination Unknown*, 63.

60. Furner, "Knowing Capitalism," 244–45.

61. Merritt, "Domestic Free Trade," 292, 277, 278; Letter of Dec. 11, 1920, quoted in Bonnett, *Employers' Associations*, 452–53; "Great Industrial Organizations of America," 11.

62. Merritt, "Strikes and Public Utilities," 88.

63. Merritt, "Closed Shop," 73. Merritt spelled out his views on the effect of *Adair* in *Labor Legislation*, 20–21. These followed his position on why strikes could be outlawed notwithstanding the Thirteenth Amendment. As Merritt saw it, Harlan's opinion only voided laws preventing *individual* employers from discriminating. It left the field of *combinations* for that purpose open to regulation.

64. Merritt, "Closed Shop," 73–74. Merritt parted company with "the most active spirits" in the AALL over minimum wages and unemployment insurance. Merritt, *Labor Legislation*, 10, 16–17. For Merritt's views on the ACWA, see "A Constructive Union Agreement," 202–3.

65. Merritt, *Labor Legislation*, 4, 18, 20. Proprietorships, partnerships, and closely held corporations still preponderated in the metal-working industry at the time. Soltow, "Origins of Small Business Metal Fabricators."

66. Merritt, *Some Recommendations*, 22.

67. U.S. Senate, *Industrial Relations*, 2:1624, 1632–33, 1636.

68. Merritt, *Some Recommendations*, 18–19. Merritt preferred not to make incorporation mandatory, on the theory that incorporation was "a privilege." Make unions suable, he reasoned, and unions would be "compelled" to seek that privilege themselves. Merritt to Walter Drew, March 17, 1917, box 1, Walter W. Drew Papers; see also "Talk of Incorporating Labor Unions," 30–31.

69. U.S. Senate, *Industrial Relations*, 11:10651–53.

70. Merritt, *Some Phases*, 8.

71. AABA, *Individual Agreements in the Open Shop*.

72. Nockleby, "Tortious Interference," 1510–539.

73. Huffcut, "Interference with Contract Relations," 273–94; "Enjoining Argument by Persuasion to Induce One to Join a Labor Union," 315–16.

74. Associated Hat Manufacturers v. Baird-Unteidt Co., 88 Conn. 332, 91 A. 373 (1914); AABA, *Bulletin*, July 27, 1914; Merritt, "Open Shop Contracts," 23–24; Merritt, "Remedies for Strikes," 21.

75. Merritt, "Open Shop Contracts," 23–24; AABA, *Bulletin*, May 1, 1917; "Suggestions as to Forms of Individual Agreements," 15–16.

76. Hitchman Coal & Coke Co. v. Mitchell, 245 U.S. 229 (1917); Merritt, *Des-*

tination Unknown, 124–25; Harvard College Class of 1902, *Twenty-fifth Annual Report,* 457.

77. David E. Lilienthal to Felix Frankfurter, May 5, 1925, reel 30, American Association for Labor Legislation Papers; "A New Labor Enslaving Device," 231.

78. Merritt to Walter Drew, Dec. 6, 1917, box 1, Walter W. Drew Papers. Merritt made this comment in reference to an interview published in the conservative New York *Sun,* Dec. 2, 1917, in which he called employers' refusal to recognize unions "indefensible."

79. Merritt, *Road to Industrial Peace,* 12, 9–10, 16, 8. A speech before an un-named employer's association restating these views was published by the AABA as a pamphlet in July 1918: *Labor Unions and the Law.*

80. Merritt, *Destination Unknown,* 125; Danbury *News,* April 4, 1918; *Who Was Who in America,* 1:1375; Henry S. Drinker to Walter Wood, April 11, 1917, reel 1, Walter Gordon Merritt Papers, Duke University; AABA, *Bulletin,* Dec. 11, 1917.

81. Danbury *News,* April 4, 1918. Walter Gordon Merritt was almost certain-ly in Danbury at his father's death, having cancelled a trip on April 1 in light of his father's worsening condition. Merritt to Drinker, April 1, 1918, reel 1, Walter Gordon Merritt Papers, Duke University.

82. Danbury *News,* April 4, 1918.

83. AABA/League for Industrial Rights [hereafter cited as LIR], *Bulletin,* n.d. [1918]; LIR/AABA, *Bulletin,* Dec. 18, 1918; LIR, *Constitution.*

84. Elizabeth *Daily Journal,* Nov. 19, 1919; Toledo *Times,* Dec. 27, 1919; Cin-cinnati *Enquirer,* June 25, 1920; Denver *News,* Sept. 5, 1921; LIR, *Proposed Legisla-tion;* "The President's Industrial Conference, Thirty-Fifth Session," Jan. 20, 1920, chronological files, William B. Wilson Papers; Millis and Montgomery, *Organized Labor,* 659–60; Merritt, "New Ideas," *Iron Age,* June 19, 1919, 1627–29; "Coopera-tion in Labor Matters Imperative," *Iron Age,* June 26, 1919, 1705–9; and "Anti-So-cial, Militant Methods Condemned," *Iron Age,* July 3, 1919, 9–12, all reprinted as Merritt, *Factory Solidarity or Class Solidarity?*

85. Merritt, *History,* 99; William H. Barr to Justus Schwacke, April 5, 1922, box 1, Walter W. Drew Papers; see Wakstein, "Origins of the Open-Shop Movement," 460–75.

86. *New York Times,* Dec. 20, 1946; "Unionization and Employe Representa-tion in Competition," 253; Merritt to John B. Andrews, Dec. 4, 1924, reel 30, American Association for Labor Legislation Papers. Merritt's interest in compa-ny unionism and other corporate personnel policies dated at least to his celebra-tion of National Cash Register as a "modern utopia of wage earning and careful provision for those in its employ" in his 1902 essay. Merritt, *Neglected Side,* 141. He sent an AABA member a copy of the Colorado Fuel and Iron Company's employee representation plan soon after it appeared. Merritt to James K. Gearhart, Oct. 18, 1915, reel 1, Walter Gordon Merritt Papers, Duke University. Company unionism did not become a substantial component of his reform program until after his encounter with shop committees in Bridgeport's munitions industry during pro-ceedings before the National War Labor Board. LIR, *In re National War Labor Board* (New York: LIR, [1918]), 218–19. See Nelson, "The Company Union Move-ment," 335–57.

87. Bedford Cut Stone Company v. Journeymen Stone Cutters' Ass'n, 274 U.S. 37 (1927); Allen Bradley Co. v. Local Union No. 3, 325 U.S. 797 (1945). On Arnold, see Ernst, "Common Laborers?" 90–97.

88. LIR, *Memorandum of League,* 2; see also "Committee Hearing on Issuance of Injunctions in Labor Disputes," 191–95.

89. "Brief of Walter Gordon Merritt," in U.S. National Labor Relations Board, *Legislative History,* 1:1056–58; *New York Times,* July 4, 1937.

90. Max Zaritsky to Merritt, Jan. 6, 1947, Walter Gordon Merritt Papers, Great Hollow; *New York Times,* Nov. 11, 1954.

91. "Reuther v. GM," 22; Ingraham interview; Danbury *News-Times,* Sept. 14, 1968.

92. Merritt, *Destination Unknown,* 143; Commonplace Book, Walter Gordon Merritt Papers, Great Hollow; Merritt, "Take and Give," 125.

Bibliography

UNPUBLISHED COLLECTIONS

American Association for Labor Legislation. Papers. Labor-Management Documentation Center. New York State School of Industrial and Labor Relations, Cornell University.

Baldwin, Simeon E. Papers. Yale University Archives.

Beck, James Montgomery. Papers. Seeley G. Mudd Manuscripts Library, Princeton University.

Borah, William E. Papers. Library of Congress.

Brissenden, Paul F. Papers. Labor-Management Documentation Center. New York State School of Industrial and Labor Relations, Cornell University.

Connecticut. Constitutional Convention of 1902. Stenographic Record. Connecticut State Archives, Hartford.

Drew, Walter W. Papers. Michigan Historical Collections. Bentley Historical Library, University of Michigan.

Dun, R. G., and Company Collection. Baker Library, Harvard University Graduate School of Business Administration.

Eidlitz, Marc, and Son. Papers. New York Public Library.

Eliot, Charles W. Papers. Harvard University Archives.

Foraker, Joseph B. Papers. Library of Congress.

Gompers, Samuel. Letterbooks. Library of Congress.

Harvard University. Students Records. Harvard University Archives.

Merritt, Walter Gordon. Papers. Mary Shawah Merritt, Great Hollow, New Fairfield, Connecticut.

———. Papers. William R. Perkins Library, Duke University.

Mitchell, John. Papers. Catholic University of America.

New York. Supreme Court, Appellate Division, First Department. Savage v. Potter, 159 A.D. 729, 145 N.Y.S. 78 (1913). Trial Transcript. Vol. 2,836, Case No. 527. Library of the Association of the Bar of the City of New York.

Post, C. W. Papers. Michigan Historical Collections. Bentley Historical Library, University of Michigan.

Roosevelt, Theodore. Papers. Library of Congress.
Root, Elihu. Papers. Library of Congress.
Taft, William Howard. Papers. Library of Congress.
United Hatters of North America. Papers. Robert F. Wagner Labor Archives, Tamiment Institute Library, New York, New York.
U.S. Department of Justice. Records. Record Group 60. National Archives.
U.S. Interstate Commerce Commission. Records. Record Group 134. National Archives.
U.S. Senate. Records. Record Group 46. National Archives.
Walsh, Frank P. Papers. New York Public Library.
Wilson, William B. Papers. Historical Society of Pennsylvania, Philadelphia.
Witte, Edwin E. Papers. Labor-Management Documentation Center. New York State School of Industrial and Labor Relations, Cornell University.
———. Papers. State Historical Society of Wisconsin, Madison.
Yale University. Student Records. Yale University Archives.

Collections on Microform

Addams, Jane. *The Jane Addams Papers.* Ann Arbor: University Microfilms International, 1985.
American Bureau of Industrial Research. *American Bureau of Industrial Research: Manuscript Collections on the Early American Labor Movement, 1862–1908.* Frederick, Md.: University Publications of America, 1985.
American Federation of Labor. *The American Federation of Labor Records: The Gompers Era.* Sanford, N.C.: Microfilming Corporation of America, 1981.
Holmes, Oliver Wendell, Jr. *American Legal Manuscripts from the Harvard Law School Library: The Oliver Wendell Holmes, Jr., Papers.* Frederick, Md.: University Publications of America, 1985.
Pamphlets in American History: Labor. Sanford, N.C.: Microfilming Corporation of America, 1982.
U.S. Commission on Industrial Relations. *U.S. Commission on Industrial Relations, 1912–1915: Unpublished Records of the Division of Research and Investigation: Reports, Staff Studies and Background Research Materials.* Frederick, Md.: University Publications of America, 1985.
U.S. Supreme Court. *United States Supreme Court Records and Briefs.* Englewood, Colo: Information Handling Services.
Eastern States Retail Lumber Dealers' Ass'n v. United States, 234 U.S. 600 (1914).
In re Pennsylvania Co., 137 U.S. 451 (1890).
Lawlor v. Loewe, 235 U.S. 522 (1915).
Paine Lumber Co. v. Neal, 244 U.S. 459 (1917).

Personal Interviews

Ingraham, Henry Gardner. Northport, N.Y. Jan. 5, 1987.
Merritt, Mary Shawah. New Fairfield, Conn. Jan. 13, 1987.

Published Government Sources

Connecticut Bureau of Labor Statistics. *First Annual Report (Second Series) of the Bureau of Labor Statistics of the State of Connecticut, for the Five Months Ending November 30, 1885.* Hartford, 1885.

──────. *Third Annual Report of the Bureau of Labor Statistics of the State of Connecticut for the Year Ending November 30, 1887.* Hartford, 1887.

──────. *Sixth Annual Report of the Bureau of Labor Statistics of the State of Connecticut for the Year Ending November 30, 1890.* Hartford, 1891.

Illinois Bureau of Labor Statistics. *Fourth Biennial Report of the Bureau of Labor Statistics of Illinois.* Springfield, 1886.

──────. *Eighth Annual Report of the State Board of Arbitration of Illinois.* Springfield, 1904.

New Jersey Bureau of Statistics. *Twenty-Fifth Annual Report of the Bureau of Statistics of Labor and Industries of New Jersey for the Year Ending October 31, 1902.* Somerville, 1902.

New York. *Assembly Journal.* N.p., 1911.

New York Bureau of Statistics of Labor. *Third Annual Report of the Bureau of Labor Statistics for the Year 1885.* Albany, 1886.

──────. *Fourth Annual Support of the Bureau of Statistics of Labor of the State of New York, for the Year 1886.* Albany, 1887.

──────. *Fifth Annual Report of the Bureau of Statistics of Labor of the State of New York, for the Year 1887.* N.p., 1887.

──────. *Seventh Annual Report of the Bureau of Statistics of Labor of the State of New York for the Year 1889.* Albany, 1890.

──────. *Eighth Annual Report of the Bureau of Statistics of Labor of the State of New York for the Year 1890, Part II.* Albany, 1891.

──────. *Ninth Annual Report of the Bureau of Statistics of Labor of the State of New York for the Year 1891, Part II.* Albany, 1892.

──────. *Tenth Annual Report of the Bureau of Statistics of Labor of the State of New York for the Year 1892, Part II.* Albany, 1893.

New York. *Senate Journal.* N.p., 1911.

U.S. Anthracite Coal Commission. "Report of the Anthracite Coal Commission." *Bulletin of the Department of Labor,* no. 46. Washington, D.C.: Government Printing Office, 1903.

U.S. Bureau of the Census. *Compendium of the Eleventh Census: 1890, Part I: Population.* Washington, D.C.: Government Printing Office, 1892.

──────. *Statistics of Manufacturers, 1900.* Washington, D.C.: Government Printing Office, 1900.

──────. *Twelfth Census of the United States, Taken in the Year 1900: Population.* Washington, D.C.: Government Printing Office, 1901.

U.S. Commission on Industrial Relations. *Final Report of the Commission on Industrial Relations.* Washington, D.C.: Government Printing Office, 1915.

U.S. Commissioner of Labor. *Twenty-first Annual Report of the Commissioner of Labor, 1906: Strikes and Lockouts.* Washington, D.C.: Government Printing Office, 1907.

U.S. Congress. *Congressional Record.* 63d Cong., 1st sess., 1914.

U.S. Congress. House. Committee on Appropriations. *Danbury Hatters' Judgment.* 63d Cong., 3d sess., 1915.

———. House. Committee on Labor, *Eight Hours for Laborers on Government Work.* 58th Cong., 2d sess., 1904.

———. House. Committee on Labor. *Eight Hours for Laborers on Government Work.* 60th Cong., 1st sess., 1908.

———. House. Committee on Labor. *National Arbitration Bill.* 58th Cong., 2d sess., 1904.

———. House. Committee on the Judiciary. *Anti-Injunction Bill.* 58th Cong., 2d sess., 1904.

———. House. Committee on the Judiciary. *Argument of Mr. T. C. Spelling in Favor of the So-Called Anti-Injunction Bills and All Labor Bills.* 60th Cong., 1st sess., 1908.

———. House. *Daniel Thew Wright.* 63rd Cong., 2d sess., 1914.

———. House. Committee on the Judiciary. *Hearings . . . in Relation to Anti-Injunction and Restraining Orders.* 59th Cong., 1st sess., 1906.

———. House. Committee on the Judiciary. *Hearings on House Bill 19745, an Act to Regulate Commerce, etc.* 60th Cong., 1st sess., 1908.

———. House. Committee on the Judiciary. *Hearings on Trust Legislation.* 63d Cong., 2d sess., 1914.

———. House. Committee on the Judiciary. *Injunctions.* 62d Cong., 2d sess., 1912.

———. House. Committee on the Judiciary. *Report on a Hearing on a Bill "to Limit the Meaning of the Word 'Conspiracy.'"* 56th Cong., 1st sess., 1900.

———. House. Select Committee. *Charges against Members of the House and Lobby Activities of the National Association of Manufacturers of the United States and Others.* 63d Cong., 1st sess., 1913.

U.S. Congress. Senate. *Industrial Relations: Final Report and Testimony Submitted to Congress by the Commission on Industrial Relations Created by the Act of August 23, 1912.* 64th Cong., 1st sess., 1916. S. Doc. 415.

———. Senate. Committee on Interstate Commerce. *Control of Corporations, Persons, and Firms Engaged in Interstate Commerce.* 62d Cong., 3d sess., 1913.

———. Senate. Committee on Interstate Commerce. *Hearings Pursuant to S. Res. 98 Before the Senate Committee on Interstate Commerce.* 62d Cong., 3d sess., 1913.

———. Senate. Committee on the Judiciary. *Hearings Before Subcommittee on the Committee on the Judiciary, U.S. Senate, during 60th, 61st, 62nd Congresses, Compiled for Consideration of H.R. 15657.* 63d Cong., 2d sess., 1914.

———. Senate. Committee on the Judiciary. *Limiting Federal Injunctions.* 62d Cong., 2d sess., 1912.

———. Senate. Committee on the Judiciary. *Maintenance of a Lobby to Influence Legislation.* 63d Cong., 1st sess., 1913.

———. Senate. Committee on the Judiciary. *Amendment of the Sherman Antitrust Law.* 60th Cong., 1st sess., 1908.

U.S. Industrial Commission. *Final Report of the Industrial Commission.* Washington, D.C.: Government Printing Office, 1902.

U.S. National Labor Relations Board. *Legislative History of the National Labor Relations Act, 1935.* Washington, D.C.: Government Printing Office, 1949.

Wisconsin Bureau of Labor and Industrial Statistics. *Second Biennial Report of the Bureau of Labor and Industrial Statistics, 1885–1886*. Madison, 1886.

Published Primary Sources

Abbott, Lyman. "Trust Laws and Labor." *Outlook* 107 (June 13, 1914): 334.

"Advance in Hat Prices." *American Hatter* 32 (Jan. 1903): 39.

"The A. F. of L. Convention." *New Republic* 15 (June 8, 1918): 164–66.

Alger, George W. "Taft and Labor." *McClure's* 31 (Sept. 1908): 597–602.

Allen, A. C. "The Legal Phase of the Labor Question." *Open Shop* 4 (June 1905): 264–71.

Allison, Andrew. "The Rise and Probable Decline of Private Corporations in America." *American Bar Association Reports* 7 (1884): 241–56.

American Anti-Boycott Association. *The Anti-Injunction Bill: Excerpts from the Remarks Before the Committee on the Judiciary Made by the Hon. James M. Beck and Mr. Daniel Davenport*. New York, 1904.

———. *The Application of the Sherman Anti-Trust Law to Labor Boycotts*. New York, n.d.

———. *Arguments in Contempt Proceeding*. New York, [1909].

———. *Arguments in Support of Petition to Have Samuel Gompers, Frank Morrison, and John Mitchell, Defendants, Adjudged Guilty of Contempt*. New York, n.d.

———. *The Boycott and Public Opinion: Editorial Comment upon the Recent Unanimous Decision of the United States Supreme Court*. New York, [1908].

———. *Buck's Stove and Range Company v. AFL: Copies of Affidavits Filed in Court by Plaintiff for Use on Hearing of Application for a Temporary Injunction*. N.p., 1907.

———. *Coercion of Congress, as Attempted by Organized Labor: A Combination to Enforce Class Nominations, Elections, and Legislation*. New York, 1906.

———. *Collective Bargaining, Is It Desirable, Practical or Possible?* New York, [1906].

———. *Constitution of the American Anti-Boycott Association*. N.p., [1902].

———. *Convention Number, February Bulletin*. New York, 1907.

———. *Danbury Hatters' Case: The Following Documents Relative to the Collection of the Judgment in this Case Are Self-Explanatory*. N.p., [1915].

———. *Davenport Testimonial*. N.p., [1915].

———. *Decision of Justice Gould of the Supreme Court of the District of Columbia Granting a Preliminary Injunction in the Buck's Stove and Range Co. vs. the American Federation of Labor*. New York, n.d.

———. *Decision of Justice Wright in Contempt Proceedings against Samuel Gompers, Frank Morrison and John Mitchell, Adjudging Them Guilty of Contempt of Court and Imposing Sentence Therefor; Together with Newspaper Editorial Expression of the Country Thereon*. New York, n.d.

———. *Extracts from Addresses Delivered at the Convention of the American Anti-Boycott Association Held the 29th Day of November, 1904*. N.p., [1904].

———. *The Federal Courts and the Writ of Injunction in Labor Controversies: Brief for the Judiciary Committee of the Senate, Submitted in Behalf of the American Anti-Boycott Association, in Opposition to the Gilbert Bill*. New York, 1906.

———. *In Memory of Charles Hart Merritt*. N.p., [1918].

————. *Individual Agreements in the Open Shop*. New York, [1907].

————. *Jacob Christensen, et al., vs. Kellogg Switchboard and Supply Co., Brief and Argument and Decision of Appellate Court of Illinois, Reprinted from the Corporations Auxiliary Company Bulletin, Vol. II. No. 3, for the American Anti-Boycott Association*. Cleveland, 1903.

————. *June Bulletin: Collecting the Danbury Hatters' Judgment*. June 7, 1915.

————. *A Legal Victory for Free Labor: Decision by Judge Adams, Judge Windes, and Judge Ball, of the Illinois Appellate Court, May 1904*. New York, 1904.

————. *"A Liberty League": Convention Bulletin, March 1908*. New York, 1908.

————. *The Loewe Case or Danbury Hatters' Case*. New York, [1910].

————. *Million against One: A Conspiracy to Crush the "Open Shop."* 2d ed. [Danbury, 1904].

————. *The Morals and Law Involved in Labor Conflicts*. New York, [1908].

————. *November Bulletin*. New York, 1905.

————. *Quarterly Bulletin: February 1906*. N.p., 1906.

————. *Reason for Existence*. New York, [1906].

[American Federation of Labor.] *Report of Proceedings of the Twenty-Ninth Annual Convention of the American Federation of Labor*. Washington, D.C., 1909.

Ames, James Barr. "How Far an Act May Be a Tort Because of the Wrongful Motive of the Actor." *Harvard Law Review* 18 (April 1905): 411–22.

"Annual Meeting, American Anti-Boycott Association." *American Industries* 15 (April 1915): 28–29.

"Another Important Chicago Decision." *Square Deal* 1 (Feb. 1906): 25–26.

"The Anti-Boycott Suit." *Men's Wear* 15 (Oct. 9, 1903): 61–69.

Atkinsen, Mabel. "Trusts and Trade Unions." *Political Science Quarterly* 19 (June 1904): 193–223.

Baker, Ray Stannard. "Capital and Labor Hunt Together." *McClure's Magazine* 21 (Sept. 1903): 451–463.

Ballard, Frederic L. "Injunction—Strike for a Closed Shop." *University of Pennsylvania Law Review* 59 (Feb. 1911): 34–44.

————. "Right of Labor Unions to Strike for the Enforcement of the Closed Shop." *Columbia Law Review* 13 (Jan. 1913): 66–68.

Barnett, George E. "Report on the Agreement between the Molders' International Union and the Stove Founders' National Defense Association." Dec. 21, 1914. *Reports of the United States Commission on Industrial Relations*. University Publications of America, 1985.

Beach, Charles Fisk. *A Treatise on the Law of Monopolies and Industrial Trusts*. St. Louis: Central Law Journal, 1898.

Beck, James Montgomery. "The Supreme Court and Organized Labor." *American Industries* 7 (March 1, 1908): 21.

————. "The Supreme Court Decisions: The Quandary." *North American Review* 194 (July 1911): 55–70.

Becker, Tracy C. "Is Boycotting Criminal?" *New York State Bar Association Reports* 10 (1887): 148–65.

Bigelow, Melville M. *Elements of Law of Torts for the Use of Students*. Boston: Little, Brown, 1878.

————. "The Extension of Legal Education." In *Centralization in the Law.* Boston: Little, Brown, 1906.

————. *The Law of Torts.* 8th ed. Boston: Little, Brown, 1907.

Bishop, Joel Prentiss. *Commentaries on the Non-Contract Law and Especially as to Common Affairs Not of Contract or the Every-Day Rights and Torts.* Chicago: T. H. Flood, 1889.

Blackstone, William. *Commentaries on the Laws of England.* 4 vols., 1765–69. Reprint. Chicago: University of Chicago Press, 1979.

Blum, Solomon. "Trade-Union Rules in the Building Trades." In *Studies in American Trade Unionism.* Edited by Jacob H. Hollander and George E. Barnett. New York: Henry Holt, 1906.

Boocock, Frederick R. *The Abuses of Organized Labor and Their Remedy. Address Delivered Before the National Association of Hardware Manufacturers.* N.p., [1906].

————. "The American Anti-Boycott Association." *Square Deal* 3 (May 1908): 47–51.

————. *Law and Reason, Labor's Two Best Friends; Address Delivered at the Annual Convention of the National Association of Manufacturers, May 18, 1909.* N.p., [1909].

"The Boycott and Free Speech." *Outlook* 93 (Nov. 20, 1909): 607–8.

"The Boycott Illegal." *Outlook* 88 (Feb. 15, 1908): 342–43.

"Boycotting: Its Employment in the United States within Two Years." *Bradstreet's* (Dec. 19, 1885): 394–97.

Brandeis, Louis D. *Business: A Profession.* 1914. New York: Augustus M. Kelley, 1971.

————. *The Curse of Bigness: Miscellaneous Papers of Louis D. Brandeis.* Edited by Osmond K. Fraenkel. New York: Viking Press, 1934.

————. "The Incorporation of Trade Unions." *Green Bag* 15 (Jan. 1903): 11–14.

————. *Letters of Louis D. Brandeis.* Edited by Melvin I. Urofsky and David W. Levy. Albany: State University of New York Press, 1971.

————. "The Preferential Shop: A Letter from Louis D. Brandeis, Esq." *Human Engineering* 2 (Aug. 1912): 179–81.

Brewer, David J. "Government by Injunction." *National Corporation Reporter* 15 (Feb. 24, 1898): 848–50.

Brissenden, Paul F. "The Labor Injunction." *Political Science Quarterly* 48 (Sept. 1933): 413–50.

Bryan, James Wallace. *The Development of the English Law of Conspiracy.* Baltimore: Johns Hopkins University Press, 1909.

————. "Proper Bounds and the Use of the Injunction in Labor Disputes." *Annals of the American Academy of Political Science* 36 (Sept. 1910): 288–301.

Bryce, James. *The American Commonwealth.* 2d ed. 2 vols. New York: Macmillan, 1891.

"The Buck's Stove Case." *Typographical Journal* 31 (Dec. 1907): 603.

"Buck's Stove and Range Company's Agreement with Organized Labor." *American Federationist* 17 (Sept. 1910): 807–8.

Burdick, Francis M. "Conspiracy as a Crime, and as a Tort." *Columbia Law Review* 7 (April 1907): 229–47.

————. *The Law of Torts.* 4th ed. Albany, N.Y.: Banks, 1926.

Burke, William Maxwell. *History and Function of Central Labor Unions.* New York: Macmillan, 1899.

Burton, Richard, ed. *Men of Progress: Biographical Sketches and Portraits of Leaders in Business and Professional Life and of the State of Connecticut.* Boston: New England Magazine, 1898.

Carter, Orrin N. "Address." *Report of the Thirty-Eighth Annual Meeting of the American Bar Association, Held at Salt Lake City, Utah, August 17, 18, and 19, 1915.* Baltimore: Lord Baltimore Press, 1915.

"The Case of the Danbury Hatters." *Outlook* 97 (April 22, 1911): 847–49.

"Changing the Trust Laws to Suit Labor." *Literary Digest* 48 (June 6, 1914): 1345–47.

"Charles H. Merritt." *American Hatter* 48 (May 1918): 98.

Chenery, William L. "War and Peace at Rochester." *Survey* 44 (May 1, 1920): 185.

Cheyney, E. P. "Decisions of the Courts in Conspiracy and Boycott Cases." *Political Science Quarterly* 4 (June 1889): 261–78.

Cicero. *De Officiis.* Translated by Walter Miller. New York: Putnam, 1928.

Citizens Industrial Association of America. "The Third Annual Convention of the Citizens Industrial Association of America, Held in St. Louis, Mo., on the 15th and 16th Days of November, 1905." *Square Deal* 1 (Dec. 1905): 3–30.

City of Bridgeport. *Municipal Register.* N.p., 1878, 1886, 1895.

Civic Federation of Chicago. *Chicago Conference on Trusts.* Chicago: Civic Federation of Chicago, 1900.

Clark, Charles Hopkins. "The Connecticut Convention." *Yale Review* 11 (Aug. 1902): 146–63.

Clark, J. B. "The Theory of Collective Bargaining." *American Economic Association Quarterly* 10 (April 1909): 24–39.

Clark, Lindley D. *The Law of the Employment of Labor.* New York: Macmillan, 1911.

———. "The Present Legal Status of Organized Labor in the United States." *Journal of Political Economy* 13 (March 1905): 173–200.

Clifford, Henry G. "St. Louis' Pre-eminence in Stove Making and the Man Who Gained It." *American Business-Man* 2 (Aug. 1908): 412–17.

"The Closed Shop." *Open Shop* 4 (July 1905): 328–37.

Cogley, Thomas S. *The Law of Strikes, Lockouts and Labor Organizations.* Washington, D.C.: W. H. Lowdermilk, 1894.

Commemorative Biographical Record of Fairfield County, Connecticut. Chicago: J. H. Beers, 1899.

Commerce Clearing House. *The Federal Antitrust Laws, with Summary of Cases Instituted by the United States, 1890–1951.* Chicago: Commerce Clearing House, 1952.

"Committee Hearing on Issuance of Injunctions in Labor Disputes." *Monitor* 15 (March 1929): 191–208.

Commons, John R. *Labor and Administration.* New York: Macmillan, 1913.

———. "New York Building Trades." *Quarterly Journal of Economics* 18 (May 1904): 409–36.

"The Conviction of Labor Leaders." *Outlook* 91 (Jan. 2, 1909): 3–6.

Cook, Walter Wheeler. "Boycotts on 'Non-Union Materials.'" *Yale Law Journal* 27 (Feb. 1918): 539–42.

Cooke, Frederick Hale. *The Law of Combinations, Monopolies and Trade Unions.* Chicago: Callaghan, 1898. Revised edition. Chicago: Callaghan, 1909.

———. *The Law of Trade and Labor Combinations as Applicable to Boycotts, Strikes, Trade Conspiracies, Monopolies, Pools, Trusts, and Kindred Topics.* Chicago: Callahan, 1898.

———. "Solidarity of Interest as Basis of Legality of Boycotting." *Yale Law Journal* 11 (Jan. 1902): 153–58.

Cooley, Thomas M. *A Treatise on the Law of Torts.* Chicago: Callaghan, 1879. Revised edition. Chicago: Callaghan, 1888.

Coolidge, Anne H. "Michael Stern & Co. vs. The Amalgamated." *Nation* 110 (June 5, 1920): 759–61.

"The Coronado Coal Case." *Yale Law Journal* 32 (Nov. 1922): 59–65.

Croly, Herbert. *The Promise of American Life.* 1909. Reprint. N.p.: Archon Books, 1963.

Crossley, F. B. "Orrin Nelson Carter, 1854–1928." *Illinois Law Review* 23 (Dec. 1928): 371–74.

Cunniff, M. G. "Labor in Politics." *World's Work* 12 (Oct. 1906): 8130–35.

"The Danbury Hatters Case Finally Settled." *Carpenter* 37 (Nov. 1917): 19.

"Danbury Hatters Lose." *Literary Digest* 48 (Jan. 10, 1914): 53–54.

"The Danbury Labor Suits." *Bulletin of the National Metal Trades Association* 2 (Oct. 1903): 849–50.

Darrow, Clarence. *The Open Shop.* Chicago: Charles H. Kerr, 1904.

Darrow, Clarence, and Edgar Lee Masters. *Brief and Argument of Appellants on Consolidated Records: Jacob C. Christenen v. People ex rel. Kellogg.* N.p., n.d.

Davenport, Daniel. Address. *Annual Report of the State Bar Association of Connecticut.* 1912: 28–43.

———. *Address of Daniel Davenport, of Bridgeport, Connecticut, against Political Railroad Rate Fixing, Delivered Before the Chautauqua at Clarinda, Iowa, August 16, 1905.* N.p., n.d.

———. "An Analysis of the Labor Sections of the Clayton Anti-Trust Bill." *Central Law Journal* 80 (Jan. 15, 1915): 46–55.

———. *An Analysis of the Unanimous Decision of the Supreme Court of Massachusetts Declaring the Anti-Injunction Law of the State Unconstitutional.* New York, 1916.

———. "The Anti-Boycott Movement." *Bulletin of the National Metal Trades Association* 2 (Aug. 1903): 676–78.

———. *Arguments of Daniel Davenport, Esq., General Counsel for the American Anti-Boycott Association Before the United States Supreme Court in Support of the Decision of Justice Wright Adjudging Samuel Gompers . . . Guilty of Contempt.* New York, 1911.

———. *Arguments of the Hon. Daniel Davenport, General Counsel for the American Anti-Boycott Association, at the Hearing Before the Committee on the Judiciary of the House of Representatives on the Various Bills Seeking to Regulate Judicial Procedure in Cases of Contempt of Court.* Washington, D.C., 1912.

———. "The Boycott and How It Can Be Destroyed." *Iron Age* 72 (July 23, 1903): 54–55.

————. "The Clayton Anti-Trust Bill." *American Employer* 2 (May 1914): 581–85.

————. "Employers, Union Men, Non-Union Men, Farmers, Citizens—All Must Stand for the Open Shop." *Open Shop Supplement to American Industries* 3 (Sept. 1, 1904): 1–4.

————. "For the Open Shop, in the Heart of the Coal Regions, Before Employers, Citizens and Union Miners." *American Industries* 3 (Oct. 15, 1904): 9–11.

————. *The Two Hundredth Anniversary of the Settlement of the Town of New Milford, Connecticut, June 17, 1907.* Bridgeport, n.d.

Dicey, A. V. *Lectures on the Relation between Law and Public Opinion in England during the Nineteenth Century.* 2d ed. London: Macmillan, 1920.

Duffy, Frank. "Another Sweeping Court Decision in Favor of the United Brotherhood of Carpenters and Joiners of America." *Carpenter* 38 (Jan. 1918): 4–7.

Dunn, Jacob P. *Greater Indianapolis: The History, the Industries, the Institutions, and the People of a City of Homes.* Chicago: Lewis Publishing, 1910.

"The Duplex Case." *Law and Labor* 3 (Feb. 1921): 30–32.

Eddy, Arthur J. *The Law of Combinations.* 2 vols. Chicago: Callaghan, 1901.

Edwards, Alba M. "The Labor Legislation of Connecticut." *Publications of the American Economic Association* 8 (Aug. 1907): 413–734.

Eliot, Charles W. *American Contributions to Civilization, and Other Essays and Addresses.* New York: Century, 1897.

————. "Employers' Policies in the Industrial Strife." *Harpers' Monthly Magazine* 110 (March 1905): 528–33.

"Enjoining Argument by Persuasion to Induce One to Join a Labor Union." *Central Law Journal* 69 (Oct. 29, 1909): 315–16.

Ford, Guy S. "Rural Domination of Cities in Connecticut." *Municipal Affairs* 6 (Summer 1902): 220–33.

Four Cities and Towns of Connecticut, Illustrated. New York: Acme Publishing and Engraving, 1890.

Frankfurter, Felix. "The Coronado Case." *New Republic* 26 (Aug. 16, 1922): 328–30.

————. *Felix Frankfurter Reminisces.* Edited by Harlan B. Phillips. New York: Reynal, 1960.

————. "The 'Law' and Labor." *New Republic* 25 (Jan. 26, 1921): 245–48.

————. "The Law and the Law Schools." *American Bar Association Journal* 1 (1915): 532–40.

Frankfurter, Felix, and Nathan Greene. *The Labor Injunction.* New York: Macmillan, 1930.

Freund, Ernst. "Historical Jurisprudence in Germany." *Political Science Quarterly* 5 (Sept. 1890): 468–86.

————. "Malice and Unlawful Interference." *Harvard Law Review* 11 (Feb. 25, 1898): 449–65.

————. *The Police Power: Public Policy and Constitutional Rights.* Chicago: Callaghan, 1904.

————. "Recent Illinois Decisions Regarding Injunctions Issued in the Course of Strikes." *Journal of Political Economy* 14 (Jan. 1906): 43–46.

Gavin, Frank E. "The Mutability of Social Institutions." *Papers and Addresses of the State Bar Association of Indiana.* 1913: 115–35.

"George Wakeman Wheeler." In *Representative Men of Connecticut, 1861–1894*. Everett: Massachusetts Publishing, 1894.

Gibbons, John. "Legislation for the Protection of Labor." In Illinois State Bar Association, *Proceedings of the Annual Meeting of the Illinois State Bar Association*. 1893, 131–41.

Gompers, Samuel. "The A.F. of L. and the 'Boycott.'" *American Federationist* 9 (Nov. 1902): 808–10.

———. "The Boycott as a Legitimate Weapon." *American Federationist* 6 (Oct. 1899): 192–95.

———. "The Charter of Industrial Freedom—Labor Provisions of the Clayton Antitrust Law." *American Federationist* 21 (Nov. 1914): 957–74.

———. "A Damage Suit or Prosecution to Scare or Intimidate Us—Well!" *American Federationist* 10 (Oct. 1903): 1038–39.

———. "A Fair Injunction Decision—Labor Aims to Make It the Law of the Land." *American Federationist* 13 (Oct. 1906): 816–18.

———. "Free Speech and the Injunction Order." *Annals of the American Academy of Political and Social Science* 36 (Sept. 1910): 255–64.

———. "Invading Labor's Rights." *American Federationist* 11 (Feb. 1904): 129–30.

———. "Is the Boycott Un-American?" *American Federationist* 14 (Nov. 1907): 875–80.

———. "Judicial Jumble on the 'Open Shop.'" *American Federationist* 11 (July 1904): 585–88.

———. "Justice Wright's Denial of Free Speech and Free Press." *American Federationist* 16 (Feb. 1909): 130–32.

———. "Labor and Its Attitude Toward Trusts." *American Federationist* 14 (Nov. 1907): 880–86.

———. *Labor and the Common Welfare*. 1919. Reprint. New York: Arno Press, 1969.

———. "Labor Organizations Must Not Be Outlawed—The Supreme Court's Decision in the Hatters' Case." *American Federationist* 15 (March 1908): 180–92.

———. "Labor's Rights Judicially Upheld." *American Federationist* 24 (April 1917): 295–97.

———. "A New Labor Enslaving Device." *American Federationist* 28 (March 1921): 229–32.

———. *Seventy Years of Life and Labor: An Autobiography*. 1925. Reprint. New York: Augustus M. Kelley, 1967.

———. "Van Cleave Hales Us to Court for Contempt." *American Federationist* 15 (Aug. 1908): 614–15.

"Great Industrial Organizations of America: The League for Industrial Rights." *Industry* 1 (Nov. 15, 1919): 11–13.

Grinnell, Frank W. "An Analysis of the Legal Value of a Labor Union Contract." *American Law Review* 41 (March-April 1907): 197–214.

Groat, George Gorham. *Attitude of American Courts in Labor Cases*. 1911. Reprint. New York: AMS Press, 1969.

Guthrie, William D. "The Constitutionality of the Sherman Anti-Trust Act of 1890." *Harvard Law Review* 11 (May 25, 1897): 80–94.

Hale, Richard W. "Injunctions and Pardons: In re Gompers." *American Law Review* 43 (March-April 1909): 192–204.

Hale, Robert Lee. "Coercion and Distribution in a Supposedly Non-Coercive State." *Political Science Quarterly* 38 (Sept. 1923): 470–94.

Hallam, Henry. *Constitutional History of England from the Accession of Henry VII to the Death of George II.* New York: W. J. Widdleton, 1877.

Hamburg, Alexander M. "Torts: Secondary Boycott." *Cornell Law Review* 1 (Jan. 1915): 133–36.

Hammond, William A. "The Evolution of the Boycott." *Forum* 1 (June 1886): 369–76.

Hard, William. "A History of the Kellogg Strike." *Bulletin of the National Metal Trades Association* 3 (Jan. 1904): 23–26.

Harriman, Edward A. "Melville M. Bigelow." *Boston University Law Review* 1 (June 1921): 157–67.

Harvard College Class of 1902. *Fiftieth Annual Report.* Cambridge: Harvard University, 1952.

———. *First Class Report.* N.p., 1903.

———. *Twenty-fifth Annual Report.* N.p., n.d.

Harvard University Catalogue, 1900–1901. Cambridge: Harvard University, 1900.

"Hat Chat." *American Hatter* 35 (Feb. 1906): 71.

"The Hat Trust." *American Hatter* 31 (Aug. 1901): 50.

"Hatting in Connecticut." *Hat Review* 29 (Dec. 1901): 58.

Hicks, Frederick C., comp. *Famous American Jury Speeches: Addresses before Juries and Fact-Finding Tribunals.* St. Paul: West Publishing, 1925.

Hilbert, F. W. "Employers' Associations in the United States." In *Studies in American Trade Unionism.* Edited by Jacob Hollander and George E. Barnett. New York: Henry Holt, 1906.

Holdom, Jesse. *Legal and Historical Progress of Trade Unions.* N.p., [1905].

———. "Some Comments on Chicago Strikes and Injunctions." *Open Shop* 4 (Dec. 1905): 551–56.

Holmes, Oliver Wendell, Jr. *Collected Legal Papers.* Edited by Harold J. Laski. New York: Harcourt, Brace and Howe, 1920. Reprint. New York: Peter Smith, 1952.

———. *The Common Law.* Boston: Little, Brown, 1881.

———. *The Holmes-Einstein Letters: Correspondence of Mr. Justice Holmes and Lewis Einstein 1903–1935.* Edited by James Bishop Peabody. New York: St. Martin's Press, 1964.

———. *Holmes-Pollock Letters: The Correspondence of Mr. Justice Holmes and Sir Frederick Pollock 1874–1932.* Edited by Mark deWolfe Howe. Cambridge, Mass.: Harvard University Press, 1946.

———. *Justice Oliver Wendell Holmes: His Book Notices and Uncollected Letters and Papers.* Edited by Harry C. Shriver. New York: Central Book, 1936.

———. "Law in Science and Science in Law." In *Collected Legal Papers.* Edited by Harold J. Laski. New York: Harcourt, Brace and Howe, 1920. Reprint. New York: Peter Smith, 1952.

———. *The Occasional Speeches of Justice Oliver Wendell Holmes.* Compiled by Mark deWolfe Howe. Cambridge, Mass.: Harvard University Press, 1962.

———. "Privilege, Malice, and Intent." *Harvard Law Review* 8 (April 1894): 1–14. Reprinted in *Collected Legal Papers.* Edited by Harold J. Laski. New York: Harcourt, Brace and Howe, 1920. Reprint. New York: Peter Smith, 1952.

"Hon. Henry Clay Caldwell." *American Law Review* 30 (March-April 1896): 282–86.

"Hon. Horace Henry Powers." In *Genealogical and Family History of the State of Vermont.* Compiled by Hiram Carleton. New York: Lewis Publishing, 1903.

"H(orace) Henry Powers." In *Who Was Who in America,* 1:990. Chicago: A. N. Marquis, 1981.

Howe, Alfred F. "Connecticut's Labor Mayors." *Independent* 55 (May 28, 1903): 1259–64.

Hoxie, Robert F. "The Principle of Uniformity." In *Current Economic Problems.* Edited by Walton Hale Hamilton. 3d ed. Chicago: University of Chicago Press, 1925.

———. *Trade Unionism in the United States.* 2d ed. New York: D. Appleton, 1923.

Huber, William D. "The Fight in the Courts for the 'Open Shop' and Anti-Boycott." *Carpenter* 30 (Sept. 1910): 22, 57.

Huebner, Grover G. "Definitions, Laws and Judicial Decisions Regarding Boycotting." *Government* 1 (June 1907): 36–47.

Huffcut, E. W. "Interference with Contract Relations." *American Law Register* 37 (May 1898): 273–94.

———. "Interference with Contracts and Business in New York." *Harvard Law Review* 18 (April 1905): 423–43.

"Hundreds of Unions Haled to Court." *American Industries* 2 (Oct. 1, 1903): 5–6.

"An Illegal Boycott." *Outlook* 94 (Feb. 19, 1910): 370–71.

"Indicting a Labor Trust." *Literary Digest* 46 (June 1913): 1365–66.

Injunction Data Filed by Samuel Gompers. Washington, D.C.: Goverment Printing Office, 1908.

"The Injunction in Labor Disputes Must Go." *American Federationist* 13 (April 1906): 228–30.

"Injunctions in Labor Disputes: For and Against." *Survey* 31 (Feb. 7, 1914): 575–82, 602–4.

"Is the Closed Shop Illegal and Criminal?" *National Civic Federation Monthly Review* 1 (July 1904): 1–6.

Ives, J. Moss. "Connecticut in the Manufacturing World." *Connecticut Magazine* 7 (1902–3): 627–46.

"James M. Beck's Promotion." *Law Student's Helper* 11 (July 1903): 206.

"James Wallace Van Cleave, New President of the Manufacturers." *American Industries* 4 (June 15, 1906): 12–13.

James, William. "On a Certain Blindness in Human Beings" (1897). Reprinted in *Pragmatism and Other Essays.* Edited by Joseph L. Blau. New York: Washington Square Press, 1963.

———. *Writings, 1902–1910.* New York: Library of America, 1987.

Jenks, Jeremiah W. "Trade Unions and Wages." *Journal of Social Science* 28 (Oct. 1891): 49–53.

Journal of the Constitutional Convention of Connecticut of 1902. Hartford, 1902.

"Judge Irving G. Vann." *Green Bag* 22 (Nov. 1910): 611.

"Justice Wright's Decision and Sentence in the Gompers, Mitchell, and Morrison Case: The Appeal and Judge Parker's Magnificent Argument." *American Federationist* 16 (May 1909): 438–54.

Keller, Albert Galloway. *Reminiscences (Mainly Personal) of William Graham Sumner.* New Haven: Yale University Press, 1933.

Kennedy, John C. "An Important Labor Injunction." *Journal of Political Economy* 16 (Feb. 1908): 102–5.

Kintner, Earl W., ed. *The Legislative History of the Federal Antitrust Laws and Related Statutes: Part I: The Antitrust Laws.* New York: Chelsea House Publishers, 1978.

"Knocked into a Cocked Hat." *Virginia Law Register* 20 (Feb. 1915): 785–87.

Kocourek, Albert. "Labor Unions—Threatened Strike to Procure Discharge of Non-Union Employees." *Illinois Law Review* 7 (Dec. 1912): 323–24.

Labatt, C. B. *Commentaries on the Law of Master and Servant.* 2d ed. Rochester: Lawyers Cooperative, 1913.

"Labor Is Not a Commodity." *New Republic* 9 (Dec. 2, 1916): 112–114.

"Labor Leaders Sentenced." *Independent* 65 (Dec. 31, 1908): 1585–86.

"The Labor Lobby in Washington: An Enlightening Interview with Mr. Daniel Davenport, General Counsel of the American Anti-Boycott Association." *American Employer* 2 (Sept. 1913): 84–87.

"Labor Unions as Monopolies Imposing Illegal Restraints upon Trade and Commerce." *Central Law Journal* 65 (Oct. 4, 1907): 261–62.

"Labor's Influence over Congress." *Literary Digest* 48 (June 13, 1914): 1423–24.

Laidler, Harry W. *Boycotts and the Labor Struggle: Economic and Legal Aspects.* New York: John Lane, 1913.

Lalor, John J. ed. *Cyclopedia of Political Science, Political Economy, and the Political History of the United States.* 3 vols. New York: Maynard, Merrill, 1895.

Langdell, Christopher C. *A Selection of Cases on the Law of Contracts.* Boston: Little, Brown, 1871.

Laski, Harold J. "The Personality of Associations." *Harvard Law Review* 29 (Feb. 1916): 404–26.

"The Late Judge George L. Phillips." *Ohio Law Reporter* 19 (Jan. 23, 1922): 570.

"Law for Unionists in Chicago: To See if There Is Plenty of It." *American Industries* 2 (Sept. 1, 1903): 11.

"The Law of the Closed Shop." *The Nation,* July 21, 1904, 46–47.

"Law Partnership Established." *American Industries* 13 (July 1913): 14.

League for Industrial Rights. *Constitution of the League for Industrial Rights, as Revised May, 1919.* New York, 1919.

———. *In re National War Labor Board.* New York, [1918].

———. *Memorandum of League for Industrial Rights in Opposition to Bill Limiting the Power of Federal Courts in Equity.* N.p., 1932.

———. *Proposed Legislation on Public Policy and Industrial Warfare Submitted to Industrial Conferees, Washington, D.C.* New York, [1919].

Legal Aid Society of New York. *Annual Report.* 1920, 1928.

"Legal Fight against the Boycott." *American Hatter* 33 (Sept. 1903): 31.

"The Legal Status of the Boycott." *Iron Age* 72 (Oct. 1, 1903): 22–23.

"The Legality of the Closed Shop." *Yale Law Journal* 20 (Jan. 1911): 216–19.

Lewis, William Draper. "The Closed Market, the Union Shop, and the Common Law." *Harvard Law Review* 18 (April 1905): 444–51.

————. "The Modern American Cases Arising out of Trade and Labor Disputes." *American Law Register* 53 (Aug. 1905): 465–508.

————. "A Protest against Administering Criminal Law by Injunction: The Debs Case." *American Law Register and Review* 33 (Dec. 1894): 879–83.

————. "Some Leading English Cases on Trade and Labor Disputes." *American Law Register* 42 (March 1903): 125–60.

————. "Strikes and Courts of Equity." *American Law Register* 37 (Jan. 1898): 1–12.

Lieber, Francis. *On Civil Liberty and Self-Government.* Philadelphia: J. B. Lippincott, 1859.

Lincoln, Abraham. "Address Before the Young Men's Lyceum of Springfield, Illinois." In *The Collected Works of Abraham Lincoln.* Edited by Roy P. Basler. Vol. 1. New Brunswick: Rutgers University Press, 1953.

Lippmann, Walter. *Drift and Mastery: An Attempt to Diagnose the Current Unrest.* 1914. Reprint. Englewood Cliffs, N.J.: Prentice-Hall, 1961.

Lord, Arthur. *An Illegal Boycott: Argument of Arthur Lord of Counsel for the Plaintiff in the Case of Benjamin S. Atwood v. Brockton Central Labor Union et als.* [sic] *and the Findings of the Master as Set Forth in His Report to the Court.* Boston, 1906.

————. *The Writ of Injunction in Labor Disputes. Argument of Arthur Lord Before the Joint Special Committee on Labor of the Massachusetts Legislature.* New York, [1910].

Low, Seth. "The Contempt Cases of Messrs. Gompers, Mitchell and Morrison." *National Civic Federation Review* 3 (March 1909): 13.

Mack, Edwin S. "The Revival of Criminal Equity." *Harvard Law Review* 16 (April 1903): 389–403.

Marks, Marcus M. "The Employer and the Labor Union." *Independent* 68 (May 26, 1910): 111–15.

Marcosson, Isaac F. "The Fight for the 'Open Shop.'" *World's Work* 11 (Dec. 1905): 6955–65.

————. "Labor Met by Its Own Methods." *World's Work* 7 (Jan. 1904): 4309–14.

Martin, John. "Labor Unions and the Boycott." *Charities and the Commons* 21 (March 6, 1909): 1046–48.

Martin, W. A. "Conspiracy." In *Cyclopedia of Law and Procedure.* Vol. 8. New York: American Law Book, 1903.

————. *A Treatise on the Law of Labor Unions.* Washington, D.C.: J. Byrne, 1910.

Mason, James M. "The Legal Aspect of the Strike and Boycott." *Kansas Law Journal* 3 (June 12, 1886): 273–79.

McClennen, Edward F. "Some of the Rights of Traders and Laborers." *Harvard Law Review* 16 (Feb. 1903): 237–54.

McMurtrie, Richard. "Equity Jurisdiction Applied to Crimes and Misdemeanors." *American Law and Register and Review* 31 (Jan. 1892): 1–15.

McNeill, George E., ed. *The Labor Movement: The Problem of Today.* New York: M. W. Hazen, 1890.

McWilliams, Robert L. "Evolution of the Law Relating to Boycotts." *American Law Review* 41 (May–June 1907): 336–42.

Megaarden, Theodor. "The Danbury Hatters Case—Its Possible Effect on Labor Unions." *American Law Review* 49 (May 1915): 417–28.

"Members of the Trade Union Group in Congress." *American Federation of Labor Weekly Newsletter* 2 (Sept. 14, 1912): 4.

Merritt, Charles H. "Employers' Associations." *Bulletin of the National Metal Trades Association* 2 (Nov. 1903): 880–81.

Merritt, Walter Gordon. *Anti-Injunction Legislation: Some Arguments Directed More Particularly against Section 266c of the "Clayton Anti-Injunction Bill."* N.p., [1915].

——. "Are the Present Aims and Methods of Organized Labor Contrary to Public Policy—More Particularly from a Legal Standpoint?" *Report of the Proceedings of the Meetings of the State Bar Association of Wisconsin* 12 (1918): 315–32.

——. "The Boycott as a Conspiracy." *Literary Digest* 25 (Oct. 18, 1902): 478–79

——. "The Class Conflict and the War." *Unpopular Review* 8 (July-Sept. 1917): 11–32.

——. "The Closed Shop." *North American Review* 195 (June 1912): 66–74.

——. *Destination Unknown: Fifty Years of Labor Relations.* New York: Prentice-Hall, 1951.

——. "Domestic Free Trade and Organized Labor." *Unpopular Review* 6 (Oct.-Dec. 1916): 276–93.

——. *Factory Solidarity or Class Solidarity?* New York, [1919].

——. *History of the League for Industrial Rights.* New York: AABA, 1925.

——. "Industrial Peace and World Peace." *Unpopular Review* 9 (Jan.-June 1918): 21–38.

——. "Is Labor's Criticism of the Courts Warranted?" *American Business-Man* 2 (June 1908): 243–48.

——. *Labor Legislation.* 2d ed. New York, 1914.

——. *Labor Unions and the Law.* New York, [1918].

——. "The Law of the Danbury Hatters' Case." *Annals of the American Academy of Political and Social Science* 36 (Sept. 1910): 265–76.

——. *Limitations of the Right to Strike.* New York, [1908].

——. "The Neglected Side of Trade Unionism." *Bulletin of the National Metal Trades Association* 1 (Oct. 1902): 140–50.

——. "Open Shop Contracts." *American Industries* 16 (Aug. 1915): 22–23.

——. "Organized Labor and Democracy." *Unpopular Review* 5 (April-June 1916): 254–74.

——. "Remedies for Strikes on Public Utilities." *American Industries* 17 (March 1917): 20–21.

——. *The Road to Industrial Peace: An Address Delivered Before the New York State Bankers' Association, January 18, 1918.* N.p., 1918.

——. "The Significance of the Loewe Decision." *American Industries* 10 (March 1910): 22–23; (April 1910): 25–27; (May 1910): 28–29, 46.

——. "Social Control of Industrial Warfare." *The Consensus* 6 (March 1921): 3–12.

——. *Some Phases of the Federal Industrial Commission Report.* New York, 1915.

——. *Some Recommendations Submitted to the United States Commission on Industrial Relations by the American Anti-Boycott Association.* New York, 1914.

——. "Strikes and Public Utilities: A Remedy." *Outlook* 94 (Jan. 8, 1910): 85–89.

————. "Take and Give: Free Enterprise and Altruism." *American Bar Association Journal* 43 (Feb. 1957): 123–26, 186–89.

————. "Trade Unions and the Law: A Reply." *Survey* 31 (Jan. 31, 1914): 524–25.

"Miners' Union as a 'Labor Trust.'" *Literary Digest* 47 (Dec. 20, 1913): 1214–15.

Moderwell, Charles M. "The Bituminous Coal Industry and the Sherman Law." *Colliery Engineer* 34 (April 1914): 569–70.

National Association of Manufacturers. *Proceedings of the Eighth Annual Convention of the National Association of Manufacturers, Held at New Orleans, La., April 14, 15, 16, 1903.* N.p., [1903].

————. *Proceedings of the Ninth Annual Convention of the National Association of Manufacturers of the United States of America Held at Pittsburgh, Pa., May 17, 18 and 19, 1904.* New York, [1904].

————. *Proceedings of the Tenth Annual Convention of the National Association of Manufacturers of the United States of America, Held at Atlanta, Ga., May 16, May 17, and May 18, 1905.* New York, [1905].

————. *Proceedings of the Twelfth Annual Convention of the National Association of Manufacturers of the United States of America, Held at New York, New York, May 20, 21, and 22, 1907.* New York, [1907].

————. *Proceedings of the Thirteenth Annual Convention of the National Association of Manufacturers of the United States of America, Held at New York, May 18, 19, and 20, 1908.* N.p., [1908].

National Civic Federation. *A Discussion of the Boycott Problem: Meeting of the New York Council, the National Civic Federation, at the Rooms of the New York Board of Trade and Transportation, Friday, April 2, 1910.* N.p., n.d.

Neal, Eldridge H. "The 'Open' Shop." *North American Review* 195 (May 1912): 618–29.

Nelles, Walter. "Commonwealth v. Hunt." *Columbia Law Review* 32 (Nov. 1932): 1134–69.

Nelles, Walter, and Samuel Mermin. "Holmes and Labor Law." *New York University Law Quarterly Review* 8 (May 1936): 517–55

Official Report of the Proceedings of the Democratic National Convention. N.p., [1908].

O'Hara, William H. "Obituary Sketch of Daniel Davenport." *Cases Argued and Determined in the Supreme Court of Errors of the State of Connecticut* 114 (1932): 742–47.

Olney, Richard. "Discrimination against Union Labor—Legal?" *American Law Review* 42 (March–April 1908): 161–67.

"The Open Shop an Open Question." *Shoe Workers Journal* 5 (Sept. 1904): 9–10.

Osborn, N. G. *Men of Mark in Connecticut.* 5 vols. Hartford: William R. Goodspeed, 1906–10.

Peabody, Francis Greenwood. *Jesus Christ and the Social Question.* 1901. New York: Macmillan, 1908.

————. "The People." In *Organized Labor and Capital.* Philadelphia: George W. Jacobs, 1904.

"Permanent Injunction in Wood Trim Case." *American Industries* 12 (July 1912): 18.

Perry, Arthur Latham. *Elements of Political Economy.* New York: Charles Scribner's Sons, 1871.

Perry, John H. "Constitutional Convention of 1902." In *History of Connecticut in*

Monographic Form. Edited by Norris Galpin Osborn. 5 vols. New York: States History, 1925.

Pollock, Frederick. *The Law of Torts.* Philadelphia: Blackstone, 1887. Revised edition. London: Stevens and Sons, 1904.

Porter, Noah. *Address at the Inauguration of Noah Porter, D.D., LL.D., as President of Yale College.* New York: Charles Scribner, 1871.

————. *The American Colleges and the American Public.* 2d ed. New York: Charles Scribner's Sons, 1878.

————. *The Elements of Intellectual Science: A Manual for Schools and Colleges.* New York: Charles Scribner's Sons, 1871.

————. *The Elements of Moral Science: Theoretical and Practical.* New York: Charles Scribner's Sons, 1885.

————. *Fifteen Years in the Chapel of Yale College.* New York: Charles Scribner's Sons, 1888.

Post, Philip S., Jr. "Trusts and Trade Unions: Does Justice to Both Require That Our Antitrust Laws Be Amended?" *Outlook* 88 (March 21, 1908): 631–35.

Pound, Roscoe. "Law in Books and Law in Action." *American Law Review* 44 (Jan.–Feb. 1910): 12–36.

————. "Mechanical Jurisprudence." *Columbia Law Review* 8 (Dec. 1908): 605–23.

————. "The Scope and Purpose of Sociological Jurisprudence." *Harvard Law Review* 25 (April 1912): 489–516.

"Proceedings of the Fifth Annual Convention." *Bulletin of the National Metal Trades Association* 2 (July 1903): 450–91.

"Protest against Injunction." *Carpenter* 32 (July 1912): 33–35.

Putnam, Frank. "What's the Matter with New England: Connecticut, the State Ruled by Its Uninhabited Country Towns." *New England Magazine* 37 (Nov. 1907): 267–90.

"The Question of To-Day." *Men's Wear* 15 (Sept. 25, 1908): 65–66.

"Regrettable Error in the Contempt Cases." *Law Notes* 15 (June 1911): 43.

"Report of General President Kirby for Months of February and March 1913." *Carpenter* 33 (May 1913): 16–21.

"Respectability Screens Anti-Union Assaults." *Journal of Electrical Workers and Operators* 29 (May 1930): 259–60, 320.

"Responsibility of Labor Unions Before the Law." *Law and Labor* 1 (June 1919): 64–67.

"Reuther v. GM." *New Republic* 114 (Jan. 7, 1946): 22.

"Right to Restrain the Right of Free Speech or a Free Press When Necessary to Make Effective the Terms of an Injunction Restraining a Boycott." *Central Law Journal* 68 (March 19, 1909): 207–8.

Robbins, Hayes. "The Employers' Fight against Organized Labor." *World To-Day* 5 (May 1904): 623–30.

"Robert E. DeForest." In *Representative Men of Connecticut, 1861–1894.* Everett: Massachusetts Publishing, 1894.

Robinson, Philip Alexander. "The Labor Trusts." *Conservative Review* 5 (March 1901): 11–29.

Rockel, William M. "Boycotting." *National Law Review* 1 (April 1888): 149–60.

Rogers, W. P. "Government by Injunction." In Indiana State Bar Association, *Proceedings of the Annual Meeting of the Indiana State Bar Association.* 1898: 103–16.

Roosevelt, Theodore. *The Letters of Theodore Roosevelt.* Edited by Elting E. Morison. 8 vols. Cambridge, Mass.: Harvard University Press, 1954.

Seager, Henry R. "The Attitude of the State Towards Trade Unions and Trusts." *Political Science Quarterly* 22 (Sept. 1907): 385–400.

———. *Labor and Other Economic Essays.* New York: Harper and Brothers, 1931.

———. "Trade Unions and the Law." *Survey* 31 (Jan. 10, 1914): 448–49.

———. "Trade Unions and the Law: A Rejoinder." *Survey* 31 (Jan. 31, 1914): 525–26.

Seligman, Edwin R. A. *The Economic Interpretation of History.* New York: Columbia University Press, 1902.

———. "Liberty, Democracy, Productivity and the Closed Shop." *National Civic Federation Monthly Review* 1 (July 1904): 9, 16.

———. *Principles in Economics.* New York: Longmans, Green, 1905.

Shepard, Alan G. "Boycotts." *Case and Comment* 17 (Sept. 1910): 159–66.

Simkhovitch, Mary K. *Neighborhood: My Story of Greenwich House.* New York: W. W. Norton, 1938.

Smith, Jeremiah. "Crucial Issues in Labor Litigation." *Harvard Law Review* 20 (Feb. 1907): 253–79; (March): 345–62; (April): 429–55.

Steffee, Jonathan G. "The Taff Vale Case." *American Law Review* 37 (May–June 1903): 385–94.

Stimson, F. J. *Labor in Its Relations to Law: Four Lectures Delivered at the Plymouth School of Ethics.* New York: Charles Scribner's Sons, 1895.

Stockton, Frank T. *The Closed Shop in American Trade Unions.* Baltimore: Johns Hopkins University Press, 1911.

———. *The International Molders Union of North America.* Baltimore: Johns Hopkins University Press, 1921.

Stoner, Gordon. "The Influence of Social and Economic Ideals on the Law of Malicious Torts." *Michigan Law Review* 8 (April 1910): 468–81.

"Stove Founders Again Succumb." *Review* (Feb. 1909): 7–12.

"Stove Founders and Molders Union Agree to Restrain." *Review* (March 1909): 5–12.

Stowe, Lyman Beecher. "Paying the Penalty in Danbury." *Outlook* 110 (July 14, 1915): 612–15.

"The Straight Stuff About Those Danbury Hatters and About Boycotting." *Everybody's Magazine* 33 (July 1915): 121–23.

"Strike Injunctions and Picketing in Illinois." *Chicago Legal News* 40 (March 7, 1908): 241.

Sturges, Wesley A. "Unincorporated Associations as Parties to Actions." *Yale Law Journal* 33 (Feb. 1924): 383–405.

"Suggestions as to Forms of Individual Agreements." *Law and Labor* 1 (April 1919): 15–16.

"Suit Entered against the United Brotherhood." *Carpenter* 30 (June 1910): 2–33.

Sumner, William Graham. "Cairnes's Political Economy." *The Independent* 26 (Oct. 8, 1874): 9–10.

———. *The Challenge of Facts and Other Essays*. Edited by Albert Galloway Keller. New Haven: Yale University Press, 1914.

———. *Collected Essays in Political and Social Science*. New York: Henry Holt, 1885.

———. *The Forgotten Man and Other Essays*. Edited by Albert Galloway Keller. New Haven: Yale University Press, 1918.

———. "Industrial War." *Forum* 2 (Sept. 1886): 1–8.

———. "Protective Taxes and Wages." *North American Review* 136 (Summer 1883): 270–76.

———. *War and Other Essays*. Edited by Albert Galloway Keller. New Haven: Yale University Press, 1911.

———. *What Social Classes Owe to Each Other*. 1883. Reprint. Caldwell, Idaho: Caxton Printers, 1952.

Sweet, Ada C. "A Great Plea for Free Speech and Free Press." *National Civic Federation Review* 3 (July 1909): 15, 27.

"Synopsis of the Proceedings of the Eighth Annual Convention of the National Metal Trades Association, Cleveland, Ohio, March 21 and 22, 1906." *Open Shop* 5 (June 1906): 249–92.

Taft, William Howard. "Address of the President." *American Bar Association Reports* 39 (Oct. 1914): 359–85.

———. *The Anti-Trust Act and the Supreme Court*. New York: Harper and Brothers, 1914.

———. "The Right of Private Property." *Michigan Law Journal* 3 (Aug. 1894): 215–33.

"Talk of Incorporating Labor Unions." *Law and Labor* 4 (Feb. 1922): 30–31.

Tarleton, B. D. "Some Reflections on the Relations of Capital and Labor." *Proceedings of the . . . Annual Sessions of the Texas Bar Association*. N.p., 1894.

Taussig, Frank W. *Principles of Economics*. 2 vols. New York: Macmillan, 1911.

———. "The Southwestern Strike of 1886." *Quarterly Journal of Economics* 1 (Jan. 1887): 184–222.

Taylor, Charles W. *Biographical Sketches and Review of the Bench and Bar Indiana*. Indianapolis: Bench and Bar, 1895.

Thacher, Sherman D. "Boycotting." *New Englander and Yale Review* 45 (Dec. 1886): 1038–42.

"The Threats of Labor." *Nation* 86 (April 9, 1908): 324–25.

"The Trusts Not the Employers." *American Employer* 1 (Jan. 1913): 323–24.

Tuley, Murray F. "Compulsory Arbitration: Is it Practicable or Is It Advisable?" *Illinois State Bar Association Proceedings*, pt. 2 (1902): 77–144.

Tunison, J. S. *The Cincinnati Riot: Its Causes and Results*. Cincinnati: Keating, 1886.

"Twenty Years in the Harness." *Buck's Shot* (Jan. 1908): 16.

"Two Bills for the Better Protection of Public Welfare against Unwarranted Strikes and Lockouts." *Law and Labor* 1 (Oct. 1919): 143.

Ullery, Jacob G., comp. *Men of Vermont*. Brattleboro: Transcript Publishing, 1894.

"Union Men to Pay Boycott Damages." *Literary Digest* 50 (Jan. 16, 1915): 86–87.

"Unionization and Employe Representation in Competition." *Law and Labor* 6 (Sept. 1924): 253.

United Brotherhood of Carpenters and Joiners of America. *Proceedings of the Nineteenth General Convention of the United Brotherhood of Carpenters and Joiners of America, Held at Fort Worth, Texas, September 18 to 28, 1916.* N.p., [1916].

———. *Proceedings of the Seventeenth Biennial Convention of the United Brotherhood of Carpenters and Joiners of America, Held at Washington, D.C., September 16 to October 1, 1912.* N.p., [1912].

———. *Proceedings of the Sixteenth Biennial Convention of the United Brotherhood of Carpenters and Joiners of America, Held at Des Moines, Iowa, September 19–30, 1910.* N.p., [1910].

———. *Proceedings of the Twentieth General Convention of the United Brotherhood of Carpenters and Joiners of America, Held at Indianapolis, Indiana, September 20 to 29, 1920.* N.p., [1920].

United Hatters of North America. *Proceedings of the Convention of the United Hatters of North America [May 11–22, 1903].* N.p., n.d.

"United Hatters vs. C. H. Merritt & Son." *American Hatter* 35 (Oct. 1905): 41–42.

Van Cleave, James W. "The Boycott Abandoned." *American Industries* 7 (March 15, 1908): 18.

Walter, Carroll G. "Incorporation of Labor Unions." *Albany Law Journal* 68 (March 1906): 68–70.

Walton, F. P. "Motive as an Element in Tort." *Harvard Law Review* 22 (May 1909): 501–19.

Wambaugh, Eugene. "Should Trade Unions Be Incorporated?" *Green Bag* 15 (June 1903): 260–65.

Want, Samuel. "Right to Strike for the 'Closed Shop.'" *Law Notes* 14 (Oct. 1910): 128–29.

"War on Boycotters." *Bulletin of the National Metal Trades Association* 2 (Sept. 1903): 738–40.

Watson, Warren. "Henry Clay Caldwell." In *Distinguished American Lawyers.* Edited by Henry W. Scott. 1891. Reprint. Littleton, Colo.: Fred B. Rothman, 1989.

Welford, Walker L. "Only Trouble in Recognition of Unions Militant as Now." *American Industries* 2 (April 15, 1904): 13.

White, Henry. "The Issue of the Open and Closed Shop." *North American Review* 180 (Jan. 1905): 28–40.

———. "The Labor Unions in the Presidential Campaign." *North American Review* 188 (Sept. 1908): 372–82.

White, William Allen. "Cleveland." *McClure's Magazine* 18 (Feb. 1902): 322–30.

Wickersham, George W. "Labor Legislation in the Clayton Act." *American Federationist* 22 (July 1915): 493–503.

Wigmore, John H. "Boycott—Action by Non-Union Employees to Enjoin a Union from Compelling Their Discharge." *Illinois Law Review* 7 (Dec. 1912): 320–22.

Williston, Samuel. "Freedom of Contract." *Cornell Law Quarterly* 6 (May 1921): 365–80.

Willoughby, William Franklin. "Employers' Associations for Dealing with Labor in the United States." *Quarterly Journal of Economics* 20 (Nov. 1905): 110–50.

Wilson, Woodrow. "Mr. Cleveland as President." *Atlantic Monthly* 79 (March 1897): 289–300.

————. *The Papers of Woodrow Wilson.* Edited by Arthur S. Link. Vol. 31. Princeton: Princeton University Press, 1979.

————. *War and Peace: Presidential Messages, Addresses and Public Papers (1917–1924) by Woodrow Wilson.* Edited by Ray Stannard Baker and William Dodd. New York: Harper, 1927.

Witte, Edwin E. "The Clayton Bill and Organized Labor." *Survey* 32 (July 4, 1914): 360.

————. "Early American Labor Cases." *Yale Law Journal* 35 (March 1926): 825–37.

————. *The Government in Labor Disputes.* New York: McGraw-Hill Book, 1932.

————. "Injunctions in Labor Disputes." Appendix D: "Injunctions and the Outcome of Strikes." Appendix E: "Injunctions and Trade Union Boycotts." Feb. 27, 1915. *Reports of the United States Commission on Industrial Relations.* University Publications of America, 1985.

————. "Section Twenty of the Clayton Act." *New Republic* 9 (Dec. 30, 1916): 243–44.

Wolman, Leo. *The Boycott in American Trade Unions.* Baltimore: Johns Hopkins University Press, 1916.

————. *The Growth of American Trade Unions, 1880–1923.* New York: National Bureau of Economic Research, 1924.

"Would Have Killed This Lawyer: Other Enterprises of Gallagher, Union Slugger." *American Industries* 3 (July 15, 1904): 1–2.

Wright, Philip G. "The Contest in Congress between Organized Labor and Organized Business." *Quarterly Journal of Economics* 29 (Feb. 1915): 235–61.

Wright, Robert Samuel. *The Law of Criminal Conspiracies and Agreements . . . to which Is Added, the Law of Criminal Conspiracies and Agreements as Found in the American Cases.* Edited by Hampton L. Carson. Philadelphia: Blackstone, 1887.

Wyman, Bruce. "The Law as to the Boycott." *Green Bag* 15 (May 1903): 208–15.

————. "The Maintenance of the Open Shop." *Green Bag* 17 (Jan. 1905): 21–29.

Yale College. *A Biographical Record of the Members of the Class of 1873.* New York: Rogers and Sherwood, 1880.

————. *Fourth Supplement to the History of Yale Class of 1873.* N.p., n.d.

Yarros, Victor S. "The Labor Question's Newer Aspects." *American Monthly Review of Reviews* 31 (May 1905): 589–93.

Published Secondary Sources

Adams, Graham, Jr. *Age of Industrial Violence, 1910–1915: The Activities and Findings of the United States Commission on Industrial Relations.* New York: Columbia University Press, 1966.

Ahlstrom, Sydney E. "Peabody, Francis Greenwood." *Dictionary of American Biography.* Supp. 2. New York: American Council of Learned Societies, 1958.

————. "The Scottish Philosophy and American Theology." *Church History* 24 (Sept. 1955): 257–72.

Atiyah, P. S. *The Rise and Fall of Freedom of Contract.* Oxford: Clarendon Press, 1979.

Atleson, James B. *Values and Assumptions in American Labor Law.* Amherst: University of Massachusetts Press, 1983.

————. "Wartime Labor Regulation, the Industrial Pluralists, and the Law of Collective Bargaining." In *Industrial Democracy in America: The Ambiguous Promise*. Edited by Nelson Lichtenstein and Howell John Harris. New York: Woodrow Wilson Center Press and Cambridge University Press, 1993.

Bailey, James Montgomery. *History of Danbury, Conn., 1684–1896, from Notes and Manuscript Left by James Montgomery Bailey*. Edited by Susan Benedict Hill. New York: Burr Printing House, 1896.

Baney, Terry Alan. *Yankees and the City: Struggling over Urban Representation in Connecticut, 1880 to World War I*. New York: Garland, 1993.

Barber, William J. "The Fortunes of Political Economy in an Environment of Academic Conservatism: Yale University." In *Breaking the Academic Mould: Economists and American Higher Learning in the Nineteenth Century*. Edited by William J. Barber. Middletown, Conn.: Wesleyan University Press, 1988.

Barenberg, Mark. "The Political Economy of the Wagner Act: Power, Symbol, and Workplace Cooperation." *Harvard Law Review* 106 (May 1993): 1397–496.

Barnett, George E. *The Printers: A Study in American Trade Unionism*. Cambridge, Mass.: American Economic Association, 1909.

Barrow, Clyde W. "From Marx to Madison: The Seligman Connection in Charles Beard's Constitutional Theory." *Polity* 24 (Spring 1992): 379–98.

Bauder, Russell S. "National Collective Bargaining in the Foundry Industry." *American Economic Review* 24 (Sept. 1934): 462–76.

Bendix, Reinhard. *Work and Authority in Industry: Ideologies of Management in the Course of Industrialization*. New York: Harper and Row, 1956.

Benedict, Michael Les. "Laissez-Faire and Liberty: A Re-Evaluation of the Meaning of Laissez-Faire Constitutionalism." *Law and History Review* 3 (Fall 1985): 293–331.

Bensman, David. *The Practice of Solidarity: American Hat Finishers in the Nineteenth Century*. Urbana: University of Illinois Press, 1985.

Bercovitch, Sacvan. *The American Jeremiad*. Madison: University of Wisconsin Press, 1978.

Berman, Edward. *Labor and the Sherman Act*. New York: Harper and Brothers, 1930.

Bernstein, Irving. *The Lean Years: A History of the American Worker, 1920–1933*. Baltimore: Penguin Books, 1966.

Bickel, Alexander M. *The Judiciary and Responsible Government, 1910–1921: Part One*. New York: Macmillan, 1984.

Biographical Directory of the United States Congress, 1774–1989. Washington, D.C.: Government Printing Office, 1989.

Blodgett, Geoffrey. "A New Look at the Gilded Age of Politics in a Cultural Context." In *Victorian America*. Edited by Daniel Walker Howe. Philadelphia: University of Philadelphia Press, 1976.

Bonnett, Clarence E. *Employers' Associations in the United States: A Study of Typical Associations*. New York: Macmillan, 1922.

Botein, Stephen. "Cicero as a Role Model for Early American Lawyers: A Case Study in Classical 'Influence.'" *Classical Journal* 73 (April–May 1978): 313–21.

Brandeis, Elizabeth. "Labor Legislation." In *History of Labor in the United States, 1896–1932*. Edited by John R. Commons et al. New York: Macmillan, 1935.

Brody, David. *Workers in Industrial America: Essays on the Twentieth Century Struggle.* New York: Oxford University Press, 1980.

Brown, Nelson Courtlandt. *The American Lumber Industry, Embracing the Principal Features of the Resources, Production, Distribution, and Utilization of Lumber in the United States.* New York: J. Wiley and Sons, 1923.

Buenker, John D. "Progressivism in Connecticut: The Thrust of the Urban New Stock Democrats." *Connecticut Historical Society Bulletin* 35 (Oct. 1970): 97–109.

Carstensen, Peter. *The Content of the Hollow Core of Antitrust: The Chicago Board of Trade Case and the Meaning of the "Rule of Reason" in Restraint of Trade Analysis.* Working Paper No. 2-6. Institute for Legal Studies, University of Wisconsin–Madison Law School, 1987.

Chandler, Alfred D. *The Visible Hand: The Managerial Revolution in American Business.* Cambridge, Mass.: Harvard University Press, 1977.

Chomsky, Carol. "Progressive Judges in a Progressive Age: Regulatory Legislation in the Minnesota Supreme Court, 1880–1925." *Law and History Review* 11 (Fall 1993): 383–440.

Christie, Robert A. *Empire in Wood: A History of the Carpenters' Union.* Ithaca: Cornell University Press, 1956.

Cmeil, Kenneth, *Democratic Eloquence: The Fight over Popular Speech in Nineteenth-Century America.* Berkeley: University of California Press, 1990.

Cochran, Thomas C., and William Miller. *The Age of Enterprise: A Social History of Industrial America.* New York: Macmillan, 1942.

Commons, John R., et al. *History of Labour in the United States.* 4 vols. New York: Macmillan, 1918–35.

A Compilation of the Messages and Papers of the Presidents. New York: Bureau of National Literature, 1917.

Compton, Wilson. *The Organization of the Lumber Industry with Special Reference to the Influences Determining the Prices of Lumber in the United States.* Chicago: American Lumberman, 1916.

Comstock, John B. *History of the House of P. & F. Corbin.* N.p., 1904.

Cooper, John Milton. *The Pivotal Decades: The United States, 1900–1920.* New York: W. W. Norton, 1990.

Cummings, Homer, and Carl McFarland. *Federal Justice: Chapters in the History of Justice and the Federal Executive.* New York: Macmillan, 1937.

Curtis, Bruce. *William Graham Sumner.* Boston: Twayne, 1981.

Davis, Pearce. *The Development of the American Glass Industry.* Cambridge, Mass.: Harvard University Press, 1949.

Dell, Christopher. *Lincoln and the War Democrats: The Grand Erosion of Conservative Tradition.* Rutherford, N.J.: Farleigh Dickinson University Press, 1975.

Dewey, John. *Characters and Events: Popular Essays in Social and Political Philosophy by John Dewey.* Edited by Joseph Ratner. New York: Henry Holt, 1929.

Dewhurst, Frederic, and Paul W. Stewart. "Hat Industry." In *Industrial Planning Under the Codes.* Edited by James B. Galloway. New York: Harper and Brothers, 1935.

Dickman, Howard. *Industrial Democracy in America: Ideological Origins of National Labor Relations Policy.* La Salle, Ill.: Open Court Press, 1987.

Dictionary of American Biography. 17 vols. New York: Charles Scribner's Sons, 1927–81.

Dombrowski, James. *The Early Days of Christian Socialism in America*. New York: Columbia University Press, 1936.

Dorfman, Joseph. *The Economic Mind in American Civilization, 1606–1865*. 5 vols. New York: Viking, 1946–59.

Dorn, Jacob H. "The Social Gospel and Socialism: A Comparison of the Thought of Francis Greenwood Peabody, Washington Gladden, and Walter Rauschenbusch." *Church History* 62 (March 1993): 82–100.

Dulles, Foster Rhea, and Melvyn Dubofsky. *Labor in America: A History*. 4th ed. Arlington Heights, Ill.: Harlan Davidson, 1984.

Eggert, Gerald G. *Railroad Labor Disputes: The Beginnings of Federal Strike Policy*. Ann Arbor: University of Michigan Press, 1967.

Epstein, Richard A. "A Common Law of Labor Relations? A Critique of the New Deal." *Yale Law Journal* 92 (July 1983): 1357–408.

Ernst, Daniel R. "Common Laborers? Industrial Pluralists, Legal Realists, and the Law of Industrial Disputes, 1915–1943." *Law and History Review* 11 (Spring 1993): 59–100.

———. "The Critical Tradition in the Writing of American Legal History." *Yale Law Journal* 102 (Jan. 1993): 1019–76.

———. "Free Labor, the Consumer Interest, and the Law of Industrial Disputes, 1885–1900." *American Journal of Legal History* 36 (Jan. 1992): 19–37.

Eskridge, William N., and Philip P. Frickey. *Cases and Materials on Legislation: Statutes and the Creation of Public Policy*. St. Paul, Minn.: West Publishing, 1988.

Faulkner, Harold U. *The Decline of Laissez Faire, 1897–1917*. New York: Holt, Rinehart and Winston, 1951.

Feinstein, Estelle F. *Stamford in the Gilded Age: The Political Life of a Connecticut Town, 1868–1893*. Stamford: Stamford Historical Society, 1973.

Ferguson, Robert A. *Law and Letters in American Culture*. Cambridge, Mass.: Harvard University Press, 1984.

Fine, Sidney. *Laissez Faire and the General Welfare State: A Study of Conflict in American Thought, 1865–1901*. Ann Arbor: University of Michigan Press, 1966.

———. "The National Erectors' Association and the Dynamiters." *Labor History* 32 (Winter 1991): 5–41.

Fink, Leon. "Labor, Liberty, and the Law: Trade Unionism and the Problem of the American Constitutional Order." *Journal of American History* 74 (Dec. 1987): 904–25.

Forbath, William E. "The Ambiguities of Free Labor: Labor and Law in the Gilded Age." *Wisconsin Law Review* 1985 (July 1985): 767–817.

———. *Law and the Shaping of the American Labor Movement*. Cambridge, Mass.: Harvard University Press, 1991.

Fox, Richard Wightman. "The Culture of Liberal Protestant Progressivism." *Journal of Interdisciplinary History* 23 (Winter 1993): 639–60.

Freidel, Frank. *Francis Lieber: Nineteenth-Century Liberal*. Baton Rouge: Louisiana State University Press, 1947.

Friedman, Lawrence M. *A History of American Law*. 2d ed. New York: Simon and Schuster, 1985.

Furner, Mary O. "Knowing Capitalism: Public Investigation and the Labor Question in the Long Progressive Era." In *The State and Economic Knowledge: The American and British Experience*. Edited by Mary O. Furner and Barry Supple. New York: Cambridge University Press, 1990.

———. "The Republican Tradition and the New Liberalism: Social Investigation, State Building, and Social Learning in the Gilded Age." In *The State and Social Investigation*. Edited by Michael J. Lacey and Mary O. Furner. New York: Cambridge University Press, 1993.

Galanter, Marc. "Why the 'Haves' Come Out Ahead: Speculations on Limits of Legal Change." *Law and Society Review* 9 (Fall 1974): 95–151.

Galenson, Walter. *United Brotherhood of Carpenters: The First Hundred Years*. Cambridge, Mass.: Harvard University Press, 1963.

Gitelman, H. M. *The Legacy of the Ludlow Massacre: A Chapter in American Industrial Relations*. Philadelphia: University of Pennsylvania Press, 1988.

Gordon, Colin. *New Deals: Business, Labor and Politics in America, 1920–1935*. New York: Cambridge University Press, 1994.

Gordon, Robert W. "'The Ideal and the Actual in the Law': Fantasies and Practices of New York City Lawyers, 1870–1910." In *The New High Priests: Lawyers in Post Civil War America*. Edited by Gerard W. Gawalt. Westport, Conn.: Greenwood Press, 1984.

Green, Charles. *The Headwear Workers: A Century of Trade Unionism*. New York: United Hatters, Cap and Millinery Workers International Union, 1944.

Green, John B. "Labor's Fighting Legionaries on the Legal Field: A Retrospect and Prevision." *Case and Comment* 19 (Sept. 1912): 233–39.

Greenberg, Irving. *Theodore Roosevelt and Labor, 1900–1918*. 1959. Reprint. New York: Garland Publishing, 1988.

Gregory, Charles O. *Labor and the Law*. New York: W. W. Norton, 1946.

Grossberg, Michael. "Institutionalizing Masculinity: The Law as a Masculine Profession." In *Meanings for Manhood: Constructions of Masculinity in Victorian America*. Edited by Mark C. Carnes and Clyde Griffen. Chicago: University of Chicago Press, 1990.

Haber, Samuel. *The Quest for Authority and Honor in the American Professions, 1750–1900*. Chicago: University of Chicago Press, 1991.

Haber, William. *Industrial Relations in the Building Industry*. Cambridge: Harvard University Press, 1930.

Hammack, David C. *Power and Society: Greater New York at the Turn of the Century*. New York: Columbia University Press, 1987.

Hanson, John Mark. "The Political Economy of Group Membership." *American Political Science Review* 79 (March 1985): 79–96.

Harris, Howell J. "Getting It Together: The Metal Manufacturers' Association of Philadelphia, c. 1900–1930." In *Masters to Managers: Historical and Comparative Perspectives on American Employers*. Edited by Sanford M. Jacoby. New York: Columbia University Press, 1991.

Harter, Lafayette G. *John R. Commons: His Assault on Laissez-Faire*. Corvallis: Oregon State University Press, 1962.

Hartog, Hendrik. "Mrs. Packard on Dependency." *Yale Journal of Law and Humanities* 1 (Dec. 1988): 79–103.

Hattam, Victoria C. "Courts and the Question of Class: Judicial Regulation of Labor under the Common Law Doctrine of Conspiracy." In *Labor Law in America: Historical and Critical Essays.* Edited by Christopher L. Tomlins and Andrew J. King. Baltimore: Johns Hopkins University Press, 1992.

Hawley, Ellis W. *The Great War and the Search for a Modern Order: A History of the American People and Their Institutions, 1917–1933.* New York: St. Martin's Press, 1979.

Hedges, R. Y., and Allan Winterbottom. *The Legal History of Trade Unionism.* New York: Longmans, Green, 1930.

Helfand, Barry F. "Labor and the Courts: The Common-Law Doctrine of Criminal Conspiracy and Its Application in the Buck's Stove Case." *Labor History* 18 (Winter 1977): 91–114.

Herbst, Jurgen. "Francis Greenwood Peabody: Harvard's Theologian of the Social Gospel." *Harvard Theological Review* 54 (Jan. 1961): 45–69.

Higham, John. *History: Professional Scholarship in America.* Baltimore: Johns Hopkins University Press, 1989.

——. "Multiculturalism and Universalism: A History and Critique." *American Quarterly* 45 (June 1993): 195–219. "Rejoinder," 249–56.

Hilliard, Francis. *The Law of Torts or Private Wrongs.* Boston: Little, Brown, 1859.

Hofstadter, Richard. *The Age of Reform From Bryan to F.D.R.* New York: Random House, 1955.

——. "What Happened to the Antitrust Movement?" *The Paranoid Style in American Politics and Other Essays.* New York: Alfred A. Knopf, 1965.

Holmes, Anne Middleton. *Algernon Sydney Sullivan.* N.p., 1929.

Holt, James. *Congressional Insurgents and the Party System, 1909–1916.* Cambridge, Mass.: Harvard University Press, 1967.

Horwitz, Morton J. *The Transformation of American Law, 1870–1960.* New York: Oxford University Press, 1992.

Hovenkamp, Herbert. *Enterprise and American Law, 1836–1937.* Cambridge, Mass.: Harvard University Press, 1991.

——. "Labor Conspiracies in American Law, 1880–1930." *Texas Law Review* 66 (April 1988): 919–65.

——. "The Sherman Act and the Classical Theory of Competition." *Iowa Law Review* 74 (July 1989): 1019–65.

Howe, Daniel Walker. "Classical Education and Political Culture in Nineteenth-Century America." *Intellectual History Group Newsletter,* no. 5 (Spring 1983): 9–14.

——. "Victorian Culture in America." In *Victorian America.* Edited by Daniel Walker Howe. Philadelphia: University of Philadelphia Press, 1976.

Hunter, Robert. *Labor in Politics.* Chicago: Socialist Party, 1915.

Hurst, James Willard. *The Legitimacy of the Business Corporation in the Law of the United States.* Charlottesville: University Press of Virginia, 1970.

Hurvitz, Haggai. "American Labor Law and the Doctrine of Entrepreneurial Property Rights: Boycotts, Courts, and the Juridical Reorientation of 1886–1895." *Industrial Relations Law Journal* 8 (1986): 307–61.

Jacoby, Sanford. *Employing Bureaucracy: Managers, Unions and the Transformation of Work in American Industry, 1900–1945.* New York: Columbia University Press, 1985.

James, Lee M. "Restrictive Agreements and Practices in the Lumber Industry, 1880–1939." *Southern Economic Journal* 10 (Oct. 1946): 115–25.

Jones, Alan. "Thomas M. Cooley and 'Laissez-Faire Constitutionalism': A Reconsideration." *Journal of American History* 53 (March 1967): 751–71.

Jones, Dallas L. "The Enigma of the Clayton Act." *Industrial and Labor Relations Review* 10 (Jan. 1957): 201–21.

Kalman, Laura. *Legal Realism at Yale, 1927–1960.* Chapel Hill: University of North Carolina Press, 1986.

Kaplan, Sydney. "Taussig, James, and Peabody: A 'Harvard School,' in 1900?" *American Quarterly* 7 (Winter 1955): 315–31.

Karson, Marc. *American Labor Unions and Politics, 1900–1918.* Carbondale: Southern Illinois University Press, 1958.

Kazin, Michael. *Barons of Labor: The San Francisco Building Trades and Union Power in the Progressive Era.* Urbana: University of Illinois Press, 1987.

Keller, Morton. *In Defense of Yesterday: James M. Beck and the Politics of Conservatism, 1861–1936.* New York: Coward-McCann, 1958.

———. *Regulating a New Economy: Public Policy and Economic Change in America, 1900–1933.* Cambridge: Harvard University Press, 1990.

Kelley, Patrick. "Holmes on the Supreme Judicial Court." In *The History of the Law in Massachusetts: The Supreme Judicial Court, 1692–1992.* Edited by Russell K. Osgood. Boston: Supreme Judicial Court Historical Society, 1992.

Kelley, Robert. *The Transatlantic Persuasion: The Liberal-Democratic Mind in the Age of Gladstone.* New York: Alfred A. Knopf, 1969.

Kerny, James. *The Political Education of Woodrow Wilson.* New York: Appleton-Century-Crofts, 1926.

King, Willard L. *Melville Weston Fuller: Chief Justice of the United States, 1888–1910.* New York: Macmillan, 1950.

Klare, Karl. "Labor Law as Ideology: Toward a New Historiography of Collective Bargaining Law." *Industrial Relations Law Journal* 4 (1981): 450–82.

Klarman, Michael J. "The Judges versus the Unions: The Development of British Labor Law, 1867–1913." *Virginia Law Review* 75 (Nov. 1989): 1487–602.

Kloppenberg, James T. *Uncertain Victory: Social Democracy and Progressivism in European and American Thought, 1870–1920.* New York: Oxford University Press, 1986.

———. "The Virtues of Liberalism: Christianity, Republicanism, and Ethics in Early American Discourse." *Journal of American History* 74 (June 1987): 9–33.

Kolko, Gabriel. *The Triumph of Conservatism: A Reinterpretation of American History, 1900–1916.* New York: Free Press, 1963.

Kraines, Oscar. *The World and Ideas of Ernst Freund: The Search for General Principles of Legislation and Administrative Law.* University: University of Alabama Press, 1974.

Kuritz, Hyman. "Criminal Conspiracies in Post-Bellum Pennsylvania." *Pennsylvania History* 17 (Oct. 1950): 292–301.

Kutler, Stanley I. "Chief Justice Taft and the Delusion of Judicial Exactness—A Study in Jurisprudence." *Virginia Law Review* 48 (Nov. 1962): 1407–26.

———. "Chief Justice Taft, Judicial Unanimity, and Labor: The Coronado Case." *Historian* 24 (Winter 1961): 68–83.

————. "Labor, the Clayton Act, and the Supreme Court." *Labor History* 3 (1962): 19–38.

Lacey, Michael J., and Mary O. Furner, eds. *The State and Social Investigation*. New York: Cambridge University Press, 1993.

Lamoreaux, Naomi R. *The Great Merger Movement in American Business, 1895–1904*. New York: Cambridge University Press, 1985.

Leonard, John William, comp. *Who's Who in Jurisprudence*. Brooklyn: John W. Leonard Corp., 1925.

Letwin, William. *Law and Economic Policy in America: Evolution of the Sherman Antitrust Act*. New York: Random House, 1965.

Licht, Walter. "Studying Work: Personnel Policies in Philadelphia Firms, 1850–1950." In *Masters to Managers: Historical and Comparative Perspectives on American Employers*. Edited by Sanford Jacoby. New York: Columbia University Press, 1991.

Ligasor, Nancy, and Frank Lipsius. *A Law unto Itself: The Untold Story of the Law Firm of Sullivan & Cromwell*. New York: Morrow, 1988.

Link, Arthur S. *Wilson: The New Freedom*. Princeton: Princeton University Press, 1956.

————. *Wilson: The Road to the White House*. Princeton: Princeton University Press, 1947.

Livingston, James. *Origins of the Federal Reserve System: Money, Class, and Corporate Capitalism, 1890–1913*. Ithaca: Cornell University Press, 1986.

————. "The Social Analysis of Economic History and Theory: Conjectures on Late Nineteenth-Century American Development." *American Historical Review* 92 (Feb. 1987): 69–95.

Loomis, Dwight, and J. Gilbert Calhoun. *The Judicial and Civil History of Connecticut*. Boston: Boston History Company, 1895.

Lorwin, Lewis L. *The American Federation of Labor*. Washington, D.C.: Brookings Institution, 1933.

Mandel, Bernard. *Samuel Gompers: A Biography*. Yellow Springs, Ohio: Antioch Press, 1963.

Mason, Alpheus T. "The Labor Decisions of Chief Justice Taft." *University of Pennsylvania Law Review* 78 (March 1930): 585–625.

————. *Organized Labor and the Law*. Durham: Duke University Press, 1925.

Matzko, John A. "The Best Men of the Bar: The Founding of the American Bar Association." In *The New High Priests: Lawyers in Post Civil War America*. Edited by Gerard W. Gawalt. Westport, Conn.: Greenwood Press, 1984.

May, Henry F. *The End of American Innocence*. Chicago: Quadrangle Books, 1964.

————. *Protestant Churches and Industrial America*. New York: Harper and Row, 1949.

May, James. "Antitrust Practice and Procedure in the Formative Era: The Constitutional and Conceptual Reach of State Antitrust Law, 1880–1918." *University of Pennsylvania Law Review* 135 (March 1987): 495–593.

Mayer, David N. "The Jurisprudence of Christopher G. Tiedeman: A Study in the Failure of Laissez-Faire Constitutionalism." *Missouri Law Review* 55 (Winter 1990): 93–161.

McCormick, Richard L. *From Realignment to Reform: Political Change in New York State, 1893–1910*. Ithaca: Cornell University Press, 1981.

———. *The Party Period and Public Policy: American Politics from the Age of Jackson to the Progressive Era*. New York: Oxford University Press, 1986.

McCurdy, Charles W. "American Law and the Marketing Structure of the Large Corporation, 1857–1890." *Journal of Economic History* 38 (Sept. 1978): 632–49.

———. "Fuller, Melville W. (1833–1910)." *Encyclopedia of the American Constitution*. Edited by Leonard Levy. Vol. 2. New York: Macmillan, 1986.

———. "The *Knight* Sugar Decision of 1895 and the Modernization of American Corporation Law, 1869–1903." *Business History Review* 53 (Summer 1979): 304–42.

———. "The Roots of Liberty of Contract Reconsidered: Major Premises in the Law of Employment, 1867–1937." *Supreme Court Historical Society Yearbook* (1984): 20–33.

McFarland, Gerald W. "The Breakdown of Deadlock: The Cleveland Democracy in Connecticut, 1884–1894." *Historian* 31 (May 1969): 381–97.

McLaughlin, Doris B. "The Second Battle of Battle Creek—The Open Shop Movement in the Early Twentieth Century." *Labor History* 14 (Summer 1973): 323–39.

McLean, Iain. *Public Choice: An Introduction*. Oxford: Basil Blackwell, 1987.

McNulty, Paul J. *The Origins and Development of Labor Economics: A Chapter in the History of Social Thought*. Cambridge, Mass.: MIT Press, 1980.

McSeveney, Samuel T. *The Politics of Depression: Political Behavior in the Northeast, 1893–1896*. New York: Oxford University Press, 1972.

Mendel, Ron. "Cooperative Unionism and the Development of Job Control in New York's Printing Trades, 1886–1898." *Labor History* 32 (Summer 1991): 354–75.

Meyer, D. H. *The Instructed Conscience: The Shaping of the American National Ethic*. Philadelphia: University of Pennsylvania Press, 1972.

Meyers, Marvin. *The Jacksonian Persuasion: Politics and Belief*. Stanford: Stanford University Press, 1957.

Miller, Geoffrey P. "Public Choice at the Dawn of the Special Interest State: The Story of Butter and Margarine." *California Law Review* 77 (Jan. 1989): 83–131.

Millis, Harry A., and Royal Montgomery. *Organized Labor*. New York: McGraw-Hill, 1945.

Mink, Gwendolyn. *Old Labor and New Immigrants in American Political Development*. Ithaca: Cornell University Press, 1986.

Montgomery, David. *The Fall of the House of Labor: The Workplace, the State, and American Labor Activism, 1865–1925*. New York: Cambridge University Press, 1987.

Murray, Robert K. "Public Opinion, Labor, and the Clayton Act." *Historian* 21 (May 1959): 255–70.

———. *Red Scare: A Study in National Hysteria, 1919–1920*. New York: University of Minnesota Press, 1955.

National Cyclopedia of American Biography. 75 vols. New York: James T. White, 1898–1984.

Nelson, Daniel. "The Company Union Movement, 1900–1937: A Re-examination." *Business History Review* 56 (Autumn 1982): 335–57.

Nelson, William E. *Americanization of the Common Law: The Impact of Legal Change on Massachusetts Society, 1760–1830.* Cambridge, Mass.: Harvard University Press, 1975.

Niven, John. *Connecticut for the Union: The Role of the State in the Civil War.* New Haven: Yale University Press, 1965.

Nockleby, John. "Tortious Interference with Contractual Relations in the Nineteenth Century: The Transformation of Property, Contract, and Tort." *Harvard Law Review* 93 (May 1980): 1510–39.

Novak, William J. *Intellectual Origins of the State Police Power: The Common Law Vision of a Well-Regulated Society.* Legal History Working Paper No. 3-2. Institute for Legal Studies, University of Wisconsin–Madison Law School, 1989.

Olson, Mancur, Jr. *The Logic of Collective Action.* New York: Schocken, 1968.

Ozanne, Robert W. *The Labor Movement in Wisconsin: A History.* Madison: State Historical Society of Wisconsin, 1984.

Parker, James R. "The Business of Politics, the Politics of Business: The Career of John C. Spooner, 1868–1907." *Maryland Historian* 17 (Fall–Winter 1986): 39–53.

Parrini, Carl P., and Martin J. Sklar. "New Thinking about the Market, 1896–1904: Some American Economists on Investment and the Theory of Surplus Capital." *Journal of Economic History* 43 (Sept. 1983): 559–78.

Parrish, Michael E. *Felix Frankfurter and His Times: The Reform Years.* New York: Free Press, 1982.

Paul, Arnold M. *Conservative Crisis and the Rule of Law: Attitudes of Bar and Bench, 1887–1895.* 1960. Reprint. Gloucester, Mass.: Peter Smith, 1976.

Perlman, Selig, and Philip Taft. *History of Labor in the United States, 1896–1932.* New York: Macmillan, 1935.

Persons, Stow. *American Minds: A History of Ideas.* New York: Henry Holt, 1958.

———. *The Decline of American Gentility.* New York: Columbia University Press, 1973.

Petro, Sylvester. "Injunctions and Labor Disputes: 1880–1932. Part I: What the Courts Actually Did—and Why." *Wake Forest Law Review* 14 (June 1978): 341–576.

Piott, Steven L. *The Antitrust Persuasion: Popular Resistance to the Rise of Big Business in the Midwest.* Westport, Conn.: Greenwood Press, 1985.

Porter, Glenn, and Harold C. Livesay. *Merchants and Manufacturers: Studies in the Changing Structure of Nineteenth-Century Marketing.* Baltimore: Johns Hopkins University Press, 1971.

Poulson, B. W. "Criminal Conspiracy, Injunctions and Damage Suits in Labor Law." *Journal of Legal History* 7 (Sept. 1986): 212–27.

Pringle, Henry P. *The Life and Times of William Howard Taft.* New York: Farrar and Rinehart, 1939.

Rabban, David M. "The First Amendment in Its Forgotten Years." *Yale Law Journal* 90 (Jan. 1981): 514–95.

———. "The Free Speech League, the ACLU, and the Changing Conceptions of Free Speech in American History." *Stanford Law Review* 45 (Nov. 1992): 47–114.

———. "The IWW Free Speech Fights and Popular Conceptions of Free Expression before World War I." *Virginia Law Review* 80 (August 1994): 1055–158.

Ramirez, Bruno. *When Workers Fight: The Politics of Industrial Relations in the Progressive Era, 1898–1916.* Westport, Conn.: Greenwood Press, 1978.

Robinson, Donald B. *Spotlight on a Union: The Story of the United Hatters, Cap and Millinery Workers International Union.* New York: Dial Press, 1948.

Rodgers, Daniel T. *Contested Truths: Keywords in American Politics since Independence.* New York: Basic Books, 1987.

———. "In Search of Progressivism." *Reviews in American History* 10 (Dec. 1982): 113–32.

———. *The Work Ethic in Industrial America, 1850–1920.* Chicago: University of Chicago Press, 1978.

Rogers, James Grafton. *American Bar Leaders.* Chicago: American Bar Association, 1932.

Rogers, Joel. "Divide and Conquer: Further 'Reflections on the Distinctive Character of American Labor Laws.'" *Wisconsin Law Review* 1990 (Jan.–Feb. 1990): 1–147.

Rogin, Michael. "Voluntarism: The Political Functions of an Antipolitical Doctrine." *Industrial and Labor Relations Review* 15 (July 1962): 521–35.

Ross, Dorothy. "The Liberal Tradition Revisited and the Republican Tradition Addressed." In *New Directions in American Intellectual History.* Edited by John Higham and Paul Conkin. Baltimore: Johns Hopkins University Press, 1979.

———. *The Origins of American Social Science.* New York: Cambridge University Press, 1991.

Scoville, Warren C. *Revolution in Glassmaking.* Cambridge, Mass.: Harvard University Press, 1948.

Scranton, Philip. "Diversity in Diversity: Flexible Production and American Industry." *Business History Review* 65 (Spring 1991): 27–90.

———. *Figured Tapestry: Production, Markets, and Power in Philadelphia Textiles, 1885–1941.* New York: Cambridge University Press, 1989.

———. *Proprietary Capitalism: The Textile Manufacture at Philadelphia, 1800–1885.* New York: Cambridge University Press, 1983.

Scranton, Philip, and Walter Licht. *Work Sights: Industrial Philadelphia, 1890–1950.* Philadelphia: Temple University Press, 1986.

Siegel, Stephen A. "Historism in Late Nineteenth-Century Constitutional Thought." *Wisconsin Law Review* 1990 (Nov.–Dec. 1990): 1431–547.

Silbey, Joel. *A Respectable Minority: The Democratic Party in the Civil War Era.* New York: W. W. Norton, 1977.

Singer, Joseph W. "The Legal Rights Debate in Analytic Jurisprudence from Bentham to Hohfield." *Wisconsin Law Review* 1982 (Nov.–Dec. 1982): 975–1059.

Sklar, Martin J. *The Corporate Reconstruction of American Capitalism, 1890–1916: The Market, the Law, and Politics.* New York: Cambridge University Press, 1988.

Skocpol, Theda. "Political Response to Capitalist Crisis: Neo-Marxist Theories of the State and the Case of the New Deal." *Politics and Society* 10 (1980): 155–201.

Skolnik, Richard. "Civic Group Progressivism in New York City." *New York History* 51 (July 1970): 411–39.

Smith, Wilson. *Professors and Public Ethics: Studies of Northern Moral Philosophers before the Civil War.* Ithaca: Cornell University Press, 1956.

Sollors, Werner. *Beyond Ethnicity: Consent and Descent in American Culture.* New York: Oxford University Press, 1986.

Soltow, James H. "Origins of Small Business Metal Fabricators and Machinery Makers in New England, 1890–1957." *Transactions of the American Philosophical Society,* no. 55 (1965).

Starr, Harris E. *William Graham Sumner.* New York: Henry Holt, 1925.

Steigerwalt, Albert K. *The National Association of Manufacturers, 1895–1914: A Study in Business Leadership.* Ann Arbor: University of Michigan, 1964.

Stevens, Robert S. *Law School: Legal Education in America from the 1850s to the 1980s.* Chapel Hill: University of North Carolina Press, 1983.

Stevenson, Louise L. *Scholarly Means to Evangelical Ends: The New Haven Scholars and the Transformation of Higher Learning in America, 1830–1890.* Baltimore: Johns Hopkins University Press, 1986.

Stigler, George J. "Free Riders and Collective Action: An Appendix to the Theories of Economic Regulation." *Bell Journal of Economics and Management Science* 5 (Fall 1974): 359–65.

Stone, Katherine Van Wezel. "The Post-War Paradigm in American Labor Law." *Yale Law Journal* 90 (June 1981): 1509–80.

Strum, Philippa. *Louis D. Brandeis: Justice for the People.* Cambridge, Mass.: Harvard University Press, 1984.

"Symposium on the Renaissance of Pragmatism in American Legal Thought." *Southern California Law Review* 63 (Sept. 1990): 1569–853.

Taft, Philip. *The A.F. of L. in the Time of Gompers.* New York: Harper, 1957.

Taylor, Albion Guilford. *Labor Policies of the National Association of Manufacturers.* Urbana: University of Illinois Press, 1928.

Thelen, David P. *The New Citizenship: Origins of Progressivism in Wisconsin, 1885–1900.* Columbia: University of Missouri Press, 1972.

Thorelli, Hans B. *The Federal Anti-Trust Policy: Origination of an American Tradition.* Baltimore: Johns Hopkins University Press, 1955.

Tobin, Eugene M. *Organize or Perish: America's Independent Progressives, 1913–1933.* Westport, Conn.: Greenwood Press, 1986.

Tomlins, Christopher L. "Criminal Conspiracy and Early Labor Combinations: Massachusetts, 1824–1840." *Labor History* 28 (Summer 1987): 370–85.

———. *Law, Labor and Ideology in the Early Republic.* New York: Cambridge University Press, 1993.

———. "The New Deal, Collective Bargaining, and the Triumph of Industrial Pluralism." *Industrial and Labor Relations Review* 39 (Oct. 1985): 19–34.

———. *The State and the Unions: Labor Relations, Law, and the Organized Labor Movement in America, 1880–1960.* New York: Cambridge University Press, 1985.

Tushnet, Mark V. *The NAACP's Legal Strategy against Segregated Education, 1925–1950.* Chapel Hill: University of North Carolina Press, 1987.

Ulman, Lloyd. *The Rise of the National Trade Union.* Cambridge, Mass.: Harvard University Press, 1966.

Vandevelde, Kenneth M. "A History of Prima Facie Tort: The Origins of a General Theory of Intentional Tort." *Hofstra Law Review* 16 (Winter 1990): 447–97.

Van Tine, Warren R. *The Making of the Labor Bureaucrat: Union Leadership in the United States, 1870–1920.* Amherst, Mass.: University of Massachusetts Press, 1973.

Vatter, Harold G. *The Drive to Industrial Maturity: The U.S. Economy, 1860–1914.* Westport, Conn.: Greenwood Press, 1975.

Vesey, Laurence R. *The Emergence of the American University.* Chicago: University of Chicago Press, 1965.

Vittoz, Stanley. *New Deal Labor Policy and the American Industrial Economy.* Chapel Hill: University of North Carolina Press, 1987.

Wakstein, Allen M. "The Origins of the Open-Shop Movement, 1919–1920." *Journal of American History* 51 (Dec. 1964): 460–75.

Waldo, George C., Jr., ed. *History of Bridgeport and Vicinity.* New York: S. J. Clarke, 1917.

Wandesee, Winifred. "'I'd Rather Pass a Law Than Organize a Union': Francis Perkins and the Reformist Approach to Organized Labor." *Labor History* 34 (Winter 1993): 5–32.

Watts, Sarah Lyons. *Order against Chaos: Business Culture and Labor Ideology in America, 1880–1915.* Westport, Conn.: Greenwood Press, 1991.

Weinstein, James. *The Corporate Ideal in the Liberal State, 1900–1918.* Boston: Beacon Press, 1963.

Wellington, Harry H. *Labor and the Legal Process.* New Haven: Yale University Press, 1968.

White, G. Edward. *Tort Law in America: An Intellectual History.* New York: Oxford University Press, 1980.

Who Was Who in America. 11 vols. Chicago: Marquis–Who's Who, 1963–93.

Who's Who in America, 1903–1905. Chicago: A. N. Marquis, 1905.

Wiebe, Robert H. *Businessmen and Reform: A Study of the Progressive Movement.* Cambridge, Mass.: Harvard University Press, 1962.

Wigdor, David. *Roscoe Pound: Philosopher of the Law.* Westport, Conn.: Greenwood Press, 1964.

Wood, Gordon S. *The Creation of the American Republic, 1776–1787.* Chapel Hill: University of North Carolina Press, 1969.

Wunderlin, Clarence E., Jr. *Visions of a New Industrial Order: Social Science and Labor Theory in America's Progressive Era.* New York: Columbia University Press, 1992.

Zieren, Gregory. "The Boycott and Working-Class Solidarity in Toledo, Ohio in the 1890s." In *Life and Labor: Dimensions of American Working-Class History.* Edited by Charles Stephenson and Robert Asher. Albany: State University of New York Press, 1986.

Unpublished Dissertations and Papers

Bellomy, Donald Cecil. "The Molding of an Iconoclast: William Graham Sumner, 1840–1885." Ph.D. diss., Harvard University, 1980.

Bensman, David Harlan. "Artisan Culture, Business Union: American Hat Finishers in the Nineteenth Century." Ph.D. diss., Columbia University, 1977.

Boemke, Manfred F. "The Wilson Administration, Organized Labor, and the Colorado Coal Strike, 1913–14." Ph.D. diss., Princeton University, 1983.

Church, Robert LaValley. "The Development of the Social Sciences as Academic Disciplines at Harvard University, 1869–1900." Ph.D. diss., Harvard University, 1965.

Eggert, Gerald G. "Richard Olney, Corporation Lawyer and Attorney General of the United States, 1835–1895." Ph.D. diss., University of Michigan, 1960.

Ernst, Daniel R. "The Lawyers and the Labor Trust: A History of the American Anti-Boycott Association, 1902–1919." Ph.D. diss., Princeton University, 1989.

Green, Marguerite. "The National Civic Federation and the American Labor Movement, 1900–1925." Ph.D. diss., Catholic University of America, 1956.

Greene, Julia Marie. "The Strike at the Ballot Box: Politics and Partisanship in the AFL, 1881–1916." Ph.D. diss., Yale University, 1990.

Heath, Frederick Morrison. "Politics and Steady Habits: Issues and Elections in Connecticut, 1894–1914." Ph.D. diss., Columbia University, 1965.

Hoyt, Richard M. "The Danbury Hatters Case." B.A. honors thesis, Yale University, 1965.

James, Walter T. "The Philosophy of Noah Porter (1811–1892)." Ph.D. diss., Columbia University, 1951.

Jones, Dallas Lee. "The Wilson Administration and Organized Labor, 1912–1919." Ph.D. diss., Cornell University, 1954.

Katz, Joseph. "The Legal Profession, 1890–1915: The Lawyer's Role in Society." M.A. thesis, Columbia University, 1954.

Kelly, Arthur H. "The History of the Illinois Manufacturing Association." Ph.D. diss., University of Chicago, 1938.

Merrihew, Henry Merton. "Government by Injunction." LL.B. thesis, Cornell Law School, 1898.

Moore, Michael Anthony. "The AFL and the Anti-Trust Laws, 1890–1932." Ph.D. diss., Case Western Reserve University, 1964.

Myers, Howard Barton. "The Policing of Labor Disputes in Chicago." Ph.D. diss., University of Chicago, 1929.

Niven, John William, Jr. "The Time of the Whirlwind: A Study in the Political, Social and Economic History of Connecticut from 1861 to 1875." Ph.D. diss., Columbia University, 1954.

Index

propriations bill rider and, 174–78; indictments against United Mine Workers and,
176–78, 179; progressive position on, 181–
82; Seager's article in *The Survey* and, 178–
80; Senate debate on Clayton Act and,
178–82. *See also* Hepburn bill (1908); Sherman Antitrust Act
A priori tendency, jurisprudence of: in *Buck's
Stove*, 133, 145; debate over antitrust laws
and, 180; Gray's opinion in *Jacobs* and,
100–102; of the Great Upheaval, 107;
Holmes and, 83–85
Atomistic theory of justice. *See* Individual
rights
Atwood, Benjamin S., 62, 67
Auburn Draying Co. v. Wardwell (1919), 212,
228

Baker, Ray Stannard, 222
Baldwin, Simeon, 38, 42
Barnes, Mahlon, 134
Barnum, William H., 40, 42
Bathwick, E. R., 185–86
Beach, John Kimberly, 117, 118–20, 149
Beattie, Charles Maitland, 196–99, 209, 227
Beck, James Montgomery, 58, 110, 117–18, 136,
139, 144, 167
*Bedford v. Journeymen Stone Cutters' Associa-
tion* (1927), 234
Bentley, Arthur, 4
Berg and Company, F., 15
Berger, Victor, 134
Berle, Adolf A., 234
Berry v. Donovan (1905), 100, 259n.56
Bigelow, Melville M., 78, 80, 86
Blackmar, Abel, 194, 197, 199, 210–11
Blum, Solomon, 200
Bonaparte, Charles J., 124
Boocock, Frederick, 54, 59, 102, 139
Booth & Brother v. Burgess (1906), 205
Borah, William E., 174, 181, 187–88, 275n.59
Bossert v. Dhuy (1917), 197, 199, 209, 211, 212
Bowen, Charles, 81, 82, 200–201
Boycotts, 7, 56, 71–72, 222–23. *See also Buck's
Stove and Range Company v. Gompers;
Loewe v. Lawlor;* "Materials" boycotts;
Secondary boycotts; Woodtrim War
Boyle, Michael, 175, 228
Brandeis, Louis D.: on *Berry*, 100; on *Chris-
tensen*, 99, 107; closed shop and, 11, 99;

dissent in *Duplex*, 210; incorporation of
trade unions and, 160–61, 162; jurispru-
dence of a priori tendency and, 107; view
of labor unions, 11–12
Brewer, David J., 76–77, 113, 117, 226
British Trade Disputes Act of 1906, 88, 178
Bryan, James Wallace, 88, 256n.82
Bryan, William Jennings, 42, 44, 135
BTCs. *See* Building trades councils
Buck's Stove and Range Company v. Gompers
(1907–14), 109, 124–46; AABA and, 7, 130,
132, 136, 139, 141–44, 146; compared with
Loewe, 110–12; cost of litigation in, 57;
Gompers and, 130–35; national politics
and, 111, 125–26, 131–32, 135–37, 145–46; oc-
casion for suit, 127–28; significance of,
110–12; Van Cleave and, 125, 126–30
Buck v. Bell (1927), 37
Building trades councils (BTCs), 200–208,
210. *See also Moores & Co. v. Bricklayers'
Union No. 1*
Burdick, Francis M., 255n.48

Caldwell, Henry Clay, 201, 258n.20
Cannon, Joseph, 131, 132, 146, 166, 167, 174
Carpenter, Elisha, 73–76, 106, 107
Carter, Orrin Nelson, 103–5, 106, 107
CCF. *See* Central Competitive Field
Central Competitive Field (CCF), 177, 179
Champerty, law of, 196–97
Chase, Emory, 211
Cheyney, Edward P., 157, 158, 270n.40
Christensen v. Kellogg Switchboard and Supply
(1903), 95–99, 100, 107, 168
Christian virtue. *See* Moral philosophy
CIAA. *See* Citizens' Industrial Alliance of
America
Cigar making industry, 14, 71, 240n.37
Cincinnati Court House Riot of 1884, 137, 139
Citizens' Industrial Alliance of America
(CIAA), 98–100
Civic humanism, 67–68, 74; Davenport and,
25, 26, 27–28; W. G. Merritt and, 227
Civil liberty, 35
Clark, Charles H., 46
Clark, William, 41
Clayton Act (1914), 8, 165; Cummins's
amendment and, 188; Gompers's view of
Loewe decision and, 167–70, 183; Gomp-
ers's vs. Davenport's views on, 165–66;

Daniel R. Ernst is professor of law at the Georgetown University Law Center. He received a Ph.D. from Princeton University in 1989, an LL.M. from the University of Wisconsin in 1988, a J.D. from the University of Chicago in 1983, and an A.B. from Dartmouth College in 1980.

BOOKS IN THE SERIES
THE WORKING CLASS IN AMERICAN HISTORY

Southern Labor and Black Civil Rights: Organizing Memphis Workers
Michael K. Honey

Radicals of the Worst Sort: Laboring Women in Lawrence, Massachusetts, 1860–1912 *Ardis Cameron*

Producers, Proletarians, and Politicians: Workers and Party Politics in Evansville and New Albany, Indiana, 1850–87 *Lawrence M. Lipin*

The New Left and Labor in the 1960s *Peter B. Levy*

The Making of Western Labor Radicalism: Denver's Organized Workers, 1878–1905
David Brundage

In Search of the Working Class: Essays in American Labor History and Political Culture *Leon Fink*

Lawyers against Labor: From Individual Rights to Corporate Liberalism
Daniel R. Ernst